ISLANDS OF STORM

For Marian and Bill

ISLANDS OF STORM

EILEÁIN ANNRAIDH

JAMES CHARLES ROY

"Si tollis hostem, tollis et pugnam;
si tollis pugnam, tollis et coronam."
St. Columbanus

DUFOUR EDITIONS

First published in the United States of America 1991 by
Dufour Editions Inc.
Chester Springs, Pennsylvania 19425-0449.

Library of Congress Cataloguing-in-Publication Data:

Roy, James Charles, 1945-
    Islands of storm : Inishmurray, Iona, Inishkea North / James
Charles Roy
        p. cm.
    Includes bibliographical references and index.
    ISBN 0-8023-1293-4 : $30.00
        1. Inishmurray (Ireland)—Antiquities. 2. Inishkea North
(Ireland)—Antiquities. 3. Ireland—Church history—To 1172.
4. Christian antiquities—Ireland. 5. Iona (Scotland)—Antiquities.
6. Monasteries—Ireland. 7. Celtic Church. I. Title.
DA990.I54R69 1991
274.15'02—dc20   90-48646
                                                              CIP

U.S. ISBN 0 8023 1293 4

Printed and bound in the United States of America

Table of Contents

I

iNishMURRAy

"Who could show me a solitude,
a place without roads?"
Evagrius of Antioch

N

W   E

S

Donegal bay

shaddan■ ■bomore
rock   rock

mullaghmore

ballyshannon →

Inishmurray

the foul grounds   dernish
island

spanish rocks

black rock

clashymore
harbor

monastery

streedagh point   Inishnagore

moneygold

the haven   conor's island

●grange

staad
abbey

benbulbin

cloonagh

●drumcliff   sligo →

IRISH PROVINCIAL TOWNS like Sligo are generally daylight places. Shoppers have finished their chores by early evening, offices have cleared out and cottage industries such as car repair and gravestones, often run from alleyway store-fronts or garage space, all barred, grated, locked away. In the sheen of a steady drizzle the abandoned streets reflect more an air of gloom than they probably deserve. Behind the dank, unpainted concrete walls of houses on either side of the street I can well imagine grates full of coal, or electric fires purring away. But somehow my experience with Ireland tells me not to fool myself. In how many foreboding hallways, heavy with the wet chill of outdoors, leading to rooms just as bare and sodden, have I spent so many nights either as a guest or transient stranger? How many evenings before an enormous hearth, with a winter storm passing through, and only the heatless flicker of a dying piece of turf to light the barren walls? As I walk through town, counting the endlessly changing shades and tinctures that the color gray so miraculously provides this misty country, and pass over the surging, frigid Garavogue, cutting Sligo in half as it runs down from Lough Gill to the sea, I see two truths in perverse harmony. This is a God-awful place, and I love it.

It's not too late to buy a few provisions. Although I am not going far one can never be sure that anyplace out in the countryside will be open, and if they are, what interesting fare might be for sale. When looking for food I can generally muster little enthusiasm for the shoe-laces, rock candy, paraffin, detergents and assorted pails that often make up the inventory of rural groceries. This is not to say that Sligo or places like it have much better to offer: commercial bread and cheese of very poor quality, ham, oranges from Spain or Israel, thirty to fifty brands of cookies and crackers, the new sort of milk that requires no refrigeration until opened. One does not shop in such places, one breathes a sigh of relief that at least one has found the basics. I have never come to Ireland in search of good things to eat.

The main road to Donegal from Sligo is familiar to me in a rather unspecifiable fashion, if only because I've travelled this way countless times, hurrying for the northern reaches of the Slieve League plateau and Glencolumbkille — O'Donnell country. When I was younger and more impressionable I habitually stopped at the monastic site at Drumcliff, just five miles out of Sligo, to pay my respects to William Butler Yeats, who though initially buried in France after his death in 1939 was reinterred here in the old graveyard nine years later. The atmospherics of the place are immense, almost gaudy. A superb high cross from the ancient Celtic monastery, a fragment of round tower still standing, lovely vistas of windy Drumcliff Bay to the west and, towering over everything beyond the crow-infested trees lined up as an avenue to the nineteenth-century Protestant chapel, the monolithic profile of "bare Ben Bulben's head". Though a scant 1700 feet or so in height, this little hill is Ireland's Everest, a dominating, aged, fiercely aristocratic presence that reminds one of a sage or prophet of old. It was to Yeats's credit, mere poet and mere man, that he could subjugate all this splendor with just a few strokes of the pen, words etched plainly on his tombstone,

> Cast a cold eye
> On life, on death.
> Horseman, pass by!

Two of the finest epitaphs ever written were those by Yeats and Swift, Irishmen of vastly different temperament but perhaps equal brilliance. Swift, of course, wrote his in Latin, something of a barrier for today's tourist, and his remains lie wedged away in the musty confines of St. Patrick's Cathedral in Dublin, the kind of place one visits perfunctorily, like the Poets' Corner in Westminster, where the Dean's vitriolic ill temper seems smothered in churchly decorum. But Yeats is the wild man in death, his vivid sense of the supernatural and the eerie, romantic, electricity of his style both merging to bottle up, in one or two wonderfully constructed phrases, the enormous possibilities that a scene such as Drumcliff presents. I always felt that in those few lines Yeats had dwarfed nature.

I still enjoy the poem, and I can still appreciate the almost Jacobean

Benbulbin
County Sligo

___

flare that Yeats could impart to old Gaelic tidbits that he saw lying about, unused and despised by most literate people, during the course of his writing life. Dean Swift, I think, would have considered Yeats a superficial man, a foppish figure of enormous pretension and mock profundity. There is, perhaps, some truth to that, for we all see ourselves in a particular and flattering sort of way (if we are human) and some of us indulge that self-esteem more ostentatiously than others. Yeats was not a modest person. I can recall the reminiscence of a graduate from the college I attended when Yeats came by on a lecture tour in 1932. The poet, learning that the president of the institution had planned a small dinner party in his honor, sent word ahead that he was not to be spoken to by anyone unless Yeats himself initiated the conversation. Such grandeur may perhaps annoy us, but the same power and assertiveness that fuel a personality can, in the case of an artist peculiarly gifted, linger on for centuries in the work left behind. Yeats's simple and elegant epitaph is proof of that.

But I no longer stop at Drumcliff, the only part of this road, as I said before, that I know anything about. It is one of those places or sights, like the Rock of Cashel, the megalithic necropolis above the Boyne at Newgrange, the Book of Kells or the Hills of Killarney that are overwhelming necessities for the casual visitor to Ireland. They are, in fact, totally self-sufficient and fulfilling. A person can say (and be completely correct) that he has really taken in the country if he ticks off a few such prerequisites from his list, which I think is not the case for some other well-abused European war horses such as Stonehenge, Notre Dame Cathedral, the Mona Lisa or the Roman Forums. The problem with Drumcliff, after awhile, is that you want more, and thankfully Ireland is a land of plenty, a land that in its several parts can both overwhelm a Drumcliff, even with Yeats as its guardian angel, and at the same time, in more subtle fashion, ease it aside with blows as soft as pillows.

THROUGH THE COURSE of many trips (and many years) passing back and forth through the backwaters of this country, I have had recourse to a wider than usual variety of vehicles (including my own two feet, which I suppose do not count) that have tended, in their own quite individual fashion, to amaze the locals. This was never my intention though always the result. For some reason, and perhaps simple clumsiness is more the explanation, I have never achieved the sublime goal of being unobtrusive, of slipping into town like an unseen cipher and sliding out again afterwards with no one so much as aware that I had been there. I have come into various little crossroad villages by truck, bus, haycart, motorcycle, caravan, rented Mercedes, tractor, bicycle and all variations in between. I have never failed in receiving looks of catatonic bewilderment, and as the years pass by my hopes for anonymity fade ever more quietly away. I blame this on my current vehicle, a small Citroën station wagon purchased new in 1972. It was, back then, a rather plain but not undistinguished car, having as its progenitor the classic *deux chevaux* that every farmer in France used to husband along for at least thirty years (quite fantastic for a piece of tin) and which the company elongated by two or three feet to create extra space in the rear. It was euphemistically launched as the *Ami* or Friend. My wife and I, tired of the inevitable washouts and unwelcome attention from sheep and cattle that tenting so heroically invites in this teeming land, had cleared out the back seat to build a platform, and there we could sleep in comfort wherever we wished as the gales passed by overhead. In 1972 we garnered attention by the very fact that the car was new, a condition unheard of in Ireland no matter the artifact: farm tractor, suit of clothes, house, fishing vessel, whatever. Now, with over a decade of Common Market prosperity happily behind it, the exact reverse is true. I have become the ancient mariner of the roadway, something of a menace, in fact, at 45 mph (my top speed) with impatient, then furious farmers screeching past me in elegant, expensive, honking road cars. The oddity of the scene is manifest, to my disadvantage, by the Citroën's now decrepit and idiosyncratic appearance, acquired patiently over years of weathering in a farmer's hay shed near Galway where I store the car when away. One autumn he painted the barn with a rust preventative. He sprayed the car at the same time, inadvertently of course, but the effect is quite like a Jackson Pollock. Interspersed with these scattered red droppings there was soon natural vegetation. The car, in effect, sprouted. A growth of moss, nicely green, and various weed-like protrusions nearly covered the entire vehicle and resisted all our efforts of scraping and washing. We had become a travelling garden. At a gas station yesterday the attendant asked me if the car was alive. Should he water it after pumping in the petrol? How was the harvest this year? Did I use an ass for ploughing? And so on. The Irish, in their freshly acquired modernity, are now quite condescending when it comes to the ancient past, a subject they formerly treated with reverence.

The old Citroën, however, is really very useful to me, no matter its glaring personality. It serves as a barometer, a yardstick that I can use every few years to chart the steady progress of Ireland. Other people normally compare prices to find out how things have changed, others may note how many new houses or chalets have sprung up since their last visit here many years ago, where before there had been only pasture. For me, I can feel it on the road.

Coming out of Sligo town, and passing Drumcliff churchyard buried in mist, I feel a sense of dread falling over me. The great tentacles of mainstream Europe have come this far, are slithering along to the farthest reaches of a land considered in ancient times the very edge of the world. They follow the pottering lanes and twisted byways (originally cattle tracks and carriage routes), everywhere widening, straightening, bulldozing, flattening. The Ireland of yesteryear, in the euphemistic phrase, is being opened up, and modern roadways are the strategy, loaded with tractor trailers and trucking vehicles of hitherto unimaginable size going at speed that in olden times, on older roads, would have resulted in mayhem.

I can generally tell when a new stretch of highway is beginning or ending. In the ditches or breakdown lanes lie the bodies of cats, dogs, chickens, even crows, demolished by drivers with their feet hard to the gas pedal, either in reflexive anticipation of the joy ride ahead or the stubborn refusal to believe that all good things must end. I have noticed this everywhere in Ireland. Animals now know to stay off the newer highways, but still believe the familiar and antiquated roadways of yore are safe for them to lounge about, as they were when this old Citroën was king of the hill. They had plenty of time to move then. But from my creeping vantage point I can see the resultant carnage of a new and fast way of life that is deeply symbolic.

With the dark creeping in, and occasional cloudbursts soaking an already drenched succession of fields and farmsteads, the degenerating vista could well justify Thomas Carlyle's glum impression as he passed by in 1849 of "a dingy, desolate looking country. Would we were well out of it!" And indeed, if he were a modern traveller he could, after passing Benbulbin, have had a fairly brisk and carefree run straight on to Ballyshannon, the largest town between Sligo and Donegal. He would have wound his way through Grange, a shabby little place much ruined by new roadworks, which elevate somewhat north of the town to course a slight ridge for a length of ten or so miles, with views of Donegal Bay to the west, moorland and then rising mountains to the east. He might, if he wished, detour down to the sea at Mullaghmore, with a fine harbor, but more than likely he would prefer to continue on past Bundoran, a popular though rickety summer resort, to cross the River Erne at Ballyshannon. From there the road awaits future Common Market subsidies, twisting, turning and bumping all the way to Donegal, but the entire stretch from Sligo onward to the scenic north is barely two hours.

Any traveller unbiased to begin with might still agree with one Terence O'Rorke, who in 1889 wrote a highly opinionated history of Sligo, town and county, which abounds in generally depreciative assessments of this very countryside, a vista of "low moory expanse without hill or dale, without visible lake or river, without trees or other timber, except the whitethorn hedge along the sides of the highway. The seashore too is for the most part rugged, and lined with brown drift sand, still more sombre in hue than the moor of the inland. And even the sea that washes this shore shares, or seems to share, the dark and cheerless look of the land." This was a common point of view among nineteenth-century writers, and more particularly those of a Protestant persuasion, who saw in the monotonous acres of useless bog a riveting symbol for all the blight and "degraded superstition" that Roman Catholicism had exercised over

Ireland for so many centuries. On a more human level it was also the kind of comment that Victorians liked to hear who felt, like Thackeray, that a comfortable drawing room was more to be trusted than the tempestuous out-of-doors. Still, I must admit one's first impressions do tend to veer towards the bleak, especially with weather so ugly and unwelcoming. When Benbulbin drifts off behind you, so also does the Ireland of picture books and travel post cards, a dark blot indeed for a land so blessed with natural beauty

The rain this evening, however, serves the fine metaphorical purpose of demythologizing not only fabled scenery but the gloss of Irish legend as well. The Battle of Books is, at face value, a typical tale from the Celtic repertoire, and thus typically charming. It has some historical truth but not exactly where you'd expect to find it. The despicable weather tends to emphasize whatever pedestrian reality there may be to the story at the expense of its more attractive folkloric possibilities. Certainly at The Yeats Ballad Lounge where I have stopped for a sandwich and beer, the talk is all tourist fodder. " 'Twas a great fight," says the barkeep, "the greatest ever seen in Ireland. The streams flowed red with the blood of warriors slain, and all that commotion over a tiny book that St. Columcille borrowed to copy," and so on. When it came to directions, for the battle took place just above Drumcliff churchyard in a place called *Cúl Dreimne*, or "Cool of the Hillocks," the rhetoric is equally expansive, fulsome, windy, vague and, in the end, inaccurate. I am soon hopelessly turned about in a warren of lanes beneath Benbulbin, and with dark coming on fast I get out of my car at the first opportunity where I may have it right. This is the place, I say to myself, and it hardly matters. On this pasture, where a few steaming cows stand rooted in the mud, the battle may well have been fought, given a mile or two in either direction. There would be no marker in any case, no monument, statue or commemorative plaque. If all the fights in this country were so identified, then every road, field, and river ford would be littered with signage. Every step one takes here covers history.

The Battle of Books, or *Cúl Dreimne*, took place c. 561. It is of interest to me as introducing the first historical reference we have to the island of Inishmurray, nearly five miles off the coast at nearby Streedagh Point, the reason for my being here in the first place. And it features as a central character the famous, though elusive Irish Saint, Columcille, even if his role in this particular fray is deeply shrouded in mystery. The one certain fact is that a battle was fought here between a collection of clans from the northern Donegal highlands, mostly O'Donnells and O'Neills in alliance with the King of Connaught, and the forces of Diarmait mac Cerbaill, the symbolic High King who ruled from the renowned Tara Hill, one of the mythological Camelots of Celtic Ireland, where the remains of royal raths, earthworks, and banqueting halls still mark the earth, clearly visible to the traveller, at its site north of Dublin in County Meath. All of

Main Altar
Monastic Ruins of Gartan
County Donegal

16

these warriors, save the Connachta, belonged to a single generic entity known as the Uí Néill who had, in some remoter era, split into two distinct septs now referred to by historians as the Southern and Northern Uí Néill, reflective of the areas in Ireland where they wielded lordship. Between these blood related kinsmen the title High King was regularly alternated, and though its practical value was slight there were certain embellishments of a histrionic nature that regularly excited the jealousies of haughty chieftains not eligible, at any particular moment, to claim the accolade themselves. Though Columcille had some role in fomenting *Cúl Dreimne*, it is more probable that Diarmait mac Cerbaill came all this way from Tara to earn the respect and obeisance of his cousins. He was here not for profit or booty or territory, but to force them to their knees in a bloody show of force. Such was the power of vanity in ancient Ireland.

Columcille was a prince of the O'Donnells or, in the words of a later poet, "a king's son of reddened valour." His birthplace, a remote Donegal hamlet known as Gartan, was the center of O'Donnell authority but today's visitor, finding there an empty, windswept, barren landscape of bog and mountainous moorland, would be hard-pressed to envision the place as a royal stronghold teeming with courtly intrigue or romance. The Rock of Doon, where O'Donnell kings were inaugurated, remains as it has for centuries past, but if one didn't know otherwise it would hardly seem more than another stony outcrop in a landscape littered with formidable and hulking scenery. The ancient monastery founded there by Columcille has little to show for it — a small medieval stone oratory, a few extremely crude *termonn* (or sanctuary) crosses — with its abutting cemetery, the resting place of countless O'Donnell kings and chieftains, like any other in Ireland, an anonymous collection of shattered tombstones and empty flower vases. A little farm lane winding along near Lough Gartan leads to the site of his birth, an empty field marked by a large high cross of evidently modern provenance and a rough piece of stone upon which the baby was allegedly delivered. It is claimed that to sleep on this Saint's Bed before departing Ireland will relieve the pangs of homesickness for the old country. Looking over the depopulated acres all around, scenes of some of the most bitter land evictions of the nineteenth century, one can envision that this particular folk custom must have seen considerable use. My other thought was that the vistas surrounding me in Gartan held the perfect interpretative key to his various names — *Colum*, or Dove, *Cill*, of the Church. The lovely, placid lake, the harmonious patchwork of fields and ancient stone walls certainly underscore such gentle nomenclature. But menacing this entire scene is the barrier of mountainous and sinister ridges which press against the lake, a reminder of his baptismal name, *Crimthan* or Wolf. Columcille, Wolf of the Church. He was, it appears, a man of extreme character.

It is suspected that Columcille's father, watching the growth in popularity and power of the new Christian religion, sought to place an ally within the institution itself. Columcille was fostered out of the home at an early age, but instead of placement with another kingly family, joined to the O'Donnells by custom or treaty, Columcille was handed over to the Church. His youth and early manhood, if the traditions dealing with his life are at all correct, consisted of study at one distinguished monastic school after another, his teachers the most renowned of an era called by many commentators the Golden Age of Christian Ireland. Columcille, we may presume, joined in the general fervor of the times. Two of the several score monasteries that he and his disciples founded in Ireland would later become famous as far as the European mainland (Derry and Durrow) while Iona, established in 563 on a small island off Mull in Argyll, Scotland, remains without question the most influential of all the Celtic foundations.

The Battle of Books is the stuff of legends. It is alleged that Columcille, after his ordination as a priest, paid a brotherly visit to one of his favorite teachers, St. Finnian of Movilla. There he saw a newly revised edition of the Bible that excited him tremendously, and he asked for the loan of it from Finnian. Unknown to the elder monk, however, were Columcille's furtive intentions. After the evening office, when all the monks had retired, Columcille remained behind in church and copied the book. How many nights the task required we do not know, but Finnian soon discovered what he came to consider a fraudulent act, and demanded the return of both the original and Columcille's duplicate, an order his student refused. Both monks appealed to the High King for a judgment which one historian has called "the first action in the annals of the law over copyright." Columcille was infuriated at his old master for bringing charges against him. "The book of Finnian is none the worse for my copying it," he said to the King, "and it is not right that the divine words in that book should perish, or that I or any other should be hindered from writing them or reading them or spreading them among the tribes. It was right for me to copy it, seeing it was my desire to give profit to all peoples, with no harm to Finnian or his book." But Diarmait ruled against him with the famous Solomonic decision that "to every cow belongs her calf, and to every book its copy, and therefore to Finnian belongs the book thou has written, O Columcille." Instead of complying with the King's decision, however, Columcille fled the court for Donegal, taking with him the purloined manuscript. And heeding an old Irish saying that "the wrong decision of a judge is a raven's call to battle", he summoned the tribes to avenge his honor against the King, and at *Cúl Dreimne* the entire disagreement was bloodily settled in combat. The legends differ as to Columcille's role in the fighting itself, the most common description being that he stood behind his kinsmen in the classic Irish penitential posture of the cross-vigil, or arms outstretched as though nailed to the cross. St. Finnian, it is said, assumed the same position behind the King, who unfortunately reaped little benefit from these heavenly supplications, suffering a crushing defeat in which he may have lost as many as three thousand warriors. Columcille, according to some of his biographers, witnessing the carnage that pride and willfulness had caused, came to his senses in a fit of remorse. An old tenth-century Gaelic ecclesiastical calendar of saints' days known as the *Martyrology of Donegal* succinctly describes the final scene: "St. Molaise of Inishmurray, at the cross of Ath Inlai, pronounced sentence of banishment on St. Columcille." In 563 he left for Scotland as a penance, and "he made these quatrains" on the occasion of his melancholy departure:

> Derry of the Oaks, let us leave it
> With gloom and with tears, heavy hearted;
> Anguish of heart to depart thence,
> And to go away unto strangers.

> The seagulls of Lough Foyle,
> They are before me and in my wake.
> In my coracle with me they come not.
> Alas, it is sad our parting.

> Great is the speed of my coracle,
> And its stern turned upon Derry.

There are few authentic or anywhere near contemporary records that can verify any of these details as historical. Most of the colorful highlights derive from a work known as the *Betha Colaim chille*, or Life of Columcille, composed in 1532 by Manus O'Donnell, Lord of Tyrconnell (as the O'Donnells styled themselves in medieval times) in his castle at Lifford in Donegal. Manus was the epitome of Gaelic chieftain, a warrior prince fully engaged in the daily theatre of local hostings and tribal vendettas, while equally involved in a broader struggle with the abhorred authority of English interlopers from Dublin, whom he alternately courted and flouted. His career ended unhappily, the prisoner for eight years of a rebellious son, but at least he lived to a relatively mature age and died a natural death, "a thing rare in that distracted age" according to one historian. His own self-image was that of a scholar, indulging himself in the Irish passion for antiquarian study and the enjoyment of old Gaelic literature. He patronized poets, artisans, monks, academics, and held a liberal court in his various strongholds that featured music and bardic entertainments. He was the kind of man that Gaels of old saw as the ideal of kingship, a Renaissance Celt. Intrigued by the career of his clan's patron saint he ordered men of learning to gather up all the old manuscripts and saints' lives they could, and to translate these into Irish. The Latin works were fairly straightforward but many of the ancient Gaelic poems, written in a language archaic even then to the Celts themselves, proved difficult to decipher. With many disparate versions before him, Manus O'Donnell dictated to scribes his Life of Columcille.

Experts have been able to trace many parts of this work to specific older compositions — Abbot Adomnán's seventh-century Life, written at Iona, for example, and an old Irish tenth-century vita — but much of O'Donnell's recitations are the folk tales that spread from mouth to mouth through the breadth of Donegal. The whole story of Finnian and his dispute with Columcille appears to stem from oral tradition, and thus may be judged the product of a rich and very lively imagination

D IARMAIT'S REAL MISSION was one of prestige. He had followed the icy, treacherous road to kingship within his own clan, and sought at *Cúl Dreimne* to convince everyone else that he was worthy of the title High King. It seems fair to say the expedition was also intended to punish Columcille. More obscure references in the various annals suggest that Columcille had cursed the King for some violation of custom regarding the ecclesiastical privilege of sanctuary, a problem that Diarmait, a pagan, had encountered before in disputes with other clerics. In fact much of the extensive saga lore that surrounds his name involves disagreements with Christian saints. Most of these led to some disaster or another befalling the King, who in truth appears to have suffered many humiliating defeats on the battlefield in the course of his career, the last of which saw him slain in 565. We probably find in these fifth-century episodes the picture of a half converted society beset by conflict between the Church and a semi-pagan state. The legend of St. Patrick, of course, would have us believe the opposite, that by this late date the island was a Christian land, still warlike to be sure, but unified by a common and orthodox Catholic faith. This is far from the truth.

At the time of Christ, over five hundred years before the battle, Ireland was little more than a welter of diverse and competitive tribal units, all that remained of an independent Celtic culture from the European mainland. Roman conquest had smothered and Christianized the Celts of Gaul and Briton, but the legions had gone no further. The Roman General Julius Agricola, according to Tacitus, was aware that Ireland existed. Indeed, he longed to cross the Irish Sea to win her, but like the wilds of Scotland, Ireland was left alone to the savages. The Celts were an Iron Age people at that point, and war their cherished preoccupation. Early classical reporters such as Strabo, Posidonius and Diodorus Siculus have left reliable portraits of the turbulence, both mental and physical, with which the Celts pursued their fortunes. It was a way of life both static in its conventions yet ever changing: tribal dynasties expanded and contracted, grew fulsome with power or collapsed, appeared and disappeared. There were more twists of fate, reversals of fortune, betrayals and triumphs than even the *filid*, custodians of tribal lore, could keep up with in their saga tales, all oral and memorized in chant-like pedigrees, droned to an eager audience on days of celebration or remorse. These were the tides ebbing back and forth of ambitions and shattered dreams, the details of which, or the personalities of those involved, we will never intimately know. All that can be understood is that the arena of these multiple dramas, the social environment within which this turmoil thrived, never changed: men and groups of men fought and slew each other for hundreds of years. Borders changed, kings and warlords came and went, the only thing that remained constant was violence, death, the brandishing of heads.

Christians are certain to have existed in this all but pagan land by the early decades of the fifth century. We know this because an early pope, in 431, authorized a mission here "to the Irish believing in Christ". The majority of historians speculate that these Christian communities were mostly gathered in the south of Ireland, more accessible to Gaul and Romanized Britain, and it was there the papal emissaries most likely landed. St. Patrick, to his enormous credit, sought to evangelize the considerably more hostile and savage tribes of the northern reaches, where he is thought to have crossed in the early 460s. His expedition was a parochial enterprise directed from the midlands of England, prompted perhaps by the twin desires to convert the pagans as Christ had demanded while at the same time blunting, through civilized instruction, the warlike Irish ardor which had spawned so many devastating raids along their coastline. We are fortunate that two authentic writings from Patrick himself have survived from the fifth century, and while these documents are often obscure in meaning, they suggest in very graphic fashion the sinister and frightening obstacles that Patrick faced as he wandered "unaided and alone, where no one else had ever penetrated". His mission, it seems to me, was largely ineffectual (at least as compared to the legends we are so familiar with) but it was a start, just as the papal effort in the south should also be construed as an initial probe, not the heathen-smashing whirlwind that later sagas suggest. These early missionaries, after all, were demonstrably Roman in their point of view, experienced to some degree in the ways of civilized men, in how a diocese might be organized, how a church could be financed and built, instruction given, influence won within a familiar Imperial authority. But Ireland presented scenes of unimaginable barbarism. There was, to their way of thinking, no government to speak of, only vicious, predatory warlords. There were no cities in which to base a diocesan seat, only scattered raths and cattle stations. And there was no system to anything, no laws or codes or verifiable standards they could read or understand, for all business was conducted orally and in a stylized, ritualistic fashion that seemed more attuned to posture and appearance than function. Patrick and the others, by the power of their personalities and intensity of belief, managed a core of initial conversions, and it was to these native Celts, understanding as they did the trackless complexities of their system of life, that we owe the gradual transformation of Ireland from paganism to Christianity. By 561 and the Battle of *Cúl Dreimne* we finally have, after well over one hundred years of effort, a real turning towards the

Saint's Bed
Glencolumbkille
County Donegal

new religion. Second, third, and fourth generation Irish Christians are numerically significant and driven, unlike the heathen priesthood, to garner conversions. But even so, old belief and custom looms large among the people. At *Cúl Dreimne*, after all, Diarmait's army was protected by a druid barrier.

What we really see in this horrible, primeval killing ground, where men were slashed, hacked, stabbed, battered, and speared to death, is that Celtic society had hardly changed since the time of Christ. The battle itself was certainly no different in terms of weaponry or tactics. Warriors of particular ferocity might swagger back and forth in front of the enemy, boasting their prowess and belittling the virility of their opponents; individual combat between "heroes" from either side would degenerate into a general haze of free-form brawl that might last an entire afternoon; with one side finally broken, a disorganized rout could develop, with terrible slaughter amid the noncombatants and stragglers; very few prisoners taken, and no quarter for any wounded left stranded on the field. The only significant difference may well have been the religious stripe of the priest involved. Instead of druids chanting curses and spells over the enemy, we might see Abbot Columcille waving a cross or holy bell and screaming incantations against the Southern Uí Néill.[1] And among the opposing ranks, perhaps a Christian priest like Finnian carrying sword or ax, searching for an opportunity to take the Abbot's head — in other words, a scene that would have revolted Patrick, a picture of barbarism restored, not Christianity triumphant.

But Patrick, a clumsy Briton with little talent for penetrating insight, would have misread the entire situation. It was one thing for an abbot to control his flock in peace, it was another to lead them in battle, to replace the war gods with Christ. When Christians could achieve that degree of status, then change could occur more quickly.

Patrick, of course, the foreign intruder, proved incapable of fashioning a role for himself in what were, to his view, the impenetrable mores of Celtic life. To Columcille and men like him such difficulties constituted simple, everyday reality, holding no terror or confusion. They were able to take the Roman form of the first missionaries (or what little they may have understood from that tradition), twist and alter it as necessary, and fashion what was left into a very Celtic entity. The early Church therefore reflected the society itself like a mirror: it was disorganized, decentralized, individualistic, superstitious, parochial, chaotic and impassioned. It travelled first along dynastic lines, following the political contortions of any given moment — the alliances, pacts, and treaties of the various clans — that generally resulted in the identification of certain "saints" with

---

[1] Sacred appurtenances such as bells often had bloodcurdling repurcussions when used by the saints in battle. "Its sound is a drink of death," said one old poem, it "causes shortness of life. Woe to him who will defy it."

quite specific tribal alignments. Thus Columcille evangelized the clan to which he was born, the O'Donnells, branching off from there towards septs traditionally friendly with his own, and conversely avoiding those who, over generations, "had grasped our womenfolk after defeat in battle." Thus, it was always possible, in the various raids and stylized engagements of the times, to find clergy among the combatants of both sides, eagerly indulging themselves in the hereditary and sanguine passions of the clan. This extremely sectarian nature of the Celtic Church persisted well into feudal times. Indeed most ancient forms of patronage and endowment — and then the actual ownership of ecclesiastical wealth — tended to institutionalize local clan control of Church affairs. This rather unique characteristic partially explains the disproportionate pillage and siege that most Irish monastic communities endured for so many centuries. They were too clearly identified with the fortunes of petty kings, dynasties and chieftains (which Ireland seems to have produced in unwieldy abundance) to avoid becoming the plump and tantalizing targets of predatory hostings, which gloried in combining the usual depredations associated with feud, revenge and booty with the added opportunity to tarnish the reputation of patrons pledged to a particular church's defense. In Ireland, the humiliation of one's enemy was almost more enjoyable than killing him.

Ciarán of Clonmacnoise, Féchín of Fore, Comgall of Bangor, Finnian of Clonard — all these early churchmen, caught up in the fervor of Christian faith, evangelized their kinsmen and spread about the countryside, stringing together along normal Celtic lines the confederations of small monasteries and religious cells and schools for which Ireland was soon to be so famous. Columcille was, in only one respect, different from these men. He was of royal blood: not the son of a carpenter, herdsman or smithy, not a common laborer or soldier, but indisputably a prince, one who could have, had he so wished, entered the more traditional and Byzantine struggle for kingship of his clan whereby brother murdered brother, cousin slew cousin, until no other rival was left to take the prize.[1] But Columcille chose the cross, which he considered in the same martial terms that his blood relations regarded warfare. It was discipline, hardship, combat, and no one applied himself more assiduously than Columcille. He is beyond question the most enduring and legendarily gigantic of the Irish saints,[2] and I think this may reflect an historical fact that he was the most effective. Putting aside for the moment his apparent skills as an orator and preacher, which his biographers past and present

---

[1] "Woe to brothers amongst a barbarous people," as a Norman cleric observed in the twelfth century when commenting on these sanguinary intrigues. "Woe to kinsmen! When they are alive they are relentlessly driven to death."

[2] Some may question this claim by mentioning Brigit of Kildare, but considerable doubt has been cast whether, apart from myth, she ever existed. Columcille, by contrast, is verifiably historical.

judged to be considerable, the very fact of his lineage guaranteed an access to figures of authority that other missionaries could not match. The ancient Celts were status conscious as few other societies in history have been. St. Patrick realized this quickly enough when local chieftains scorned him as a beggarly fool without rank, princely attire or suitably impressive retinue. What god was worth adoring who had such a ridiculous wretch as his servant, wandering about in rags with a wooden staff? So Patrick hired a company of mercenaries, the sons of local gentry, to act as a respectable body of courtiers, an expenditure his superiors back in Britain found incomprehensibly extravagant. But Patrick, sizing up the situation, had improvised correctly, a recourse that Columcille (who, incidentally, may never have heard of Patrick) had no need of.

As the prince of a powerful (and warlike) northern tribe, many weaker or dependent chieftains had little choice but to pay him mind. He could speak to them as an equal, one of the ruling elite, or he could badger them as a superior, threatening catastrophe, a "red-draped doomsday," should they resist his message. He could also take the Bible to heart and preach among the lowest elements of Celtic life, though by upbringing he may not have wished to. This was a dual entrée that no other native Irish saint (to say nothing of Patrick) could duplicate, and a considerable achievement in a society so stratified and class conscious. I am inclined to believe, however, that despite professions of humility that characterize the alleged sayings and rules of Columcille, he did his greatest work among kings and people of rank. His career indicates this skill: beneath the common touch that devotional works by or about him selectively emphasize for the momentous events of his career, a careful analysis generally reveals a substrata of shrewd political intent. We have many instances in European history (though none on record for Ireland) of total conversion, whereby entire tribes, at the orders of their leadership, cast off old gods for new, marching down to seashore or riverside for wholesale baptism. I can envision this sort of scene for many of the northern septs, particularly those influenced by the menacing O'Donnells. We see some attempt by Columcille and other Irish saints to make this transfer more palliative by crudely channeling many pagan customs and feast days into a Christian orientation, but nevertheless I see a Celtic Richelieu in these proceedings. *Cúl Dreimne* presents much the same impression. Columcille could harangue the mob of soldiers to do the killing (if indeed they required any encouragement) but in order to have that opportunity he had to convince the chieftains to call them out in the first place. Only a prince could have done that, someone used to power. Unlike Patrick, who hired his coterie of retainers, Columcille simply gave the command. It is said that on state-like occasions he ordered forty priests, twenty bishops, thirty deacons and fifty students to precede his entry.

Naturally enough, the idea of "blood royal" and princely aristocrats, like

Columcille, seems somewhat out of place in this sodden farm field. In a lordly cathedral back in London, of course, the falling rain would be reassuring and atmospheric, a gentle backdrop for organ music, crimson robes, throne and scepter, crown and sword of state. But not here, not in the chill of this by now heavy rainfall and hacking, shivering livestock. The poet Edmund Spenser mocked these Celtic pretensions, refusing to call any of their rabble kings, preferring the sobriquet "captaine". For he saw the various tribes as "barbarous nations", mere collections of savage brigands dedicated to the fine art of murder and spoil. He would have seen in this field of *Cúl Dreimne* (a surrogate field, I am inclined to believe) something far away indeed from Runnymede. In Columcille he would have sensed a war hungry "captaine" as fierce as any, clothed in the rough garb of a kern, wild-eyed and hysterical, little different, save perhaps for a cross of gold around his neck, or an ornamented staff, maybe bell in hand, from the equally impassioned common swordsman called out from his duties as swineherd to fight again. But Spenser would have had it only partly right. The Irish were easy game for ridicule. Everyone knows the old joke that there were more kings in Erin than milkmen, and Spenser, speaking from the comparative modernity of an English point of view with its centralized monarchy and elaborate, costly ritual, would have naturally regarded the Irish, with something like three hundred petty domains or *tuaths* and that same number of kings (with perhaps hundreds more plotting to become one) as backward, primitive, vainglorious and absurd. What he missed, I think, was the sense of honor and imagination that the Irish possessed to a far greater degree than the English. True the Irish were bloodthirsty, but the same can be said of all the peoples of Europe at one time or another. They were also poor. Instead of the golden scepter of Good Queen Bess, an Irish king held a pure white wand as his symbol of sovereignty; instead of an ancient throne, with jewels and gold plate, a lonely stubbled mound of dirt littered with dung on a deserted mountain top or sacred grove; in place of dazzling crown, a green wreath of some despised and common vegetation. But this is simply form over substance: the intent of the Irish was identical. The king or "captaine" stood for honor, bravery, protection of the clan, fair dealings to all members of that clan. How faithfully such responsibilities were carried out depended, of course, on the make-up of the leader, and that is a generalization fit for all nations, big or small. Columcille was a little man from a little corner of a little island. He was not a particularly civilized individual by Roman standards, let alone Spenser's. But he and his people, by exalting themselves and their lives and their destinies in rhetoric fit for the gods, in effect dredged the good out of life, the nobility that there may be down here in the mud. This requires both a buoyancy of spirit and a certain creative urge. The Celts had more than their share of the former, and just enough of the latter to create a culture that was profound, resilient, and principled. One can find its expression in the few remains and artifacts and treasures that have survived so many centuries of turmoil; from ruined monasteries, cashels, beehive *clocháns*, and scattered hermitages; in the rather more copious saga tales, law tracts, and poems that the monks, when they sensed a coming end to old ways, preserved by writing down. Most of all, we see its worth in the long struggle to survive, not just physically but spiritually, the hundreds of years of effort by foreign intruders, incalculably superior in material resource, to extirpate their system with all its ancient values and traditions. Aside from the Jews, very few ethnic groups have fought so long and so hard. It is unfortunate that when the Irish lost their native tongue they really did lose their cultural war. Hebrew is at least a working language, Gaelic a university course.

The battlefield of *Cúl Dreimne* is a lesson in irony. It is just a sloppy field, but it is also the marrow of legend and glory. This was a mélange of filthy, violent clansmen, but they valued with similar ferocity the works of poets, musicians and artists. True it is that Columcille was no theologian, yet he reminds us of Christ more than a St. Augustine. The rain is valuable here. It will teach us, starting out, to look with particular attention at all the smallest details of what little is left from those faraway times, for they will serve as monuments equal to the Parthenon or Colosseum. This place really is the preserve of royalty. Spenser told a fairly gruesome story in his polemic *A View of the Present State of Ireland*, which he wrote in 1595-96. "I saw an old woman at the execution of a notable traitor at Limerick called Murrough O'Brien," he related, who "took up his head whilst he was quartered and sucked up all the blood running there out, saying the earth was not worthy to drink it." A vestige of barbaric perversity to some, a living act of poetry to others.

THIS MORNING HAS not been auspicious. I realized I was in trouble when the sun awoke me. Too late! I said to myself, I would miss whatever fishermen were going out that day and sure enough, leaning up in the back of the Citroën, parked on one of the two jetty arms that make up the harbor of Mullaghmore, I could see three skiffs passing the breakwater into the bay, but no other activity at all up or down on the docks. Thinking I might still catch a straggler I resist the temptation to go back to sleep and struggle out of bed, get dressed and walk around to the other quay. This is certainly where the fishermen operate. It's a mess, stacks of lobster traps and frayed nylon ropes interspersed with rusty piles of diesel-soaked machinery parts and marine-related flotsam. An air of forlorn abandonment hangs around the place, the boats tied up alongside each other having all seen better days. I notice an older man pottering about amid the debris and ask him if any other boats will be fishing today. "All that's going out be out by now," he replies, barely looking up at me. " 'Tis a lovely day to be out for sure, after yesterday's soaking, and the lads are eager to bring in the pots. Aye, winter has landed all right, time to save what you can for next year." We chat along for a minute or two. The only fishing out of Mullaghmore, I learn, is for lobsters. No trawlers or boats with any crews or processing plants around here. "In Killybegs, up there in Donegal," he says pointing off across the bay, "they have some big boats, but here it's all old times, little open skiffs like these below. We stay close by, hard to the shore, and work the pots. Not many lobsters these days, though. Not many lads out there anymore either." I ask him if anyone will take me out to Inishmurray. "Ah well now, in summer they might, for a few of them keep traps out there sometimes, when they think in along here be all fished out. But not now. Too dangerous. You can't land there you know, it's very hard. I'm off to my tea now. No, none of the lads will go out." Shuffling away he waves his hand at a somewhat larger boat tied up along the dock, which seems to my untrained eye an old-fashioned dragger, though by the looks of her she is now retired to the status of pleasure craft, having none of the battered antiquity that working boats along this coast generally exhibit. "You might try him. He'll do anything for a quid or two. Up there in the boat yard." I reply I will, though a charter captain was not what I had in mind.

Walking on top of the sea wall back to the shore, I am full of admiration for the enormous vistas across Donegal Bay and, closer at hand, the sweeping crescent of Bunduff Strand curving northward, with miles of breaking surf whipped up by a vigorous offshore wind that clears out the lingering vestiges of last night's storm. The village itself is not of much interest, however, being the artificial creation of the famous Lord Palmerstone whose ancestors, somewhere in the 1640s, had gleefully joined in despoiling the native Irish clans by purchasing 10,000 acres here from Sir Thomas Stafford, the much hated Lord Deputy who had engineered the notorious Confiscation of Connaught. Two hundred years later Palmerstone found on his estates conditions little changed from medieval times, and decided to develop the area as a "Brighton in the West," spending almost £30,000 on the harbor alone, where before there had been only a wild and unsheltered shore front. He constructed as well hotels and substantial goods shops along with peasant cottages, schools, and churches. Along an eminent bluff high above the village on the other side of this small peninsula and directly facing the open ocean, he also built a magnificently brooding Tennysonian castle, visible for miles from the main coach road. He named this pile "Classie Bawn," from the original *Clasa bana* which the Gaels called this place, the "White Hollows" or "Wilderness" of Sand. It has some contemporary interest as the former summer residence of Lord Mountbatten, who motored out of Mullaghmore Harbor in his specially designed launch on the morning of

August 27, 1979 for a day of cruising. An I.R.A. assassin, from some vantage point along the bluffs, detonated by remote control a bomb previously hidden on board, with the result that Mountbatten and several guests and employees were either killed or severely injured.

Palmerstone's enterprise never returned much on his investment, though in a modest way a few yachts come and go through the course of a summer season, with the hotels and guest houses doing just enough business to justify trying again year after year. But the place has a false look about it, a satisfaction and bourgeois sense of comfort that is extremely un-Irish. What is native about the place are the long rows of ghastly modern bungalows that lie atop the expansive plateau of farm fields west of town. Palmerstone would be pleased at the energy and apparent prosperity that could create these buildings, though perhaps his aesthetic sensibilities might be offended.

It is very early, and I can tell from the drawn blinds that my captain is still in bed. I take a seat in his garden, though the sun is hardly warm. Palmerstone, it is said, provided a front yard for every house he put up here, "a piece of civilization," according to a correspondent from *The Times* in London, "for which Irishmen as a rule do not seem to care." I can eye the superb views to seaward while also keeping watch on the bedroom blinds.

In due course, the household awakens and hard bargaining begins.

"Inishmurray is it," he says after generously offering breakfast. He turns on the radio to catch a forecast. "Winds could shift on us out there," is the first worried comment he offers. "It's a tight fit even in the best of weather, but if the sea ground comes out of the southwest it'll take all I've got to push out from her. But if you're game we can try." We beg to differ on his fare. "Well it's £40 to go out. Now if there were three or four people to share it the price would seem reasonable enough, sure you'd agree with that. But you've come here in the worst of times and alone." We agree to £30, whether I can land or not. This is an ominous precondition, but an hour or so later we churn around the point into open seas, straight for Inishmurray.

I can think of many island views more memorable than this: the coal black Skelligs, for instance, jutting theatrically from the ocean more than seven miles off Bolus Head in Kerry; the lush, modulated, melancholic Great Blasket, a shorter distance off Slea Head on the Dingle Peninsula, made famous by its extraordinary works of literature — Maurice O'Sullivan's *Twenty Years A-Growing*, Tomás O Crohan's *The Island-man*, Peig Sayers' *An Old Woman's Reflections* — which chronicled the end of Gaelic life there; or the renowned Aran Islands in Galway Bay, with cliffs on the southern edge of Inishmore, largest of the three, hundreds of feet high over the ocean with the outlined ruins of Dun Aengus, the Iron Age fortress encompassing over eleven acres, clearly visible. In contrast, Inishmurray is a low, unpresumptuous place of little feature or outline, what one early visitor uncharitably described as a "bare, barren, dreary island." It resembles a bay leaf, or stone arrowhead, and runs in a fairly true east-west line, Rue Point at the tip facing shore, Kinavally at the stem towards the Atlantic, a mile in length (at best) by a half mile at its widest part. There are no imposing physical characteristics of the type we usually associate with the wilder coastline sections of western Ireland — cliffs, mountainous terrain, sea-carved archways, stupendous gun-holes. The island does not seem to have erupted from the ocean in some fiery cataclysm from long ago; rather it carries an air of floating on the surface, a flat, undistinguished lowland table top. It stands about 40 to 70 feet above sea level; 223 acres in size, roughly a quarter of that area being arable; sandstone for the most part, with a soil depth of only 4 to 5 inches; shallow peat in the center of the island, surrounding a small tarn or bog lake, two wells that have never gone dry, no beach to speak of and a harbor notorious for its treachery. It is not the sort of place that looms before you, nor does it kindle feelings of excitement, splendor or the terror of nature.

It is a nine mile voyage out to the island, and the chilling wind encourages the captain and me to wedge ourselves in a little enclosed pilot's bridge to the rear of the boat. The close quarters generate some conversation, first about his boat. It's an old vessel, he tells me, about fifty years plying the bay, first as a sailing craft, mostly fishing for salmon, then converted to diesel sometime after the war. The major historical note about her is that three crewmen died one night off Slieve League, the enormous mountain range that plunges dramatically into the ocean as a sheer drop along the northern edge of the bay. The boat, low in the water with a full catch and her nets still out behind, was apparently barged by a whale or some such fearsome creature, which stove in the hull and caused her to flounder. He paid £80 for what was essentially a wreck and put her back together in his boat yard. "Aside from Mountbatten's boat, which really was a thing of beauty, this old tub is queen of the harbor," which causes some resentment from the locals. "I'm a blow-in, you know, not from around here. They all look at the boat and scratch their heads. They remember her as a battered old hulk."

He considers himself an expert on the island. "After all, I make my living taking people out there in the summer. Not much business in the yard, minor repairs, that's about it, so I butter up the tourists. They want to hear all the whiskey talk, how the islanders made their living from poteen and stole it into shore in the face of revenue agents in the dark of night on stormy, stormy seas, that kind of stuff. It's very romantic to most of them. Then I have the usual stories about the island superstitions and folk lore — the Gaelic angle — and after that they're always asking me about Yeats, what did he think of the place, did it inspire any of his poems and so forth. I hate to do it but I usually tell them the truth, that as far as I understand it the island doesn't figure in any of the old sagas or fairie tales, you know the Deidre of the Seven Sorrows or Cú Chulainn stuff, so it's a bit dull as subject matter, especially in comparison with all the things they have around Sligo, which Yeats did use. And then I have to tell them that Yeats was a lazy sort of devil if you know what I mean. He could spend a pleasant day lying in the sun at Innisfree rather than hacking it out here where he'd likely get drowned. Then, of course, there's the old ruins, which I'm guessing is why you're out here, and finally the birds and seals. By the time I'm finished we're usually ready to land. On the way back I'm talked out, and that's generally when they all get seasick.

"There now, there's the new jetty", he says pointing to a solid concrete walkway that sticks imprudently out into the sea off the south shore of the island, about a thousand feet from Rue Point. "That's a real insight into the natives. They refused to pay rates, saying why should they, they received no services from the County Council and they had no money anyway. They said build us a new pier and we'll pay rates. This was all back in the 1920s. So the government people came out, looked around and said ok, we'll build one here. The islanders all knew it was no good. I mean look at it, totally exposed to all the prevailing winds and the open ocean, really useless. But the islanders didn't say anything. They got six months work from the government on a project they knew wouldn't work from the start. So when Sligo sends out the rate notice, the islanders say no way, we won't pay, the jetty is no good, build us one we can use. You can imagine the exasperation back there in the bureaucracy because really, these illiterate people were very wily and had pulled one off. Though of course they never got a decent harbor. If they had they might still be there."[1]

We are motoring along the south coast, all broad blocks of rock descending like steps into the ocean; on the ridge above, clusters of peasant cottages, raw unpainted sandstone hulks, roofless and deserted. A bit over half way along we come to *Clashymore*, what passes for the harbor of Inishmurray. "Here's where you want to be fairly tidy now," says the captain, who cuts his speed and veers off the shore in order to line up the boat for a direct, headlong plunge into a shallow indentation of the coast line. On our portside is a substantial, sheltering island called *Oileán is Tiar*, on starboard a very messy looking assemblage of low water rocks, embroiled in surf, ready for the careless or unwary. "That island there is deceptive," according to the captain, "there's a channel cut through on the other side which opens direct to the southwest where the prevailing winds and currents run through, so the ground swells are

---

[1] Aversion to paying taxes was an old Inishmurray tradition. A visitor in 1883 saw the women of the island hurling stones at the rates collector as he tried to land in rough weather. After several missiles hit the boat he gave up and left for home.

usually deadly, they can throw you up on the eastern side of the anchorage in a single toss. Right now we're ok, we're fine, because the winds are northwesterly." We run into the harbor, then turn smartly starboard into a long narrow fissure where the captain eases the bow, motioning me to clamber up on shore. I can see what he means by the southwesterlies. The gap between *Oileán is Tiar* and Inishmurray lines up perfectly with this natural little slip. As he said to me later in the afternoon, on our way back, "Southwest is your enemy here. All those little *classeys* (Gaelic for furrow) face the southwest, they were carved out of the island by wave action from the prevailings. First you had a natural crack in the rock face centuries ago, and as the seas pounded them over and over again boulders kept falling away and being swept out. The back suckage is always stronger, you know, because it's falling downhill, like when the wave goes up on the rocks, it comes back down with more water force because it's falling off a hill, tearing the boulders out with it. So nature made the little anchorage and the little places where a boat could land, but in the bargain guaranteed that in most conditions you'd have your life at risk doing it." He has eased the boat back into the harbor and cast an anchor over. "Keep your eye on me now and then," he yells across. "If the winds change we'll have to get out."

I was diligent in keeping my attention on the weather for about twenty minutes. Every so often I would face Benbulbin back on the mainland and if the wind was in my face then I knew I could stay. But selfishness is undoubtedly the most human of afflictions and after awhile, as I passed through what is, on so many levels, a dreamscape here on this island, I concluded that wind and sea conditions were the captain's problems which I had paid him an exorbitant fee to take care of — not a particularly judicious frame of mind, I admit, but that's what I was thinking.

Walking along the now lushly-padded cart track, no longer tramped to dirt by the island people and their livestock, I feel as though I have entered some prestigious museum of art, a place which celebrates deadness. It's not just the abandoned farmsteads, the tumble-down small sheds and neglected stone walls, but the entire aura of the place. There is no vitality here or life. Even the birds, the one or two seals I can see larking about offshore, and the ocean's clamor, seem vestigial and gray. But of interest to me, perversely, is a feeling I have from the very first step, an enormous sense of freedom. How can a person feel free in a graveyard, which Inishmurray certainly is? How can a dead end like this make a person fresh and exuberant? I remind myself that Inishmurray is no brave new world: it is not where people in search of discovery, excitement, or raw stimulation are likely to spend time — a monumental Antarctica, a frontier Alaska, a mystical Incan site in Central America, tantalizingly overgrown by a primeval rain forest, or even the moon or outer space of current fantasy. This place is the backwater of a European land mass that no longer holds secrets of any magnitude. It is the Old

World that people have been fleeing for centuries, a nostalgic memory bank that pioneers, immigrants and explorers have spent their lives brushing away as a cumbersome, stagnant weight. One always ruminates out here in restrictive terms because the vision is a stale one from the start, mildewed crumbs from a past gone yellowed in the history books, eulogized and buried in sociological post-mortems for a vanished, though familiar, people. Only someone who lives with his back to the future can be happy here.

A few minutes from the harbor I approach the only semblance there is on Inishmurray to a crossroads. The main path runs along ahead to the remaining nine cottages (I have passed three) and the old school house, built in 1899. To my right is the ancient Church of the Women, a low unadorned rectangular building within whose enclosure is a cemetery where, in segregation, only females (whether married or not) lie buried. A narrow track separates the church from one of Inishmurray's sixteen stations of the cross, this one dedicated to Columcille and featuring an oblong standing stone incised with cross motif. Turning to my left, or inland, I follow an even narrower pathway to the monastic cashel, one of the finest examples left in Ireland today of a complex that in olden times was as common as rain.

Cashel as a generic term applies to the Celtic penchant of surrounding their dwellings, farmsteads, churches, and princely abodes with circular walls of either dirt or stone. In the midlands of Ireland, where clans generally followed their herds from one grazing ground to another, the landscape is scattered with earthen rings more specifically called raths; but in the north, and particularly the west, where the land is considerably less hospitable, boulders and slabs of rock were commonly used, and these constructions, in the purest technical sense, are cashels. There has been some debate among academics whether this particular cashel, impressively substantial by any standard (or "cyclopean" as nineteenth-century antiquarians preferred to call the style) came before or after the religious buildings that lie within. Some believe the cashel is an Iron Age fortress similar in style to the "royal palace" of Aileach in Donegal and Staigue in Kerry and was, like so many raths all over Ireland, deeded to the Church by a king or regional notable as the endowment for an ecclesiastical foundation. Aerial photographs of most Celtic monasteries, their original buildings long since obliterated or superseded by medieval construction, will nearly always reveal an outline of the original cashel or rath encircling the complex. Others have maintained, however, that the cashel on Inishmurray is either contemporaneous with the structure inside or a later, defensive addition dating from the 800s, when Viking raiders were endemic to these waters. Barring some archaeological dating device as yet uninvented (a not implausible possibility, I should add, given the incredible strides radiocarbon techniques have made these past several decades) there is likely to be no satisfactory resolution to this debate, for the written records pertaining to Inishmurray — the monastic chronicles and histories — are either silent or long since destroyed through the turbulent generations of the Irish past. As one historian said to me, "We've been, over the years, a race of pyromaniacs, putting to the torch everything we've ever written about ourselves and, in the bargain, a few of the record keepers as well. We like to see things go up in smoke."

Four gateways penetrate the cashel wall at what seem to be haphazard and arbitrary intervals, but then again everything to do with this place seems skewed and off-kilter. The wall itself, a good 8-10 feet thick and about 12-15 in height, is not a perfect circle by any means. For no reason that I can tell — the contour of the land, for example, or certain unavoidable natural obstacles such as an obdurate boulder or rocky outcrop — the cashel is more the shape of an egg, and is divided internally by lower walls into four idiosyncratic and unequal portions. The largest of these, into which I have entered, contains what is called the monastic church or Church of the Men, for it was here in this enclosure that deceased males were interred. Various tombs and grave slabs of fairly recent nineteenth-century provenance lie scattered about, along with several very ancient pillar stones, archaically incised with either crosses or crude decoration. The famous cursing stones are here as well, a collection of smooth, sea-rolled boulders of various size that have been gathered on a raised altar or platform, and which constitute the only ritual on Inishmurray that has garnered any attention in the mainstream world of touristic hyperbole. Through various spells or incantations involving these stones a disconsolate islander could avenge himself on a neighbor who had wronged him, the object of these curses suffering, within a year, some appropriate turn of ill fortune. The Irish, of course, have always been renowned for their tempestuous humors — "The men of this country are during this mortal life more prone to anger and revenge than any other race," as a Norman observed in 1188 — and no doubt these stones have a long and certainly pagan pedigree. Several of the finest specimens, carved with crosses when it came time to Christianize the various heathen customs, have been taken away either by souvenir hunters of fairly recent times or museum curators from Dublin who saw no alternative to prevent their disappearance. Such has also been the case of the finer pillar slabs, several of which lie locked away in the "House" of St. Molaise, a very small oratory tucked away near the cashel wall. This little building, only 12 by 8 feet but constructed of extremely thick sandstone slabs, is typical of the earliest Celtic stone chapels, several examples of which survive in Ireland. It is a gabled building, and one of the few left in this place, whether church or cottage, that can still claim the semblance of a roof. In the nineteenth century it was the most venerated of the monastic buildings on the island, due in part to its association with Molaise, Inishmurray's patron saint, and to his famous statue that was housed inside.

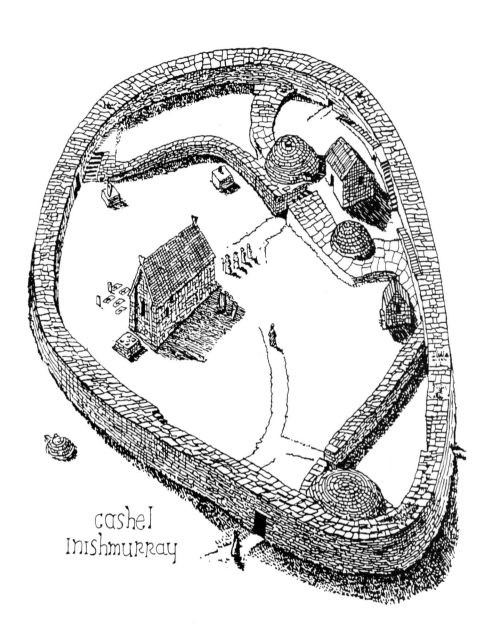

cashel
inishmurray

This is the same Molaise who served as Columcille's confessor after the Battle of *Cúl Dreimne* and who imposed on him, the cantankerous and too-impassioned royal monk, the onerous penalty of exile from Ireland. Aside from his role in that particular drama little is known of his life or career with any certainty, though story-tellers both past and present are delighted to fill in the details. We cannot be sure, for example, whether Molaise was the founder of this monastery, since Inishmurray means in Gaelic "the island of Muirdeach", and an early saint by that name was known to have established a community on the southern shores of the bay at Killala, and it could well be that to him goes the credit for setting up the original cell. On the other hand, many commentators have been fond of assigning the single man both these names, always a convenient methodology for eliminating pluralism and creating, as the end product, something easy to understand. Others have hypothesized that the Molaise of Inishmurray was the same individual as the Molaise of Devenish, a monastery of considerable wealth and temporal power that clearly out-classed the tiny hermitage we see here. This theory is slightly more plausible since Devenish, located on an island in the Lower Lough Erne, is in reasonable geographic proximity to Inishmurray. Dr. Patrick Heraughty, however, a native of Inishmurray and a physician for many years in Sligo, explained to me that "the whole thing is speculative, to say the very least. Who founded Inishmurray? Was it the same man who founded Devenish? Who can ever know? We have twelve men who called themselves Molaise, if you separate them all in the sagas and chronicles, twelve individuals carrying the same name. Now Molaise of Devenish, if only because Devenish became one of the top-flight Celtic monasteries in the country, is the star of this group, but really we know as little about him as any of the others. That doesn't stop us here in the lesser places from wanting to assign him as one and the same person. This is the trouble, no one will give up their Molaise! We say Molaise of Inishmurray and Molaise of Devenish is a single man, and who's to say we're wrong? Those early Irish churchmen travelled about from place to place a great deal because the spirit to gain conversions was on them. The country was by no means Christianized, despite the fact we like to say St. Patrick did it in so short a time. Now Devenish is very, very near Inishmurray, and between the two, in a place called Rossinver, which is in North Leitrim, we know that Molaise of Devenish, or his *coarbs*,[1] established a daughter house. It's all an obvious straight line — Devenish to Rossinver to In-ishmurray — so that I believe it makes a good circumstantial case. I haven't the courage, as many people do, to bet my life on it, but it strikes me as

---

[1] *Coarb* in Irish means "heir to" or "family of" and refers to those abbots who succeeded the original founding father of a monastery or abbey. Abbots at Devenish, for example, were known as the *coarbs* of Molaise. Daughter houses or satellites of important monastic centers banded together in federations known as the *paruchia*.

more than possible."

The lineage of the statue is equally suspect. It was first mentioned in 1779 by a French antiquarian, Gabriel Beranger, who reported that the islanders he met — "very innocent, good-natured, and devout, but at the same time, very superstitious and credulous" — pointed out to him a life-size wooden figure which they kept in the monastic ruins, purporting to be a representation of Molaise. "They have daubed him all over with red paint to make him look handsome," he noted, and spun a good many tales and legends about the saint and various island traditions, all of which "filled some pages of paper." Beranger's curiosity was not shared by the local Protestant gentry or its clergy. During periods of comparative calm, when they were not fearful of French invasion or peasant unrest, many of these landlords tried their hand at proselytizing the natives. This predilection found its greatest expression during the famine years when soup kitchens were set up and food distributed to the starving tenants, on the condition they listen to Protestant harangues on the evils of Catholicism. On Inishmurray, in fact, the landlord installed a schoolmaster, at an expense of £36 per annum, ostensibly to educate the illiterate but in fact to convert them, or so believed the islanders who, on the advice of a priest from the mainland, refused to send their children for instruction. "The Black Master", as he was dubbed, became the ready explanation for every ill to befall the island. John O'Donovan, the legendary Gaelic scholar who visited Inishmurray in 1836, wrote "the islanders believe they have not had a day's luck since he first came among them, that the land has lost that fertility which distinguished it during the Golden Age, that fishes have forsaken their shore and" — the worst calamity of all — "the still refuses to give the usual quantity." The schoolmaster, at least, took none of this personally. He was untroubled by the discontent and, so long as he received his salary, did not seem to mind such a comparative life of leisure. But several of his coreligionists felt otherwise, and the island was periodically invaded by Protestant worthies upset at rumors that the statue itself had been transformed by the islanders into a god, an idolatrous reversion to paganism which hardly surprised them. One such expedition resulted in the arms of the statue, apparently raised in supplication or thanksgiving, being hacked off with an ax, along with several other mutilations; another in its utilization as a rifle target; and a final desecration, being removed from the island and dumped at sea. It was not believed at any time that the figure might be antique, the Protestants apparently convinced they had destroyed nothing more valuable than a merchant vessel's figurehead — perhaps Neptune or some other nautical representation — washed up on shore from an unknown wreck or maritime disaster by "the waves which lash the island for its superstition." In fact, experts now date the figure as a fourteenth-century carving, clearly depicting a cleric in vestment-like robes. In a truly miraculous turn of events the saint was found several days later back where it belonged, strewn on the island's coast-line by sea and tide, a confirmation (if one was needed) of the statue's sanctity. But it was never, before or after that day, worshipped as an idol. The islanders "are greater rogues than fools," said O'Donovan, and he scoffed at the Protestant interferences. Even if they could be converted, he wrote, "it would be of no great acquisition to have these distillers reckoned amongst the elect." When Inishmurray was evacuated in 1948 the figure was removed to Dublin's National Museum, to no apparent dismay on the part of the islanders who cast it, along with most other of their traditions, to the winds as they found themselves scattered on the mainland and beyond. When I last saw the figure it certainly had a weary air about it, not ravaged I must say, but serene. It is ironic that most of its difficulties seem of fairly modern vintage.

A little corridor leads into the next largest enclosure, where a variety of interesting structures still remain: a perfect *clochán* or beehive hut; an underground passage-way or tunnel, known as a souterrain, one of two within the cashel; a curious underground chamber covered with heavy slabs of stone, and reminding me of construction originally seen in the pre-Celtic Stone Age passage graves so common in Ireland; and another small rectangular oratory known as the Church of the Fire. The tunnel and souterrains are a mystery. Exotic explanations usually concentrate on their role as hiding places in time of danger, of which there were many, whereas more prosaic analyses tend to see them as space for storage. I see no reason to doubt they played both roles. The *clochán* is an indigenous Celtic creation, a circular hut-like structure of unmortared stone that served as cell or dwelling for the monks. Some remaining examples in Ireland are quite substantial, such as those of Skellig Michael in County Kerry, where the largest is some 16 feet in height from floor to ceiling, with walls as much as 6 feet thick at its base. The dome of the roof is ingeniously designed to prevent seepage of rainwater to the interior, but the lack of any bonding agent such as cement made them easy targets for destruction or, if abandoned, victims of eventual cave-in or a slow wasting away. Even until fairly recent times these buildings were still being put up by the Irish peasantry, mostly in the Dingle Peninsula near Tralee, where they were used for tool sheds, outhouses, animal sties. This example on Inishmurray is particularly fine, though it lacks the elegance of the larger, more tapering *clocháns* of Skellig Michael, being surrounded by a secondary retaining wall which accentuates its rather squat appearance. The entrance is low, requiring one to stoop going in. This could either be a token of humility or else a break against the sea wind.

The Church of the Fire resembles the other oratories on the island, but is more interesting for its reputation as the source of perpetual flame. A certain hearthstone within the Church could always be relied upon to start a piece of turf, or any other combustible material, should domestic

The "House" of Molaise and his Statue
Inishmurray
County Sligo
c. 1875

fires on the island suddenly go out. O'Donovan relates the story, much beloved by the islanders, that a "Protestant had the profane assurance of defiling this flagstone by sitting on it to drop those excrescences which proved to Alexander the Great that he was not a God, but lo! the pure Molaise implored his God to work a miracle to confound him and his companions, for a supernatural fire issuing forth in swelling flames caught his flesh and penetrated to his marrow, so that he was consumed, to the horror of his companions who had accompanied him hither to insult and destroy the sacred ruins." Dr. Heraughty told me that when he was a child a stack of human bones was kept nearby to impress the skeptical. This vengeful piece of rock was rather callously broken up by government workers in 1880 (all Catholics I would presume) and used as building rubble when the cashel was repaired and certain other of the buildings tidied up. It seems, in fact, that quite a bit of damage was perpetuated by outsiders. Revenue agents, for example, smashed several tombs over the course of periodic raids to uncover caches of bootleg whiskey (mostly ferreted away in the bogs, according to Heraughty), and workmen sent out over the years to restore the old ruins were not adverse to undertaking drastic and unhistorical renovations. Two of the four entrances are the result of these enthusiasms, along with the addition of wall enclosures and "defensive" works on the cashel itself, all of which have prompted anguished cries of outrage from visitors more learned than the rest of us.

CLIMBING UP ON the cashel wall gives a fine view all around the bay and open ocean, the island itself with its now overgrown fields and ruined cottages and, of course, an almost aerial perspective of the monastic compound below, calculated by Dr. Heraughty as encompassing about one third of an acre. Some early Gaelic poems suggest these cashels were built as a devotional exercise, that saints "could see nothing except the heavens above" when they were finished. Places like this were often referred to as "prisons of hard narrow stone" where monks like Énda "of the high piety" could achieve "victory with sweetness". These are tidy sentiments, familiar to people like me with a Christian and, more particularly, a Catholic background, the idea of reward for pain, or paradise around the corner. But something about Inishmurray is far from tidy, and circumnavigating the monastery from my elevated vantage point a series of contradictions occur to me. The first takes the form of a recollection from childhood when I habitually clipped color photos from travel magazines and glued them into scrapbooks. The ones most appealing to me depicted the countrysides of Britain and Ireland, miles of multi-hued fields and pastures bounded by quaint stone walls and full of contented livestock. They seemed to me as soft and alluring as feathery beds, an illusion quickly lost when I started hiking and camping in Europe during college vacations. Then, of course, I discovered brambles and thorns, drainage ditches and gullies, mudholes and plough ruts, angry bulls and cow manure. Inishmurray may be sanctified ground but it is not a manicured, antiseptic property of the National Trust or the United States Park Service, removed from history by the modern care heaped upon it. This place is rough, unadorned, disquieting, and irregular. Something about it dispels whatever languid assumptions we may have brought along with us from the mainland, notions like those of John Healy, the nineteenth-century Bishop of Tuam, who took enormous satisfaction that here, at least, "no Protestant lives or is buried, and no church of the new worship desecrates the resting place of early Irish saints." But did Healy or even the Protestants have any idea what kind of men came here when the monastery was founded in the late 500s, or when the buildings whose remains we see today were built, probably in the seventh century? Did they have any real understanding of the beliefs these monks held, and whether those beliefs would have stood the scrutiny of a Vatican commission on orthodoxy? I rather doubt it. Healy and other comfortable visitors[1] would not have related the crudity of these ruins with a religious point of view that verged on superstition. They would have preferred a beautifully restored cashel wall, re-roofed oratories and beehive huts, silken lawns and uniformed custodians -- the neatness of the scene a confirmation, as it were, of dogmatic tradition and certitude, the passing of a torch direct from the Apostles. Instead we have an arrogance here in these ruins, a refusal to answer questions and a refusal, certainly, to provide unambiguous conclusions. Even the ground cover -- lumpy, uneven, dishevelled, an invitation to a bad fall or twisted ankle -- seems perverse. Why such miniscule oratories, for example, barely serviceable to more than three or four people at a time? Why the divisions within the cashel, which seem to have no rationale? The crosses, pillar stones, and stations, erected in apparent confusion -- what was the system or plan that placed them in such chaotic fashion? And beneath all of this, the central point really, what of the monks themselves? John O'Donovan wrote that "four very wild men" rowed him out to Inishmurray when he came out in 1836, echoing a strain of commentary that seems unbroken from the very first observers of the Gael who took the time to record their impressions -- even St. Patrick, who moaned that "I dwell among barbarians." Inishmurray is a reflection of these people but, in great style, it will not dignify the visitor with much of a portrait. In some ways the place ignores us.

One purpose of this book is to try and uncover the personality of this elusive figure, the early Irish monk -- what he was like, what he felt and

---

[1] The travel writings of nearly all these nineteenth-century tourists share the common trait of fulsome culinary description -- picnic baskets overflowing with delicacies, bottles of wine and spirits, afternoon naps and postluncheon difficulties clamoring over rocks or reboarding boats for the return trip, all to the astonishment, we may presume, of the islanders, whose diet was mostly salted fish.

believed, what he studied and read, the kinds of paths he may have followed. To do this, of course, we must also try to understand the origins of monasticism itself, where it first developed in the East, how it pervaded the disintegrating Roman Empire and then, in a great leap through the unknown, how it penetrated the farthest regions of Ireland, a country referred to by one seventh-century churchman as "a pimple on the chin of the world." And even beyond that we should wish to examine the very religion itself, and the person of its founder, in order to see if in Ireland, perhaps, the truest germ of Christianity somehow remained distinct from the edifice which gradually emerged on the European mainland, itself the evolutionary product of political and intellectual forces that barely touched this remote, hostile land.

Yet time frames of history — the progressions of year to year, decade to decade, century to century — are often too enormous for any of us to comprehend in the sense of a completed painting. Famous writers may attempt, like Toynbee, to make sense of this endless panorama by suggesting a pattern or cycles, epic though predictable, wherein the breadth of mankind's comings and goings can approximately be handled, absorbed, and understood. This encapsulating urge allows one to glide through generations and comfortably see beginnings and endings, definable eras and epochs, in a perfectly harmonious package. But in the more narrow sphere of Irish history this same approach has not been successful, due mainly to the lack of written source material and a firm foundation of plentiful data. It is not uncommon to read sentences like "Nothing really happened for two hundred years," a dark ages approach that, in the interest of truth, we must generally accept. If we do not, we enter the realm of fiction.

So what is left are bits and pieces, the odd bone now and then that provides us with a minor insight or revelation. These we will endeavor to pick up, turn over in our hands, examine closely and then, as has happened to me many times in Irish cemeteries, rather wonder what to do. A human bone — once the inner structure of a man or woman from God knows how long ago — is not something idly cast over one's shoulder or tossed to the ground. Instead, with funerary awareness, one looks for a nice tall patch of grass or sheltering tombstone behind which to place it, realizing of course that a dog will find the thing some day soon. The lesson here is that we are surrounded in matters of the long ago, and not just in Irish material I hasten to add, by an assorted mélange of irony, inconsistency, splintered and incomplete information, absurdist peregrinations. But these bumps and grinds, though an invitation to ruin according to the American scholar Samuel Eliot Morison, who warned "never let yourself bog down in pedantry and detail", are indeed the essence of historical experience. There is no smooth road to follow. Writers desperate for continuity or mechanisms to attract and then hold our attention — what the biographer Catherine Drinker Bowen identified as a "Will the reader turn the page?" syndrome — in many ways distort this truism. Books have beginnings and ends, but the affairs of men are rarely that neat. "This is not a time to complete anything," as Marcel Duchamps said to Anaïs Nin in 1934. "It is a time for fragments."

T HERE IS, OF course, an umbrella over this entire story, one we cannot avoid, and that is religion, though it should be noted that this excursion to Inishmurray is not a devotional exercise on the author's part, either as pilgrimage or retreat. A veteran of both these endeavors, I no longer pursue either anymore. If taken seriously, in the traditional fashion, they are meant to encourage fervor and intensity — if you will, faith — but they are not conducive to clarity.

I really do not know if Inishmurray is conducive to clarity either. The physical splendor of the place, and the almost overwhelming elements of sea and wind which monopolize one's senses and orientation, tend to be antagonistic at times to thought. But anyone coming here in the hopes of catching some hint of the tremendous force that caused men to flee their lives of secular concern for the rigors of a harsh unrelenting hermitage, must consider the individual who inspired such drastic behavior, Jesus the prophet from Nazareth.

It will not surprise me if some readers would regard any discussion of this man's life and personality with extreme irritation and contempt. I will agree that in many respects it is a trite and tiresome subject, the reminder of brainwashed childhoods or worse. But Inishmurray in its largest implications revolves around him. Surely there can be no argument on that score. To consider the place only as a collection of buildings and walls and ruined crosses would be suitable for an archaeological inventory but not much else. We would have no life to consider, only debris. And so the first bone, our initial idiosyncratic inspection, should by rights belong to Christ, if for no other reason than he is the foundation of everything here.

Ironically, however, this presents a topic of such convolution and complexity that it dwarfs the more narrow confines of rummaging about on this obscure and largely irrelevant island. I myself maintain before me the image of Christ as God whenever I consider or reflect on Inishmurray, though I often question the historiography of most Catholic canon. The monks of centuries past never did so, their faith being largely absolute and unassailable.

For the purposes of this particular voyage it does little good to debate the often fascinating questions whether Jesus was or was not the Messiah, whether he considered himself a God or merely His messenger, did or did not in fact arise from the dead after three nights, later to ascend into heaven; nor does it matter if the Apostles were a band of drunken freebooters and St. Paul, to whom credit goes for much of this religion's content, not much more than a deranged spinner of delusions. Jesus Christ, it seems to me, was a real person and Inishmurray, like Galilee, is the Holy Land. It is best to synchronize our steps with those of the accepted portrait of Christ and his career here on earth. Otherwise we come to Inishmurray as tourists and nothing more.

THE CHRONOLOGICAL PICTURE of Christianity's remarkable diffusion through the Empire is usually bench-marked by reference to the travels of St. Paul, who reached the epicenter of the ancient civilized world, the great city of Rome, about A.D. 58, albeit as a prisoner in chains, with the executioner's block his eventual fate. His digressive wanderings on the way — many years in Macedonia and the Peloponnesian peninsula — are generally considered an appropriate rite of passage, since Roman civilization owed much of its substance to the older, and eminently superior, Greek model. But in fact, by the time Paul reached the capital there were Christians at the wharf to greet him. Many of these vexed the great missionary, being true Romans, by their lack of anxiety over the fortunes of coreligionists on the more obscure outer boundaries of the Empire: "They seek their own interests," Paul wrote, "not those of Jesus Christ."

Correlating the voyages of Paul with the spread of Christianity to the West is a convenient device for the classroom and a not particularly misleading one, as many more complicated rearrangements of fact have proven to be. Paul was an energetic administrator whose talents as an underground cellular agent are deservedly praised, and his determination to focus on urban populations proved both strategically farsighted and mathematically productive. In fact, the early meaning of the word heathen — *paganorus*, "rustic" or "dweller in the wasteland" — indicates where the majority of early conversions were taking place, and much of this success is the direct result of Paul's endeavors. But to emphasize the Pauline, or Westward, mission obscures two facts of interest (at least to the theme of this book), one that is not profound, I admit, but is all the same an eternal when we read or think on matters of the ancient past, while the second is of greater importance though usually glossed over by conventional European historical consciousness. Both proceed from a similar reality: that Christianity was a perimeter religion. It did not grow and mature at the center of Empire, but rather its fringes.

Where, when and how did Christianity spread from its place of birth, the environs of Jerusalem? Aside from what we know of Paul's career there are no definitive answers. But the one constant we can rely upon for its initial transmission is so ephemeral, simplistic, and unverifiable that it mocks the portentiousness of what it seeks to explain. First,

Monastery Ruins
Inishmurray
County Sligo

Christianity spread by word of mouth. It coursed the trade routes, filtered through the slave markets, made the rounds of countless seaports, followed the marches to and fro of legionnaires. As all roads led to Rome, it arrived at the capital in grain carriers, merchant galleys, warships, and slavers. It circulated through tavern gossip, market chitchat, and salon repartee. It created the nucleus of converts to whom Paul could address his Epistles to the Romans, "You who are called to be saints, you I have often intended to visit."[1]

Christianity had to compete, of course, with the delicious wonders of other cults and mystery religions from the exotic East that travellers to Rome unfolded to friends and acquaintances. What most of these had in common with Christianity was the certain, defined, and alluring notion of life after death, something the now moribund Greek and Roman pagan religions had left amorphous. In this "twilight world" of esoterica Christianity more than held its own until, over the course of several decades, oral transmission was buttressed with a solid body of written material — the letters of Paul, the Gospels, theological commentary — nearly all of it emanating, again, from the farthest reaches of the Empire.

Second, Christianity, or more precisely, its theological gestation, was more the product of the East than of Rome, where doctrinal disputation seemed less a matter of life and death. Roman society in the era of Christ had grown indifferent to the established religion, a crude variety of superstitions dressed up in the well-known personalities of Grecian mythology. No one paid it much mind and, indeed, many "rationalistic" historians of recent times saw in this apathy the perfect explanation for Christianity's success: a people drained of their vitality and no longer capable of profound religious insight become almost willing prey, as Germanic tribes batter the Empire, to that most escapist, yet persistent, of the mystery religions, one that features a man turned god, a Stoic sense of the evil world, fantastic ritual, an appealing moral sense and, most germane of all, a glorious life in the hereafter. Edward Gibbon's melodramatic summary of *The Decline and Fall of the Roman Empire*, where he bemoaned the necessity of writing exclusively on "the triumph of barbarism and religion", is the best regarded instance of this wearied (and often wearying) attitude. It had the ironic and sometimes belittling effect of forcing our collective attentions on societal ennui, at the same time speaking sarcastically about a Christian "conquest" as though the struggle had been achieved in a vacuum with subpar or nonexistent opponents. In many cases the outcome was even termed an apathetic "surrender" which was not, as intended, flattering to the religion. It also helped to obscure the originality of the Greeks, which was anything but pedestrian.

This rather hazy interregnum between the initial gentile missions of

---

[1] As Ezra Pound phrased it, "Transportation is civilization."

Paul and the first signs of an institutionalized church springing up here and there in the major cities — let us say between c. A.D. 150 and the early 200s — is not a time in the story of Christianity that we can describe with complete assurance. "Our caution," as one historian put it, "should by now be well rehearsed." But the story of Greece and the spread of its influence through the far reaches of Empire, both East and West, is quite another matter. Hundreds of years of plotting, poisoning, campaigning, and colonizing are rather well catalogued, to the point where many people in our modern society, if they know anything at all of the general outline in ancient Mediterranean history, are probably more familiar with the specific highlights of the Grecian past than others. The esoteric intellectual peregrinations of that culture are also familiar, though of interest perhaps to specialists only. This can largely be explained by the general permeation of Greek thought in the literature, mores, and artistic expression of most civilizations in Western Europe.

By the time of Christ, of course, Greece had long given way to the authority of Rome. Her last expedition through the heady atmosphere of global power, in fact, had been as a rather unwilling partner to the extravagances of Alexander the Great and his altogether crude Macedonians — frontier barons of little sophistication as far as the Greeks were concerned. Diminution of its political role coincided with stagnation in the academies. As J. H. Robinson wrote in 1921, "After two or three hundred years of talking in the market place and of philosophic discussions prolonged through morning, such of the Greeks who were predisposed to speculation had thought all the thoughts and uttered all the criticisms of commonly accepted beliefs and of one another that could by any possibility occur." But again, we are talking here of affairs at the center. The vitality of Grecian culture had gone elsewhere, out to the horizons, much of it a byproduct to the wild career of Alexander.

During that young man's truly astonishing dismemberment of the Persian Empire, more than seventy Hellenic "cities" were established in the East. His successors founded another two hundred. These were originally little more than fortified camps or outposts, and the rate of their survival or prosperity varied greatly after Alexander's early death, as his ephemeral kingdom split apart amid the jealousies of his generals and through native resurgences. It is interesting to note the coincidence that this self-styled god who died of fever in Babylon, 323 B.C., was brought for burial to what turned out to be the most enduring of his foundations, the city of Alexandria.

When Alexander the Conquerer first came upon the site nine years before, it was little more than a fishing village and base camp for small-time pirates and smugglers — one of dozens clustered among the shifting dunes and islands of the Nile Delta, called "the gifts of the river" by an admiring Herodotus. Alexander, master of many a fine city by this stage in his career, had spent nearly a year fighting down the Levantine coast. Seven months had been occupied by the bitter siege of Tyre alone, the result of which was that city's utter ruination and the infusion of some 30,000 of its citizenry to the local slave markets. Egypt, to the contrary, had greeted Alexander enthusiastically. Anybody, it seems, was better than the Persians. Needing a maritime link to the Peloponnesus, and appreciating both the friendliness of his new subjects and the economic potential of the Nile river valley, Alexander laid the outline of a new city. Three hundred years later, in the time of Christ himself, Alexandria had become foremost in the Empire after Rome, with an estimated population of well over 300,000, the citizenry being a polyglot collection of Greeks, Jews, and Egyptians, each residing in separate quarters but co-mingling all the same in the market places, schools, temples and synagogues. It was the type of place that a St. Paul would have found quite congenial — highly urban (and urbane), religiously contentious, intellectually stimulating. It was, all at once, the very capital of colonial Hellenism, the largest Jewish community in the world, the mercantile crossroads of Egypt, the positively vital breadbasket of Rome, being that city's primary supplier of grain. More than one Imperial general had tried to strong-arm the Senate, stymie an emperor or roil the Roman street mob by closing the granary docks of Alexandria. And it was here, in this ferment, that a great deal of Christian Doctrine was imagined, developed, refined, and spread.

We owe much of this to the nimble Greek mind and the expansive possibilities of the Greek language, which in combination could both excite and yet devastate the ardor of an audience locked to the foil and counterfoil of academic debate. The subtle (and some might say, devious) Greek could find heresy anywhere, be it in the mouth of a babe or Christ himself. Conversely, nothing orthodox was ever safe, for the Greeks, with their love for abstruse and metaphysical tongue twisting, could and did play havoc with theological definitions, credos and articles of faith. The more sophisticated deviations from doctrine that plagued the early Church most grievously such as Arianism, Nestorianism, and Gnosticism, all originated and were popular with Greeks in the East.

Christianity might have forever remained a peasant religion had it not reached an accommodation, and then an expression, in Greek, and this occurred not in the Peloponnesus but largely within the confines of Hellenic city-states abroad. Alexandria, the largest of these, reflected this distinction by an Academy that dwarfed in vigor those of Greece itself, with the splendors of a library unheard of anywhere in the ancient world. Its collections are believed to have numbered over 700,000 papyrus rolls, and its major philosophic creation — what textbooks call today Neoplatonism — is in large measure the result of acquisitive librarians who translated everything of interest (in this case, Hebrew theological discourse and scripture) into Greek. Cross-fertilization between cultures, requiring not so much an open-minded attitude towards conflicting systems of thought as a disputative urge to argue, saw wholesale borrowings back and forth which drastically affected the earliest Christian theologians, who sought to enter the religious debate in a style that was worthy of the competition. No matter their polemics against the pagans, in many instances they plundered the ancients with an enthusiasm that bordered on greed.

A city such as Alexandria was a natural goal for the earliest missionaries from Jerusalem, those who were scattered when the Temple suppressed the radical Jewish Christians and martyred, among others, Stephen the Deacon. Many of the synagogues in Alexandria were extremely liberal and thoroughly Hellenized — their congregations Greek-speaking, their Testaments in Greek, their contact with pagan philosophers daily and perhaps friendly. These were certainly fertile grounds for proselytizers of the new religion to cultivate: worldly and cultivated Jews on the one hand, intellectually open and curious Gentiles on the other. While we have no specific details (here or almost anywhere) on how the missionaries fared in Alexandria, we can safely assume from the later history of this city and its attachment to Christianity that early successes here were considerable.

The background of all substantial discussion (that of intelligentsia as opposed to grocers) was of course Plato and Aristotle. It is beyond my aim, to say nothing of ability, to explain their particular notions of the universe and of whatever or whoever created it, what the role of man's sojourn on earth really was, or the intended fate of his soul. But the term Neoplatonism specifically relates to the Academy of Alexandria, and is variously categorized as the death rattle of pagan thought, the last stand of Classical Greece or, in a more studied and ironic definition, "the consummation, yet also the collapse, of ancient philosophy". It is the "collapse" that interests us here, how it affects our look at the origins of monasticism.

WHY IT FELL apart is certainly an interesting matter. The question, I suppose, is whether it toppled of its own weight or if Christianity pushed it over the edge by assimilating, at least at the start, its most prominent features. I think my own guess would be the latter. As Christianity flourished (for a number of reasons: tolerance, for the most part, by Rome, although sporadic persecutions could be severe and very bloody; the underground aspects of the religion, meeting in cells, catacombs and the like, which fostered solidarity of feeling; the high moral standards of its first leaders, together with their willingness to suffer martyrdom when required; and also for many other reasons) it settled first among the poor and despised of the urban centers, passing like a germ through tenement, barrack, and dock side. As numbers increased the sweep grew wider: liberal Jews, middle class gentiles, even the odd aristocrat now and then. In general, however, the cult was neither prestigious nor sophisticated, lacking both an ancient past or a cohesive system that could generate an answer for every question. It took imaginative, spontaneous thinkers like Paul to produce these necessities. In Alexandria, that sort of individual was Origen.

Origen was certainly not the first creative thinker to justify Christianity in Alexandria. There are records of several writers who preceded him, but none has the stature of this man, so committed to the moral precepts of his religion that as a teenager he cut off his penis with a hatchet to ensure perpetual chastity. The church historian Eusebius attributed this act to "an immature and youthful mind", and it seems that Origen himself regretted his extremism later on in life.[1]

This severe cast of mind was perhaps conditioned by his father's martyrdom in A.D. 202, an indication that even so cosmopolitan a city as Alexandria could periodically savage one or another of its religious constituencies. Origen developed a bedrock attachment to Christianity, in particular the authority of scripture, his exegesis of which was more thorough, painstaking, and voluminous as any by then undertaken. St. Jerome, in fact, who probably had a pen in hand most every working hour, later complained, "Who could ever read all that Origen wrote?" But this devotion to the Bible is basically what kept Origen attached to the real world. This might seem a rather contradictory thing to say, especially on a religious matter, but the temptations of more ethereal philosophies were immense within the circles where Origen operated, and the Bible, that solid and authoritarian repository of divine revelation, proved a counterweight that kept this most profound of the early theologians in touch with his Christian base. Because in Alexandria, at least, there was no fear or hesitation in drowning oneself in pagan thought, a situation not so just two hundred years later when the classical collections of the great library were ransacked and put to flames as heretical poison. Origen attended, and then taught, at the Alexandrian equivalent of a cathedral school, but in the traditional manner of the Greeks, the catechetical method, or question and answer. Side by side the tenets of old thought and emerging Christian doctrine were passed back and forth, compared, dissected, and debated. It was not seen as a dangerous practice, or as a possible contaminant, but rather as a useful resource. There were many principles, Origen felt, "well stated by the Greeks, which cannot be lightly dismissed, concerning the immortality of the soul, or its survival, or the immortality of the mind." This Alexandrian tradition continued all through the third century. While the great African father Tertullian was fulminating, "Away with all attempts to produce a mottled Christianity of Stoic, Platonic, and dialectical composition! We want no curious disputation", the pagan Academy in Alexandria was nominating a future bishop as professor of Aristotelian philosophy. Origen saw no problems

---

[1] An apocryphal gospel of the second century took a dim view of such extremes, admonishing those so sorely tempted to "cut off the impulse and not the member."

in a situation like that. "We can agree" with many positions of ancient belief, he wrote, "because they are rightly stated."

Origen was not, of course, a propagandist for undigested Grecian thought. Plato and Aristotle, he could formally point out, were pagan and beyond the pale. They would not achieve salvation because they were aliens to the true Church and had no knowledge of Jesus Christ. But Origen, like St. Paul in his curious love/hatred of the Law, was caressing what he loved without admitting it. Along with his contemporaries in the Alexandrian school, Origen went to great lengths to establish that Moses and the Old Testament prophets predated Plato and Aristotle. In his mind, the Grecian academies had plagiarized every decent idea they ever had from the Jews, and merely glossed them over with a pagan veneer. Origen rationalized his re-use of these Platonic jewels with the notion that he was merely recovering stolen goods. This was an exquisite means of self-justification and allowed Origen to do what he really wanted, create a Christian philosophy with Greek definitions, which was a totally Alexandrian exercise. The Jewish thinker Philo, for instance, had done the same thing in that city when he created, in Greek, a Platonic structure for Judaism. In the process, of course, as a French scholar pointed out, and again harking back to the example of Paul, Origen's system "owed nothing to the Jesus who lived, spoke, acted".

What then did Origen achieve? In a textbook sense (if you believe in the sort of authoritative and sweeping judgments common to these) he in effect short-circuited the revival of platonic thought by redirecting it into Christianity. On a more personal level the rather pedestrian content of Christianity greatly disturbed him. He realized, like any intelligent observer of his times, that every religion has a somewhat pandering exterior that is necessary for attracting the common people. For Greek and Roman religion that happened to be a pantheon of the gods to which no thoughtful person gave any credence. Beneath the crude and obvious trappings there was, however, the realization of one God, Principle, or Idea. In the words of the Platonist Maximus of Tyre, though of "one nature, the gods are many names." And it was that nature that Plato and the rest sought to conceptualize and grasp. For Origen the task was similar. He wanted the Greeks to understand that beneath the superstition of Christian practice was a base as solid, profound and attractive as Platonism. The two believed in many of the same things which were, after all, eternals, e.g. the desire of the soul to shed the encumbrances of matter and achieve, in some indefinable way, union with the eternal God (or "Good," as Plato had it). The deviations and contortions with which this journey was achieved differed widely in detail, of course, and I do not intend to try and define where all of these separate and distinguished thinkers either met on common ground or parted company, beyond to say their goal was approximately the same. Origen, unlike the pagans, subordinated all this philosophical rhetoric to the Bible, which alone commanded all before it and decreed, in a sense, what could safely be appropriated. And Origen was willing to cede the authority of interpretation to the Church, sole repository of Apostolic tradition. Origen did not consider himself as anything but orthodox.

The effect of Origen's work was to dignify the mystical nature of Christianity. Nonbelievers, looking in on a Christian service, might well equate the fervor and evident depth of faith as merely a black magic trance, feminine delusion or self-induced hysteria. Origen provided substance; he could define this spirituality, using Greek models, as something other than base or frivolous emotion. He achieved respect for the inner workings of the Christian soul by placing its contemplative struggle well within the common perspective of all sophisticated men as they search for God.

Origen died c. 254 in Tyre, and the influence of his vast body of work was immense over all facets of the early Church until well into the sixth century. By that time an inquiring attitude towards the pagan philosophers had long evaporated and Origen, steeped in the methodology and vision of that particular point of view, was condemned as a heretic and many of his writings destroyed. Earlier than that he had been deemed suspect. Rufinius of Aquileia, who translated some of Origen from Greek into Latin, confessed openly that he altered much of the master's thinking to conform with more orthodox positions. It is certainly true that as a philosophic original, one who roamed far and wide over the many problems in emerging doctrine, Origen came up with probably more ideas than was prudent, "seducing the Church," in the opinion of one critic, "making light account of the ancient simplicity of the Christian religion". Rufinius, for one, could not leave untouched Origen's thought that the Holy Ghost was not the equal of Father or Son and, like many a censor before and after, proceeded to bring him into line. And Cassiodorus, to take another example, in his well-known series of remarks to the monks he had endowed c. 551 at the Italian monastery of Vivarium, could delude himself into thinking (as barbarians marched to and fro through his country) that Origen mattered one way or the other. "I have marked *rejected* passages which have been spoken contrary to the rules of the fathers," he wrote, so his monks — or, to put things in proportion, those who might survive the military catastrophes of the age — would not be "deceived, for if caution is employed, his poison can do no harm." Probably the worst thing said about him was Porphyry's remark that "he thought like a Greek."

I N ORDER TO take some photographs of the cashel, I have been floundering about in a fierce welter of bracken and undergrowth that has taken over the small garden plots and grazing lands which once

Station of the Cross
Inishmurray
County Sligo

supported the islanders. Wading through these entanglements is rather like struggling with a wild surf, and every so often my footing plunges into deeper sinkholes full of mire. Feeling like a medieval knight trapped in his armor I finally break free to the main pathway of the island, soaked from the knees down and sweating profusely. Catching my breath and plucking off several hundred burrs and thorns from my pants and jacket, I delight in the stiff, wintry air that dries and cools me off, but all at once I can sense that something has gone awry, that perhaps I'm facing the wrong direction. Sure enough, the wind has switched, and my alarm mechanisms click into gear. Looking westward I see, to my horror, a solid wall of black on the horizon, preceded by an angry, wind-driven chop on the ocean's surface below me. I head back to *Clashymore*, but no boat. The breaking waves smack against the seaward edge of *Oileán is Tiar*, and run unimpeded into the harbor.

I cannot believe that my boat has deserted me, but from the southerly shore there's not a trace of it to be seen. The only elevation on the island is the western cliff walk, so I head for that in hopes I can spy my man from there. It is with considerable relief that just as I reach the other side of the harbor he comes into view, waving merrily. He had evidently seen me first, and perhaps enjoyed my seeming panic.

Going back to the landing I gather up my pack, noticing now that the tide has run low. I can tell the captain is going to have a tricky time of it, and in fact he jockeys about for several minutes after entering *Clashymore*, lining up the bow to slip in, trying to keep the ground swell from pushing him up on the rock where I'm standing. After awhile he no longer seems merry.

"I can't get in there," he shouts. "Throw your stuff on board, I'll keep her headed up, and when you see your chance, jump!" This is an awesome prospect — a good 12 foot drop to the boat, which the captain cannot, in these conditions, maneuver any closer than 5 or 6 feet from shore. A broken leg, or worse, is in store for me. I toss the pack over, full of fragile cameras and equipment, and hear it thunk on deck. The captain is standing out of the pilot house, one hand stretched towards the wheel inside, looking over his shoulder at the swells. He's picking one out, I guess, to let it ride him in while he plays with the throttle. He looks back at me all of a sudden, gives the nod and the boat surges up. There's nothing for it but to take a running leap, and in a perfectly executed aerodynamic triumph I land on board as she rises to greet me, tumble over in a gymnastic flip and end up on my feet with hands on the rigging just as the worthy old vessel whines in reverse. "Well done, well done!" cries the captain, as we power from *Clashymore* into the ocean.

"Where were you, laddie?" asks the captain after I've checked over my gear. "I told you to keep a weather eye out. Look at this stuff in back of us," and there's no doubt that a heavy-handed Atlantic pounding is on its way. The minute the winds had shifted, he explains, *Clashymore* was no place for him, and he had circled the island in hopes of spotting me along the shore, probably at the same time I was slogging about through the interior. I ask him if he'd have left me there. "For sure I would have," he says, "the old schoolhouse is unlocked and you could have slept in there. When the storm passed by I'd have come out for you again, and if I couldn't land I would at least have thrown some food up. Still, it being winter, I'd have felt uneasy about it. But we made it alright. You saw the island and you're alive to tell the tale."

"I barely saw the island," I reply. "I'll have to land again."

"Well at £30 a crack that might get expensive. I know a lobsterman who still has traps out here. He's a native of Inishmurray, born and bred, fishes out of Moneygold, over there," — pointing to a spot of shore directly east of the island — "that's only a five-mile run, whereas going from Mullaghmore is twice that distance. He goes out every day. He could drop you off, pick up his pots, take you back in the afternoon. Just don't get seasick on him, he just hates it, he's a real thick fellow for that." I react to this phrase and the captain bursts into laughter. "Not thick meaning stupid, oh no, I mean he's good as a friend, bad as an enemy. Just ask for Christy, Christy down there in Moneygold."

By now we're in very thick weather, plenty of rain and good-sized rollers. "This would be a good time for a kick of the dog," says the captain. I ask him what Poteen or the old bootleg whiskey is really like, having seen gaudily labeled bottles of it for sale at the Shannon Airport duty free store, interspersed with shillelagh sticks, soapstone carvings of Blarney Castle, and aprons embossed with recipes for soda bread or Irish coffee. He replies that commercial poteen is pretty sanitary. "The real thing is poison." It has no real taste, according to what he has been told, but just gives the drinker a solid burning sensation — clear, smooth, deadly, powerful. "You know, towards the end out there on the island, in the late 1940s, they had a couple of V-8 engines in their boats, and if they ran the poteen into shore and got stuck in a corner, you know, ran out of fuel and couldn't get to the pumps, they'd crack a keg, pour in a couple of gallons of poteen, and away she'd go. Over the long haul an engine would heat up too much with pure liquor in her, but no problem getting out of a jam."

"I'd hate to have that stuff go through my system," says I.

"Me too," the captain laughs, "too expensive! But you know what they say, Any port in a storm."

I ask him when the islanders abandoned Inishmurray. "Nineteen forty-eight, I think. There were around forty-five of them left, the very old and the very young. Anyone with any brains or any ambition had gone out to England or America by then. During the war, you know, there was full employment abroad, in the army and navy or the factories, whereas there was nothing here. And life on the island was all manual labor. They had heavy wooden boats, 18 to 25 footers, which had to be dragged up on shore each time they were finished with them. And then the farming and the distilling. When all the young lads took off it got to be too much for the older men, they couldn't physically do the work. And you hear them say that the turf was running out, there was no market anymore for their fish, the kelp business was done, the police too diligent in chasing the still down. But the bottom line was sugar. When the Government rationed sugar in the early '40s they couldn't make the poteen, and that's the only trade there was to put money in their pockets. They had a king out there, really what you'd call a chieftain, and he badgered the City Council to bring them all out to shore, build houses for them on the mainland and resettle the whole community, which is what happened. Six of those cottages are in Moneygold, as a matter of fact, where Christy lives. And they left without a whimper, not like some other islands out here where the Government ordered the people off. You'll hear them crying in their beer for the dear old place, but they were happy enough to leave it behind."

In a downpour we pull into Mullaghmore and dock.

S EVERAL DAYS PASS by with stormy weather and gale-force winds. The shipping forecasts are all troughs and depressions so there is little hope of reaching Inishmurray anytime soon. As Dr. Heraughty was to tell me, it was not uncommon for the islanders to be marooned for up to six weeks, sometimes longer. I have used this time to good advantage, however, familiarizing myself with the small stretch of coast that runs from Lissadell House on Drumcliff Bay, childhood home of Yeats's

> Two girls in silk kimonos, both
> Beautiful, one a gazelle,

on up to Mullaghmore itself. Touristically speaking this area is relatively obscure, and indeed if the Yeatsean associations were removed I doubt if many visitors would take the time to explore it slowly and carefully. There are several lovely beaches and stunning views of Sligo Bay to the south, Donegal to the north, but no purpose to keep a person tethered here for long.

Tracking Christy down is simple enough. Moneygold (pronounced Monneygould) is not, as I had supposed, a village, but rather the broad designation of an area encompassing two or three lengthy lanes that fall off from the main Sligo road down to the shore, and all the dwellings and farmhouses that lie therein. The six County Council cottages put up for the islanders are clustered near the mouth of a long and narrow estuary or sea gullet, drainage for the little river that runs through Grange up above. At low tide the entire embrasure, about three miles in length, lies empty save for a tiny trickle of water that passes for the main channel. The seaward arm of this miniaturized bay consists of Conor's Island, now joined to the mainland by a long spit of sand called Inishnagor. Christy's house, like those of the other islanders, sits on property that once made up a large estate owned by Protestants, the rusted gate of which still stands just across the road. He can see from his window the open sea through a gap between the tip of Conor's and Dernish Island, which guards the northern outlet of the estuary, and around whose landward shore lies the only navigable exit to the ocean. This gap is Christy's barometer, a low, natural sea barrier of rubble and sand that links the two islands. "When you see the surf crack over the rocks out there, you've no chance to get on the island," he says to me. "If you see no white at all, or if the rollers seem to wear a misty plume, which means an offshore wind is blowing the spray straight up the face of the wave, then it means you can get on. But in winter, see, we can have bad weather for two, three weeks at a time. Even in summer, for that matter." Christy's cottage is a low, snug, modest affair — whitewashed, one storey, a small and unkempt patch of lawn in front, fishing gear piled in the back, lined up in a row with a couple of identical neighbors. We are sitting in the living room, his wife and children glued to a television.

"Maybe the forecast will cheer us up", I say.

"Never listen to them myself," he replies. "I just look out the window, over there to the foul grounds in the gap." We walk down to the small pier where Christy's rig is tied up. It is surprisingly well-maintained and resembles the kind of lobster boat common to the coast of Maine. "Those lads down in Mullaghmore, I wouldn't trust them 100 yards from shore," he says. "This craft here has a hard road to Inishmurray and back, and I can count on her." He hasn't been out in over a week, however. "In cold air like this, you can have Force 7 to 9 winds forever. But even if you should get a calm day, like, it's a dicey thing. The ground swell's up now, I was noting it these past few weeks, and while we'd get across the bay all right and we could work the pots — they're in 100 to 200 feet of water — we'd never get close enough to the island for me to let you off. We call it a harbor out there, you know, but it's only a cut in the rock. And these days, in broken weather even, where we go out from this place into the ocean can sometimes be all blocked off. So I'll take you out if I can get you ashore, but don't count on it."

And so I become the gypsy of Moneygold. I park the old Citroën in a little field next to the pier and smack on the inner bay. The County Council reserves this for islanders who may wish to pull their boats up in stormy weather. A couple of derelict little curraghs lie heaped in a corner, witness to the minimal level of maritime activity still pursued here. "When the islanders came ashore," a grocer in Grange told me later, "they hauled up their boats and walked away, turned their backs on the sea and disappeared."

If I had been a real gypsy, of course, the fifteen or twenty people who live down here by the pier would have tossed me out. Instead, I'm an American curiosity. After about a week of camping in the field — and hearing Christy's daily lament about the surf — I awaken one morning to a heavily-bearded man staring me in the face through the car window. "Are ye up then?" he asks. I arrange to be. "Sure you must be bored with walking hill and dale around here. I'm going for periwinkles and you're welcome to join me." I look to the gap, see little in the way of foamy commotion, and wonder aloud if this morning will be my day. "Don't be daft," he exclaims, "the man will never take you. He'll wait you out and finally you'll get tired and be gone, and him relieved. He wouldn't want the fearsome burden of putting you on the island and then, God knows, not getting you off again. It's a frightful place, Inishmurray, I'll grant him that. Contrary in the wintertime. I was born there myself so I should know."

The only boat at the pier besides Christy's is a large and bulbous craft of, to put it mildly, curious appearance. Something on the order of a plywood shack, painted orange, floating on a bubble. "I built this myself," says Paddy Joe Brady, as he identifies himself, "up there in my mother's house. Oh she was sick to death of it, since I put most of her together in the living room. Solid oak below the water line, double keel, fifty-two hundred nails, a high double skin with five layers of paper glued and puttied in between, which gives me about a quarter inch coating around the oak, and finally twenty pounds of tar all over the bottom. She'd be hard to break her back in a wave, I can tell you, and even though you busted her now she wouldn't sink. But you can see she rides as pretty as a feather on the water, a real gem for the little bay. Cast off the line there." A tiny Seagull outboard putters us out to the estuary. We're headed for Conor's Island where Paddy Joe has stashed several sacks of shellfish. They're on the seaward shore so we'll have to lug them across the spit. The water is calm as a mirror.

"I don't suppose this boat could make it to Inishmurray?" I ask.

"No ballast in her now, though I'd planned to pour about a ton and a half of concrete in the bottom to make her seaworthy. But then I would have ruined her for the bay, she'd have sat too low, and I've decided this is where I'm going to fish, not out there," waving towards the gap. I learn that Paddy Joe's schedule is rather leisurely. Every second week he diligently puts aside six days for work, but only four hours each day. In that period he can gather about fourteen hundred pounds of periwinkles. Twice monthly a wholesaler trucks by and pays out approximately £270 for the haul, which he in turn exports to France where the shellfish are ground up at aquaculture farms for oyster feed. "It's not a bad living at all, to be honest, better than Christy's. Where's the point of going out with overhead: petrol, boxes for the fish, bait, traps, rope, hauling gear, and everyone going out at six in the morning and not getting back until four in the evening? And all that time you're on your feet, with your concentration always round on the rocks and the water and the weather and making sure your rope doesn't get wrapped on the propeller or around your leg. You're always moving about, rolling with the boat, no sitting down, no rest period, and all that heavy salt air getting into your lungs and making you sleepy. Worse than that, if the sun be hot and the vapor off the water, it's not proper for your head to be inhaling it so, it can give you such a headache. By the time you're finished with it all, you feel like you were drawing stones on your back for the whole day entirely, and that night you'd be wondering how you ever got so tired." I am now convinced the sea is not for me.

We spend most of the morning going back and forth with Paddy Joe's catch. Conor's Island is broader than it seems from shore, and cut up in the usual chaotic manner into countless little fields, the stone walls of which we must clamber over repeatedly with our heavy loads. It's a well-travelled route, however, at least by Paddy Joe, who knows exactly where the walls have fallen away or barbed wire is slack to make the going easier. "The wire around here has always bothered me," he says. "The Conors, see, they own this island. Those two houses at the tip over there, one of the two brothers used to live in it before he took ill. They've been here for centuries you know, they think they're royalty, and it's in their blood to be dominating, especially with me because I'm part of the Inishmurray crowd and they feel superior to the likes of us. And oh, it must be sixteen or seventeen years ago, there were a lot of them sea rods, they call them — did you ever see them coming in with the tide, kelp, with the big long rods? — well there were a mass of them, so I came out to put some up, there being fair good money for them then. I had about two ton gathered when himself and the brother arrived, and the brother is about fifty times more contrary, and they came down aggressive, you know, and of course I wasn't in any better mood meself. 'Who owns the shore?' says I when they start pushing me around. 'This is driftwood and no one owns the shore!' Provided you pay a shilling for trespass money, see, anyone can gather what the ocean throws up, and the sea rods was driftwood in my opinion. That's the law! Well we had an awful row and the brother, he had a cattle stick and he kept waving it at me so I left. Next thing they put up the wire, so thick you couldn't get an eight pence out of it. Well, we folk from Inishmurray can be a thick bunch, I'll tell ye, and I cut the stuff to make a point. Nice neat cuts so I could get to sea and back. And I didn't see them after that and I was here for months. I remember one fine day when I dragged four tons of kelp across. That was a proper haul."

59

By noon we've stacked a good many sacks in the boat, beached on the sandy bottom of the inlet since the tide's gone out, or "soaked away" in Paddy Joe's words. "A perfect opportunity to take a stroll," he says, "I'm a devil for roaming." We head back towards the sea.

A marvelous day this has become. Bright sun, blue sky, fiercely triumphant cloud formations hurtling overhead in a stiff wind from the west. "Ah, the state of the bay!" Paddy Joe lets out all of a sudden as we reach the shore. "But here's your problem, here's the prevailing wind. You can never get on the island with this blowing, it causes a trough to come in on you at *Clashymore*. 'Once in, never out,' like we used to say, or 'once out, never in' — same thing." We reach Black Rock, a large and twisted mass of stony pinnacles that point out to sea towards Inishmurray. Trailing off behind on either side are two lovely crescents of sandy beach, Inishnagor heading south towards another point known as Streedagh, and northwards the ocean strand of Conor's Island. From the top of Black Rock, a theatrical little mountain really, our views are expansive. "Well there she is now, dear old Inishmurray." I ask Paddy Joe how long he lived there. "My mother took me off when I was six. They said it was too dangerous, every landing was a perfect chance to go to heaven, that it was time to come out. My mom said for sure I wouldn't outlive it and she might have had a point to hang her hat on for that one. It was a hard life living out there. The winter stormy season, that was terrible now, but still we enjoyed it and didn't mind that much. We're shipwrecked over here, and that's God's truth for ye. I haven't been on the place for two years now, which is a record for me. And my mother hasn't been back since she left in 1948. She's nervous of the water, which might seem strange for an islander to say, but the place could take its toll. My granny, for instance, God rest her soul, is wedged beneath here under the rocks. She and my grandfather, oh this must be sixty years ago, delivered poteen out here. That was a grand business for us back then, you know, though I'll tell you the truth that real poteen tastes like battery acid. I made a throw myself one time, not on the island but out here on the mainland. Rigged up a worm, used barley instead of treacle, ran it through three times, not once, which can be dangerous, and came up with twenty-two bottles. You'd get about eight glasses of poison per bottle. Anyway, back then it was a real industry out on the island. Now on the other side of Streedagh Point, over there, is a place called Cloonagh. That's where the Inishmurray folk usually landed because it was about the shortest distance to the mainland there, and most all me own friends come from there now. And all through Cloonagh there were these *shebeen* houses, or unlicensed pubs, and that's where we sold our poteen. The publicans sometimes ran lemonade through it or colored it in some fashion to disguise the stuff, in case the police came, because the poteen was pure clear. One taste, though, and you knew it was the real thing. As a result, all around Cloonagh you found all the great music, the people fond of drinking, fond of singing and playing, all of them fine fiddlers and such. And the poteen fueled up the whole thing. As my mother says, 'When it comes to making pleasure, there's always drink.'[1]

"All along these beaches here is where the stuff was landed. Different people had different customs but my granddad used to hide his kegs along Inishnagor. He'd have several caches here and there so if he'd be caught they wouldn't get all his throw. But it was dangerous work. Many times they'd only do their distilling in winter, because the smoke from their fires would give them away, and they could expect a raiding party anytime. But in winter the chances of that be slim. But what I'm going to tell you now is that he and my granny were coming out with several kegs and a southwesterly gale hit them at this point where we're standing now. All of a sudden it came, and just as he was nearly about to land. It drove him straight for Black Rock, it was getting dark in the bargain and the wife — a great seawoman, you know, she was a McGovern from Cloonagh — well she forgot to switch the stay on the mast to the other side when the sea shifted, you know to strengthen the mast against the gale, and what happened the mast snapped and knocked her overboard, never seen again in body or soul. Her man was driven ashore here. He got caught up in the trough and broken surf and he couldn't sail her out against the wind into deeper water. The boat got a hole in her side from hitting the ledges and went over. It was laying there for years afterward up on the sands but I couldn't trace her now. My granddad got thrown on the beach and survived. He lived to be eighty-nine years. Lost his wife, lost his boat, but saved his poteen. They always left a little air in the kegs so that if the police caught up with them out at sea and they had to throw the stuff out, or if they went under in a storm, the kegs at least would float into shore. And that's what happened to him. Ah, those were the tough old days, as you'd say yourself it must have been a hard life."

I ask him if the authorities regularly interfered with the traffic. "Ah they did to be sure. In the last century they even had constables stationed on the island, can you believe the lonesome duty that would be? In my Dad's time, though, they more or less waited for us on the shoreline. Often if they raided the island they couldn't land or the lads would see them from afar and hide away the whiskey and the still. If the cops did make it ashore there could always be unpleasantries, however. They had long rods for searching the bogs with. And while some of them were fine lads, and would say 'Give us a couple of fish and we'll be gone' — which meant let's have a bottle or two for the ride home — some of the others could be nasty. If they uncovered any poteen they'd dump it all over the house or pour it into the cradle, when the child would be in bed, that sort of

---

[1] A history of Irish whiskey relates that "customers in *shebeens* were beggars, itinerant dealers and similarly (unrespectable) characters and the *shebeen*, therefore, was not wholly disliked by the licensed publican since it drew off the unwelcome drinkers."

thing. But generally they found it more useful to lie about on the beach, catching pneumonia I hope. The lads would usually let off a man first who'd give a signal if the coast was clear. Or else we'd run in two separate boats, one a dummy. It was cold, wet work. I even wrote a poem about it." Standing a bit taller, his beard and hair flattened by the wind, Paddy Joe orated.

'Twas on a Sunday morning
All in the month of May
A police boat was sighted
Out there in the bay
We had twenty kegs of poteen
All ready for to land
But we got no answer signal
From the lonely Streedagh Strand.

A sidecar was dashing through
The early morning gloom
A sudden fall and in the sea
They went to meet their doom
Two island lads lay dying there
Just like their hopes so grand
They could not give the signal now
From lonely Streedagh Strand.

No signal answers from the shore
King Waters sadly said
No comrades here to welcome us
Alas they must be dead
But we must do our duty
At once we mean to land
So in a boat we pulled ashore
On lonely Streedagh Strand.

The island boats were lying there
With whiskey in galore
Up came a Garda boat and spoke
"No boats to reach the shore
You are our long time enemy
We forbid you for to land
No island foot shall e're pollute
The lonely Streedagh Strand."

They sailed for Mullaghmore Harbor
Said the islanders, "We are undone
The Garda are our masters now
Man for man, son for son
We've twenty kegs of poteen here
But they will never land
We'll sink them all and bid farewell
To lonely Streedagh Strand."

"There's more to it," he says after a long pause, "but I've forgotten. I'll dig it out when we get home. There's an air to it as well, but I've no voice for singing."

Coming down off Black Rock we stumble over some old sheets of corroded tin, scattered about a small indentation in the promontory. "A hermit used to live here," Paddy Joe tells me.

"A religious hermit? Like out on the island?"

"Now that I cannot tell. I don't recall our ever talking about religion, to be honest with you, and we did have a few long chats. He was the friendliest soul in the world. You could be building a castle up the wee field beyond and he'd be there talking to you, or you could just have a match to your name and it wouldn't matter. How he survived the winters out here I'll never know. One day he just disappeared."

On the beach now, Paddy Joe leads me into the ground swell along Black Rock, the frigid water swirling about our rubber waders. Pointing to a crevice, "Here's where I found the doubloon." This takes me aback.

"A Spanish doubloon?"

"The same." Paddy Joe pats the rock and smiles. "I'm a devil for antiquities." We stand there for almost a minute without talking, Paddy Joe smiling and lightly slapping the rock. I am now aware that the tables have shifted a bit, that I am not in the company of just another charming and expansive Irishman, a spinner of tales or windy exaggerations. I have misread my man. I begin to suspect that Paddy Joe is a character of the first order, a throwback to the famous hedge scholars who conducted bardic schools out-of-doors during the penal times, when Catholics were denied the opportunities of traditional instruction. An academic, as it were, without education, diploma, textbooks, or the proper professorial demeanor.

"Ok, Paddy Joe, I'll take the bite. How did you come to find it?"

"I was just browsing," he replies, "as I often do. Now if you look out there just a few hundred yards offshore where the surf is boiling, that's called *Carricknaspania*, or 'Rock of the Spaniards.' Somewhere in this bay, and tradition says there, four Armada galleons came to grief in September of 1588. There's no question about it either, from all the stuff I've uncovered. I'll be showing it to you later." We continue up the beach to the northerly end of Conor's Island. Between here and Dernish are the foul grounds that Christy keeps his weather eye on, a rubble of sea rocks and sand just above sea level, almost a causeway between the two islands. In former times this was likely an open gap to the sea, now silted up. In the fiercer Atlantic gales this would certainly be no place for casual walking, as the ocean rollers could sweep across to the estuary. Many site names here seem specific to the Spanish disaster. To our right in the inner bay, a sinkhole from 40 to 60 feet in depth according to Paddy Joe, is called *Poll dearg*, or 'The Red Hole,' presumably from decayed or bleeding bodies trapped here by currents. On Dernish there is a *Cnoc na*

Gcorp, or 'Hill of the Corpse,' from which we can see another long beach curving northward to Classie Bawn Castle and Mullaghmore, known as Trawalua Strand or the Beach of 'Mishap' or 'Lament.' Behind the great dune wall of sand and beach-grass that looms over Trawalua is, according to Paddy Joe, a rough, unsettled patch of ground known as 'The Garden of Dead.' Tradition has it that a great pit or common grave was dug there for the many score of dead that washed up from the wrecks. As I later discovered, a letter by one Geoffrey Fenton, an Elizabethan Secretary of State for Ireland, reported that "At my late being in Sligo, I numbered on one strand of less than five miles in length above 1,100 dead corpses of men which the sea had driven upon the shore." A merciless coast line indeed.

Dernish is a monument to an Ireland long since past, a maze of narrow farm lanes wandering a crazily haphazard course from field to ruined cottage to field again. At every desolate farmstead Paddy Joe recites the fate and fortunes of the family that once lived and tilled these lands, men and women and children long since scattered to the wider world beyond — to England, America, Australia — whose descendants have no idea, more likely than not, of their origins in this wild and tempestuous setting. "There's not a soul here now, God knows," Paddy Joe says at one point. "It's a sad tale to be sure. Sometime or another a German or Dutchman will buy the whole place, I'm guessing, just for the view. They say Mountbatten was interested in it at one time. He purchased the shooting rights, I know that much, and he often cruised about in these waters. But it's an awful shame to see such a fine piece of land with such beautiful prospects all gone to waste for the common man." Dredging my own poor memory I recall a line from Synge, what some peasant said to him as he trekked through the countryside: "Now all this country is gone lonesome and bewildered, and there's no man knows what ails it."

"True words, my friend," Paddy Joe agrees, "truer words never spoken."

The tide is full by the time we return to Paddy Joe's boat at the end of day. We can hear the surf crashing away at the coastline in rather eerie contrast to the unrippled, glass-like surface of the inner bay. "Look there now below, there's a fine group of seals floating about. Coming in with the tide to feed."

"Is it true," I ask him, "the islanders would never kill a seal?"

"'Tis so. They had an old superstition that every seal was a soul in purgatory, and you came to bad luck if you killed one. The King on the island, Michael Waters, killed a seal one time and his daughter died shortly after that. I think the purgatory thing got started because seals, ah, they're kind of human. The females especially, they have a breast on them like a woman, and they have a human cry to them when they're wailing away up on the rocks. Sort of a bereaved cry, like a person in trouble or pain. I like all sorts of animals meself, even rats and mice. Those poor animals always live in fear."

Abandoned Farmstead
Kilcasey
County Donegal

F OR THE NEXT several days the weather deteriorates steadily. Taking Paddy Joe's advice I give up my pursuit of Christy and periodically pay visits to Mullaghmore Harbor, where inquiries finally produce a young man rash enough to take me out, but even I can figure that our trip may be days in coming. Paddy Joe is amused at this obsessional activity, but no more so than his mother, a small, buoyant, cheerful, roguish woman who now regards the two of us as her wards. Most evenings I spend next to the tiny fireplace in their cluttered cottage, one or two lumps of coal periodically tossed in the iron grate. "Ah, many is the character that was in here with Paddy Joe," she tells me, "but never the likes of you. Always Armada people, I can tell ye, but never anyone who could care if the dear old island just slipped away beneath the wave." And indeed, Paddy Joe's fascination with the ruined galleons is evident everywhere. In his bedroom, large and detailed maps are tacked to the wall, covered with annotations of sea currents and wind directions, plotted routes and possible shipwreck sites, underwater rocks and specific locations where Paddy Joe has uncovered artifacts. These he trundles out at odd moments: a few musket balls during the evening news, one or two coins as his mother brings out tea,[1] the barrel of an old sixteenth-century rifle as we listen to the wireless, countless cannon balls at all times of day. Once in the pouring rain I am led out to the back shed to inspect twisted pieces of oak, evidently once part of the ribbing for one of the galleons. In several ruined cottages nearby, in fact, Paddy Joe has identified in various lintels, roofing trusses and even derelict kitchen cabinets the remains of ships that had evidently been scavenged from the shoreline. "I've found a good many bones as well," he says, "mostly in the wash out there between the two islands." It turns out he has advised several teams of divers, including the Belgian Robert Sténuit, who discovered spectacular artifacts from the *Girona* off Dunluce Castle in County Antrim during the late 1960s. To date, none of the wrecks here have been uncovered, though four vessels are known to have floundered in Donegal Bay. On a Sunday afternoon on one of the dune walls overlooking Trawalua, Paddy Joe explained his theories. "You can see up to the north we have the head at Slieve League, down to the south is the Mayo promontory with Benwee and Erris Heads, and in between this great amphitheater of Donegal and Sligo Bays. The Spaniards had no idea that the west coast of Ireland had these enormous indentations in shoreline, their maps showed nothing like this at all. The Armada plan had been to sail considerably west of Ireland, then straight south and southeast for Spain,[1] but you see many of the ships had been

---

[1] These were identified by the National Museum in Dublin as an eighteenth-century copper halfpenny, inscribed "Georgius III," and a seventeenth-century token, also copper, of a kind issued by various market towns such as Sligo when coinage of the realm was in short supply due to troubled conditions in the country at large. They were "cash in kind," redeemable when fresh supplies of currency arrived from Dublin, and primarily designed to prevent the degeneration of commercial activity to the status of simple barter.

so badly mauled in their fight up the English channel they were literally falling apart, plus they had so much disease and starvation aboard that they fell away to shore, the problem being that once they entered the bay they couldn't escape. Those four ships spent days trying to sail out of here, attempting to weather Benwee Point, but the west and southwest winds had them trapped. They were terrible bad sailors in such bad ships, they couldn't sail to windward at all. Each storm that came up pushed them closer and closer to the rocks and beaches and, the biggest catastrophe of all, no anchors! Most of the galleons had cut their cables during the fire ship attack in Calais,[2] so when the southwest gales hit them they jury-rigged anchors or breaks, but no good, they couldn't hold. So they broke up on the coast. My opinion is that one went down at *Carricknaspania* as tradition holds. Those bodies washed up along Dernish and this strand here. I think the other three got beaten on Inishnagor. Most of the divers don't agree with me. They like to go down at *Carricknaspania*, spend all their time there. But you watch, you'll see I'm right."

After a few evening sessions the ceaseless Armada chatter strikes Mrs. Brady as inhospitable. "You be boring him to tears, Paddy Joe," she tells him, "You're a terrible man for repetition, like those videos in the States. Bring on the television and we'll watch a show."

"Now Maw," he replies, "the lad can watch his TV at home. He didn't come over here to look at all this crap, not at all. Don't you think now," turning to me, "that it would be a fine thing if the telly was never invented? It's just another material thing and I am no way interested in material things, because you know yourself the whole business is only dust. These Armada bits and pieces are proof of that, the iron balls, swords, muskets, jewels and all — what good were they to the Spaniards?"

"Well they're not much good to you either, and aye that's the truth," Mrs. Brady chimes in. "You should find chalices, that's where the money is."

"You wouldn't be a happy man if you had them. One of those Spanish grandees had thirty-two servants on board for himself alone. I can't believe he was a satisfied man."

"Oh drink your tea, Paddy Joe. I'll have one of those thirty-two bring you out some bread."

---

[1] "Take great care," wrote the Armada's commander, the Duke of Medina Sidonia to his captains, "not to fall upon the coast of Ireland, because of the harm that may come to you there."

[2] David Howarth, in his fine book *The Voyage of the Armada*, says that "nearly three hundred anchors were (left) lying on the sea-bed off Calais, and no doubt they are lying there still."

A N UNPREDICTABLY BRUTAL southwesterly gale hits the bay one early evening when I happen to be camping, for a change of scenery, at the old abbey of Staad. Its position is totally exposed, sitting above the coast just south of Streedagh Point on a short stretch of rocky shorefront. The remains are scanty: a small medieval stone building much ruined by nature and war, only a single wall with window embrasure still standing as a recognizable architectural entity. My pocket radio reports that fishing and coastal vessels have been scattered by the storm and those Donegal islands still inhabited such as Tory, all cut off from the mainland. The Citroën, battered by heavy gusts, rocks like a cradle back and forth as I lie in my sleeping bag, deafened by the din of crashing surf and cascades of driving rain that beat a tattoo against the roof. I can empathize with the terror those many hundreds of nameless men must have felt as their vessels broke apart in surf and storm, pushed irrevocably and fatally towards a hostile land.

Next morning the pelting rainfall has let up but the winds still complain and the sky remains a deadened mass of scudding storm clouds racing eastwards, dropping the sudden shower every few minutes. The chill expanse of the bay is a dull, menacing, grey morass of breaking waves, the kind of wild, depressing vista that would make any normal person yearn for a quiet Sunday dinner of roast beef and claret before the warming blaze of a fireplace. But in Thackeray's phrase, if the view is gloomy it is at least characteristic. So too the abbey ruins. I have spent much time in Ireland studying my various collections of maps, mostly the ordnance survey, half-inch to the mile series, trying to locate various arcane little artifacts of the past that suddenly appear, then vanish, at the odd moment in some stretch of Irish history. These are generally symbolized by the cartographers as "Cas" and "Ch" (for Castle and Church), "Monastery", "Rd Tower", "Fort" and "Abbey". Whereas in England such a lure might easily result in a collection of fine, imposing structures, or at least an evocative Arthurian ruin, the reverse is usually true for Ireland. More often than not a pile of fallen stone, or the stump of some long obliterated keep, or the ragged, indistinct walls of a little chapel despoiled centuries ago by some maurauder will be the only reward for hours spent glued to the map, following lane and cattle track through a hopeless maze of pasture. It is hard to think of Staad as an abbey, one small wall of the church all that is left, not even the size of a decent cattle shed or proper cottage — a mockery, in fact, of the ecclesiastical and medieval grandeur that our imagination would come to expect from a Europe so long glamorized by cinematic spectacles and art books. But this is precisely the value of Ireland (an unwelcome one, I would expect, for many travellers today), its appropriate human scale. There is no sense of the wondrous here, of being dwarfed by either a building or an event so long heralded by the histories that we find ourselves lost in the wake. These instead take a dimension we can readily recreate. The wonder of

Ruins of Staad Abbey
Streedagh
County Sligo

Ireland is the starkly theatrical coloring that landscape and atmosphere lend to each of its tragic stories, an element a friend of mine called "things watching you", where the distance between then and now shrinks in a natural way to nothing. The old abbey wall facing seaward, the only thing left here, stands dripping in the wet and soggy morning chill. I can see as though it were yesterday the bodies of several poor Spaniards as they lie hanging dead from iron window grates, feet just a few inches from the ground, their last sight on earth the island of Inishmurray sitting forlornly in this wretched bay they had sought to flee.

This was the gruesome sight which filled the gaze of one Francisco de Cuellar, captain of a galleon from Seville, the *San Pedro*, from whose command he had been removed in a sordid purge undertaken by bitter members of the Armada's general staff after various fiascos in the English Channel. De Cuellar had even been sentenced to death and handed over to the Advocate General for execution, but a last minute reprieve spared him the fate of a fellow officer who was hung and his body paraded about the fleet as an example. De Cuellar wrote a long and picaresque account of his misadventures to Philip II in 1589, when he had at last found refuge in Spanish Flanders, hoping ostensibly that "your Majesty may occupy yourself a little by way of amusement after dinner in reading this letter," though more likely he sought to retrieve his former rank or perhaps some reward for all the grief and pain he had suffered. There are places in his narrative where de Cuellar affects amusement or recourse to the obligatory sang-froid of stylized Knight Errantry, but in truth the dreadful squalor and unalloyed terror of his ordeal lies marked on every page.

De Cuellar went down with the Judge Advocate's ship, one of the three battered in surf off Inishnagor, having failed in its attempt to clear Benwee Head. Their anchors had strained to keep them offshore, but "on the fifth day such a great gale arose on our beam, with a sea running as high as heaven, that the cables could not stand the strain nor the sails be of any avail, and all were driven onto the beach." Here a scene of unrivalled horror ensued. De Cuellar, unable to swim, retreated to the poop deck and watched hundreds of men swept into the sea as in less than a single hour each of the galleons was pulverized into flotsam. Panic spread everywhere as spars cracked and toppled overboard, sheathing flew apart and men fell crushed by splintered decks and shifting debris. On all sides the fearsome din of raging storm and thunderous broadsides of breaking ocean rollers created havoc. Many noblemen and commanders drowned quickly, weighed down by gold coins and bars sewed to their clothing. On the horizon of the shore no better sight greeted de Cuellar. He could pick out a multitude of ragged barbarians "dancing and leaping with delight," just waiting for survivors to straggle through the surf. "I gazed my fill of this fiesta," he writes, "not knowing what to do. I never saw the like."

Finally thrown over the side in the death throes of his ship, de Cuellar managed to grab a hatch door "which God in His mercy brought within my reach," and he made it to the strand, but not before a falling timber nearly crushed his legs, covering him with blood. This gory apparition emerging from the water spared him the attentions of native Irish kerns who, in their lust for plunder, were tearing the clothes off every body washing up, in more than several cases clubbing to death those still alive. Unable to stand, de Cuellar crawled up the beach into dune grass. He records his astonishment at seeing what survivors there were in a state of pathetic wretchedness, shivering naked in the bitter cold of early winter, victims of an almost unnatural greed. He estimated that out of fourteen hundred men only three hundred escaped, as he had, off the strand.

By evening, news of the shipwrecks had spread all along the coast. Irish clansmen and their families (de Cuellar guessed almost two thousand people) were scouring the beaches for booty, and these were soon joined by English soldiers from Sligo, as equally interested in killing Spaniards as in the loot. Hobbling about in a state of near shock the next morning, de Cuellar came to Staad, and found "the deserted church, its images of saints burned, everything destroyed," along with the blood-chilling display of his slaughtered countrymen. This is a picture the sparse ruins of today, in windy, cold, desolate weather, readily convey.

De Cuellar could be well-forgiven, I think, had he given in to despair and simply gone off in the woods to die of exposure. Indeed, the catalogue of the various wounds he duly received over the next several days, to say nothing of months, is staggering, and de Cuellar had the right to say later that he suffered "the extremest misfortunes that man ever found himself in." But he displayed two characteristics typical of his race. The first was religious faith. De Cuellar was most anxious to die in a state of grace. Considering the large numbers of friars and clerics that his king had placed on board the fleet (at the expense, some claim, of more practical cargoes of food, medicines, maps, and military stores) it is amazing that anyone should lapse for long into a condition of mortal sin, but de Cuellar suggests he could not afford to die unshriven. This drove him on. And second, the fact remains that de Cuellar was a brave man. Despite tiresome English propaganda that all Spaniards were cowards, the stories of Armada crews thrown up on the coast of Ireland almost uniformly depict heroism, determination, and a stoic grittiness. In de Cuellar's case we also find a sense of humor, which sustained him in the perils that lay ahead as he shuffled from one miserable village to the next, with the English "prowling about" and treachery everywhere among the Irish. It is a wonder that after "seven months in mountains and woods and amongst savages, for in that part of Ireland where we were wrecked they are all such," he ever managed to reach Scotland and the court of James VI, and from there by ship to the Continent. Surely de Cuellar had cause for thought on the ways of futility and fate when this vessel was blown apart by the Dutch in French waters. Two hundred fifty Armada veterans were killed: just three made it to shore. De Cuellar picked himself out of the surf off Dunkirk just as he had at Inishnagor twelve months before, a fortunate gentleman indeed.

It is often debated whether the Irish, to whom the Spaniards were declared coreligionists and potential allies, were any different in their barbarity towards the Armada survivors than were the apostate English. And indeed, the carnage at Staad Abbey, certainly the work of the Sligo garrison, was more than matched by various Gaelic chieftains, some of whom freely admitted to the murder of several score of their Spanish guests. But the spectacle of Inishnagor was really one of supernatural dimensions to the Irish, most of whom had never seen such resources of material wealth and plenty in their lives. They simply lost their heads being, as de Cuellar observed, natural thieves in the first place. But after the initial gorge on plunder the Irish for the most part treated the survivors in decent fashion. De Cuellar lists many instances of kindness from the local peasantry, who endangered their own lives in doing so, and two local warlords were delighted to have Spanish soldiers swell their ranks, though both had their heads cut off as the result. "If these savages had not taken care of us as they did of themselves not one of us would still be alive," he concludes. "Though they had been the first to rob and strip naked any man cast alive on their shores, we were grateful to them."

DECIDING THAT STREEDAGH Point would present a fairly wild picture this morning I start to hike out from the abbey ruins. At a vantage point on the way I notice in the basin at the foot of the Grange estuary three fishing boats, all beached at various angles since the tide is out. I straddle several fences and slog through boggy shore line until reaching the bay itself, all sandy bottomed and relatively firm, and head for the closest. When I am about halfway a figure emerges from the cabin, hops over the side and walks in my direction. An inevitable encounter in the desert.

"Morning to ye," he calls out first as we approach. "A desperate day to be sure. Have ye the time?" I have a rough idea and tell him. He'd like to catch Mass at Grange, but considering that it's a good hour's walk away he decides he won't make it. We head back to the boat for "a wee sup of tea, as we call it here in Ireland," which is brewed on a begrimed and ancient burner at a very curious bent indeed given the boat is lying half over on its side. "I've had worse nights, believe me. At least I was safe and sound." My host is a fisherman from Killybegs, on the northern shore of Donegal Bay. The storm had surprised him off Inishmurray and at first he thought to ride it out "head to head, laddie, if you know what I mean. It was a real punching match for about a half hour or so, until I realized I could get in some real trouble. Home was too far and the seas, well, no way I says to myself, too dangerous. And I mean it was starting to blow smoke out there, getting dark too, so I headed for Dernish and the Haven. Aye, I've been in some tough weather, and so have those lads," waving to the other boats, "and I guess they came to the same conclusion I did. Went over before but they're both empty. They must be up in Grange. Have some tea, laddie. You'll have to drink it barefoot, I've no milk left. Plenty of sugar though." Sitting around for an hour or so, the fisherman decides that missing Mass is one thing, the pub another. He calculates he can be to Grange and back for a pint or two and catch the tide out to get back home. "You know, a day ago they hardly noted this storm on the wireless. Now they're saying it'll sit here for days. Might as well be at Killybegs than here." In the vast solitude of this empty bay I watch him walk to the shore and disappear on the road to town.

A N EVENING DEVOTION to Mary is taking place in the church at Grange, a fairly modern structure that sits on the edge of the new highway coming up from Sligo. A crude reproduction of the St. Molaise statue from Inishmurray, made from some sort of plastic epoxy, sits on a pedestal across the street. As the crowds pour out all the women head for shops and home, most of the men for bars.

There was, on my last trip through two years ago, a post card of a pub and grocery on the main street, with fine nineteenth-century frosted windows, burnished panelling and old-time fixtures, a warmness of feeling that was almost tactile. As a rule I seldom drank in the place, the crowd being generally a noisy one and that great enemy of Irish civilization — the television set — continuously turned on, beaming its greenish and purple discolorations into the adoring eyes of everyone present. But just in admiration I did periodically stop in to buy provisions, until I noticed workmen tearing out a wall several days ago. "There's no money in nostalgia," the bar girl tells me. "That lounge bar across the road is taking all our business so we've decided to tart up the place a little, modernize it. We're getting much more traffic now going north, truckers and all, so we're thinking of putting in an electric sign that lights up, a bigger lounge and new TVs. It's the way to go." I retreat with a look of horror that I hope is noticed.

My usual watering hole these past couple of weeks is a shabby enterprise just a few doors down, a nook that on some whim of the proprietor — a favorite saint's day, perhaps, or an early evening snooze — can more likely than not be shuttered up and closed. Tonight I find the place deserted, a not unnatural occurrence and, as directed on a previous occasion by Mr. Waters, the publican, I pour myself a pint of stout and take a seat on the hard wooden bench. There is, mercifully, not a sound to be heard in the place — no traffic from outside, no radio or television, no loud and boisterous talk. Only the wind overhead.

Mr. Waters comes in after the rosary. A small wizened man of about sixty-five, his head a shock of white thatch, fingers gnarled by arthritis, he leans across the bar with an air of ancient resignation. His sighs are deep, portentious, melancholic. He reminds me of the ruins on Inishmurray.

"Are ye still trying to go out?" he asks me.

"I am, Mickey."

"Ah, you've great ambition. When I was younger, now, I'd go out once a year. The priest from town here would go once a year to say Mass for the islanders, and I'd go to be the server. They were a grand people out there, very proud, very free with what they had, always trying to give you a drink of poteen or a twist of tobacco or a meal of fish. Thank God I don't drink, because that poteen was poison to be sure."

"You run a pub but you don't drink?"

"Aye, that's true, and my father before me not at all. This place has been in our family for over two hundred years, you know."

"It sort of looks it." We lapse into an easy silence.

"A good wind tonight. When it's wild on the land, it's calm on the sea. You'll be out tomorrow. I'll say a prayer for it." Another customer comes in.

"A pint for a gentleman, Mickey."

"Ah, gentlemen are scarce, Patrick, very scarce indeed."

Before turning in I stop at Paddy Joe's for the forecast. Mrs. Brady squeals in delight, "The Hulk be here, thanks be to God, now sit ye by the fire, I've had it going for you all the night." I had hoped, in a romantic impulse turned parody, that if Mrs. Brady were to choose a nickname for her new American friend it would be some appropriate mythological giant from the Celtic past, Cú Chulainn perhaps, or Balor of the Mighty Blows or Ferdiad, Battle Rock of Destruction. That it reflects instead her enthusiasm for the American programming that saturates Irish airwaves is to me mordantly perverse.

"It'll be mild for tomorrow," she tells me, "with very little rain."

"It's not the rain at all," says Paddy Joe, "it's the direction of the wind that matters. But still, you've a chance I think tomorrow." We talk off and on about the island. Paddy Joe is laboring me about underwater rocks to avoid and sea cliffs to watch out for and dangers everywhere that I might be swept out to deep water by a rogue wave.

"I'm not the captain," I finally tell him.

"Aye, but you're probably smarter than the lad who'll be taking you out. You watch now, you'll be forced to tell him what to do. He'll like nothing better than to motor out, say he can't put you on and then come back home. That would be some soft money for him! You'll have to put some iron up his backside, I warn you, you will."

"Don't be scaring him, Paddy Joe," says Mrs. Brady. Turning to me, "God knows — I'd be loving to go with you, and that's the truth, I be dying to get back to it. Now be sure to say a prayer at my old house, will you do that for me?" I tell her I will. "You'll find it easy now. You go out of *Clashymore* and Mrs. Heraughty's, the schoolteacher, is first, and Water's then is next, and Hart's then is up the lane, and then there's a Heraughty then again, and a Heraughty's above that again, and you go over the road and come to Boyle's, another empty house there, and I'm then again beyond that wee bit of a house of McGowen, that's where I lived. We had good times there, I'm thinking, it was a busy place one time. There was no need to be depressed. We had music and cards and story-telling, we'd walk about the town going from house to house, tour the island. And you could go down to the still, dip down in that fifty gallon wooden barrel and have a glass of beer or then, when it was distilled, whiskey. There was no need for LSD or cannabis or anything like that. Sing him your poem, Paddy Joe, on dear old Inishmurray."

"I did, maw, already."

"Let's hear it again, then."

Dear old Inishmurray, far out in the sea
Lies like a ship at anchor, the way it used to be
Sometimes it makes me wonder, why we chose to part
From our lovely, lonely island that it often breaks my heart.

For centuries it has stood erect in strong and stormy seas
And now it's like a sinner, down on bended knee
All forsaken just like a tree which sheds its many leaves
If only we could stay there, dreaming night and day
The peaceful thought will sure be sought, and we'll be back aboard some day.

"That's good," I say.

"It's very good!" Mrs. Brady agrees.

"Well it's not bad," Paddy Joe, acknowledging the praise, "not bad for a simpleton like me."

We walk down to the pier late at night, where my car is parked. Paddy Joe is in a philosophical mood. "You know now," he says, "the things you stray over and think about, the places you go to, each of us as an individual, the millions of experiences. I was often thinking what a human being goes through both in thought and in action and, oh Christ, I'd be often amazed."

NEXT MORNING AT 7:30 I am perched in a small, open seventeen-foot wreck of a boat chugging out past the Mullaghmore breakwater. Michael, a man of about twenty-five or so, is at the tiller. It is rare to find a fisherman so young still about in the West during wintertime, when most of his compatriots would likely be headed for England or Scotland in the hopes of a temporary job until spring. "I'm the only young lad here period," he tells me, "winter or summer. It's bleak wherever you look." Such despair is reflected, I hate to admit, in the present craft to which we have committed our well-being. I see no life belts or rings on board

— indeed, anything that will float — nor is there a single oar, though shattered spars that may once have been utilitarian lie randomly about. The inboard engine, started only after considerable encouragement, both manual and linguistic, is a rusted old contraption that, by the sounds of her, has received little attention over the years. And my man at the stern keeps throwing anguished looks at the sky overhead, not a menacing overcast of grey, but not a very friendly one either. As we round the point into open ocean the westerly winds smack me in the face. I decide to say nothing as to what this bodes for our chances of landing and put on my rain gear. Michael's entire body is swaddled in yellow oilskins. I cannot see his eyes and wonder if he's asleep.

During the ninety minutes that it takes to reach the island against seas, as I have noticed, that seem rougher with each passing minute, I really question whether all of this is necessary. It is very easy to talk a good game about rigor and hardship and the natural elements when you're sitting in an easy chair back home and planning an affair like this, another to be doing it. That is where pride comes in, I suppose, the notion that 'who else but me would be in this boat?' or, 'who else but me could like any of this?' These are attitudes I might have entertained a few years ago but I believe now, like the hermits of old, that a goodly sense of humility is a more attractive companion for those who undertake the personal and logistical difficulties required to visit such removed and desolate places as Inishmurray.

True, it's not the Himalayas or the jungles of Mexico or Central America; nor the mountains of Peru or deserts of the Holy Land. Ireland is only a few hours by air from New York, and here, at least, we have the language in common. But Inishmurray and the other westward islands of Ireland and Scotland, as well as the countless mountain hideaways and bog-obscured sanctuaries to the past on the mainlands of these British Isles, are separated from our mainstream by a formidable barrier, or should be if we wish to mine the most they have to offer. Considerations of the present tense should ideally be left behind, and luckily for a place like Inishmurray (which is, as Paddy Joe said, "a pain to reach for") the difficulty of access, the primitive archaism of this wheezing engine, creates the appropriate atmosphere. When you're wet, tired and miserable, the wretched coarseness of the past seems more real and intimate. One becomes less of a sightseer and more the participant. But again, humility is helpful, for it is best never to feel extraordinary. "Be as cautious as a stranger," one old hermit said, "do not desire your word to have power before you." I read that as a caution, and a necessary one, not to convey the impression that I discovered this place, or that I am singularly qualified to explain its little secrets. Many have come before me and many will come after, and a great number of these will certainly know more than I ever will about this place. I still wish to retain a single bit of vanity, however, the rather sneaky self-regard for my preferences in these matters of ancient remains. It is a source of satisfaction to me that Notre Dame, to take one example — an immense, convoluted, multi-layered statement of medieval thought and belief — has far less to say to me than the comparatively scanty traces here on this wind-swept, rather shabby little island. This may seem perverse but, drawing the line, hardly romantic. I am not a modern day Arthurian fool, searching for the Holy Grail, or dressing up in druid's robes for the summer solstice at Stonehenge. And I am not, I hope, making too much of what may seem too little.

LINKAGE BETWEEN THE sea voyage out to Inishmurray and the dusty, wind-driven tracks leaving the gates of Alexandria for the desert fastness beyond are tenuous and cannot be proven absolutely, but few have seriously doubted the connection. The Irish eremitical tradition, though idiosyncratic and its own master, owes a singular debt to the equally disordered austerities of its Egyptian role model. The similarities are not those of mould to mould reproduction, however. Ireland did not imitate in any slavish pattern its Eastern predecessor, one reason being they had no intimate, all inclusive idea or picture as to what the real thing really was. One of the fascinations to our line of inquiry, in fact, is the very tenuous business of passing information along over hundreds of miles, through several generations, then seeing what the end result has in common with the original. Ascetic practices in faraway Ireland, a country repeatedly referred to over many centuries as "truly a desert land," almost inaccessible, the ends of the earth and so on, had much in common with the principal source in Egypt, but the applicable metaphor may well be the common feeding trough. I am reminded of two images by way of explanation: the first, of Borneo head-hunters looking over issues of *Life Magazine* and styling themselves with ribbons, plastic jugs and assorted flotsam in the fashion of highly-elegant male and female models presented through its pages. How much have the two to share? The impulse seems the same, to be sure, but what a world of difference! The second was the visual plenty of punk hair fashions that I witnessed in the streets of London during my last visit there in 1984. There was no singularly primal style, though all had much in common. It would have been difficult to tell at times who was the teacher and who the pupil.

As an historical fact, and it might be refreshing at this point to present one, there is little doubt that for the origins of monasticism we must look to Egypt. The picture is not a neat one, but neither are we dealing here with a void of information. By A.D. 250 the Christian religion is an established entity and Church history, formerly a trickle, now flows as a healthy, broad river in which to fish for useful insight. One clear development we can trace is the struggle to achieve cohesion and unity. The

Church is older, maturing, consolidating, yet also experiencing the trauma of both losing members through various highly volatile disagreements over points of doctrine and interpretation, and absorbing countless new believers as Christianity spreads to different lands and cultures, who bring with them a bewildering variety in language, custom, and religious orientation. Unlike the Roman Empire which could and did, in a realistic, daily sense, accept a diversity of behavior within the general whole, the Church could not, in its infancy, afford to. Already it sought uniformity, as when St. Paul counselled his flock to "all say the same thing." St. Cyprian, Bishop of Carthage in 249, used the familiar metaphor of Christ's robe at the crucifixion, which was not torn to pieces and shared among the various soldiers present, but rather became a gambling prize, to be taken by the winner "unspoiled and undivided." This insistence that "you cannot have God for your Father if you have not the Church for your mother" produced, not unnaturally, one of the first real dichotomies to face the primitive Church. The message of Jesus had been to reject secular society but now, faced with growing evidence that in order to succeed in a practical manner it had, instead, to embrace a world it had spent a hundred years condemning. No wonder the arguments! Some of the earliest and most invigorating Christians such as Tertullian were aghast at bureaucratization and commercial development within the Church as it rose in power to rival the State. "All things are permitted to bishops!" he bitterly exclaimed, condemning his coreligionists as "sensual" and "libertines". At the same time hundreds of men and some women, adhering to the original formula, were indeed "fleeing the world".

Thirty years after the death of Origen, a young and illiterate Egyptian named Antony, of prosperous family and legitimate prospects within his community, sold all he had and gave it to the poor. In varying degrees of severity he removed himself from human society, at first choosing retreats close to his village and church, then further away in desert nooks and crannies, mostly empty and forlorn tombs long since emptied by looters and robbers. This was country that "no monk ever knew." Antony, though barely conscious of the precedent, had reinvented the willful withdrawal of John the Baptist.

For one stretch of twenty years he lived in the barricaded ruins of a Roman fort and invited the Devil, in his fashion, to do combat with him there, "for the mark of the true monk only appears under temptation." At first, thinking this young man an easy prey, Satan concentrated on the flesh, snares "that are in the navel of the belly." But mortifications, fasting, sleeping on bare ground (when he slept at all), constant vigils, and repeated supplications to the Lord subdued his body, made it weak and tiresome, but fortified the spirit in exchange. Satan moved on, appearing to Antony in frightful visions and hideous form, but again, to no effect. Next the great temptations, such as Christ endured at Gethsemane, the promises of eternal power and fame — "all lies" — that Antony rejects, triggering hysterical threats of torture and death, again ignored. The Devil then performs, shaking the old fort to and fro, tossing Antony about from wall to wall, screaming, shrieking, "hissing and hammering". "Often he struck me blows," Antony reports, but "I would say 'Nothing will separate me from the love of Christ.' And then the demons would beat each other instead!" Several times friends who delivered him bread and water every six months at the gates overheard the racket from within and would cry out their alarm. Antony sent them away. The serpents "make fools of themselves," he cried, they would flee eventually "as though hounded by the whip of that word, 'I am Christ's servant.'"

These verbatim transcripts of Antony's remarks are vivid pictures indeed of the struggles he routinely endured to achieve a goal of "daily martyrdom". They are, however, most likely the inventions of the highly intelligent Alexandrian, Athanasius, who wrote a *Life of Antony* in 357, or a year after the hermit's death. Athanasius was an extraordinary man of his age, the bishop of his city and a willing participant in all the contemporary controversies of both church and court. His career, a tempestuous one indeed, mainly hinged on the struggle against his fellow Alexandrian, the Presbyterian Arius, whose theories on the abstruse matter of whether Christ, as perfect man and perfect god, was the equal of the Father, would disturb the Church both East and West throughout the fourth century. Athanasius was deposed from his bishopric and exiled on five separate occasions, politely by the Emperor Constantine but with considerable menace from three of his successors who employed street mobs for their purpose. In one flight from Alexandria, Athanasius sought refuge in the desert, where by now considerable numbers of hermits lived, many of whom had forced themselves on Antony as disciples. Despite some accusations in the nineteenth century by Protestant commentators that Antony was a complete fabrication on the part of Athanasius, it now seems accepted that he was certainly an historical figure, though his various pronouncements and philosophical nuggets, extremely pungent and beautifully expressed, appear likely, in their finished form, to be the polished work of the cosmopolitan refugee who sat at the feet of the elder and mentally recorded his beliefs.

Thus it is hard to say who really put the spurs to this movement, Antony or Athanasius. Certainly the biography itself was a primary catalyst, written in Greek by Athanasius but soon translated into Latin and Coptic, spreading as a result all over the Mediterranean basin. And Athanasius himself, because of his various banishments now a world traveller, proved an able proponent. He had spent over seven years in Italy, Gaul, and Belgium, where interest in his tales of desert asceticism proved pandemic. To fuel that enthusiasm, in fact, he wrote the biography, specifically addressed to "the brethren in foreign parts," hoping "the rivalry you have entered on with the monks in Egypt" might explode

Hermits' Cells
Marmoutier
Le Val de Loire
France

throughout the Church and preserve, in the process, its orthodoxy. It would seem logical that the portrait of Antony as presented is an idealized blend of the many personalities that Athanasius bumped into as he wandered the desert.

These men were certainly an odd breed. Mostly unlettered Egyptians (or Copts), they lived a life of utter squalor, deprivation and eccentricity, though some of their habits which strike us as crude had a basis of justification given the time and place. Nearly all the monks, for example, took great pains never to bathe. It was a source of pride to Antony that he was continuously filthy, and the thought of washing any part of his body was abhorrent. "No one ever saw him undressed," as Athanasius marvelled, a rebuke, it has been conjectured, to the general populace who frequented the public baths of Alexandria, evidently scenes of considerable licentiousness.[1]

The pattern Athanasius presents is that of scattered elders — those who came first to the mountain of Nitria and the desert of Scete that stretched at its foot (about 60 miles southwest of the city), or the marshlands of the Nile Delta — living in isolation on whatever scanty fare they could generate, usually the produce of a miniscule garden plot or wild forage, perhaps food bartered for baskets or mats made from rushes, just about the only work these men deigned to do. Many of the holiest ascetics such as Antony gradually attracted disciples, and it was slowly deemed advisable that every week the master and his pupils gather for Mass (if any one of them happened to be a priest, that is) and then discussion. "It is well for us to encourage each other in faith and to employ words to stimulate ourselves," said Antony. "Be you, therefore, like children and bring to your father what you know and tell it, while I, being your senior, share with you my knowledge and experience." Through the course of several years we can easily imagine these gatherings developing along more formal lines, where a group of younger followers might settle around the cell of a wiser elder, venerating him and awaiting his teachings. Upon his death the memory of this man, and the oral tradition of his sayings, might continue to unify the group. Perhaps buildings would be erected and a surrounding wall built up, much like what we see on Inishmurray. So a monastery might begin, the paradox being that in this quite logical progression lay the degradation of Antony's ideal.

To Antony and the intellectual propagandists like Athanasius who wrote and lectured on his sermons, these growing numbers of disciples

---

[1] Public and private baths in the Roman world were often sensationally elaborate, and the supposedly luxurious American bathroom of the early twentieth century, more the invention of industrialist Robert T. Crane Jr. than anyone else, remains but a shadow of its ancient predecessor. When barbarian armies cut off the aqueducts to Rome they only finished off what the ascetics had begun — the complete destruction of civilized, hygienic bathing — and when society reorganized itself in the Middle Ages, "it clung to the squalor of the Orient." In H. J. Randall's words, "the ages of faith have been ages of filth."

were theoretically a burden. The arena of action for them was the individual cell, not the corporate life of an organized body of men. The Coptic monk Pachomius, a contemporary of Antony, had founded just such an entity at Tabannesi on the upper Nile near Thebes, about a ten-day sail from Alexandria. A former legionnaire, he had established a semi-military community with written rules (later translated by St. Jerome into Latin) that emphasized obedience and work. The monks wore uniforms, were organized into work groups and led a regimented life. At the height of its influence the Pachomian system, it is claimed, numbered over ten thousand monks. Again, in the same time frame, St. Basil of Caesarea in Palestine also advocated the communal life over that of the solitary, though his innovation was that monks should service the general populace with acts of charity and public prayer. In his view, the hermit laid himself open to the sin of pride by having no one nearby to correct him or keep his vainglory in check. Christ had bathed his Apostles' feet. "Whose feet wilt thou wash?" Basil asks the hermit. But these systems, to Antony and his peers, were the leaden weights of the world. It was fine, as a form of education and discipline, to live with monks of similar zeal for a period, but "perfect men, purged from every fault, ought to go into the desert. Not because they are cowards, running away from their sins, but because they desire a more sublime vision which cannot be found except in solitude." Or to put the matter more eloquently, "The monk's cell is the pillar of cloud out of which God spoke to Moses."

What we really have c. 360 is a period of chaotic groping where men or groups of men undertook in various ways to initiate a retreat from the world. The purity of Christ's message no longer seemed to them a possession of the clerical hierarchy or the day-to-day commercial Church. It was only to be found apart, either in the company of like-minded individuals or in the solitary mode. Rules of conduct, as varied as each monk, were seldom uniform. Like a meadow of wild flowers, the enthusiasm lay spread in profuse diversity through Palestine and Egypt and the far-off wilds of Western Europe, in particular Gaul, where Athanasius as early as 340 found interest already keen. His biography of Antony, no matter whose opinion it embodied, whether that of the elder himself or of the worldly bishop, served as a model both for those already on the path and also for those still grouped at the entrance. As such its impact was an extraordinary one. The figure of Antony shaped that of many who followed. Indeed, without meaning to, it infected a very significant proportion of the emerging monastic tradition with a streak of willfulness that the Church itself would expend considerable energy to extirpate.

BY THE LAST quarter of the fourth century the Egyptian desert could no longer be described as a simple piece of religious exotica known only to the few. Athanasius, both in person and through his writings, had unleashed a flood of enthusiasm for the ascetic ideal, and travellers from all over the Empire crowded the caves and hills around Alexandria,

The Monastery of Bishôi
The Desert of Scetis
Egypt
c. 1921

Founded c. 390 by Bishop Boshôi, a Copt. One of the four original monasteries of Scetis and Nitria. "These four are the stars, my beloved, which shine on the holy mountain of Scetis like jewels and precious stones in a dark place. They are like the Four Holy Gospels which shine over all the world."

searching for enlightenment.[1] Many of these, reminding me of war correspondents sending off dispatches from the front, wrote long and remarkably elegant reports of what they had seen and heard of the hermits' battles with the "Evil One and his hounds" for consumption back home, which provided, not surprisingly, excellent material for truly thunderous sermons. John Chrysostom, one of the more eloquent churchmen of this period, castigated his flock from the pulpit in Constantinople as unruly hedonists "without object or rules," who live as though "at sea, continually beaten about with winds, passing your days at the theatres and orchestras. For of these, although numberless fountains of pleasures and mirth seem to spring up, yet are countless darts still more bitter brought forth." The hermits, on the other hand, were at rest in a sheltered harbor, close to God, "and ye ought by the sight to take in these things. If thou desirest to learn about their table, be near it", which, with a zeal reminiscent of the medieval crusades, many thousands of men endeavored to do. But as one old monk in the desert lamented, in tears, "Worldly men have ruined Rome, and monks have ruined Scete."

With the turmoil of discovery came tremendous tension. The eremitical tradition, if indeed we can call it that, was young, immature, untested, the province of individual habit and pattern. The extremes of behavior, accordingly, were often mind-boggling. Many ascetics made Antony seem lax by comparison, as they hobbled through barren wastes with chains and leaden balls shackled to their belts or, like the famous Simeon the Stylite, lived for years on narrow pillars built, in some cases, over fifty feet from the ground. Whether true saints or mere charlatans, they attracted droves of unruly followers who many times, whether over ideological or even political differences, did battle with rival congregations, setting "altar against altar" in the words of a contemporary observer. And many were the instances of monks coming in contact with harlots or herdmens' daughters, with often disastrous consequences for both. Within the growing hurly-burly came a final and unhappy conflict that tore at the heart of the young monastic movement, with important consequences for the West, and even for Celtic Ireland.

Athanasius, who had died in 379, was a controversial figure in his own lifetime and not one universally admired. "Self-willed, authoritarian, ambitious and intolerant of opposition," writes a modern English historian, "a master of billingsgate." But at least a well-known master, even to this day. With John Cassian, however, one of the premier individuals of the early Church, the spotlight is far dimmer if not extinguished. No cult of sainthood followed his death, no string of miracles was recorded at his tomb, no widespread veneration given his writings, quite substantial and marked by considerable taste and insight. Cassian fell subservient to the

---

[1] One visitor estimated that on Mt. Nitria alone over five thousand hermits lived in separate cells.

84

greater figure of St. Augustine. They represented two opposing view-points that transcended an early struggle within the monastic movement by its spread into the larger universal Church. It involved the primal question of free will and Augustine's victory, even as he lay dying with barbarian armies about to breach the walls of Hippo in A.D. 430, thereby to extinguish the Christian Church in northern Africa for years to come, largely completed the Catholic canon as we know it today.

Little has been unearthed of Cassian's background, not even his country of origin, but he appears to have been well educated, fluent in both Greek and Latin, and early on a zealous participant in monastic practice. He is first seen in the Holy Land around the year 380 when he joined a community of anchorites that had settled near the site of the nativity in Bethlehem. Hearing legends of more extreme ascetic behavior in the deserts of Egypt, he and a friend named Germanus received permission to acquire information firsthand, and sailing to an eastern tributary of the Nile Delta in 385 they began a journey that some experts have determined may have lasted fourteen years. The various and celebrated saints they met, and the discussions they eagerly launched into with these masters, formed the basis of Cassian's most celebrated literary works, the *Institutes*, written c. 425, which dealt with the organizational details of a monastic community in Egypt (dress, conduct, various rules and prohibitions), as well as a catalogue of the primary sins which the monks were steeled to resist; and the *Conferences*, released just two or three years later, being conversations with the most revered of the Egyptian fathers. Cassian wrote both these books in Provence many years after the fact, and even more than in the case of Athanasius we may assume the views presented therein are largely personal to the author. We do know that the desert abbot Evagrius Ponticus, called by Thomas Merton a "prince of the Origenists", held unparalleled sway over the youthful Cassian, an admiration that was never surrendered.

If the picture of Antony created by Athanasius presented the Western world with its idealized image of the true ascetic monk, Cassian provided depth of field. In effect he intellectualized the popular notions, the almost comic-book perceptions of titanic desert fathers, by soberly charting and defining this hard road to salvation. In this and many other respects he contrasts dramatically to the style of Augustine, who literally unveiled himself in his famous *Confessions*. Cassian, instead, practiced restraint. Even when dealing with the highest ecstasies of the anchoritic pilgrimage — the point of communion with the Godhead — his language stood cold and far removed from emotion, though burning all the same with the rich possibilities of what could be within the reach of every monk. "The most eloquent Cassian," as Cassiodorus remarked, could point out the way, but not twist your arm. By discouraging a reader, he could prod him on. He was a realist.

But every man, and every work, has a weakness, and for Cassian it was

85

memory and nostalgia. The years he spent in the desert were the golden years of his youth, sitting with his friend Germanus at the feet of saints, men who had seen God with every fibre of their being. Cassian had never felt so enriched or captivated, yet he had personally seen the ideals of these men destroyed. Cassian, in the *Institutes* and *Conferences*, glorified a tradition that the desert itself had rejected. He presented it to the monks of the West, present and future, "who are indeed athirst," full knowing the goal was beyond their capabilities. Instead, he emphasized what they could handle, the "infant school" of the coenobium. With Cassian, the Neoplatonic traditions of Alexandria wither away, despite lingering and romantic persistence in presenting them as the highest pinnacle of achievement, and thereby unattainable. Only in Ireland, I think, did Cassian's memories of old find a people who could not be discouraged.

IT WOULD BE hard even to guess the nationality of the first individual who left Alexandria "for the desert". Was he a Greek, a Jew, a native Egyptian? Was he an educated man or illiterate? Did he abandon his family and give away his possessions, or did he leave the city gates as poor as he was the day before? No one knows. It seems a likely guess, however, that as the migration swelled, as the word passed around, more of the city's (and region's) less affluent members provided the numerical bulk, and these would have been the Copts. Certainly the organized monastic communities founded to the south by the Egyptian Pachomius were predominantly Coptic, and from our knowledge of the later difficulties we can say that in the north, in the valley of Nitria and the Scete desert, large numbers here were also the native populace. And like Antony, many of these could neither read nor write.

The Greeks, however, fascinated participants of all religious trends and theories, soon appreciated the possibilities of what initially appeared to them a rather fruitless pursuit. They perceived that withdrawal from society meant also withdrawal from a Church gone wild with the competitive appetite for glory, status, and financial substance. Solitude, not the company of men, seemed the place where an individual could put in practical application the more theoretical ideas of Origen and the Neoplatonists. There, undistracted, they could in the words of their chief theologian, Evagrius Ponticus, "shed all matter, attain perfect formlessness, draw near the immaterial Being, and attain to understanding." They quickly appropriated the vehicle of retreat to serve their own philosophical system, caring little, if at all, what their ignorant Egyptian counterparts might think.

Evagrius in particular saw what the desert meant — "freedom". In that sense he could empathize with rugged individualists like Antony who, indifferent to the opinions of his fellows, simply disappeared from regular life. They were the paragons, the men who refused to leave their hidden cells, gladly accepting the invitation of Satan to battle. There was a thrill for Evagrius in that challenge. These were the hermits, he said, whom

The Tree of Obediance
Monastery of John the Little
The Desert of Scetis
Egypt
c. 1921

"An old hermit took a dry stick and plunged it in the sand. He said to John, 'Water this every day until it shall bear fruit.' Now the water was far distant from them, so that when John went out in the evening he did not return until the morning. But after three years the stick lived and bare fruit. And the old hermit took it and brought it to the church, saying to the brethren,
'Take and eat the fruit of obedience.'"

the Devil respected and was prepared to fight in the open, whereas monks who lived in communities under a rule were less worthy opponents. The Evil One "arms the more careless of his brethren" against the cenobites, for that encounter "is much lighter than the first." Above all, the solitaries never run away. "To flee and to shun such conflict schools the spirit in awkwardness, cowardice and fear."

Their aim was to purify the soul, to prepare it for the mystical encounter with God. Sin had to be trampled, in particular the wasting cancer of *accidie*, identified by Cassian as the midday demon of the 90th Psalm, "the dejection that wasteth at noonday," or more simply put, spiritual despair. Evagrius, like all the hermits, considered this satanic snare far more insidious than lust or anger or gluttony. "*Accidie*, like some fever, makes it seem that the sun barely moves, if at all." It encourages malaise, the impulse to abandon one's cell for another, just for the change, a desire for company or reinforcement from fellow monks. Evagrius sternly counsels that "then is not the time to leave. Instead, with tears, divide your soul in two. One part is to encourage, the other is to be encouraged."[1]

Evagrius, like Origen condemned as heretical one hundred and fifty years later, was best known in these early decades of the monastic movement for his eloquent treatise on prayer, the *Praktikos*, written between 390 and 395. It is unabashedly Origenist in tone, thoroughly Alexandrian and typically Greek. It enthralled Cassian, Germanus and the other Greek-speaking disciples in his entourage, who flocked to his word. And what he gave them proved enormously attractive, even sensual: the promise that prayer would provide the truly worthy man with "continual intercourse with God, living constantly with him without intermediary". First, said Evagrius, "strive to render your mind deaf and dumb at the time of prayer," for when the monk's spirit "knocks at the door hard enough it will be opened." No Church, no priest, no sacrament, no grace from God is required, only the fierce will of the supplicant who must not waver in his assault, for "if your spirit still looks around at the time of prayer, you are no better than a man of affairs engaged in landscape gardening."

The objective was to reach a mental formlessness, whereby no visual image or picture of God is established. "Avoid allowing your spirit to be impressed with the seal of some particular shape, but rather, free yourself from all matter." This, of course, is Plato almost verbatim and the goal of many contemplative, mystical disciplines such as Zen Buddhism. But to monks like Antony, it was nonsense.

Years later, as an old man — indeed, an exile — Cassian could probably

---

[1] Whitehead observed, "The great religious conceptions which haunt the imaginations of civilized mankind are scenes of solitariness: Prometheus chained to his rock, Mahomet brooding in the desert, the meditations of the Buddha, the solitary Man on the Cross. It belongs to the depth of the religious spirit to have felt forsaken, even by God."

review the events that took place in Egypt with a more understanding eye. The Greeks, he may have felt, had been arrogant in their presumptions of superiority over the Coptic monks, too self-assured and abrasive. Nevertheless, it was probably inevitable, given the argumentative nature of the Alexandrian academic community, that disagreements within the city would flow out into the desert and back again. Certainly in many instances politics and religion were so intertwined that upheavals in one sphere could and did infect the other. The career of Athanasius was certainly a case in point, where street mobs under political control could tip the balance of a religious dispute. And even Antony himself on occasion travelled to the city to participate in partisan turmoils. But just the same, Cassian may have thought, it was probably unwise to taunt the Copts in their ignorance.

Antony had had that experience. He related to Athanasius how Greek philosophers from Alexandria had searched out his lair in the desert in order "to experiment with him, because he had not received any schooling." But Antony said to them, in a burst of argumentative logic all his own, "'What do you say, which is first, the mind or letters? And which is the cause of which — the mind of letters, or letters of the mind?' When they stated that the mind is first and the inventor of letters, Antony said: 'Therefore, one who has a sound mind has no need of letters.'"

The occasional debating loss notwithstanding, to an average Greek the Coptic view of things required radical alteration. Though numerically inferior to their Egyptian coreligionists, desert theologians such as Evagrius had indelibly stamped the experience with a Greek point of view. They assumed, as though by right, the philosophical leadership, propounding mostly Neoplatonic principles that baffled men like Antony. With puritanic zeal the Greeks sought to bring uniformity to the desert, and no item seemed more in need of their correction than the Coptic habit of visualizing the Godhead. Simplicity, while a virtue in the pious monk, could also be the occasion of sin. Ignorance, perhaps, was a more normal, even understandable human condition, and while it was regrettable that some Coptic monks did not seem to understand, for example, which Testament came first, the Old or the New, that was certainly not a sin. It was a sin to pray to an image of God, however, a human image more likely than not with most offenders, a direct contravention of the warning in Romans not "to change the glory of the incorruptible God into the likeness of corruptible man." Instead, the more sophisticated procedure of praying to God "with the inner eyes of the soul" was prescribed, where the monk will not allow himself "the memory of a name, the appearance of an action, or the outline of any character." In other words, transcend the body and expunge mental familiarity.

Cassian, in his second *Conference*, tells the story of Abbot Sarapion, "a man of long-standing strictness of life, altogether perfect in actual discipline" but, unfortunately, a victim of what the Greeks called anthropo-morphism, or giving human form to something which by "nature is incorporeal and uncompounded, what can neither be apprehended by the eyes nor conceived by the mind". When God threw bolts of lightning to the earth, a man like Sarapion would recreate the scene literally, God as a hero, with beard and flowing hair, personally directing the thunder-ous missiles in a patriarchal, Homeric rage. For the Greeks, all was metaphor and symbol. Surrounded by more educated brothers, Sarapion is forced to alter his practice, but the pressure of deviating from a lifetime's habit breaks him in the end. There is a wild scene among the monks where he falls to the dirt groaning, "Alas! Wretched man that I am! They have taken away my God from me, and I have none now to lay hold of; and whom to worship and address I know not!" Cassian, who witnessed the heartrending event, wrote later that he was "terribly disturbed".

The resolution of these conflicts was swift and, for the Greek party, painful. Yet to us, as distant observers, it provides a clarity of insight (ignored by several modern writers) into the character of these men. These philosophical differences between Greek and Copt were deadly serious, far more destructive in their potential than a conflict between, let us say, town and gown. In the end a veritable army of Egyptian ascetics descended on Alexandria and, in effect, laid siege to the bishop who, frightened for his safety (and properly so), reversed his own original and "definitive" judgment on anthropomorphism that had been favorable to the Greeks, and issued an order expelling them from the desert. Under continued browbeating from the Copts he even petitioned the Pope in Rome to condemn the teachings of Origen and Evagrius. Cassian and his friends were forced to flee for Constanti-nople. Their entire school of thought, and the apparatus that sup-ported it, crumbled to dust.

These were life and death matters in large measure because the hermits – men of character so bold and determined they could embrace with relish a life we would consider unrelievedly distasteful – were not content, or sufficiently humble, to be told how to believe. This hardened attitude has been misunderstood by two schools of modern interpreta-tion which have tended to overlook or simplify the racial divisions that marked this desert community. The distinguished historian Philip Schaff, for instance, who oversaw in the late nineteenth century the translation into English of several dominant works from the primitive Christian Church, had little respect for the crudity of ascetic practice. The hermits had "no affinity with the morality of the Bible, and offend not only good taste, but all moral feeling," he wrote. In particular their predilection for filth repelled him. "The ascetic holiness is incompatible with cleanliness and decency." The desert fathers, as he saw them, were deluded curmud-geons. Disgust (or fascination) with some of the more extreme hygienic and devotional habits of the monks do, however, tend to obscure their incredible resolution. The physical details, distasteful to a Victorian ethos, should be seen as a projection of mental toughness that we can only imagine, a strength of conviction untamperable by outside authority. No wonder that differences of opinion resulted in various ecclesiastical brawls, themselves fueled by a violence of conviction that today we would probably associate with Iranian mullahs or Protestant fundamentalists caressing snakes. There was nothing pretty about ascetic obstinacy, but to confuse it as solely a matter of outward appearance, as did the fastidious Schaff, is misleading. The hermit was a fearless loner. Even his tone with God was imperious, demented, superior. When the Lord spoke to Antony, "he was not bewildered." Nor were the Irish.

Thomas Merton contrasts with Schaff by idolizing the desert fathers. For Merton, aspiring hermit that he was, the sayings and prophesies of the ascetics provided a romantic reinforcement of an impulse already strong in his soul. Merton was predisposed to be charmed by their writings — which are both wise and simple in their almost folk art naivete — but he tended to overlook the violence of their pride by over-projecting an image of serenity more suited to a Francis of Assisi. The hermits were not, as their history confirms, particularly gentle or timid. Schaff realized that. Nor were they concerned, as Merton wished, in protecting anyone's soul but their own. Merton's enormously popular humanistic and ecumenical vision, which was the right sort of thing for an era of nuclear dread, saw the monks as interceders in the heavenly court, the saviors, through prayer, of fallen humanity. "There can be no other valid reason for seeking solitude or for leaving the world," he wrote. "And thus to leave the world is, in fact, to help save it by saving oneself."

> This is the final point, and it is an important one. The Coptic hermits who left the world as though escaping from a wreck, did not merely intend to save themselves. They knew that they were helpless to do any good for others as long as they floundered about in the wreckage. But once they got a foothold on solid ground, things were different. They then had not only the power but even the obligation to pull the whole world to safety after them.

But it was an old maxim of the fathers, "Do not lose yourself in order to save another." The hermits were not humble men. They resorted to violence when necessary, threats and coercion too. They were strong individuals and, really, men of their times. We should neither exalt their character unduly nor exaggerate their failures of style. As the Church matured it did both, elevating the one extreme into the realm of miracle while redirecting the other into the moderate monastic tradition that we have today.

For Cassian, the road to exile was suitably melodramatic. In Constantinople he became the protege of John Chrysostom, a brilliant though emotionally erratic individual full of "imprudent" sympathy for the Origenists cast out from Egypt. When Chrysostom fell just three years later, Cassian, by now a deacon and in charge of the cathedral's treasury, watched helplessly as mobs broke into the great building and burnt it to the ground. From yet a second pile of ruins he fled to Rome, itself under immense pressure from barbarian invaders, and then to Provence. There, as a mature churchman, he would battle Augustine on the issue of free will, and inaugurate a monastic ethos which would influence the entire progression of this movement through Western Europe. But for him, the sad though glorious past proved haunting, a time and place he could never recapture, the joys of youth and its enthusiasms. A modern Catholic historian, disapproving of the semi-pagan flourish with which Evagrius imbued all his work, gives Cassian considerable credit for pruning "the coarse excretions of an overseverity" from the master's work, but this is false or misconceived praise at best. Evagrius, and indeed Origen, were the best the desert could produce, the ideal — indeed, the perfection — that Cassian saw was no longer attainable. In older age he counseled his readers to regard their exploits as "beyond the capacity of ordinary goodness". Their lives should not be held up to inspire reproduction, in a monastic rule for instance, because their achievements were "outside the condition and nature of human weakness, and should be brought forward as a miracle rather than an example".

A N EVENT OF unimagined catastrophe took place in the dead of night August 24, A.D. 410. A gate in the outer walls of Rome was treacherously opened from within (by break-away slaves, according to some), and Gothic barbarians under the leadership of Alaric poured through city streets to the utter shock and confusion of defending legionnaires and citizenry. This was the infamous sack of Rome, a pillaging that Alaric could not control until three entire days had passed. In that span of time several fires destroyed numerous residential quarters of the city, started by the barbarians on that initial night, it is alleged, so they could see what they were stealing. Considerable slaughter ensued, though many Christians who had gathered in their churches and holy places were evidently spared. The loot was prodigious, though Roman monuments and public buildings, of sufficient solidity to require more time than Alaric evidently felt open to him for lingering, resisted destruction. And according to Gibbon in *Decline and Fall* even the rapine was less than might have been expected, "the want of youth, or beauty, or chastity protecting the greatest part of the Roman women" from outrage. Rome would suffer worse terror in 455 when Vandals occupied the city for two weeks, but by then over three-quarters of its population had long since ebbed away. And in fact Catholic troops of Charles V in their pillage of 1527 exceeded every horror visited upon Rome by the fifth-century heathens. But Alaric was the first, an illiterate chieftain "subject to no royal authority", leading a mob of warriors "content with the disorderly government of their important men, and led by them through every obstacle".

As most schoolboys know (or used to know) the fall of Rome was no sudden disaster. The ill-omens of the age, and their import in full and multicolored gloom, were certainly apparent to anyone who cared, in a reflective way, to give them any thought. The Western Empire was *in extremis* and most observant men knew it. I say this because the process of demise – one tumultuous disaster to another – had beneath the noisome din of terror, pillage, and frightful battle, a certain calm thread of inevitability that became, over one or two decades, dreadfully obvious. In particular, Imperial policy regarding the Rhine and Danube frontiers proved defective. Accommodations with the various Germanic tribes, made dangerous by the combination of their own quite natural warlike truculence and the pervasive, often hysterical fear they felt for more powerful migratory peoples pressing them from the East, insured a fluid volatility just waiting for a spark or a panic for ignition. Many recent commentators on the Western Empire have also chosen to emphasize the moral and intellectual decay then pervasive within the ranks of Roman leadership – indeed, the society at large – as a precondition to this vacillating posture towards the Germans, and no doubt there is considerable merit to their theory. Others point to the monetary difficulties facing Rome but this results again, I think, from the "moral vacuum" approach whereby the circus flourished, along with mind-boggling graft and corruption, at the expense of proper appreciation and attention to the integrity, morale and make-up of the Army, which was by then largely mercenary and without particular zeal for Rome. Whatever the explanation, the specific cause for its fall did lay at the frontier.

It is ironic that Rome's collapse can directly be traced to the follies of an Eastern Emperor, Valens, who ruled from Constantinople just thirty years before Alaric's startling victory. As a matter of fact, it is widely forgotten that Rome's disintegration was not reflected by a similar breakdown in the East. The Byzantine Empire, remnant of the wider Roman authority, remained indestructible until Constantinople fell to the Turks in 1453. Through many of those centuries Rome, a provincial backwater, was of no importance in world affairs. Still, in charting the specific series of events that led to Alaric's adventures in Italy, we must start with an Eastern fiasco.

Ammianus Marcellinus, a military staff officer of Greek origin born c. 330 in Syrian Antioch, turned his attentions later in life to chronicling the dwindling fortunes of Empire through the final years of the fourth century. He is regarded by most historians as remarkably trustworthy – Gibbon, in fact, swore by him – and his somber foreboding at the ineptitudes of Imperial policy no doubt reflect the thinking of all intelli-

Roman Citizens of Aquincum
Province of Pannonia
The Danube Frontier
Present-day Budapest
Hungary

gent contemporaries. But the clearest origin of the Empire's problems he perceived as no one's fault. "The seed of all the ruin and various disasters that the wrath of Mars aroused, putting in turmoil all places with unwonted fires, we have found to be this: the people of the Huns, but little known from ancient records, dwelling near the ice-bound ocean, exceeding every degree of savagery." These wild and unrestrained tribesmen, "glued to their horses" since birth, had wandered the Asiatic and Russian steppes for generations, but not until the 370s did anyone in the West have any knowledge of them. According to Gibbon they initially ravaged two German tribes, the Ostrogoths and Visigoths, settled for many years in territories adjacent to the Black Sea, north of the traditional Roman frontier of the Danube. "The numbers, the strength, the rapid motions, and the implacable cruelty of the Huns," writes Gibbon, "were felt, and dreaded, and magnified by the astonished Goths, who beheld their fields and villages consumed with flames and deluged with indiscriminate slaughter." The Visigoths turned to Valens, pleading for sanctuary south of the Danube. Valens, a man of little substance, saw the opportunity here for profit: manpower for his army, gold for the Imperial treasury. "The affair", said Marcellinus, "caused joy, not fear", an astounding reversal for common sense as Valens unlocked the frontier enabling, it is estimated, more than one million refugees to enter, two hundred thousand of whom were able- bodied warriors. "Diligent care was taken that no future destroyer of the Roman State should be left behind."

Various measures had been contemplated to control this immense migration. All weaponry was to be handed over, a proper count undertaken of those coming across the river, and a dispersal throughout the Empire of every male child for proper indoctrination in the ways of a civilized society. Only the last requirement was enforced with some vigor, with tragic consequences for those who were in fact separated from their families and shipped away. After news of the disaster at Adrianople, these youths were herded together in assorted market squares and butchered. As for the census, it was deemed "a vain attempt", the numbers being so immense. And the Gothic soldiery, "who considered their arms as the ensigns of honor and the pledges of safety consented, with some reluctance, to prostitute their wives and daughters" for the privilege of keeping their swords and spears and shields.

Roman venality did not, unfortunately for the Empire, stop there. Rather than provide the Goths with emergency food supplies to tide them over temporarily, officials created a condition of "artificial famine" which resulted in a highly lucrative market for dog meat and "unclean animals that had died of disease" which, again, the Goths were forced to purchase through bribery and a debasing trade in young girls and boys. To further embitter these people the Roman Army sought to assassinate their leaders at an elaborate, though treacherous, festivity, a plot that was bungled irretrievably when survivors were allowed to escape and spread about the tale of massacre. It is small wonder that the tribes exploded in fury. Valens, again through vanity impervious to sound advice, with "unseasonable bravery" engaged the Goths in battle fifteen miles outside of Adrianople, just a short march from his capital city and the Bosporus. Taken in by the crudest of ruses, Valens allowed his forces to stand about in the searing sun in full armor without food or water for most of August 9, A.D. 378. At mid-afternoon the full brunt of Gothic cavalry "trampled down horse and man" and a rout ensued. Some forty thousand men were slain, almost two-thirds of the army. The Emperor's body guard "all scattered in flight over unknown paths", leaving Valens behind. In the general panic he was wounded by an arrow; so thick was the dust that these deadly missiles could not be seen approaching. He was carried to a nearby cottage and abandoned by most of his retinue. The Goths, not knowing the Emperor lay wounded within, burned it to the ground in their hysteria for destruction. "With such stormy eagerness on the part of insistent men," complained Marcellinus of Valens and the Imperial Court, "was the ruin of the Roman world brought in."[1]

Reading the history of Western Europe and the Empire for the succeeding few decades presents a picture of unrivalled complexity. The engine of state did not overheat and explode, but rather shed its various nuts and bolts until eventually the entire contraption fell apart in a welter of ruin. The comings and goings of numberless heathen tribes makes for a dizzying catalogue of catastrophes — frontiers pierced, armies destroyed, cities besieged, broken, put to the torch. While some commentators have doubted whether any individual tribe could ever muster forces of more than twenty to thirty thousand armed men, alliances among warlords and, more common, spontaneous intrusions of several tribes at once (universally pressured as they were by Huns at their backs) could place hundreds of thousands within the frontier at any single moment. The calamitous breakthrough at the Rhine in 407, for example, was apparently the work of several independent peoples taking advantage of freakish winter conditions that saw the river freeze solid.

In the Western Empire there was no possibility of an adequate defense. The Rhine and Upper Danube wall, hundreds of miles to cover and guarded, for the most part, by unreliable barbarian mercenaries (as likely to join the invaders as to obstruct them) put intolerable pressure on Rome's resources.[2] Byzantium, in contrast, had a relatively defined arena for its defense. Barbarian hordes regularly crossed the lower Danube and

---

[1] Gibbon noted with his usual elegance that "A Gothic chief was heard to declare, with insolent moderation, that, for his part, he was fatigued with slaughter; but that he was astonished how a people who fled before him like a flock of sheep could still presume to dispute the possession of their treasures and provinces."

[2] As Toynbee observed, "When a frontier between civilization and barbarianism stands still, time always works in the barbarians' favor."

ravaged at will through Thrace. But tiring of that, they had no choice but to contest Imperial forces at the Strait which, guarding as it did the capital city itself, was always adequately garrisoned. Valens's reversal was due more to a shoddy performance on the battlefield than to a generic fault in the thinking of his command staff. And though the Visigoths shattered his forces on that dismal afternoon, they did not succeed in taking Constantinople.

If Rome had been located in the middle of Gaul perhaps the story there may have been different, with more opportunities for a unified front to face the Rhine. Instead, the geographical position of the city hindered an effective military response. Troops were withdrawn from the unwieldy frontier to protect the Italian homeland, thereby preventing any quick resolution (and punishment) to invasion from without. The most incredible saga of the Vandals is illustrative of the general vacuum into which many invaders happily blundered. A collection of Teutonic tribes settled around the river Oder in Silesia; they had skirmished with Imperial troops in an ancient Roman territory called Pannonia, along the upper Danube. In 406 they crossed the Rhine, razed Mainz and surged into Gaul, nowhere opposed by Roman troops. In the span of just fifty years, and with more than their share of reversals (due in large measure to internal feuds and defeats at the hands of other barbarian freebooters) they still managed to fight and bull their way through the southern provinces into Spain, cross the Straits of Gibraltar into North Africa, reducing every city along its coast, finally taking Rome itself in a daring attack from the sea in A.D. 455.

The Vandals, of course, are fairly well-documented, surviving for us in the descriptions and histories of the time, which cannot be said for many of the smaller groups of foragers — just as hungry, desperate, and warlike to be sure — that surged like a flood tide through the western districts before them and after. These are peoples the chroniclers either knew nothing about or ignored, weary perhaps of monotonous stories heaped with carnage and destruction whereby the flesh of countless dead, in Gibbon's mordant phrase, "was greedily devoured by the birds of prey, who in that age enjoyed very frequent and delicious feasts." Roman authority gradually wore away, no longer able to cope even in Italy, the victim of exhaustion and splintered ambitions. In 410 six individuals of varied, de-stabilizing power claimed possession of the title Emperor. Between their sanguinary struggles and the depredations of barbarian hordes, it was inevitable that "final and long impending punishment should reach a fearful Rome". When Jerome heard the news in faraway Jerusalem he said, "The city which has taken captive of the entire world is itself taken captive. My voice chokes, and sobs interrupt me as I dictate this."

It is interesting to speculate what influence this aura of impending doom, and then the calamitous event itself, may have had on the citizens

Ruins from a Pillaged Town
Vaison-la-Romaine
La Vallée du Rhône

of the Empire, both in Rome and abroad, and particularly its effect on the emerging practice of monasticism in the West. Certainly the sense of gradual foreboding must have had considerable impact, and that is an emotion we can, I believe, faithfully recreate. In our own twentieth-century, intimate to all of us in a way no other epoch in recorded history can claim, we are able to examine, read, see and even feel the anxieties so many individuals experienced prior to the hostilities of both World Wars. Perhaps an even more telling comparison might be the era we live in now, with its drift of seeming inevitability (which none of us, like the Romans, can tolerate believing in totally) to some unspecified nuclear disaster. At the turn of the fifth century what did people think the world would be like without Rome and Empire? We saw what Jerome felt: sackcloth and ashes. But Augustine, on the other edge of the spectrum, seemed calm and undisturbed. His attitude in the *City of God*, a work expressly written to discuss the catastrophe, seems to this reader quite detached. Rome's fate, more or less, was what it deserved, and his interest lay more in the future, to build upon the ruins a new Rome, one more worthy of God's beneficent attentions.[1] Augustine, however, being an original, should be considered a rule unto himself, an exception to the norm. Jerome's reaction was certainly typical of the age, though his grief lay less with the physical details of shattered aqueducts and slaughtered citizenry than it did towards psychological impact. The authority of Rome, its immense prestige and sense of continuity, its order and now, most importantly, its role in the Christian world: site of the martyrdoms of Peter and Paul, head of Empire and thus of the Church, a growing repository of spiritual power — all gone! Who could be blamed for "running away" from a world now in ruins?

Against this background — indeed, wandering about in the very streets of Rome itself — we can finally introduce a Celtic voice. Not necessarily an Irish voice, I hasten to add, more likely British, but a Celt nonetheless, the "snakeling bred in black caverns," Pelagius.

THE CONFLUENCE OF personalities and ideas and causes at this particular juncture in our narrative is strangely ironic to me. For in the largest sense this story is indeed little more than backwater debris, hardly scheduled (if at all) for more than a line or two in the general historical surveys, and even that but the meagre reward for brushing the cloak once and again of some monster figure of the period like an Augustine or a Jerome. It is of little note or importance to anyone that perhaps John Cassian and that corpulent dog from the Celtic wilds of Britain or Ireland named Pelagius may have passed one another in a narrow Roman alley-way, possibly had a discussion or two, maybe an argument. No matter that the subject more than likely concerned the

---

[1] Gibbon goes so far as to say that Augustine "took peculiar satisfaction" in the city's fall.

pre-eminent intellectual topic of the day, free will, nor even that the implications and outcome of the struggle which ensued touched, in significant fashion, our lives in the West today. This is all dead issue from the past. Even Augustine hardly matters today.

I do not mean to launch what would be, and deservedly so, a largely futile diatribe against the priorities and directions of our modern society. It is just my own belief that a place like Inishmurray is really quite irrelevant, not only to the average man in the street (whether in the guise of a tourist out here on the island, or at large) but even to those who occasionally do wonder about some of the more torturous and obscure particles from mankind's past. For Inishmurray has no handle to grab, not even the artistic hint or pretended sensibilities of a primitive art going in its favor: no African masks or Incan statues, to say nothing of polished marble gods. Inishmurray is a pile of rubble, stones upon stones, a few crude huts, a weirdly egg-shaped wall, some sketchy crosses hammered crookedly into coarse slabs of rock. There is nothing here but spirit, a very hazy thing indeed to hold, and though we may be products of what that spirit sought to understand or define, we reject it as meaning anything to us because its monuments, its forms, are ephemeral. It is difficult indeed to carve a thought.

It is appropriate that Inishmurray, dead in the Atlantic Ocean as it is, should preserve for those who wish it the spiritual minutae of ancient history — both from Rome, at the meeting between a Cassian and Pelagius that might never have taken place, and here on the island itself where monks, for hundreds of years, personified the issues that grew in dispute to embroil much of Western Europe, then to subside, over time, into another molecular substructure of twentieth-century thought. Free will means something to Inishmurray. So does John Cassian and Pelagius, Augustine too, as well as Antony and all the ignorant Copts in his train.

CASSIAN FOUND REFUGE in Rome c. 405 A.D. By then, most experts agree, Pelagius had been in residence for at least five and perhaps as much as twenty years, though the exact circumstances of his life there remain unknown, as indeed are any but the scantiest details of his youth and early manhood. It is presumed proven, however, that Pelagius was a Briton, since most of his theological opponents referred to him as "Britannicus noster", and the vast majority of commentators both past and present assume as well that he was a Celt, though one or two rogue opinions place him variously afield in Ireland or "north of the wall" among the Scots. It seems possible, in fact, that Pelagius may have been, all in one, an Irishman, a Celt and a natural-born Briton, since Irish counter-migrations and subsequent settlements eastward to the Cornish peninsula (and, indeed, into Wales, remote though that wild land was from the more heavily Romanized southeastern portions of the island) are known to have been ongoing since the turn of the fourth century. It appears to me the safest course that we grant Pelagius a British and Celtic origin and just wish him the luck, if not the certainty, of an Irish heritage as well. Two rather generalized, and perhaps dubious, assertions about the man have also been widely debated, the first that he was a talented student of law who had been sent to Rome by pious, literate, and prosperous parents to further his education amid the encouraging atmosphere of the Imperial court; and the second that he was a large and heavily-built individual, of imposing presence, though afflicted in later age by an ever expanding waistline. There is really little foundation to the former theory, while the latter owes most of its justification to the vituperative writings of St. Jerome, a man characterized by Rebecca West as "a literary genius of repellent disposition", who detested Pelagius and attacked him according to the rhetorical standards of the age as "a most stupid fellow, heavy with Irish porridge," "an Alpine dog, huge and fat" and so on.

While perhaps not an aspiring lawyer, and evidently not a priest either, Pelagius was nevertheless a man of formidable intelligence, agile of mind and assertive, though diplomatic and acute when circumstances warranted caution, which was often enough in the last years of his life when he found himself hounded by critics such as Jerome and Augustine. The titanic reputation of these two men in particular should not obscure from us the realization that in fifth-century terms this struggle was one between equals. Augustine, for example, though a prominent figure in North Africa and well-known to the various popes and prelates of the Empire, was no more or no less influential than Jerome or Pelagius himself, both of whom had recourse to similar familiarities among the hierarchy of the Church. Pelagius, in fact, frequently won the pope of the particular moment to his side during various stages of the controversy, and successfully defended himself more than once before councils called to judge his orthodoxy. In Jerusalem, where he fled after Alaric's frightening menace to Rome (Cassian, meanwhile, having left the city in the opposite direction to Marseilles) Pelagius demonstrated his intellectual credentials by presenting his case in Greek, when his accusers could do no better than employ interpreters. Pelagius was not a man to be taken lightly, as Augustine himself fully realized in his judgment that the Briton had a "very strong, active mind" and who, with a quill in his hand, "wrote with much power".

Our first reference to Pelagius making a nuisance of himself, in fact, comes from Augustine himself, and can be dated no earlier than 405. This tends to support the notion that for at least a decade, possibly two, Pelagius had lived a fairly quiet life in Rome and had eschewed the role of theological controversialist. Like many of his contemporaries he had withdrawn from the world, though not to a cave or empty tomb but within an urban monastic environment, surrounded by brothers and students who were, like himself, engaged in biblical study and contemplation. But Augustine's *Confessions*, completed in 397, began circulating in the city and when Pelagius came to read it he evidently exploded

— or, in Augustine's words, became "excited" and "nearly came to a quarrel" with a bishop who was friendly with the African father. The tone of the *Confessions*, whereby the young Augustine is mystically drawn by God's mercy to see the error of his life, to repent and convert and, finally, to open his heart to the Lord's unbearable love, was thoroughly exasperating to a man like Pelagius who was attempting through example and preaching and advice to counter the nihilistic sensuality that he saw out of control in this, the greatest city in the world. With pagan armies as a pessimistic backdrop, the citizenry of Rome — many of these Christian only because the law now forbade any other allegiance — had apparently given themselves over, once again, to the evils of mindless pleasure. (I cannot recall in my readings, as both a child and an adult, when I ever saw the people of Rome depicted as doing anything else.) In particular, Pelagius was irritated by the excuses he heard, things like, "The flesh is weak, how can I resist it, poor man that I am", or "It's not my fault, I can't control myself", or again, "What can I do, it's fate, we're lost, why not sin?" Pelagius saw that this general tone of surrender, of near helplessness, permeated the *Confessions*, in particular in Augustine's famous prayer in Book X where he cries, "Give what Thou commandest, and command what Thou willest." This was abject defeatism, the notion that a man or woman could not deal with sin or with God himself on his own terms, however human and miserably inadequate these might be. Man as a robotistic piece of stone, inert and passive, seemed insulting to both the Creator (why would he make such a pathetic creature?) and to man himself. Pelagius evidently concluded that without effort on the individual's part, without the will to avoid sin and approach God, there was no practical way to convince anyone, least of all the fickle, world-weary, jaded Roman mob, to consider a moral or godly life. In this fashion the argument commenced.

It crystallized for both men in the person of a wealthy Roman socialite, evidently quite beautiful, by the name of Demetrias. A younger Augustine, back in the days when he ambitiously sought his fortune in Rome and Milan, had been hired to supervise her education, and later in life she had sought the counsel of Pelagius and even corresponded with Jerome. Coming of age she decided not to marry, but instead sought admission to what we would today call a convent. Pelagius took the opportunity to write her an open letter of congratulation, which emphasized his delight that of her own true freedom of choice she had sought God and not the world, an option open to all. He also remarked that goodness and virtue knew no bounds, that heathen and Christian alike were capable of achieving a state of righteousness, just as they were equally able to choose the reverse, a life of sin. "Everything good and everything evil is not born with us but done by us: for we are born not fully developed but with a capacity for either conduct, and we are procreated as without virtue, so also without vice."

To Augustine these views were flippant and "fatally opposed to our salvation." In a letter and then a follow-up polemic, both notably lacking in graciousness or good manners, Augustine admonished Demetrias and her mother, Juliana, that pride in this decision, and the virtue it suggested for their aristocratic family, should not obscure the fact that without God's grace no forward movement was at all possible. It seemed dangerous to ever assume that Demetrias, on her own initiative, could follow the path towards God. For if she had that ability or strength or power of will — call it what you wish — then what became of prayer, what was the point of it? "Why should I ask God for that which he has set in my own power?" Juliana, angered by Augustine's cheerless pedantry, severed communications with him.

It is not my intention in this little travel book to give a detailed account of how this long and portentous controversy progressed — from battle to battle, wound to wound — even though the particularly Celtic vehicle of saga tale presents itself as an appropriate model to follow, especially those involving the hero Cú Chulainn which drag along for what seem several hundred pages before the final, relief-giving denouement when the victor takes his enemy's head and brandishes it aloft. In this particular instance, no verifiable or even theatrical conclusion is permissible since Pelagius, around the year 420, simply disappears from view. He had clearly foreseen the fall of Rome, leaving in 410 for Sicily, then North Africa (where Augustine, "to the best of my recollection," caught a glimpse of him "once or twice") finally reaching the Holy Land. There he engaged in petitions to Rome and was forced to attend what were, in fact, trials, but he emerged from these unscathed. At some point, sensing more trouble, he fled again, and that is all we know.

But one or two highlights of the dispute we should take time to note, since the point of contention between these two holy men — one an indisputable pillar of the Catholic canon as we know it today, the other our eventually despised Celtic outcast — vividly illustrates the most primal tension inherent to all organized religion, the question of free will: does man have it or not, is he a pawn of forces beyond his control or does he initiate his own fate, either for good or for evil? In the view of Pelagius the answer was quite simple. "We say," he wrote, "that man is always able both to sin and not to sin." While clear-cut, basic, free of artifice, structure or complication, this hardly compares with the ingenuity of an Augustine, whose response to the problem was his own personal neuroses disguised, or disfigured, into dogma. Augustine's mental prowess could dismember a Pelagius, however crafty and elusive he might be in front of ecclesiastical tribunals. In intellectual terms the answers provided by both to the issue of free will hardly bear comparison. Pelagius, like Christ, built a road so straight and without feature that it bored the individual man of whom it thought so highly. Augustine, like St. Paul, created a labyrinth which both satisfied himself and presented to gener-

103

ations of believers to come a structure at once so unreasonable yet perversely logical that it demanded attention and eventually, bewildered acceptance. Men do not really want to worship something simple. That is why we no longer pray to the sun.

Augustine, of course, is the man we should most wish to discuss. About sixty years of age at this time, he had led a long and active career as Bishop of Hippo, much of it spent in the mundane difficulties of administration and local politics, interspersed with campaigns against the schisms and heresies of the century, some of which, such as Arianism and Donatism, were already of considerable age. The Pelagian matter was different. It had no lineage, it was fresh, it demanded a vigor of thought and response that his tired, argumentative diatribes against the old-line deviations could not supply. At first, in fact, he paid it little mind. A holy man in Rome, "good and praiseworthy, who has made no small progress in the Christian life" as Augustine was forced to admit, had offered some arguable notions that appeal to the pride of man. Augustine, a man of letters, had composed various tracts in response that his allies in Rome and elsewhere could use in debate, though Pelagius was spared a direct attack, not even mentioned by name. But the followers of both men heat the kettle ever more dangerously until we see in Augustine a hardening conviction that the simple-minded beliefs of a misguided monk in Rome are more insidious than he realized and stray towards the realm of heresy (a word derived, ironically, from the Greek for "free will"). "My hesitation," he writes, "has received its limits. I must open the wound in order to cure it," for the Pelagian error is both strong and subtle, thus more menacing. It does not batter the walls of a city to dust, but "creeps into houses".

Augustine's response, under more or less direct provocation, was to create, in effect, a system. This is not as neat as it sounds, because nowhere in his tracts do we find any large body of succinct or logically sequential propositions capable of easy recall or summary. Augustine was not a Thomas Aquinas. Having few idle moments, his attention devoured by whatever controversy, religious or worldly, that happened to be troublesome at the moment, he wrote in the manner of a man running out of time. We have in many of his compositions, in fact, what may be sermons. Perhaps the greatest pressure on Augustine was his daily obligation to preach in the basilica, usually thronged for the occasion. In those days of almost standardized ecclesiastical violence when the mob, to express its pleasure, might forcibly (as it did with Augustine) ordain a man to orders or churchly position, and just as randomly, to record displeasure, burn a church to the ground, sermons took on exaggerated importance. It is hard for us to imagine, inured as we are to the most banal and perfunctory orations from the modern pulpit, how much these congregations from the earliest eras of the Church depended on their preachers to elevate them from everyday concerns. The sermon served the identical function for them that television does for us. It blended together entertainment, news, comment, farce, excitement, nostalgia, and even civil defense. It provided a daily "white noise" — comforting and dependable, yet urgent, stiffening. In times of crisis it could give even more: the up-to-the-minute bulletin, the urgent appeal, the thunderous denunciation. It was, in other words, a vital force, and Augustine came to realize, as did all the famous preachers of his time, the terrible truth behind the entire performance: that the audience could not be trusted. Religion was not a distant or even polite topic. It was meat and drink to a people keen for the subject; a minister out of favor, his ratings in a slump, could find his life very much in danger. As a result, many of Augustine's writings bear the mark of hurried effort, as though of secondary importance to the real task of the day, facing his congregation. Or else perhaps we see, let us say in his immense *City of God*, a turgid though often richly-textured discourse of truly heroic theme, the record of Augustine's daily inspirations as he composed, maybe on the spur of the moment, on his feet, extemporaneously, each of his sermons day after day, month after month which later, when he had a free moment, could be jotted down on paper.[1] A diary of his passing meditations, like the weather, varied greatly: uneven, spasmodic, often inspired, many times angry or perverse, sometimes just tired. But the viewpoints emerge with enough frequency to justify our use of the word system to describe his mental picture of the universe. The Pelagian affair, the last of his great theological wars, genuinely invigorated his being like fresh air. It spurred him to finish painting his great canvas, to apply the little details which could (and did) enrich beliefs that he had formulated from the earliest days of his conversion. It made him add the necessary complexities which, in the long run, helped to solidify the position of Christianity "as a powerful threat to reason", a vision of the future that Augustine obstinately enjoyed.

He took up where St. Paul left off. It comes as no surprise that these two most inventive Christians should have so much in common, or that Augustine looked admiringly to the man he referred to simply as "the Apostle" for stimulation. St. Paul, the whirling dervish of enthusiasms, had littered the religious landscape with a wide variety of grand and tantalizing conceptions, many of which he never developed to conclusion. Augustine searched on his hands and knees the fields that Paul had trampled, hurling seed in all directions, and nurtured those individual plantings that had survived and which appealed to him. Thus it is only partly correct to attribute, as many scholars do, the discovery of theories like predestination or original sin to Paul, when in truth it is Augustine

---

[1] Apparently Augustine's secretaries recorded some of these sermons more or less verbatim at the time of their delivery, for they include as a kind of audience barometer many of the congregation's response, most of an approving nature, such as "It's his favorite pun again!"

who took these lumps of clay and fashioned them into finished and decorative pieces.

For whatever psychological reasons one wishes to choose, and the voluminous literature on Augustine predictably offers us a multitude, he began with the premise "that all men, as long as they be mortals, must needs also be wretched." This unseemly condition, the result of Adam's sin in the Garden of Eden, forced upon us the need for a redeemer, a being "human but also divine" who could mediate between God and his now abject creation. Augustine, like Paul woefully mistaken in his ideas concerning the historical Christ, saw in quite a pagan fashion the need for bloody sacrifice. The redeemer became Jesus, the acts of his death and resurrection the necessary circumstances of atonement. Pelagius, without apparent intention, offended both these propositions by encouraging a notion that men could accept or reject God as they willed — "All are governed by their own free choice," in his own words — but Augustine saw this as "rendering the cross of Christ to no effect". The crucifixion, in other words, became irrelevant, a conclusion suited only to those "insane". Venemously turning on Pelagius now, calling him a "deceiver" and "propounder of lies", Augustine actively sought his condemnation. Pelagius became for him the epitome of the snake who offered Eve her greatest temptation.

Augustine's notions of a stricken and flawed humanity are not exceptionally original, being common to many philosophers past and present who have objected to the easy optimism in more aggressive promotions of human ability. But Augustine went further. Finding rough guidance in Paul, he envisioned a system of dependencies and glacial, awe-inspiring irrationalisms which glued man to God. These stemmed inevitably from Adam. Augustine was the first to stress the overwhelmingly negative implications for all mankind in Adam's fall — in effect, the irrevocable stain, or Original Sin. The fact that Jesus made no reference to such a condition little mattered to Augustine, nor had it to Paul.[1] Gifted as he was with enormous intelligence and being "the complete egotist", he plunged through inconsistencies with no alarm. A prodigious biblical scholar (though not on St. Jerome's level) he culled the great book — as indeed did all the combatants — to find those sayings which could buttress his positions. Unfortunately, he unearthed many of these in Paul, his fellow explorer, who tended to confirm all of Augustine's darker suspicions. From Original Sin it was but a short distance to grace.

Pelagius, throughout his long history in Christian literature as the insidious heretic, was referred to most often with the sobriquet "enemy of grace", a title (if he ever heard it) which he might have treasured.

---

[1] Likewise baptism, which Jesus never saw as more than a symbol, that later became the necessity to remove Original Sin.

Augustine, searching scripture, had found ample quotations to establish man's reliance on the Almighty — "You, O God, are my stronghold" and so forth. In Paul he discovered more than that: "It is God," wrote the Apostle, "who of his good pleasure works in you both the will and the performance", suggesting that some sort of heavenly gift — mysterious, powerful, essential, gratuitous — alone enabled man to reach God. Augustine dubbed it "prevenient grace" and it became the foundation stone of his most ambitious theory, predestination, that supreme barrier between reason and faith that said God had chosen an elect: just a few human beings, in relation to the numerical majority, who would be saved. No rational explanation as to who the select might be, no process capable of decipherment by the mind, no telltale marks of heavenly favor. God is "inscrutable".

These brief encapsulations of Augustine's thoughts must not encourage the reader to regard them as empty trivialities or slack in any way, dependent as they seem to be on incredulity and rigid faith. The scope of this book is limited and no doubt considerable violence has been done, unwittingly on my part, to the sophistication which Augustine brought to many of these problems. But in a modern world they may seem sophomoric, though I would consider such a conclusion in itself equally slight. If Augustine were alive today he would not be thinking about free will. He would, towering over the rest of us, probably be pondering some highly abstruse theological proposition even as we sit drinking our morning coffee and dismissing, in our casual boredom, a Jerome or Abelard or Aquinas as inconsequential. As the great medieval scholar Etienne Gilson remarked, he "was condemned to being original". The problem for a modern reader looking at Augustine is the proverbial bottom line. What, for example, is the character of theological speculation? It can be seen I think, as a science (like engineering) or a discipline (like mathematics). Each problem, as in a theorem, leads on to another more complicated problem. But unlike engineering, science, even mathematics, which theoretically can be proven, theology is embarked on questions which cannot be answered, indeed, that confront matters beyond what man can really know. Augustine and the others were genetic architects of the soul. And while their thought processes are brilliant and fascinating to follow they are, in the end, futile because the final result does not materialize for us to touch and examine, seemingly a prerequisite for our assertive and detail-oriented society. It is really the St. Thomas problem all over again, "Unless I see, I cannot believe." Given the lack of a finished product, and given the terms of reference which were vital to the fifth century but extraneous today, no wonder that talk of predestination or prevenient grace may strike many of us as absurd and superficial. But Augustine was neither. His writings necessarily tell us more about the man than they do about God. In terms of what today we might call common sense, Pelagius may well have been closer to the mark than Augustine, no matter the odium with which he is still officially regarded.

Pelagius certainly realized he was wading into ever deeper waters. His performances before tribunals in Jerusalem were disarming and cautious, even though the propositions offered by Augustine struck him as outrageous inventions. If anything, Augustine was the heretic! But he knew how to curb his tongue, a restraint many of his followers failed to share as they bandied arguments back and forth with the Augustinians. Primarily they could not abide the notion of Original Sin. The only bequest of Adam to the rest of us was a horrific bad example, damaging enough to be sure, but his own particular burden and not ours to share. We enter life *tabula rasa*, with a clean slate, and honor God by coming to him — "Draw near to the Lord, and He will draw near to you." The Pelagians had no need for the novelty of Grace.

It is clear this was essentially an argument between reason and faith or, put another way, thinking and belief. These are, of course, irreconcilable polarities, impossible to harmonize in a single proposition, though Augustine gave it a try only to lose himself in a somewhat mystical swamp where reason, in ecstasy at its limitation, surrenders the field. Augustine, if nothing else, had a blind faith in faith. But as Kirsopp Lake remarked, "We cannot, except in intellectual chaos, combine the two", and the history of Christianity for the next thousand years essentially records the enshrinement of Augustinian gloom into the core of Catholic, and then Protestant dogma. Pelagius proved less stubborn than Pelagianism itself, which I suppose we could call the pervading spirit of our society today, but this did the peripatetic monk little good. I think it safe to guess that Pelagius ran for cover in 420 never — purposely — to be heard from again, living to the fullest his own favorite quotation from the Bible, "And so the Apostles departed, rejoicing that they had been counted worthy to suffer disgrace for the name of Jesus."

WE PASS THROUGH a large and grimy oil slick from some tramp steamer, perhaps flushing its bilge into the open ocean beyond. The problem with oil, of course, is its refusal to break apart into several definable pieces, like a broken bottle, that we can neatly collect or sweep away into the dustbin. Oil lingers, caresses, permeates; as the waves fall and roll and recede, it conforms to every motion. A difficult mess to clean up. Augustine did not regret his successful rout of Pelagius. As a professional terror to all the heresies, he gloried in battle and its outcome, having the certain conviction that he was better than all the rest and indisputably correct in his speculations. But the resilience of these Pelagian ideas, no matter that he had crushed their inventor, haunted the final years of his life and, like the greasy water around our boat, he could not dispatch it with an easy wring of the mop. Inexorably enmeshed in the secular politics of his province, complicated by a deadly conflict with heathen Vandal tribes that had crossed in A.D. 429 from Spain into North Africa (and headed now directly for Hippo) Augustine found himself haggled from within the Church by a gang of "proud and haughty people". These dismembered his writings, subjected every sentence to a scrutiny never intended, drawing in far too many instances a conclusion or two hardly contemplated. And so, like an aged stag separated from its herd, he discovered hounds nipping at his feet, beasts of prey that themselves rejoiced in the hunt, equally convinced that not they, but Augustine was a fool in these matters, the "lord of all donkeys".

Augustine had only himself to blame. The various tracts and pamphlets written against Pelagius had circulated widely through what remained of the Empire, and some had clearly been prepared in haste. Monks in Africa, reading a letter he had composed on prevenient grace, deduced not unreasonably that since the die had been cast — one was either among the elect or else damned — what was the point of work? This "joyful conclusion" Augustine corrected with an epistle of further explanation, which of course told the brothers to resume their weaving. But another monk could inquire, in a vituperative essay spread throughout Gaul, as to the purpose of uttering the words "Thy will be done", when that "will," *a priori*, ordained their damnation. As a matter of fact, why pray at all, or bother to ask forgiveness or seek a proper penance? These were the aggravating, specific consequences of his grand designs, and as many as he could answer were incorporated in letters of correction or amplification. Many times he leaned on an old favorite, that God is beyond our understanding, in a different realm, and we demean ourselves trying to apply our own inadequate powers of intuition to the task of fathoming his behavior: "How incomprehensible are his judgments and how unsearchable his ways!" But the affair had lost its excitement. It became pedantic, trying, and paltry, one of those nagging chores that required his attention when least convenient. With Hippo under siege in A.D. 430, argumentative pamphleteering seemed the least of his priorities. There was, for instance, the matter of deciding whether to flee or face death with his parishioners here in the doomed city he had lived in almost forty years. He chose to stay, but died, possibly from nervous exhaustion given his age and fragility, before the final disaster. I think it fair to assume that to the end he felt most secure in his ideas on grace. He had sensed its workings in his own life, after all, the long experience, as one churchman eloquently put it, "of resistance to, and then a yielding to, the drawings of God's grace, giving him a clear apprehension of the great evangelic principle that God seeks men, not men God."

But to John Cassian in the far distant port of Marseilles, equally steeled, we may suppose, to the terrible insecurities of the age, these formulations were untenable. Had not even Paul said, "Work out your own salvation with fear and trembling", and the Book of Proverbs warned, "Survey your path for your feet, and let all your ways be sure"?

It seems incredible that amidst alarm and horror, as the civilized world broke into isolated pockets amid the surge of barbarian migrations through the Empire, enough men like Cassian could put aside the appalling news of the day, with all its sinister implications, to pursue a topic that most men would consider, under the circumstances, extraneous. But religions, as a rule, have an explanation for everything, and in this case the calamities of the time had long been predicted and were now, perhaps, even welcomed. Jesus had preached an apocalyptic vision that the end was near. The Apostles, we may recall, expected it imminently, spending the remainder of their careers in quiet prayer awaiting the day — "With one mind," as the Book of Acts has it, "they kept up their daily attendance at the temple." Surely, many now thought, the temporal world was finished. Rome a plundered ruin, God's Empire sundered, savages loose in the land. More now than ever, men should turn to God. Who could say how much longer anything could last?

Cassian, of course, was fully aware of the Pelagian controversy. I suspect he heard about it first in Rome, possibly from Pelagius himself who was certainly well-known in the capital and a logical attraction for the eager and by now experienced ascetic newly arrived from Constantinople. The badge of the hermit, after all, whether Greek or Copt, was that of spiritual independence. "Virtue", as Antony had preached, "has need only of our will, since it is within us and springs from us. If we remain as we were made, we are in a state of virtue, and we came into being fair and perfectly straight." The idea of a blighting Original Sin, or of "irresistible" grace, ran contrary to more than a hundred years of experience in the desert. If Cassian disliked the extremes to which Pelagius (or the disciples who followed him) pushed the implications of his theories — such as the largely symbolic, as opposed to redemptionist, character of Christ's death — he had at least no quarrels with its drift.

For thirteen years since leaving Rome Cassian had followed the monastic life, first on the offshore hermitage of Lérins, later in an establishment he himself founded in Marseilles, nearby to a community for women that he ran along similar lines. This enclave managed to survive the depredations of passing Germanic tribes, the disturbances of constant alarm and the confusion engendered by thousands of refugees, to emerge as the theoretical think-tank of Western ascetic practice. Lérins especially achieved considerable renown as a center of learning and piety, and particularized its theological bent by actively nurturing those soon to be labelled the "semi-Pelagians." To the despair of those who worshipped Augustine, these monks and hermits were above moral reproach. "We are no match for these men of high standards," one wrote to Hippo, "they far surpass us in the sanctity of their lives." They also had taken Augustine's challenge to heart — "That each may arrive at knowledge,

Chapel of the Trinity, 5th century
Iles de Lérins, La Côte d' Azur, France

first bend our necks to the authority of Holy Scripture" — and there they had found nothing to substantiate "the call of the elect" or prevenient grace. Indeed, mining the Bible carefully, they had unearthed much to the contrary, that Augustine's proposals were clearly "against the teachings of the Fathers and the faith of the Church", in other words, fanciful inventions. A monk from Lérins proclaimed, quoting a third-century pontiff, "Let there be no innovation — nothing but what has been handed down." In Cassian and his followers, Augustine was clearly matched with individuals near his own level.

Cassian most assuredly found Augustine's theories personally repellent. The perversity lay in their unprovoked disgust with efforts of many simple men, Christian and heathen alike, to better themselves morally and lead godly lives. Cassian had seen enough in Egypt to know that only strength of will and purpose of single-minded proportions were sufficient to deal with Satan in the melodramatic wastes of the desert. It was because of this immensely individual effort that singular monks could achieve sublime communion with God, rarely achieved as Cassian knew full well, but certainly possible. No monk, Cassian conceded, could reach that goal unaided. Cassian was no Pelagian, he admitted the need for grace (if only to justify prayer, the true joy of the ascetic) but the idea that such grace could not be resisted struck him as superstitious and a prescription for indolence. Grace is a gift of God, not an intravenous lifeline mechanically plunged in a vein. It is something we can ask for and God can give. It coexists with our own freedom of choice, it seeks the spark within us which needs God's help to reach fruition. "When God sees in us some beginnings of a good will, He at once enlightens it and strengthens it and urges it on toward salvation, increasing that which He Himself implanted or which he sees to have arisen from our efforts. For He says 'Before they cry, I will hear them' . . . And again: 'As soon as He hears the voice of the crying, He will answer thee.'"

It is ironic that Cassian the recluse, the hermit, the ascetic — with an attitude towards life that most of us would consider misanthropic at best — appears demonstrably more confident in the energies of man than did the more sublime Augustine. And also strange that a man who spent years in solitude should have a keener sense of human nature than one who had spent all his life in the company of fellow citizens. The degree of contrast between Gaul and North Africa may partially explain this. Augustine's basilica represented a tradition now three centuries old. Some commentators have theorized that perhaps a stale familiarity had settled in, things had become routine, people resigned and fatalistic to the barbarian threats around them. They may have had too much faith (or reinforcement from the pulpit) in the apocalyptic finality of events which seemed inevitable with the general military collapse. But in Gaul, faced as well with calamity, some degree of hopeful opportunity seemed to present itself. Zeal for monastic life was exploding, in part the result of tales, both oral and written, describing the ascetic exploits of Egyptian monks like Antony. Cassian, the veteran, wrote his *Institutes* and *Conferences* in direct response to appeals from his Gaulish brethren who wished to duplicate the Egyptian experience in Gaul. He also saw, in direct correlation, a sudden spur of enthusiasm to evangelize the newly-arrived barbarians, a desire not evident among his African coreligionists. Missionaries risked torture and death in the belief that preaching to the heathen both fulfilled the command of Christ and brought the bounty of the saved to ever-increasing numbers. St. Patrick, one of these, leaving Britain to cross the Irish Sea for a land "remote where there was no one before", to work among a race "wild and rough", did so expressly "that many people through me should be born again to God". For that, he was "ready to lay down my life unhesitatingly". How could Cassian or any of the Gaulish clergy reconcile the goodness and energy they saw so manifest about them with Augustine's sterile "predestination of the saints"? Why bother with heathens when their doom was self-evident? Why forsake the pleasures of the world by joining a monastery? St. Patrick claimed he was a "debtor" to God for the grace he had asked for and received, to do the good work of "fishing well". He saw himself as making a difference.[1]

Augustine was neither a missionary nor, for practical purposes, a monk either. He had become a man of affairs for whom the monastic life was an idea he either refused, out of duty or circumstance, to embrace fully, or else simply feared. We certainly know he regarded it as an ideal, and perhaps the failure to ever follow that life in its truest severity fashioned his bitterness. He spent his free time instead creating the mystical though melancholic *City of God*, and contemplating the various shapes that angels might take. Miracles held a fascination for him. To Cassian, these were subjects to avoid, "ministering to the reader nothing but astonishment and no instruction in the perfect life".

The reader may well inquire what all this has to do with the monks of Inishmurray. Not an unfair question given the distance of this rocky spur from the shores of the Mediterranean and a Roman Empire that never reached this far. Yet these *clocháns* and sharp, penitential tracks from shrine to shrine are directly Egyptian, it seems to me, and the Celtic monk a fossilized remain of very ancient lineage. He shared the stamina and primitive faith of Antony, and suffered many of the same delusions that snared Pelagius. He agreed with Cassian on the joys of hermitage and gloried in the expansiveness of free will, albeit subconsciously in most cases. All this we will see in future pages. It is possibly true that we have spent too much time discussing the great Augustine, who surely would

---

[1] As Peter Brown notes in *Augustine of Hippo*, "The response of utterly foreign peoples to the message of Christianity reassured (missionaries) that God wishes all men to be saved."

have regarded this island as a miserable place indeed. So too may have Pelagius who made, to the best of our knowledge, no effort to return home when events broke around him. Like many an émigré before and after he may have regarded such an option with repugnance. He had, after all, seen the great world, what use had he for such a backwater? But Cassian would have understood this place, as indeed the monks, in reciprocity, understood him. He would have relished the obscurity, and seen in the faces of these wild men of God a true reflection of John the Baptist. I doubt if Augustine would have gleaned so much, though of course it is Augustine whose reputation survived over generations as a glory to his Church.

There are several explanations for this, one being the nature of the Pelagian heresy. Pelagius, essentially a teacher of morals, was hardly what we would call a complicated theologian. His propositions would not turn the heads of many intellectuals, however threatening (to the control of the faithful) his heretical positions might be. To the Greeks and Orientals, in fact, the controversy over free will was child's play. When the Greeks decided to concoct a heresy it was usually something so abstruse and complicated that few innocent bystanders were capable of fathoming it. On the other hand, their disputes were generally far removed from tangible, everyday concerns, whereas free will is about as primal a question as mortal men can ask, a veritable poison to the religion, whereas speculations regarding the Trinity or the Logos or the divinity of Christ are not. And it was Augustine who caged it, who subordinated free will to the power of the Almighty Creator. Pelagius he had swept aside, leaving the man "dazed" in Jerome's view from the struggle. And with Cassian he achieved a draw, no minor accomplishment given Augustine's introduction of major (some would say violent) change to the body of Catholic canon. And by 494, when the Church produced its first index of forbidden books, some sixty-four years after Augustine's death and fifty-nine after Cassian's, it was the semi-Pelagian manifestoes that fed the pyre, formally proscribed and condemned. Augustine stood alone in the West. Given the enormous success of monasticism and Cassian's undisputed influence on that movement, how could this be so?

The fall of Rome, which the Bishop of Hippo perversely refused to mourn, presented a perfect and contemporary mirror that befouled the public's consciousness with an almost irrefutable pessimism. The *City of God*, in fact, consciously exploited to tremendous effect the bitter vicissitudes of the era by linking the ancient Christian theme of the world's inherent evil — something to flee — with Augustine's individual conviction that mankind was equally contaminated. Each infected the other unceasingly or, to put it another way, Rome's collapse reflected on all men. Both were temporary and paltry affairs, worthy of scant confidence. As civilized life evaporated before the barbarian onslaught, in some instances with a speed and totality that left many observers numb, so too did the Pelagian faith in natural ability. Augustine's pessimism seemed more justifiable, as did his theory on dualities, the City of Man and the City of God, both in conflict, day vs. night. "The one city," he writes, "loves its own strength shown in its powerful leaders; the other says to its God, 'I love you, my Lord, my strength.'" What powerful leaders could Western Europe look to for relief when tribal chieftains as fierce as their names — Gunderic, Frithigern, Alaric, Attila — marched about at their pleasure sowing havoc? In the vacuum, only God remained. Man's achievements, his capabilities, became puny by comparison.

Augustine's influence on the spread of centuries that we commonly call the Dark Ages is almost unique in human history. Had he lived at the height of Empire he might have been ignored as a raving provincial hyena from sun-baked Africa, but instead he stood alone at its demise and thus evolved into the prophet vindicated. Events had justified his otherworldly notions, his faith and dependence on God. Inquiry stifled, free will disparaged, a sense of human worthlessness endorsed, Original Sin codified — he achieved all this in monumental writings praised by Cassiodorus as "clear, charming, abstruse, richly packed with usefulness". He presents us with a case frequent in history: the man who turns on his own gifts. Augustine the fresh and innovative writer, a philosopher of great brilliance, sought in the end to demolish what he loved, and did it with great style.

Cassian, the man who eschewed flamboyance, could not keep pace with the literary giant of his age. Although a superior writer to many of the early Fathers, Cassian shared the similar, gray, unrelievedly one-dimensional approach that was a standard for the age, a style devoid of personality and warmth of feeling. What a contrast to the expressive and ultimately endearing quality of the *Confessions*, where the author wore his heart on a sleeve for all to see. And although Cassian's plea was certainly the more aggressive and uplifting of the two, Augustine's splendid form could overwhelm the senses, making the message (and the intent) less insistent or obnoxious, and thus more palatable. The poetry of surrender is more appealing, I believe, than the prose of assertive dominance. Augustine is most eloquent when he describes our subservience to God, and with disaster in the air everywhere in Europe, the theme of an abject man's submission to omnipotent God struck a sympathetic chord. Total reliance on our maker, after all, is an easier road to follow than a stark and brazen free fall into the unknown.

There are more specific rationales as well. Augustine was an eminently quotable author, easily abstracted by monastic chroniclers and teachers looking for a concisely expressed truth or axiom. Cassian, by contrast, could be discursive, rambling, repetitious, veiled, often boring. In the sixth century St. Benedict of Nursia turned to Cassian's writings, which he referred to as "tools of virtue," and thoroughly plundered them in composing his simple little rule "which we have written for beginners."

Cassian did not lend himself to direct quotation, and thus not a single sentence can we attribute specifically to him, even though the body of ideas therein are largely his. But to Benedict goes the credit for preserving Cassian, at least as a monastic influence, for his particular Rule overshadowed all others in the course of time. And interestingly enough most of Cassian was translated into Greek, a distinction rarely given by the East to Fathers of the Roman Church. But in general as the years of the fifth century passed by, with puppet emperors installed and deposed at will by feuding Germanic warlords, Cassian's reputation fell victim to concerns for orthodoxy. "You ought to exercise caution in reading a man who oversteps the mark", advised one critic in 551, and expurgated editions of Cassian, tame and pallid, circulated in place of his complete writings. But the real cause of his demise lies in the confluence of Augustine's peculiar and fatalistic vision with "the end of the world" as most men saw it. Each fed off the other, dramatically propelling Augustinian thought as the predominate moral viewpoint for several hundred years.

It may be difficult to recreate for ourselves how vitalized this disagreement was. One reason is that most basic and primal theological disputes — the behavioral ones like free will — have all been "solved", at least to the satisfaction of mainstream religions and encyclopedias, and are enshrined as fact. What we have really inherited as our common points of reference, however, are the survivors, the winners, those like Augustine who are now saints and presumably in heaven. We hear nothing of a Pelagius or a Cassian. We have instead, once battle is over, the monuments, which do not reflect much of anything except the formalized rites of canonization. Like a military cemetery in Flanders Field — lush, landscaped, manicured, and so beautiful they give combat a serene glow — we hardly discern any of the mud or carnage of wartime bloodletting. Nor, as contradictory as it may seem, any of the excitement. Stale, musty books are the theological battlefields we can explore today, the "military memoirs" of the principals. That is why Inishmurray is so attractive. Unlike Ypres, this place is more or less unchanged. The curtain between us and the past necessarily exists — it would be romantically simpleminded to think otherwise — but it is translucent enough to allow the vision of what was a mortal struggle.

T HE WINDS ARE fresh indeed as we near *Clashymore* after a wet ride, the seas a choppy succession of three-footers, embroiling the island in foamy turmoil. Clearly these are less than ideal conditions for an attempted landing on Inishmurray, a feeling that Michael seems prepared to embrace without any encouragement from me. "Look at that lug," he groans, tentatively nosing into *Clashymore*, "that's bad, we'll get ourselves thrown on the rocks for sure. Let's try the pier."

"That's no good, Michael. The ladder's all rusted away. If we got alongside it there's no way I could get up from the boat. Try it here."

Michael's indecision is pretty much what Paddy Joe predicted, and it strikes me as dangerous. We are tossing back and forth at the mouth of *Clashymore*, neither in nor out, the engine is sputtering and the rocks invite us to ruin. "We'll have to go back," he shouts, "we can't land here."

"No choice, Michael," I tell him, "bring her in. We can fit in that furrow there with no problem. Go on!"

Poor Michael. Against his better judgment, and mine too I suppose, he thrusts the engine into forward and plows ahead. We do a nice slip to starboard and run to the fissure. I yell to him for reverse, he gears down and we make a perfect landfall. "Good man, Michael!" and indeed, a look of pride creases his face.

A little taken aback at my peremptory assumption of command, I ask him how long I can have of the afternoon. "Oh take your time," he replies, "we got in so we can get out." I hop ashore and look down to the boat. I note the absence of any lunch pail or bag. "Did you bring anything to eat, Michael?" He shakes his head. I split my sandwich, peel an orange and divide that, toss him a bottle of Guinness as well. "We'll not starve today!" he cries, as I turn in to the pathway.

After an hour or so of going through the cashel again, and paying my respects to the Brady homestead, I start to circle the island, passing the various stations erected by monks hundreds of years ago. Every stone ledge, tidal pool and *clasaí* has an old Gaelic name for it — "the hollow of the ridges", "the rock of the current", "the crooked wave" and so on — but I find myself today somewhat more relaxed than on my first visit, less concerned with details than with soaking up a general feel of the place. Looking northwards up towards Donegal I can see a squall obliterate, then leave behind, a group of tidal rocks and shoals that are located about two miles off the island. One of these is called *Bomore*, the other *Shaddan*, or "the splashing one". These were favorite fishing grounds of the islanders — indeed, of all the fishermen in the bay — but the area is treacherous. Paddy Joe told me of a crew out of Donegal some seventy years before who were caught out at *Bomore* by a sudden southwesterly. "They decided to try for Inishmurray, to gain over to the front of the island to make a landing, but the winds played their tricks on them. They rowed and rowed and rowed, a big long open boat it was, a twenty-six footer with three oars out on either side, twenty-foot long oars they were and you know the pressure they can bring to bear. So these six men were rowing and rowing for about three hours, and no way could they make any ground up on the gale, and misfortunately they had no anchor so they couldn't try and ride it out. After three hours, when they were completely collapsed and the gale getting worse and all the rest, they just hung up their oars. The island people, all out on the shore, could see them and

Brady House
Inishmurray, County Sligo

were praying for them, but they just hung up their oars as if to say, 'That's it.' They were all taken up to the northern shore by Slieve League, where it's mostly mountains crashing down sheer to the sea, very few places that the ground is low enough to get up on a cliff or ledge, and they were smashed, smashed to pieces."

Coming full circle back to *Clashymore* I see Michael sitting on the rocks unperturbed. I reverse my direction and walk back around the island the way I came. Late afternoon, the skies open up. The tide is out so I have another good jump to make down to the boat, but we get out into the ocean without mishap. The entire trip home is a drenched affair indeed.

Pulling into Moneygold I put my trust in the expectation that Mrs. Brady has a fire going. "Ah, *musha*, you're safe returned, thanks be to God, we were praying for ye all day. But look at you now, wet to the skin! Paddy Joe, throw some coal on the fire, the Hulk be soaked."

"Did you get on now, Jim, did you get on?" Paddy Joe asks. "I couldn't have done it for you today, I'm certain of that." I report my experiences, including Michael's inclination to try the pier instead of *Clashymore*. "Oh, he's a great lad, God love him, but that pier you know yourself is useless, meets the waves head on, ledge all around, an ugly affair indeed, no place to get caught. What did you tell him?"

"I told him he was crazy."

"Good lad for that, Jim. He only wanted to gander about, not land at all."

"Well, we landed in *Clashymore*."

"He wiped his brow when he got in there, I'll wager," says Mrs. Brady. "Is that you burning? Paddy Joe, the Hulk be on fire!"

"His clothes are just steaming, maw."

"Well change them right now, change into dry clothes right away."

As I string my gear along a line in front of the fireplace, Paddy Joe gives me a wink. "That lad earned his money today, I'd say."

"He thinks so, too," I reply, and we both have a good laugh.

I AM SITTING the next morning in the offices of Dr. Patrick Heraughty in Sligo, a large, high-ceilinged room in a not very old Georgian building. The place is spartan and cold, as though a prescription in and of itself for good health. No elaborate high-tech machinery or collections of disposable gloves, jars, bags, syringes, seat covers, and wipes greet the eye, only a single stethoscope, wash basin and jug, a neat, ordered desk. Dr. Heraughty comes in after a short wait, a tall spare man in what I take to be his early seventies, dressed immaculately in a dark business suit. A native of Inishmurray, he seems a different sort from the Bradys and some of the other islanders whom I have met. "Well, my mother was not native to the place, born and bred," he tells me. "She came in 1902 as school-mistress and undoubtedly would have returned to the mainland after her tour of duty there had she not met and married my father, whose family had lived on Inishmurray for years. Being in the field of education, she realized that schooling was better provided for back on shore, and after my twelfth birthday I was sent away for my studies. I came back for summer holidays, of course, until I was twenty-one, the year I qualified, but still I had a world of advantages placed before me in comparison to the other children and I suppose our later careers, if compared, would tend to show that in fairly graphic fashion."

I ask Dr. Heraughty how many generations of his father's family had lived on Inishmurray. "Not as many as you probably think. There's a popular notion that all these islands like the Arans and Clare and Tory have been continuously inhabited since time immemorial, but In-ishmurray was in fact practically deserted in the early 1800s, and it was a landowner from the mainland who convinced one of his tenants, Domhnall O'Heraughty, to settle there. He took along a Seán Brady as a partner, and together with their wives they in effect resettled the place. Over the years they offered shares in the arable fields and the peat bogs to other folk, either as dowry settlements or because they wanted more help (or just some company, for it was a lonely spot to be sure), so much so that by 1841 the census shows a population of eighty-five. Forty years after that it reached a peak at one hundred and two."

"What about the famine years?"

"The population did take a fall, but the oral tradition out on the island when I was a child said they were not affected, particularly because of the seafood, and this was pretty typical of the islands that were not overpopulated, for unlike the mainland peasant they did not rely so heavily on the potato. As a matter of fact you never had any cousin marriages on Inishmurray until the 1920s, because the notion of emigrat-ing out to Inishmurray — marrying one of the island girls and staying — was quite appealing to mainland lads. Life would have been as good materially in terms of having enough food and all, maybe even better considering some of the poorest holdings in Ireland were around Sligo. And there was a real society out there, a real village life. By the depression, however, all that had changed. The economics were different — the market for salted fish was done thanks to refrigeration, kelp was finished and poteen — well, poteen was always problematical. And the people now were literate, especially the youngsters. They read more, they could see in books and newspapers there was more to the world than Inishmurray, a better life over the hill, or at least they thought so. Canada was the real trend then. By the second war only the very young and the very old were left, and when the youngsters got to be twenty or so they'd be gone."

"Nostalgic for the old place nonetheless I would suppose."

"Some of them, perhaps, though I've found it's more the women who sentimentalize the place. The men, that great image of themselves as sea dogs and pirates, whiskey smugglers and rogues, all evaporated once they came to shore in 1948, which I find very hard to understand myself. They dropped their seafaring the moment they pulled up their boats and left them on the beach to disintegrate. Maybe the handouts on shore made life too easy for them, I don't know, but it was fatal to the twenty-year olds, the young bucks. How could you get them to inherit the old Inishmurray tradition of going to sea if they hadn't any elders to emulate? It's a fragile thing, tradition. Hard to develop but easy to lose."

"How good were they on the sea?"

"At first I gather they were pretty poor. You have to remember those first few settlers were farming people who knew nothing about the ways of the sea or boats or fishing. You can see that in the working vocabulary on the island. These people were all Gaelic speakers so if they were talking along and said, 'Put out the oars,' all the words would be in the Irish except 'oars,' which they'd say in English. They were not originally a maritime people, probably didn't know what an oar was, and certainly didn't know what the Gaelic for it was. So all the shipping terminology was in English out there, because whoever supplied them with their gear was English speaking, perhaps the agent of their landlord.

"The first thing they learned to do was row, which of course takes little skill at all. They apparently didn't catch on to sailing for years. And no doubt about it, it took a couple of generations to get a feel for the seas and figure out the weather, most especially what was dangerous about each. My great-grandfather was drowned just a few yards off the shore, and it was a question of just not knowing a certain characteristic about a certain piece of water. But they gradually developed their seamanship, developed a sense of prognostication, winds and waves and so forth. This is it now, if you put me back out and left me there, I could tell you pretty soon what the weather was going to be, I'd have no need for a wireless! Of course, all that sort of orientation is lost now. I think Christy down at Moneygold is the only Inishmurray lad left who really goes out to sea anymore, and he's in it only as a business, not from the fact that he loves the island ways more than anyone else."

"If people like Christy and his family still lived on Inishmurray, would their life be much different from what it was a hundred years ago?"

"I've wondered that myself and think not, though some of the changes might likely seem considerable. I would guess, for example, that the Government would have made a better harbor for them at *Clashymore*,

121

poured some concrete down there between *Oileán is Tiar* and the island itself to keep the groundsea out, despite that being a pretty uneconomical thing to do for just a dozen families and really wouldn't have increased the fishing potential in terms of speeding the catch to market. And they'd be better informed, naturally, what with television for news and weather, though I think in the end those sorts of media would have made it difficult to keep the youngsters wanting to stay. But essentially the basics would be the same. They'd be subsistence farmers and part-time fishermen, just like the old days, dependent for most of their staples on the shops in Grange and Sligo. I mean, what else could they do?"

"I've heard some of them say they should run a hotel or something like that, develop their cottages for the tourist trade."

"That's a good one," Dr. Heraughty laughs, "a folk village sort of thing? It amuses me sometimes, this whole mythology on the islanders that is there to be cashed in, their rugged individualism and disdain for mainland ways. They never could have survived without the people on shore, they were totally reliant on them. All these Gaelic peasant buffs, they deify the islanders far too much. They were just ordinary people who lived on the coast, and when it got too bleak for them they left, no fuss about it, it didn't matter to anyone. The newspapers gave it little notice at all, as I remember, and once on shore the King no longer acted as their spokesman. They didn't have a unified point of view by then, they were just absorbed into the general population."

Dr. Heraughty walks me to the door after our talk. He has kindly arranged with the local stationery shop to reserve me a copy of his own book on Inishmurray, hard to come by due to its popularity, and is giving me directions. I ask him which aspect of the islands, its ancient history or the more recent demise of the island traditions, interests him more. "They're really one and the same to me. I'm keen for the islanders, of course, the way I am for my own family, and the ruins and all the old monastic legends are the same too, as intimate to my own self as a living room with its furniture, if you see what I mean. Now the monks themselves, that's a different matter because it's hard to picture exactly what they were like. I have a rather perverse notion that they were not what we have idealized them as being. They went out to Inishmurray to get away from the world and its fleshpots and to avoid, I think, the specific command of God to save souls. I guess they didn't clearly get the message that they were the ones to spread the good news, deciding instead to keep it to themselves, turn inwards, save the soul that mattered most, their own. Rather selfish, don't you think?"

"Where did they get that notion?"

"Egypt."

HOW DID THE ideals of the Egyptian desert reach Ireland? "That's a murky bog to be sure," an historian in Dublin told me some years ago, "intrinsically connected with that other finely abstruse question of how Christianity itself came to our shores — who brought it and when? You could have a wondrous feud with all manner of interesting people depending on your views, but just remember two things. The first, wherever you discuss these matters, whether in a bar or university classroom, do not expect civilized behavior. The rules that apply are those you'd find for a Night of the Long Knives. And secondly, the only definitive conclusion possible is that no one can hope to prove whatever it is that he or she believes. There are no certain answers. None. Only attractive possibilities."

The first and most prominent of these is naturally the legend of St. Patrick, but it now seems apparent that Christianity had some degree of influence in Ireland well before his mission of the 460s, and that the contact points were multitudinous. Prehistoric trade routes with the Continent, while generally theoretical, seem beyond serious doubt. Irish hunting dogs were highly valued and regularly exported, and mainland demand for precious gold was partially satisfied by finds in Wicklow and Wexford. Conversely the Irish bartered tin from Cornwall to meld with their own quite plentiful deposits of copper to produce bronze weapons and implements. Their taste for wines from Aquitaine was a long tradition, illustrated in one particular instance by the ancient assignation *Bordgal* for the place name of two separate localities (most probably markets) in Leinster, meaning in the Gaelic "Bordeaux". As we enter the era of more or less recorded history the opportunities for educated guessing increases progressively. The Irish shoreline is visible from several points along the British coast, and Roman legions knew of Ireland as early as A.D. 83 when Agricola contemplated its invasion. His biographer, Tacitus, felt that Ireland was a "convenient" enough place to visit, and indeed the fabulous megalithic tomb of Newgrange, if the various Roman coins recently unearthed in its vicinity by archaeologists are any proof, was evidently a tourist attraction even then.

Current professional theories generally postulate the likelihood of some communication with Spain, most particularly the northern coast of Galicia; substantial contact, mostly trade, with Gaulish communities, primarily on the Brittany peninsula in general, as well as those located near the rivers Garonne and Loire; and a thoroughly familiar intercourse with Britain, both as trading partner and wartime adversary, the latter in the form of raids in search of plunder and glory, but often the result of migratory expeditions when whole tribes went east to dispute for swordland in Wales and Cornwall. In the midst of all these social cross-stitchings various religious seeds were surely planted. Although a British monk writing in the sixth century claims that his fellow countrymen received the tidings of Christianity with something less than joy (in his words, "tepidly"), Tertullian, looking on from North Africa in c. 200 A.D., claimed knowledge that the religion had permeated in Britain to regions "inaccessible to the Romans". And Gaul, to an even greater extent, was substantially converted a century before Patrick's time. It seems inconceivable that Ireland, in contact with all these shores, should not, in the remark of one historian, find itself "infiltrated" by the new religion. And indeed, the long tradition of pre-Patrician Celtic saints in Munster would seem to indicate that at least in the lower half of the island, with several important river valleys and natural ports facing southward towards Cornwall and the Gaulish mainland, the process of conversion was well advanced by the year 400.

What form of belief did the Irish hold? What part the British experience, what part the Gaulish, what part from Spain made up the body of doctrine and practice that would rule a man like Columcille a century or so later? Only the most daring could answer that with certitude, but if we look at the end result — Columcille and his contemporary Celtic coreligionists who occupy what is commonly called the Golden Age of Ireland's Christian past — the pattern, though faint, seems apparent. The desert came to Ireland from Gaul, and its transmission to this remote and warlike island roughly corresponds with the disintegration of Roman rule on the Continent.

Along with portions of Spain, the province of Gaul had long been nearly the equal of Italy as an integral partner of the Western Empire. The brutal campaigns of Caesar and successive generals had at first left the Gauls little better than a slave population, but over generations, eager Gauls, whom even the conquerors saw as "quick of mind and with good natural ability for learning", were gradually entrusted with the administration of Roman authority. Gaulish aristocrats filled the majority of Imperial positions, educated their children in classical tradition at the "flourishing academies" later so admired by St. Jerome, worshipped Roman gods and spoke Latin instead of the native dialects. They were more proud of their Citizenship than were most Romans of the period.

Christianity permeated their society in the slow and gradual manner that we have come to associate with the means of its spread: verbal reports from passing traders, soldiers, diplomats, the occasional papyrus roll from the East, fast disintegrating in the moist and inhospitable climate of central Europe, and perhaps copied onto more suitable vellum or parchment. The religion progressed, we may surmise, in fits and starts, as efficiently or as awkwardly as the first proponents were successful in random conversation with friends, acquaintances, strangers. It certainly followed the pathway of Roman occupation, sprouting first in the cities and administrative centers established along all the major river systems in Gaul, most notably the Rhône, Garonne and Loire, then branching off to the forests of the hinterland where heathenism was especially fixed. One of our first reports of concerted missionary activity features one

Irenaeus, Bishop of Lyon in c. A.D. 200, who preached to the Celts in their own language. He viewed himself as a contemporary of the Twelve Apostles. Significantly, he came from the East and spoke Greek.

The great catalyst for Christianity, of course, was the conversion of the Emperor Constantine the Great and his famous Edict of Milan, A.D. 313, which issued tolerance to the religion and in effect granted it the royal favor, events "entirely unexpected" in the view of one historian. Constantine was a complicated man whose motives come down to us today as an impossibly confused amalgam of the personal and political. It seems that he saw in Christianity, when he viewed it dispassionately, a unifying force of great vitality for an Empire so large and diverse that it appeared incapable of management. His desire to eradicate the various heresies of the day stemmed largely from this streak of practicality and the Council of Nicea, called by the Emperor in 325, was his renowned attempt to extract unanimity of opinion from a collection of suspicious bishops, earning him the distinction of being the first Emperor to master "the art of holding, and corrupting, an international conference". But it is important to stress that however impressive Imperial decrees or the litany of Church councils, agreements, and judgments may seem, they should not deceive us into thinking of the Empire in terms of our own day and age, nor of the spread of Christianity as a neat and tidy progression from one triumph to another. Hilary, Gaulish Bishop of Poitiers in c. 353, an educated man of affairs and a traveller to the East himself, said it was twenty years after the Council adjourned before he ever heard of the celebrated Nicene Creed. Christianity fought many battles, hidden from us, in countless hamlets and alley-ways, farm communities and country crossroads before it subjugated Gaul entirely by the year 400. With no uniformity of pattern it is not surprising that various independent variations grew side by side and, when joined together, proved inimical.

A rudimentary diocesan system is known to have been in place for Gaul by A.D. 250, essentially a duplicate of the Roman secular mechanism centered in cities and market towns. Many early bishops, in fact, were officials in the bureaucracy, either governors, tax collectors or administrators, a reflection of their regard for civic duty, being, as the majority of them were, landowners of substance or titled gentry of the higher classes, where the distinction between God's service and Caesar's was slight indeed. Some observers sense that as the fourth century progressed the new religion settled comfortably among the people, neither disturbing nor roiling popular sensibilities, especially as the memory of various early persecutions receded in the distance. A professor of rhetoric in Bordeaux crystallized the accommodation in a poem composed c. 390 when he wrote, after his morning devotions, that "I have prayed enough to God. Boy! Bring me my coat. I must have lunch."

What disturbed these serene complacencies were rumors from the East of the new asceticism, the ideals of Antony in the Egyptian desert.

Athanasius, Bishop of Alexandria, was probably the first to propagandize reform in the West during his exile in Trier, 335, in the wake of which we may suppose that several score of enthusiastic Gaulish youth trekked eastwards to see for themselves. As they returned to Gaul in the course of one or two decades, repeating their stories, writing down what they witnessed and heard, perhaps laden with precious manuscripts, the urge to emulate the desert masters became endemic.

It is perhaps unscientific to credit the rise of monasticism in Gaul to mere rumor and the odd book carried home, but such is probably the case. Sulpicius Severus, the biographer of St. Martin of Tours, gives a graphic example of "being carried away by delight" on the return from Egypt of his friend Postumianus, brimming with desert lore. "I will hang on your lips", he blurts out, almost desperate for information. And we have ample evidence for the exchange of books. Certainly in Egypt itself the habit of transcription was firmly established among the more literate anchorites. The revered Evagrius, for example, earned "the price of what he ate" from copying manuscripts, "for he wrote gracefully" and his work was much in demand. Many tales from the Egyptian wastelands emphasize that books and manuscripts were routinely read, exchanged, lent, translated, bartered, taught from, and even stolen by envious brothers. Pride of ownership was often judged sinful, in fact, by more puritanical hermits. "Better than all else is to possess nothing," was the advice one gave to a prospective monastic librarian. The majestic biography of Antony by Athanasius reached the West within two decades of its composition. It spread through Gaul as quickly as copies could be made, "read with a passionate interest," in the opinion of the distinguished British historian Nora Chadwick, "similar to that aroused in the eighteenth and nineteenth century by fiction."

By 385 the Egyptian phenomenon was cresting, and a regular traffic of tourists back and forth to Gaul had swelled proportionately, with the result that men and women in the West could be found withdrawing from society, either to town houses in the city or obscure hideaways on country estates. But it was an undistinguished former soldier from Hungary, St. Martin of Tours, who evidently established the first identifiable communities of monks in the West: Ligugé, outside of Poitiers, in 361, and a few years later, the more renowned Marmoutier, a collection of some eighty solitaries gathered together near Tours on the river Loire. As in Egypt the emphasis was on the individual, with few if any established rules or onerous manual labor. "The elders had their time free for prayer," according to Sulpicius Severus, "rarely was anyone found outside his own cell, except when they came together at the place of prayer." He adds, significantly, that "no art was practiced there, except that of transcribers."

The secret for these early saints like Antony and Martin, of course, was to have an eager biographer nearby. Athanasius was certainly a best-seller

Abbey Ruins of Marmoutier
Le Val de Loire
France

in the ancient literary world, but outpourings from the pen of Sulpicius Severus far outdid even the vita of Antony. Once again an obscure, poorly educated, impoverished individual ostensibly of no worth, aside from a capacity for faith and stamina, was elevated to the rank of a supernatural warrior for Christ. Nothing of Martin is known except what Severus has to say about him, leading us to wonder if, as in the case of Athanasius, what we read is more the creation of an admiring disciple than the words and deeds of the subject himself.

In many ways the *Life of St. Martin* represents a foil to the sobriety of a Cassian who, after all, was a practiced veteran of the desert and perhaps inured to the type of youthful enthusiasms exhibited by Severus and his friends, whose letters and writings sometimes suggest a kind of delirium with the new ascetic disciplines. Severus, though a nobleman from Aquitaine and far from a rustic, unregenerate Gaulish tribesman, nonetheless reminds us of the high-spirited excitability that most classical reporters of ancient times found characteristic of the Celtic race, what St. Jerome summarized as their "exuberance and glitter". Severus was no theologian. His purpose in writing a biography of Martin was to show that Antony, most famous of all the Egyptian saints, now had a rival in Gaul, someone of equal power, sanctity, and favor in the eyes of God. What!, he asks his visitors from Egypt in astonishment, no reports from the Eastern deserts of dead men raised to life? No visions of Christ, no conversations with angels? "This compels us to recognize that no one is comparable to Martin." And indeed, his vita reads in the tradition of an ancient Celtic saga tale, as Martin confounds the pagans with spectacles aplenty. Unlike the biography of Antony, where subcurrents reflecting religious disputes and spiritual subtleties lie scattered about like precious stones, there is little intellectual content to be found in the work of Severus. We find ample expression of devotional fervor, the kind of spiritual intensity later so noteworthy of the Irish Church, but no glimpse of an inner life of learning. This is miracle mongering of the type so typical to the medieval Church of Western Europe, and so distasteful to a Cassian.

Of more interest in Severus' account is his depiction of friction between the ascetics and the established Church as represented by the aristocratic Gallo-Roman bishops. St. Martin, as portrayed by Severus at any rate, is notably opposed to ecclesiastical authority, which views the ascetic regime as antithetical to order and uniformity. St. Martin, in fact, is dragooned by the people of Tours and made a bishop against his will, a condition that diminishes his capacity to perform miracles, which puzzles and saddens him at first, implying a demotion on the part of heaven. His fellow bishops, not surprisingly, are appalled. They consider Martin "contemptible" and "unworthy, a man despicable in countenance, his clothing mean and his hair disgusting". He, in turn, having no social position to protect or family business to cultivate, considers the bishops "mad" and scorns their "degenerate submissiveness" as they fawn on the

Emperor of the moment. "Angels were very often seen near him," but "furious Bishops" rarely.[1]

This conflict between zealousness and complacency was exacerbated by the breakup of Empire. The dark and frozen hinterlands beyond the Rhine teemed with anarchistic tribes, and their depredations into the provinces and beyond threw thousands of refugees onto roads heading south. These met thousands more heading north out of ravaged Italy, creating a confused and miserable welter of displaced persons searching for pockets of comparative safety away from the suddenly well-travelled invasion routes or tempting urban meccas for heathen siege and plunder. It is small wonder that religious deviations could seem confused and almost treasonable to certain parties, in particular the bishops, as they attempted to cope with the disintegration about their ears of everything that mattered most to themselves and their class. There are many records of these aristocratic churchmen, having lost station, estates, family, and wealth, refusing to abandon their ecclesiastical command of city and town, preferring instead to remain at their post organizing, as the situation dictated, resistance, accommodation, or surrender to barbarian warlords. The idea of retreating to the desert for a private war with Satan when his bloodthirsty minions were greedily wrecking Christ's Church in the very real world seemed cowardly. "Stand in line of battle," said one, "put on your armor and resist your foes, so that having overcome, you may wear the crown."

Yet, in the end, the subterranean nature with which Christianity spread undermined the bishops of Gaul. They could not redirect the new religious fervor into something tangible for them, a defense of the old order and the classical past. "Hearts consecrated to Christ are closed to Apollo," said one nobleman as he retreated from the world and his disconsolate friends into a private solitude. "To spend time on empty things, whether in pastime or pursuit, he forbids." Nor could they staunch the almost underground transmission of ideas and notions from the East. Vagabond churchmen such as Martin, Cassian, Pelagius, Athanasius — cast about like chaff as they literally fled for their lives from one disturbance to another — had too much to say and too many willing listeners, who themselves spread the principles further along down the amorphous highways that new thought, rumors, belief and gossip most generally flow, creating many strands of diverse and probably disjointed teaching that caused tremendous displeasure in the established Church. These "wanderers and strangers act contrary to the Church's usages,"

---

[1] In Nitria, A.D. 420, the monk Ammonius was also approached by a mob of villagers who wished to annoint him their bishop. "While they were looking on he took a pair of shears and cut off his left ear, right to the back of the head, and he said: 'From now on be assured that it is impossible for me, as the law forbids a man with his ear cut off to be ordained priest. And if you compel me, I will cut out my tongue as well.' "

one exasperated pope complained in 428. "Coming from other customs they have brought their traditional ways with them," following practices of those who "pass their lives far from fellow men." Even the monk Severus found himself challenged by priests of the established Church, who claimed to bear him "ill will for the many lies you have told in that book of yours". But the pioneers of monasticism in the West were indifferent to these animosities. "This is an old maxim of the Fathers," wrote Cassian, "that a monk ought by all means to flee women and bishops."

At the end of this imagined roadway of ideas lay Ireland, by the 430s significantly Christian, at least in the south. The one hundred or so years between that era and the careers of Columcille and the other great monastic abbots of Celtic Ireland is ample time for the spread of a seminal ascetic tradition, no matter the turbulence of the era. It has often been said that with the execution of Boethius in c. 525 both the classical era of noble literature and vigorous philosophical speculation came to an end, giving way to the copying of knowledge from the past, saving what did not go up in flames as heathen armies marched by. It has also been noted that as cities and trade declined amid social chaos, men returned to the basics of precivilization, adopting the attitude of survivor from shipwreck, fending independently and without recourse to money, banking, credit, central authority, or municipal institutions. The growth of monasticism duplicated this tendency, avoiding for the most part an urban setting, which it did not require, instead developing into a self-sustaining agricultural entity whose initial foray into commerce was probably simple barter. Here alone learning survived, yet it did so in sterile fashion. The scriptorium becomes a symbol to some historians of this decay, the lack of intellectual vigor disguised by the very industry of the monks as they labored to produce copies of the Bible, religious instruction, and even secular work. In some ways this is a harsh, unsympathetic conclusion that fails to consider the fragility of these times and ignores the dedication of many wise men who saw it as an obligation to save what they could. As the famous Cassiodorus encouraged his monks, "Every word of the Lord written by the scribe is a wound inflicted on Satan."

This may seem to us, from the vantage point of our modern era with its instantaneous flood of communication available at all hours of the day, as an improbability, but in the ancient world — the pre-printing press world, we should bear in mind — the laboriously hand-produced manuscript was a commodity beyond value to those of the literate classes. Even though many of us can comfortably understand and agree to such a proposition, we probably fail to grasp it totally, a conclusion I reached after various discussions with friends about Umberto Eco's novel *The Name of the Rose*, who felt the plot went soft when it was revealed that the many murders, unnatural doings, and general destruction were the direct result of one man's fear of the written word, in this case those dealing with laughter in the second book of Aristotle's *Poetics*. "No one would kill a person over a book", I was told by one disappointed reader who desired a motive more compelling. But a man like Sidonius Apollonius, a bishop of the much-despoiled Clermont-Ferrand in Auvergne, seeing the world fall to ruins, would certainly have understood. To him, manuscripts were a deadly serious matter — "It is high time for you to send the book back!" he chides one of his laggard friends — and indeed, one important reference in a letter written c. 475 is a very clear indication of how information most probably passed from Gaul into Britain and Ireland. A Celtic monk from somewhere in the British Isles (exactly where we do not know) is marooned in the household of Sidonius for more than two months due to the impossibility of travelling safely through the countryside as marauders threaten the city. Sidonius refers to him as "twice a stranger and pilgrim in this world," meaning the journey is the second undertaken by this cleric into Gaul, and indeed it turns out that his previous stopover had been the famous Lérins, chief stronghold of John Cassian, located on an island in the Mediterranean off Provence, and that in his pouch are provocative semi-Pelagian writings especially attractive to the Celtic temperament. Sidonius can hardly contain himself and hastens to "make lengthy excerpts from all the important chapters, dictating as fast as I could." Due "to the skill of my secretaries" he feels no further need to invent excuses for lengthening the monk's stay, and congratulates himself on the acquisition of such "booty". Once that particular book reached its destination, we can well imagine that further copies were made and spread about by other nameless *peregrini*. With so much turmoil in Gaul throughout the fifth century, in fact, it takes little to envision hundreds of fleeing churchmen and scholars, all searching, as Cassian had done, for some hideaway from violence and corruption. An interesting notation from a possibly fifth-century glossary now housed in Leyden, though much disputed by historians, directly mentions Ireland as one such refuge. "The devastation of the whole Empire was completed by Huns, Vandals, Goths and Alans," it states, "at whose devastation all the learned men on this side of the sea took flight, and in transmarine parts, namely, in Ireland, and wherever they betook themselves, brought about a very great increase in learning to the inhabitants of those regions." Whether contemporary to the events described or a later interpolation, this intriguing little footnote would seem to suggest a likely turn of events, that either singly or in twos and threes, perhaps in larger contingents, learned men most certainly followed the footsteps of that solitary Celt who so enriched the library of Sidonius. Britain and Ireland were well-known countries to the Gauls — indeed, the southern portions of the British Isles and the western coast of Gaul represented an almost Celtic amphitheater — and it would appear logical that some diffusion of clergy would pass from the Continent along the usual trade routes. In all certainty, with them went the legends of St.

131

Monks' Garden
Isles de Lérins, La Côte d' Azur, France

Martin, venerated for centuries in Ireland more highly than any other saint. His background as a soldier appealed especially to the warlike Irish, and his career as a monastic bishop directly influenced the development of Columcille. So too did the writings of Cassian, Athanasius, and Pelagius. There can be really no other satisfactory explanation for places like Inishmurray and the durability of eremetic tradition which they embody. Many legends concerning St. Patrick stipulate that he spent many years in study at Lérins, the ideological capital of asceticism in the West. And while Patrick more than likely never visited the Continent, the association of the two does seem to represent the distant memory of a link, however chimerical. But again, there is no proof. We can only look to the Irish themselves, to men like Columcille, to see if the resemblance is merely coincidental.

MRS. BRADY HAS given me a large soda bottle full of holy water that I am to give my mother. "God send you luck," she says as I climb into the Citroën, "it's very lonely here now, I think, with you be going." Paddy Joe and I shake hands, Christy waves from his doorway. I ask him how the surf looks out there beyond. "When you see it breaking like that, no way!" he replies with a big smile.

I have one last stop to make, a friend of the Bradys' who lives in a "tumbledown" over at Cloonagh and has some old photographs that everyone says I should see. Driving over through heavy torrents of rain I arrive at a common sight in modern Ireland, an enormous, new, expensive hacienda-type building with a thick coating of unpainted stucco lathered over its core construction of concrete block. The yard is a hopeless sea of mud with planks thrown about for a catwalk to the front door. A large, rusting cement mixer stands blocking the entrance, full of rain water and corroding shovels. The doorbell doesn't work, and after five minutes of fruitless knocking I wade around to the back, where one of a numerous family lets me in. The house is one enormous hallway after another, leading to several perfectly square and bare rooms, many with frosted windows that block any view there might be. In one of these a small turf fire and two stuffed easy chairs are the only signs of habitation. Flora Brady, seventy-one years old, joins me there with a folder of pictures under her arm. "Don't get up now," she says, "I'll bring them to your hand."

Most of the photos are island scenes showing arrivals and departures down at *Clashymore*. "This is where the boat comes in and anchors here," she says pointing, "and there's another island boat there, but not anchored, can ye see that, because the ground swell be all wrong. There's another place for a landing, see the peg, you can go round that way, the bold way we called it, on up the ledge. My uncle is standing by the boat, and that's King Waters, you've heard of him, and that's Matty, my man's brother, and that there is another island lad, I can't remember his name, and that's a fellow in from the country, not an islander, and I don't know who he is. That's the husband, he's pulling in the boat. Ah, he was a good man, an honest man. Many years before a whiskey fella[1] had given the King a copper still, not a flimsy tin one, but sturdy copper, and the King hid it so the police would never find it, and the only soul he told was me husband, and he had it down to the grave with him. He never told us, and I was married fifty years to him, but never a word, he kept his oath to the King. Ah, that man was straight as a road. If he was alive today and talking with you, you'd be glad to hear him.

"Now there, that's the priest, Fr. Casey. He came into us every twelve months, aye, to say the mass. He would talk and talk there was no sin on us, that's the truth, no sin on us, we had done nothing wrong. He told us to say the rosary every Sunday at the same time he was saying mass in Grange, and we did that and all. It was a good place, the old island, a holy place. We lived a rough life, but a healthy one."

"When did you come off?"

"In 1930, my husband and I came out here to this country, got married and set up home here. And I cried when I went away, the shock of leaving me house and all. And to hear the cursing out here, which was never on the island, I don't know what they be saying but the floods of cursing. It was not a holy place to be here. On the island we had our home, our cattle, our pigs, our fowl, our grain, which we brought out here to this country to the mills for our flour. We'd have whole flour bread and porridge for the morning, five or six big bags of salted dry fish for dinner-times. No tin food we used in our house anyway. Plenty of bogs and there were wells. Happy times we used to have. This girl here in the photo, she used to play the melodeon, and we'd go dancing, the half-sets, the sixes, the jigs and all them things we did on the island, but ye won't see that today. It's that other kind of thing, disco.

"You kind of wonder why, but we all came away from the island at last, in the end because of the rationing. There was only a few pounds of flour and an ounce of sugar, so some of the lads went out to this country, and then out a ways into a new life altogether. My sister and every one of me aunts and uncles all be over in America. My uncle, who was a Hart, and two sons make their money playing music in Holly . . . what do ye call it?"

"Hollywood?"

"Aye! Out in America. We be always praying for them."

Mrs. Brady looks vacantly at the fire. "A grand spot. I'd go back tomorrow morning if the houses were fit."

---

[1] John Powers of Power's Whiskey fame.

Inishmurray Boats
Cloonagh
County Sligo

"When were you last back?"

"I was never back since 1935. You'd be in heaven to be on it, but it's been a long time. Did you ever bring anything out with you when you came? No? Funny you wouldn't take a wee bit of clay and bring it out, put a wee bit in your handkerchief, it would bring you luck and nothing would ever happen to you." Before I leave, Mrs. Brady decides to give me a piece of wood from Inishmurray, a chip from a block that the statue of St. Molaise used to stand on. Sitting by the fire, I can see her chopping it loose on the kitchen table with a large butcher's knife. As I go out the door she tucks a handwritten prayer to St. Joseph in my pocket, which promises that I "shall not be overpowered in Battle."

TWO ISLAND BOATS, gutted and splitting apart, lie mouldering in the grass above the beach at Cloonagh — island tombstones that Paddy Joe wanted me to see. Before heading off towards Ulster I drive south to a vantage point at the foot of this protrusion into the sea and leave the car behind. It is very cold, with winds bitter off the ocean. The sun has set, but in the deepening fall of dusk the green of the fields, the gray of the stones, the textures of storm clouds flying low in the sky take on the richest of hues. Sligo Bay is an enormous froth of chaos, the slender lighthouse out on Black Rock, guarding an entryway to the city's harbor, the only artifact by man in sight that seems bold, headstrong, foolish. The few cottages I can see from here lie folded to the earth, hunkered against the storm, and the small breakwater of a tiny cove below me shelters but two or three fishing boats firmly tied to shore. This is not a view to calm the spirit. It's the stuff of headaches, all dread and tumult and shrieking dissonance. Out to the west, surrounded by whitecaps, I can barely pick out the profile of Molaise's Island. I recall something Paddy Joe said about the old-timers who would sit around their fireplaces on demented nights like this, reminiscing about the ancient times, and the ways long gone, on dear old Inishmurray. "It sort of haunts them," he said, "their memory be hooked with it."

II

'PERSEVERANCE'

IONA

"It is time for me to pass
from the shelter of a habitation,
To journey as a pilgrim over the waves
of the bold and splendid sea."
Celedabhaill, Abbot of Bangor

N
W — E
S

ulva

staffa

atlantic
ocean

mull

iona

a'mhachair — dun
the abbey
bay at the back — graveyard of the
of the ocean — kings
the
carn cul rí eirinn — great
city
port of the coracle

ross of mull

oban (by sea) ——→

ulster
↓

HE WELSH ANTIQUARIAN Edward Lhuyd was disgusted in 1699 that a man could think of charging him five shillings to row from Ballycastle in County Antrim to the Kintyre peninsula of the Scottish mainland, a distance of twelve miles. "That is too much!" he shouted at the poor wretch, stalking off to find someone else who would put in the six hours or so that such a trip required. In those days, at least, Lhuyd had one certain advantage: the shortest route was the only one available, a far cry from the woes facing a modern traveller.

It will take me over forty-eight hours to reach the island of Iona, a voyage that in nautical terms is about seventy miles northwards from Ulster. I have spent all of a day just driving from Sligo to the Northern Irish port town of Larne. Another day will be taken up reaching Oban in Argyll, then several more hours before I will actually set foot on the island. And there will be nothing very direct about any of it.

I crossed into the North at the frontier village of Pettigo, then traversed the picturesque and rambling country roads of Tyrone until reaching Lough Neagh, which to my amazement is described by Walter Muirhead as the largest lake in all the British Isles. It is a vapid body of water, largely marsh and liable to flood, with few islands to speak of and hardly a town or community of any consequence on its shores. With an hour or so to spare I have searched out the old abbey of Arboe, noteworthy for its 18 foot high cross, but when there I found myself duped yet again by the high expectations that historical literature sometimes feeds. Surrounded by a decrepit iron fence, in miserable scrubland worn to dirt by God knows what (I cannot imagine a single tour bus ever coming here), the cross itself exudes a downtrodden, wasted air, its twenty-two scriptural panels weathered away to near illegibility. Of more contemporary interest were the little villages I drove through on my way to the county seat of Antrim, and from there to Larne, thankfully avoiding the war zones of Belfast itself. Each proclaims its allegiance without, it seems, fear or foreboding. The shabbier the place, the more likely it is to be Catholic, with tricolors hanging from buildings or painted on curbstones, and threatening warnings to informers daubed on walls — HONKS BEWARE — along with the more common IRA RULES, UP THE REPUBLIC, BRIGHTON BOMB WASN'T BIG ENOUGH. In more suburban and prosperous communities the undoubted Protestantism of their inhabitants is manifest through hydrants gaily painted as Union Jacks, hundreds of tiny British flags crisscrossing the streets from lamppost to lamppost and often elaborate wall murals depicting King William of Orange or the present Queen. Some display the usual favored dates — 1688, 1690 — others show the red hand of Ulster, usually dripping blood, or more enigmatic symbols such as black keys, ladders and billy goats. The standard rallying cry here is the familiar "No Popery!" Graphically speaking, Protestants hold the edge I think, though few of these efforts will find their way into the annals of memorable propagandistic art.

By the time I reach Larne the late afternoon ferry is in some jeopardy of leaving on time, if at all. A surly winter storm is thrashing about down the North Channel and so, with a few other rather abject travellers, I hang out in a rank, smoke-filled, beer-sodden waiting room until the whole thing is called off a few hours later. Larne itself is utterly depressing. I walk through its two or three streets looking for a place to eat a survivable meal and settle, mistakenly, on a Chinese restaurant, where the oriental waiter takes my order in as heavy an Ulster accent as one could possibly find. My fellow diners are third or fourth echelon punks, with ears so mutilated by rings and assorted metallurgical droppings that the only suitable image that I can come up with is the Dachau death camp. My Chinese food, which coagulates in front of me into a greasy lump of mush, comes with an enormous side order of french fried potatoes that lie in an ocean of oil. This is such an odd experience that I find my mood improving. Iona — the name itself has such a melodious, pristine tinge to it — lies just over the sea.

The next morning is fresh, clear, sunny, cold, perfect. Security at the depot is nonexistent: no papers checked, no baggage rifled. The only prohibition worth noting is that "Football supporters will not be allowed to board displaying their club 'favors' in any shape or form." The Sealink ferry then twists and turns past a breakwater into the North Channel, breaks into open water and plots a direct course for the Rhinns of Galloway in Scotland, some thirty miles distant. Except for a few diehards who congregate in the bar, most of the passengers find a sheltered spot on deck and bask in the thin sunlight.

As this mighty, twin-stacked barge ploughs through the Channel with an effortlessness and speed that somehow personify a nostalgic affection for Britain's maritime past, I lean on the rail and consider, from this highly powerful vantage point, what a curragh might seem like below with its small company of passengers and crew, their gear piled high here and there. The image seems a puny one in many respects, though we should not fool ourselves into thinking these craft were simply larger than usual rowboats that seldom left the sight of land. Maritime scholars believe these vessels may have been quite substantial, though sleek and devoid of the clumsy superstructures that characterized, for example, many of the craft that meekly hugged the shorelines in Mediterranean travel. The coastal peoples of Ireland were skillful sailors and their boats of hides sewn together, stretched across a wooden framework and then tarred, proved resilient and seaworthy. Whether they could carry more than twenty people is problematic, however, and the memorable statement by the British monk Gildas in c. 540 that the Irish in their "tiny curraghs" reminded him of "a dark swarm of worms" as they crossed the sea in raiding parties, seems to conjure the picture of a numerically impressive flotilla of small craft, packed with men and equipment, but nothing on the architectural order of a Spanish Armada.

Columcille was not charting new, exploratory ground when he left Lough Foyle for Scotland. Historically, the Celts were a migratory people. Entire tribes had transferred themselves, against the flow of earlier peregrinations, from Ireland back to Wales and Cornwall. In what historians calculate to have been a fourth-century uprooting, an Ulster tribe known to us as the Dál Riata, facing famine at home and relentless pressure from more powerful neighbors, sent warriors north across the Channel to what is known today as Argyll in Scotland. These colonists, in battle with the indigenous Picts, eventually succeeded in establishing themselves on a coastal strip of swordland in the vicinity of Islay, Jura, and Mull. By the time of Columcille's voyage, this Irish foothold had impressively expanded into a distinct kingdom known as Dál Riata, especially entrenched on the islands and tidal zones of Argyll, but also ranging many miles inland at several junctures along the shore.

What did Columcille think he was doing as he too sailed north? He was certainly not, as I am, travelling for the sake of it, indulging his sense of curiosity. This Sealink ferry befits the security of leisure time, whereas to me the notion of a curragh in this expanse of contrary winds and surging currents, immediately suggests a more austere objective. No matter that the curragh is a fine, seaworthy craft, capable of handling the often foul conditions of deep water sailing. No matter that the Irish did not fear the sea. Looking down beneath me, feeling the frigid, salty sea air, the world seems frail and dangerous, the ocean vast and muscular, Columcille and his imagined vessel a plaything of Plato's implacable universe.

Such a picture both praises Columcille and demythologizes him at the same time. The perverse influence of legend, for instance, distorts various aspects of Columcille's life that were not, in fact, extraordinary saga. The Venerable Bede records that Columcille "converted that people" (meaning the Picts, whom he found in Dál Riata) "to the faith of Christ", thereby portraying him as the Apostle of Scotland. This tends to magnify his voyage to something it was not, a missionary enterprise of some complexity, the end result of which, the salvation of an entire people, might tend to color our mental reconstruction of the sea voyage as something akin to walking on water. I prefer the image of Columcille bobbing erratically through this great panorama, in a craft no more telling to the eye than several sea buoys that I can barely pick out amid the undulations of ocean rollers and the glare of reflecting sunlight. No trumpets seem to herald such a scene. It is too lonely, bleak and harsh, too insignificant in a seascape this immense.

Columcille did not travel far from home as an evangelist, as St. Paul did. He left as St. Antony did from his village in Egypt, to save himself, impelled, as Dr. Heraughty suggested to me in Sligo, by the twin motivations of the desert: selfishness and dread. "For the fear of hell," as one old poem put it, "he went into Scotland." This may seem incongruous and contradictory, for Columcille's fulsome career, hardly devoid of its share of excitements and dangers, seems more the expression of a bold adventurism than timidity. But as Whitehead observed, "Christianity preaches a doctrine of escape. It is a neat little system of thought which over-simplifies its expression of the world. It overcomes evil with good", proceeding initially not from some abstruse and metaphysical system (like Buddhism) but with the simplest sayings and actions of a single man. The religion, quite basically, is "the tremendous fact of Christ". But to dread wickedness, to react or to live with the unremitting cloud of "fearing hell", was not an act of cowardice to a man like Columcille. As St. Jerome put it, "What saint ever won his crown without contending for it?" Fleeing evil in Irish terms meant, perversely, the deliberate collision with Satan, a combat eagerly sought with arms flailing, teeth gnashing, blows struck and received. All the imagery of the early Irish saints' lives reflect the martial strife of Celtic society. Hermits were armed to the teeth with "helmets of salvation, shields of faith, swords of the spirit". Columcille was an "island soldier" in the words of his biographer, the Abbot Adomnán, "a warrior and cleric" both according to another poem, "pure and fierce". Where Whitehead sought to denigrate Christianity with his notion of timidity, Columcille gives the word a bold veneer. Escape is something daring, risky, romantic, a Monte Cristo's intrepid break from the Château d'If, not the calamitous rout of a Dunkirk. We must accustom ourselves, in discussing the Celts, to think in terms of contradictions.

If he left not as a missionary, then, in what garb did he go? As we have previously seen, some of the legends suggest that Columcille abandoned Ireland as a penance imposed by his confessor, Molaise of Inishmurray, for the unnecessary carnage and havoc of *Cúl Dreimne* fought beneath Benbulbin in Sligo. Others explain it differently, that he sought a voluntary, private burden, and the worst he could imagine was exile from "the sweet district of Ireland". Either theory is plausible, though the latter variation is, strictly speaking, more historical. As a ninth-century chronicler from the Continent would say, "The custom of travelling into foreign lands" was "almost second nature to the Irish people", and indeed the picture we gather from saga lore of the earliest Celtic Saints, men like Brendan the Navigator, is one of wanderlust.

In typically grandiose fashion, the Celts regarded such flights from the motherland as a form of death. This satisfied both their highly developed sense of melancholy with a fidelity to the principles of desert theology, which morbidly urged every monk to think only of the grave — "Rest like a doomed man," said one old anchorite, "short hazardous sleep on a cold, fearsome bed." The separation from *tuath* and kin was sincerely felt. It was a painful step to take, and the Irish suitably ennobled the experience by making it a very precious gift to God, the *ailithre cen tintud*, or "pilgrimage without returning". In terms more immediately recognizable to a warlike people, it was also known as the White Martyrdom, to distinguish it from the Red or "bloody" Martyrdom which of course pertained to those who had actually suffered death for the faith. Some historians speculate that this notion was a direct transference from Gaul, and point to Sulpicius Severus's reference in his *Life* of St. Martin of Tours where the Saint "achieved martyrdom though he shed no blood", a justification for the rigors of monasticism. To the Celts this hardship frequently required divine assistance to cure, God in his mercy performing a miracle to obliterate the ache of nostalgia for Erin. It certainly weighed heavily on Columcille, who coasted from island to island until he could no longer see Ulster over his shoulder. When he landed at Iona, traditionally in the little rocky cove known as the Port of the Coracle, he first climbed the highest hill on its southern edge to make certain he was far enough away. There he built a great pile since known as the *Carn Cul rí Eirinn*, or the Cairn of the Back Turned to Ireland.

From an Irish perspective, the considerable Dál Riatic kingdom that he found was now akin to a Sixth Province, so close were its racial, political, and psychological ties with Ireland itself. Nevertheless, in keeping with the strictures of a White Martyrdom — "the abbot of a strange tribe over you, estrangement from your family to the day of your death, foreign earth over you at the end of your road" — it was new territory to Columcille. The Dál Riata, after all, were traditional enemies of

Cairn Cul rí Eirinn
Iona
Scotland

Columcille's people, the Northern Uí Néill. These latter tribesmen had largely been responsible for the relentless pressure which drove the Dál Riata to such perilous extremes a century and a half before, the forced emigration into Argyll. He came ashore as no friend.

Having said that, I rather doubt he suffered from any lack of confidence in his abilities, though to be honest there are no writings or descriptions of him that are anywhere near contemporary portraits, and nothing from his own pen has survived. The famous biography of Columcille by Adomnán, for example, the ninth abbot of Iona who died in 704, is more noteworthy for what it says about the author than about his subject. And the equally memorable (to Irish scholars, that is) *Amrá* or "Eulogy" of Columcille, possibly dating from the sixth century, is so obscure and archaic in its structure and language that even Irish monks of the 800s were confused — "The meaning is difficult", one copyist scribbled in the margin next to one perplexing sentence. Even so, these works and a fair supply of reverential poetry ranging from the seventh to twelfth centuries are all we have, though the hints they give us, when compared to the actual events of Columcille's life with which we are familiar, provide a foundation for at least some educated guesswork. And one characteristic of Columcille on which they all seem to agree is the ferocity of his temperament. "A brave man over the ridge of the sea," says one of these, "it was not on soft beds he undertook elaborate prayers. He crucified his body — it was not for crimes — on the green waves. Brave is the host whose toughness is his."

"HE PARTED WITH true words, with fair tidings, on his lips for kings," wrote one poet in c. 697. It is not immediately clear to whom he first gave these counsels upon landing in Scotland. The Dál Riata and the Picts, the latter people even today almost totally enshrouded in mystery, had over generations fought each other along a continuously amorphous frontier of bog and highland wilderness, usually to the de-lighted indifference of the semi-Romanized Britons living to the south, who noticed the affairs of these heathen barbarians only when their bloodthirsty attentions were turned on them in the form of sporadic, though often very deadly, raids and thieving. It is not clear, for example, who it was that granted the island to Columcille for his monastery. Two chiefs (or kings) are mentioned, and Columcille had dealings with both: Brude mac Maelchon of the Picts, who surrounded himself with druids and wizards in a mountain top rath, and Aedán of the Dál Riata, a man known as "The Wily", whose disdain for Columcille was evident from the first when he paraded his daughter in front of the cleric as bait. "Good is her blushing", said Columcille as the ruse collapsed, aware that to be seen as a "liar and fool" among people so influenced by superficial impressions would be dangerous. I surmise that Columcille carried himself in the imperious fashion that befitted his birth and pedigree. Aedán's wife reputedly distrusted Columcille, a "tricky cleric" with "haughty words", which earned her the peculiar curse of being transformed into a crane, crippled forever with a broken wing. (Vengeance, in Irish circles, was a prerogative the Lord had to share with his unruly Celtic servants.) When disputed or provoked in any way he is usually described "with face afire and blazing eyes". One poem claims that the air over his head seemed "full of demons", so possessed with pride was he. I suspect (especially given the contrasting portrait of Patrick, who initially displayed an Apostolic humility) that Columcille won his grant of Iona through bluster, threat, and malevolent prophecy, confident that "whatever business he loved would incur no reproach from angels."

IT IS TEMPTING to fall into step with the familiar and glorious parameters of what guidebooks call "The Golden Age of the Saints" when we discuss these early decades of the Christian Church in Ireland. For the most part, men like Columcille present attractive figures: simple, direct, charitable, determined, brave, zealous men, alight with faith and devotion. But in fact the picture is more complicated. At the time of Columcille's exile, the religion had clearly made gigantic inroads through a society previously dedicated to glacial immobility in religious mores. How was this transformation really accomplished? A friend of mine in Dublin answered the question by pointing out the famous letter of Pope Gregory the Great, a pragmatist of the first order, advising his monks in the Anglo-Saxon kingdom of Kent on the arts of improvisation:

> My brothers, you are familiar with the usage of the Roman Church in
> which you were brought up. But if you have found customs, whether in
> the Church of Rome or of Gaul or any other that may be more accept-
> able to God, I wish you to make a careful selection of them, and teach
> the Church of the English, which is still young in the Faith, whatever you
> have been able to learn with profit from the various Churches. For things
> should not be loved for the sake of places, but places for the sake of
> good things. Therefore select from each of the Churches whatever
> things are devout, religious and right; and when you have bound them,
> as it were, into a Sheaf, let the minds of the English grow accustomed to
> it.

Columcille and the other early Celtic zealots intuitively did the same thing, my acquaintance suggested, except they had no diverse collections of Christian habit to choose from, only pagan. As such, in his opinion anyway, the Celtic achievement was far greater and considerably more creative.

There is something to this line of argument, but it divides the Christian and pagan partitions of Columcille's make-up far too decisively. Columcille saw himself as a druid. He certainly behaved like one and, indeed, might have achieved nothing within Celtic society if people hadn't recognized in his posturings little to distinguish him from a pagan priest. It was the similarity that guaranteed his success. What was the Christ

146

story, after all? Little more than another cycle from traditional and familiar saga lore, replete with miracles, Satanic enemies, good and evil, and the Word made Flesh. This last attribute of Christianity was especially potent in a society so grounded in oral culture, where the power of a magician or poet to mock a king was virile enough to disfigure his face with warts and blisters, or in some extreme cases to explode a person's body entirely into pieces. Columcille inherited this proficiency, as Adomnán recalled in his story of the ferocious boar that was "slain by the power of his terrible word". In most facets of his ministry Columcille bore himself in the mode of a pagan conjurer: prophesizing the future, casting spells, cursing the seed of recalcitrant chieftains, destroying his enemies through witchcraft and, lastly, giving his sanction to Kingship. Columcille was the first Christian cleric to crown the king of a Celtic realm, the first to shoulder aside the customary druidic cantors. He could not have assumed that honor in a land so conservative as the Irish if he had come as an outsider with a doctrine too bizarre.

This is not to say, of course, that features of Columcille's behavior did not mystify his countrymen. Poverty and chastity, the mainstays of Cassian's system, were notions utterly foreign to the Celts. Their love of ostentation and lavish adornment signalled a vanity that nearly all classical reporters on Celtic tribes universally deprecated. And the pervasive lack of constancy in sexual matters was clearly seen as a barbarian trait, the men depicted as promiscuous and having no real interest in their wives ("although they are beautiful"); the women as wanton and salacious, who "carelessly yield their virginity to others, regarding this not as a disgrace, but as a freely offered favor." Columcille could justify his peculiar and aberrant behavior with but a single reputable authority, and I would submit that his religion's ultimate acceptance, more than any other factor, depended on the Bible.

This was the item of special sanctity that men like Columcille used to powerful effect in distinguishing their variety of hero worship from that of the native sagas. Though an illiterate people whose wise men did not write,[1] the Irish were by no means ignorant. The Romans in particular had been astonished by the complexity of Celtic culture: the enormous amount of poetry, law, and canon committed to memory by its intelligentsia, and the extravagant respect given all practitioners of scholarship (poets, bards, druids, and later the brehons) by the entire populace, whether peasant or king. Even the lowest level of entertainment, the sagas (which translates as "those things said") were rich in variation and telling detail, spinning plots and turns of action that at times seemed dizzying in their inventiveness. The Bible, convincingly, could compete on every level with all this corpus of material. It contained the story of a

---

[1] The famous ogham code was not a utilitarian script, but a ceremonial hieroglyphics.

warlike, disputatious, robust people; it chronicled the rise and fall of kings, queens, heroes, knaves, false gods and balmy prophets; it told tales of wonder with the same zest and certitude; it preached a law and priestly code; it paraded more than a few tales of a lurid nature; and it climaxed with stories of the greatest God of them all.

Generally speaking, these two separate cyles can almost be viewed as interchangeable. The Old Testament fathers, though a shade less blood-thirsty and vindictive than Cú Chulainn, Ferdiad, Fergus, and Aillil, in fact shared most of the same barbarian qualities. Where Celtic saga figures took the heads of their enemies to preserve in jars, producing them during drunken feasts to boast of their prowess, Salome danced ob-scenely round the head of the Baptist, and David cut off as war trophies the foreskins of two hundred Philistines; where the Celtic patriarches took several wives, so too did Abraham; as the Celtic firmament split asunder with the wondrous works of nature, the Red Sea parted. Con-chobar, legendary King of Ulster, could think of the crucifixion in a thoroughly Celtic context that Columcille would certainly have encour-aged. "It is a pity Jesus did not appeal to me, a valiant High King," Conchobar declares when told the dreadful news by his druid, "for with Christ should my assistance be, a hardy champion, my lips quivering, bitter the slaughter. It crushes my heart to hear the voice of wailing for my God. Beautiful the combat I would wage avenging the Creator."

Most impressive of all, the Bible was there to be seen; it was tangible. When Columcille took the book from his satchel and showed it to the tribesmen, he did so as though it were a talisman, God Himself on the pages, The Word, made Flesh, visible to all. It is no wonder that in a comparatively short span of time Irish clans appropriated the Scriptures for use less exalted than perhaps Christ may have envisioned. A patron saint's psalter would be paraded around their army three times sun-wise prior to battle, to cast a powerfully protective spell or to rob their enemies of fighting spirit. The book that inaugurated the fateful battle of *Cúl Driemne*, in fact, the book Columcille copied from St. Finnian's original, had by the sixteenth century been deprived of nearly all its devotional function, encased in a casket made of gold, studded with jewels and locked shut. "To open it is not lawful", said Manus O'Donnell. Its role became purely one of slaughter, known to O'Donnell gallowglasses, armed with ax and sword, only as "The Battler".

WRITING, OF COURSE, was a novelty with which the Celts in Ireland were barely familiar. It came to them only through the efforts of foreign missionaries and thus was irretrievably related to Christianity, becoming the elemental factor that separated their God from those of the Celts. To the idiosyncratic Irish commentator Constance Fitzgibbon, the very fact of innovation was enough. The archaic Celts "must have longed for almost any form of novelty," he writes, "which they rewarded with an abundant, soon to become traditional, hospitality."

M Y ENTIRE DAY after debarking in Scotland is spent on trains, traversing countryside largely devoid of life and habitation, with one rather prolonged layover in Glasgow fitted in the middle for contrast. It is well past ten in the evening before my arrival in the seaside town of Oban, a port of considerable activity if the many small fishing boats anchored in the harbor are any indication. Lined along the curved breakwater are innumerable hotels, mostly boarded up for the winter. Previous to 1700 Oban consisted of one thatched cottage with five inhabitants, but the transformation of Scotland from a lair of illiterate thieves and murderers[1] to that romantic hideaway created by Sir Walter Scott and Robert Louis Stevenson for Jacobean heroes and soldiers of fortune, gradually encouraged people from England to see the place for themselves. The nineteenth century in particular witnessed a real onrush of tourists, and most of Oban's waterfront was developed to receive them. Walking outside to the edge of town I trust my instincts that I'll find a bed and breakfast there, away from the commercial district, and do. Unlike in Ireland, where such an accommodation would be a cold and rather dank room, unprepared for the winter visitor, this one is baking hot. I borrow an alarm clock, for the ferry to Mull leaves at 5 A.M.

I believe, in all my travels over the years throughout the British Isles, I have never seen a world so perfectly still and crystalline as that which passed before me the next morning. The ferry, virtually empty of passengers, pulls out from a harbor totally asleep. No fishing boats out, no bustle on the quays, no activity of any kind as we slowly pass the ruins of Dunollie Castle at a headland past Oban. Scott, whose romanticism could be more turgid than most, wrote some nicely evocative lines describing the scene of this stone tower crumbling to ruin:

> And bring from out the murmuring sea,
> And bring from out the vocal wood
> The sound of Nature's joy to thee,
> Mocking thy solitude.
>
> Yet proudly 'mid the tide of years
> Thou lift'st on high thy airy form —
> Scene of primeval hopes and fears —
> Slow yielding to the storm.

Coming out to the Firth of Lorn, the entire spread of the sea lies flat and smooth, a mirror to catch the first dull break of day as it shoots through overcast at various gaps on the horizon. The thin beam of a lighthouse periodically flashing to us, the mountains towering over bay and tiny lochs, the grey, wet stone of another castle coming up at Mull — this is

---

[1] Lhuyd had been told that it was a Highland custom "to knock men in ye head for a threadbare suit of clothes."

all solemn theatre. Not the cold, icy, existential feeling of the Alps, but rather a fulsome, melancholic celebration of dour foreboding. In many ways Scott underplayed all this. Even he may have felt that it was all too much, that one could fall into a parody describing such beauty for page after page. Who could possibly believe it.

The Lady's Rocks are just a few hundred feet off our port side, barely above water at low tide, as now. The legend here is that the followers of MacLean of Duart, whose castle on Mull is before us, were so infuriated with his wife, "a witch of deep seduction" who also happened to be the daughter of their hereditary foe, the powerful Earl of Argyll, that they forced the unfortunate man to row her out one evening and leave her on these rocks. As the tide came in she screamed for mercy and fishermen heard the cries, saving her just as the water reached her throat. Several days later MacLean appeared at Argyll's castle, in severe mourning attire, to inform him of his daughter's tragic loss. When he knocked at the door, however, his thought-to-be-deceased wife opened it before him and ushered the wretch in. Medieval vendettas between powerful lords and their ladies were fairly common, and Argyll may have sympathized to some degree with his vassal for he spared him, though MacLean was later assassinated in Edinburgh by Argyll's son.

At Mull, the four of us travelling on to Iona transfer to an unheated bus. Mull is a substantial island some thirty miles long by twenty broad with numerous loughs, coves and bays which indent its coastline so severely that its total circumference totals three hundred miles. We pass several attractive houses and parks for twenty minutes or so along the coast, but turning inland on a single lane road all that fades behind as we enter a wilderness of bog and mountain.

For the next two hours we fail to encounter a single car or truck, see only a few isolated farm buildings or crofts, hardly any sign of herds, either cattle or sheep, and not one human being. This lifeless panorama amazes me. In Ireland, no matter where the road ends, no matter how barren the landscape, I am usually aware that people have been, or are, about. But the depopulation of Scotland is more extreme than anything I have seen in a Gaelic countryside. No ruined buildings or cottages remind us of past emigrations, no cemeteries, overgrown churchyards or any impress of man. "O Sir," in Dr. Johnson's words, "a most dolorous countryside."[1]

By the time we reach the sea for one last boat ride, the morning has degenerated into a windy, squall-ridden afternoon. We are all chilled to the bone but Iona is before us, a scant mile away. This particular ferry is a truly haphazard affair. It docks by keeping the motors full throttle forward with a drawbridge apparatus plunked down on a concrete

---

[1] Keats did the whole trip on foot in 1818, "a most wretched walk of 37 miles."

Port of the Coracle
Iona
Scotland

slipway awash in waves and swirling seawater. There is no ferry schedule per se. The bus arrives; we board the boat and are off. Any notion of taking in Iona from the deck evaporates in thirty seconds, or just the amount of time it takes for the captain to head our craft into the wind. Waves cascade over the bow soaking everyone foolish enough to be outside. We descend into the bowels where the stench of diesel fuel and vomit is almost overpowering. Luckily, only a mile separates Iona from the western shores of Mull.

In about the length of time it took me to fly from New York City to Tokyo several years ago, I have finally reached this place from nearby Ulster. That particular irony does not disturb me, since I enjoy trains and boats, and the isolation and inconvenience of an Iona is more helpful to its preservation than any other single factor. What also fails to trouble me are the expectations that I have created for this place. In libraries far away, in books torn and disintegrating with age, I have read thousands and thousands of words on Iona. Unlike an Inishmurray or a place like Arboe that I visited two days ago, relatively obscure in the annals of history, unimportant to travellers either past or present, Iona played a role of considerable significance in the affairs of men. Ecclesiastical successors to Columcille roamed from this stony outpost in the Atlantic Ocean to the lowlands of Scotland and Northumbria in England to proselytize the heathen. Their converts in turn contributed to the evangelization of Germanic tribes on the Continent and to the intellectual renaissance of Charlemagne. But there will be no Eternal City to greet us here, no St. Peter's Basilica or triumphal archways to illustrate these former glories, no matter whether obscured by lichen and nettles or scrubbed clean like a park. I know enough from my reading not to expect grandeur, a mistake Boswell made when the famous Graveyard of the Kings turned out to be a miserable welter of weeds instead of the marbled monuments of Westminster Abbey that he had anticipated. It is the incongruity of the Celtic landscape that for every grandiose boast there is, generally speaking, less to meet the eye than is even barely sufficient. It is the aura of the past that we must seek out.

One example of exaggeration meets the ferry — *Baile Mór*, the principal street on the island laid out in 1800 which translates as "The Great City". One or two barely stocked grocery stores, a couple of guest houses and a hotel (all closed), a post office, school, and assorted other dwellings make up what can only be charitably described as a village, though it certainly does represent what little business activity there is here. My fellow passengers and I walk up through this assemblage of houses until the pathway forks at a collection of ruins known as the Nunnery, a Benedictine foundation of c. 1200. They all head north towards the Abbey proper, while I take the southerly route that twists and turns towards *A'Mhachair*, The Great Meadow.

Iona is a small island only three miles long and approximately one and a half wide encompassing an area of two thousand acres, of which only two hundred are arable, the rest being rough pasture, bog, and little hills. From the 1690s until 1979 Iona was the hereditary possession of the Earls, later Dukes, of Argyll, who won it and most of the neighboring islands from the MacLeans of Duart.[1] Argyll superintendents, known in Scotland as factors, divided the island into two separate farms comprising sixteen crofts or rental units. In the seventeenth and eighteenth centuries the rent was generally paid "in kind" with produce, generally barley, potatoes, milk products, sheep or beef. It does not give the impression of being a prosperous sort of place. In modern times, 1842 saw the island's peak population of 500 souls, but the potato famine reduced that number by half in just twenty years. Today's figure stands at about ninety-five inhabitants.

The northern portion of the island is dominated by the *Dun* or Fort, a substantial hill of about three hundred feet, the top of which was used as a refuge or citadel during the Iron Age. To the west and south of the *Dun* is a series of smaller hillocks divided from each other by waterlogged gullies and passes; to the north and east of it lies sloping pasturage that terminate at an attractive, beach-lined shore. The principal monastic remains lie on this eastern edge.

In the middle of Iona, on the western shore, is *A'Mhachair*, a long expanse of relatively open field. It is now a fairly ridiculous looking golf course, though from the looks of things this is an enterprise in the process of abandonment. The beach-front here is sweeping and impressive, facing on what is called the "Bay at the Back of the Ocean". Iona's entire southern half is wilderness: no paths, signs, fields, pasture or cultivation of any sort. The lay of the land rises sharply into sea cliffs and bluffs of predictably savage beauty, interspersed by several coves with pebbly beaches, one of which is the Port of the Coracle where Columcille supposedly first landed. All around the island are strong and dangerous eddies and currents. The surf is usually rough, most particularly on the western shore.

Passing from croft to croft I find a place to stay with a young farmer and his family, who normally let rooms during the summer but haven't had a visitor in some months. The kitchen is the warmest room in this house, but I am gravely shown the front parlor, which I can use, with its thin and shallow fireplace, good for a lump or two of coal but not much else. I am to receive one meal a day, breakfast. I am also told there is no place to eat on the entire island. Changing out of my wet gear, and with a short drink from a bottle of port that I thankfully have brought along, I head back to *Baile Mór* and from there walk along to the Abbey.

---

[1] By a series of complicated transfers, the island in that year was conveyed to the National Trust for Scotland.

I think there can be little argument that of all the islands and sanctuaries related to the Celtic story, none is so charming and evocative as Iona. It is true that few remains from the Celtic era are to be found here, nothing on the order of the ancient monastery on Inishmurray. It is also true that an Inishmore of the Aran Islands off Galway is in many ways the equal to this in natural splendor, and has its fair share of ruins and antiquities as well. But Iona somehow transcends the others. Peace, tranquillity, the absence of people, automobiles (for the most part), and commercialism is something all these islands share. But only Iona has the tremendous backlog of a recorded history, so rare in the annals of the Celtic past, coupled with the personality of a founder/patron that is not some poorly sketched, semi-obscure totem remotely glimpsed in one or two archaic genealogies. Whether the lore of Columcille is predominantly legend makes little difference to the island itself. We have been handed a body of material that somehow, over generations, caused a flow of people to come and settle here, along the wilds of an Atlantic shoreline, to foster a communion with God and later, through missionary endeavor, with foreign men far away. The lore is a fact. We have it, read it, study it for clues. It probably represents only a fraction of the material as it once might have been, but the pertinent reality is that the man, then the myth of the man, produced on Iona the premier manifestation of a purely Celtic religious system. All we lack, ironically enough, are the actual physical ruins.

Clonmacnoise, Kells, Glendalough, to mention but three monastic "cities" that still preserve significant remains, cannot touch Iona. Perhaps because they are not islands, perhaps because their experience now includes the peripheral distractions of souvenir stands, tour busses, traffic, and helicopter pads for papal visitations. I don't know why, but they are not the same fine vintage of wine that we have here. Bethlehem, Jerusalem, Golgotha itself present a similar problem: inextricably related to Christ himself, desperate to show us something amid the blur of modernity and all its encroachments, but destined to fail. So too the countless medieval monasteries of the Continent, resonant with fame, that cannot recreate for us now their simple beginnings. Iona seems unchanged from those primitive years of the sixth century. Back beyond, into the obscure wilderness of tangled thickets, tiny glens, marshy bogland, Iona lies mutely delineated by its nomenclature: the Hermit's Cell, a watery hideaway near the *Dun*; Paul's Retreat, in the hollow of a sheltering hill; the Landing to the Desert, on the eastern shore; Sacred Hollow, in the southern bog; Hill of the Angels, overlooking *A'Mhachair*. These are views and places that require no ruins, buildings, crosses, manuscripts, Bibles or even signs. What we see is what Columcille and his monks saw. Finally, I am reminded here of St. Patrick's association with the mountain that bears his name in County Mayo, Croagh Patrick. From afar it casts a spell, there is not another word for its power. Without it, the place is just another peak, its drama half leaked away.

Wednesday, Oct. 20. — Early in the morning we surveyed the remains of
antiquity at this place. As I knew that many persons had already exam-
ined them, and as I saw Dr. Johnson inspecting and measuring several of
the ruins, my mind was quiescent; and I resolved to stroll among them at
my ease to take no trouble to investigate minutely, and only receive the
general impression of solemn antiquity, and the particular ideas of such
objects as should of themselves strike my attention.

James Boswell
A Tour to the Hebrides

A WINTRY GALE blows heavily about the island as afternoon progresses.
I am the only person out on the lanes, the only person on this entire
island from the look of things, but Iona past and present deceives me
here amidst the worsening weather. People more adventuresome than I,
in countless numbers, have come before me to trod along this path. They
have slogged through manure, ruminated among the ruins, measured and
photographed every nook and cranny, dug ditches and trenches to
unearth corroding artifacts of bone and coin hordes, written poetry to
the monks of long ago and symphonies to the varying moods of tempestuous nature, always performing at full bore here along the ocean. Sir
Walter Scott, John Keats, William Wordsworth, Joseph Turner, James
Boswell, Samuel Johnson, Felix Mendelssohn — all made the trek, some
at the peak of their prowess (Mendelssohn's *Third Symphony*, "The
Scotch", and *Overture to the Hebrides* are two striking results), others
at the end of the road (Wordsworth's Iona verses are dreadful). Many
famous, though certainly less intelligent tourists also noted their impressions for better or worse. Queen Victoria did not make the effort to leave
her yacht when cruising these waters on August 18, 1847. "I and the
ladies sketched", she noted in her diary, as Albert went ashore. And one
Honorable Mrs. Murray of Kensington reserved her astonishment for the
natives, who appeared to her as "innocent, simple, and crouching, like
spaniel dogs approaching their masters. If fear had not deterred them, I
verily believed the poor things would have gladly fondled us." Her
discomfort was assuaged by tossing a few shillings about, which afforded
the islanders "a transient joy not easily described". Only Samuel Johnson
penned anything of a memorable nature on what he saw, and his remarks
remain among the most familiar of all that he wrote. "Whatever withdraws us from the power of our senses," he noted,

whatever makes the past, the distant, or the future, predominate over
the present, advances us in the dignity of thinking beings. Far from me,
and from my friends, be such frigid philosophy as may conduct us indifferent and unmoved over any ground which has been dignified by wis-

dom, bravery, or virtue. That a man is little to be envied, whose patrio-
tism would not gain force upon the plain of Marathon, or whose piety
would not grow warmer among the ruins of Iona.

Boswell was equally impressed with his companion's summation, including verbatim the same passage in his own, more popular journal.

The remains that so moved these many, relatively recent, visitors are
the same today as then, but few have any relevance to the theme of this
book, however interesting they certainly are in their own right. The
Reilig Odhráin, or Graveyard of the Kings, was greatly sought. Legend
has it that forty-eight Scottish, four Irish and eight Norwegian monarchs
are buried here, along with several score of the lesser nobility: Lords of
the Isles, varied scions of the MacDonalds, MacLeans, MacKinnons,
assorted warriors of unusual fame. "Where is Duncan's body?" as a
character in Macbeth inquires. "Carried to Colme-kill," answers the
unfortunate MacDuff, "the sacred storehouse of his predecessors, and
guardian of their bones." But the great carved head markers that allegedly
adorned these graves are mostly gone now — indeed, have been for
centuries — either worn away by the weather, destroyed by the attentions
(and avarice)[1] of countless visitors or simply thrown into the ocean by
zealous Protestant reformers in the sixteenth century. There is nothing
here of a royal or majestic nature to justify an heroic aura. The only
identifiable graves are recent interments: local ministers and landowners,
various bodies rolled up by the sea and "Known Only Onto God"; sixteen
sailors lost on the American vessel, *The Guy Mannering*, that broke up
on the last day of December, 1865. Johnson noted the irony. The graves
are many but anonymous, he wrote, "men who did not expect to be so
soon forgotten."

Within the confines of *Reilig Odhráin* stands St. Oran's Chapel, a small
stone oratory exhibiting but "a general rudeness" in the words of one
disappointed tourist, but now handsomely restored. Some of the earliest
visitors to Iona hopefully attributed this early building to the Celtic
period, but in fact it dates to the twelfth century and was probably built
by the MacDonalds, Lords of the Isles, as a private chapel for their dead.
The dedication to St. Oran brings to mind a variation on the legend of
this close disciple to Columcille that Thomas Pennant, the well-known
traveller and writer recorded in his *Tour in Scotland* published in 1774.
We shall see that Oran sanctified this ground by allowing himself to be
ritually killed and then buried. "At the end of three days," as Pennant
heard, "St. Columcille had the curiosity to take a farewell look at his old
friend, and caused the earth to be removed. To the surprise of all

---

[1] Thomas Pennant, the eighteenth-century travel writer who discovered on Iona "the most stupid
and the most lazy of all the islanders," managed through "fair words and a bribe" to have several
monuments cleared of manure. He was so taken with some of the uncovered altar carvings that
he "purloined a piece of it."

156

beholders, Oran started up, and began to reveal the secrets of his prison-house; and particularly declared, that all that had been said of hell was a mere joke. This dangerous impiety so shocked Columcille that with great policy he instantly ordered the earth to be flung in again, poor Oran was overwhelmed, and an end forever put to his prating."

Continuing north along an ancient roadway of smooth, water-rolled boulders dragged up from the beaches below, I approach the medieval Cathedral and its monastic appendages of cloister, refectory, kitchen, chapter house, and dormitory, with the great, standing St. Martin's Cross at the entrance. This is, to use the terminology of the nineteenth century, a noble prospect indeed, and especially so given a panorama of field, ocean, and distant mountains that seem devoid of life. This entire complex of buildings, however, is not more, nor less, impressive than many of the monastic ruins that exist in the British Isles. It is not, architecturally speaking, a pure or stylistically unified collection as are, for example, many of the Franciscan friaries in Ireland. It is rather more of a hodge-podge. Designed and first built by Benedictines in the 1200s it saw more than a few reversals in fortune, see-sawing between periods of great prosperity and even more severe declines. At one point in its long history the Abbey held income-producing estates throughout the Hebridean islands, at others it lay empty, disused, bankrupt. It was redesigned on several occasions, added to, expanded, rebuilt, torn away, neglected, renewed, deserted, left to ruin, restored. The result today is thus a fantastic puzzle to historians who try to link certain features of style in windows, doorways, arches and decoration to certain periods and patrons, all the while interpreting these changes as reflecting the vicissitudes that documents, charters, annals and depositions have recorded.

The Benedictines who came here at the turn of the thirteenth century to found their community did so at the expense of the few Celtic monks they found still here. The Irish *Annals of Ulster* record for the year 1204 that the newcomers essentially squatted in their midst, and for some time two opposing factions vied for the site. But the great orders of medievalism, the Benedictines, Cistercians, Augustinians, joined later by Dominicans and Franciscans, were the style of the times, blessed by Rome and more glamourous to patrons of the local nobility. By this late date the Celtic system had largely evaporated as an independent religious phenomenon, and their struggle with the continental Benedictines was a losing one, ending over seven centuries of Irish predominance here. This cruciform cathedral of stone eventually obliterated the ancient Celtic construction of wood and wattle.

Climbing the *Torr an Aba*, a small rocky protrusion just a few yards west of the present Abbey, gives one a fairly good overview of the site, although aerial photography, more than any other modern tool, has delineated the monastic boundaries in a way that just walking about cannot do. A great *termonn* or sanctuary wall surrounded the Celtic community. At Inishmurray the *termonn* was its stone cashel, but Iona was more the monastic metropolis than a retreat, one enormous rath of some twenty acres encircled by a ditch and earthen bank — in effect, a dry moat. One expanse of this barrier is still perfectly evident north-north-west of the Abbey, and from the air one can plausibly trace the rest of it. This site on the eastern shore of the island was almost certainly selected by Columcille himself: its relatively easy stretch of sandy beaches made for safer landings, and the various rocky hillsides that spill off from the *Dun* provided shelter from westerly gales. Most experts agree the first chapel was probably built where the medieval Abbey stands today, for the Benedictines would have chosen the spot of greatest sanctity for their new cathedral, and that was Columcille's grave, most likely beneath the altar of the principal Celtic church that was founded by the Saint himself. As medieval construction proceeded and sprawled laterally to the north, it no doubt brushed aside ancillary chapels, the Irish having a traditional preference for multiple buildings of worship as opposed to a single grand edifice. As these were built of wood and plaster they were easily knocked down. Final evidentiary remains are the three high crosses grouped in front of the present Abbey which pre-date that building by over four centuries, evidence that the spiritual hub of Columcille's Iona was not drastically changed by the Benedictines.

To prove all this, archaeologists would have to dig up the Benedictine Abbey. They would be searching for timber post holes and other structural testimony to reveal outlines of the various huts and buildings that the earliest monks constructed, yet all these traces were probably destroyed as the great stone monastery was built. As a result, most excavations undertaken to date have concentrated on the peripheral areas of the rath rather than the center, and thus have revealed more of the day-to-day and mundane activities of the monks. These, when compared with the clues that Abbot Adomnán revealed in his biography of Columcille, written in c. 685, and other monastic documents give us a fairly good picture of what life was like at Iona.

The great rath was probably subdivided by lesser raised banks into several partitions or working areas. Little pottery or ceramic pieces, so useful in dating a dig, have been found on Iona, but the detritus of a woodworking shop — particles of waste, bucket staves, posts, cores from bowls and cups — reveal that implements of daily work and utensils for eating were home-grown and fashioned on the site. Evidence has been unearthed for a leather shop that produced sandals and shoes, satchels for books and manuscripts, perhaps rough tunics or aprons. There were also facilities for working in metal, for making chalices, patens, book and shrine covers, along with more utilitarian pins, brooches, abbatical rings and so forth. Farm sheds and barns no doubt accounted for many buildings within the rath. Meat was available, evidenced by finds of animal bones here and there, and a maritime proficiency illustrated by

Irish Abbot, Jerpoint Abbey
County Kilkenney

the profusion of fish scales found in various trash piles. Adomnán notes the comings and goings of over fifty-five boats to the monastery and it is unthinkable that the monks did not fish extensively. *A'Mhachair*, in the middle of the island, was not idle pasture but thoroughly cultivated, as carbon dated cereal pollens reveal. Many Irish monasteries routinely brewed "princely malt", and occasionally stronger spirits, though how much of this was consumed by the monks is hard to say. The matter of alcohol, like so many inconsistencies in the Celtic attitude, caused dissension among the saints. "As long as I shall give the rules," said one abbot, "the liquor that causes forgetfulness of God shall not be drunk here." But another replied, "My monks shall drink it, and they shall be in Heaven with thine!"

After their churches and sanctuaries, the most important building of an Irish community was its guesthouse, a facility that combined customary standards of hospitality with a religious imperative that strangers at the door might be angels in disguise or Christ himself. Many a hermit, though desirous of solitude "in a hard prison of stone", is recorded settling "where the seven roads meet" in order to provide for those far from home, and of these monks some were famous musicians who needed but little encouragement to strike up a merry and secular tune. Various domestic buildings rounded out the monastery, built as time, stability and patronage allowed: sleeping quarters, larders, storehouses, infirmary, refectory and, later, schools and a scriptorium.

We can only hypothesize on the average day of an Irish monk. Work of some sort made up a portion of it, however distasteful that might have been. Like St. Antony in the Egyptian desert, the earliest Irish saints were indifferent to food and drink: "Dry bread and cess is pure food for sages." But as a monastery grew and attracted brothers, certainly a diet more appealing than weeds was provided, though increasing numbers of monks allowed many of the more talented or studious to avoid manual chores, which was certainly their goal. "Without ploughing or reaping or drying," prayed one monk, "without work save study." Columcille himself supposedly disapproved of herding — "Where there is a cow there must be a woman, and where there is a woman there must be mischief" — and his daily toil described by Adomnán and others was that of a copyist, for "thirty victorious, lasting, bright, noble books he wrote." Nonetheless, later monastic tradition gives ample proof that students were generally required to bring along their keep and tuition in the form of a dairy cow. St. Ciarán, for example, deciding to study at the famous school of Clonard in Meath, asked his father for help to defray expenses. "Go through the herds," he was told, "and what will follow thee, take." We are left with the rather idyllic picture of Ciarán leaving home for Clonard at the even pace of his dun cow. It is fair to say that fields we see today on Iona with grazing livestock of various kinds present much the same scene as that of a millennium ago.

Certainly the rites of worship absorbed much of the monk's attentions. As was the case in the Eastern deserts, the mysteries of the Mass were celebrated but once a week on Sunday, with greater daily emphasis on the saying of divine office and private prayer. We have many poems describing the trials and tribulations of answering the summons for service on a winter's night. "To go and say the office, great labor," wrote a monk. "The wind stings my two ears. Were it not dread of the blessed lord, though sweet the bell, I would not go to it." "Shame to my thoughts, how they stray from me," another weary monk laments. "During the Psalms they wander on a path that is not right. They run through eager assemblies, through companies of wanton women, through woods, through cities — swifter they are than the wind." The respect given elders and hermits was particularly strong, and most of the larger communities like Iona supported a peripheral melange of anchorites who dwelled apart in hidden wastelands close by, enjoying in Cassian's phrase "the freedom of the desert, a dangerous liberty." Their rigors of mortification were the legends that glorified their sponsors and thrilled their fellow monks. Novices in particular made it a habit to go on rounds, from one hermit to another, to receive a blessing or a scrap of heavenly insight. "Senán loved lasting illness, thirty diseases in his body", read one Martyrology. "Noble Iarlaithe loved three hundred genuflections every night, three hundred genuflections every day." Some performed cross vigils without ceasing. Sagas relate that certain hermits stood for so long in this penitential posture that birds made nests in their upturned hands, or stood on the cleric's head as though a rock or tree.[1]

A monastery, of course, was a collection of men and thus not a perfect place. We see in the various ecclesiastical rules the most commonplace problems with which abbots had to deal and none is too surprising. "What should be shunned by a holy person?" asks an eighth-century devotional piece:

> "It is not hard to say. Growing angry frequently, unruliness towards a superior, tardiness at answering the bell, secret plotting, derision of brethren, impure words, asperity of reply, resistance against a prior, unruliness at reproof, rivalry with fellow monks, and frequency of disputation."
>
> "What does all that do to you?"
>
> "It is not hard to say. Rejection from Heaven."

Sagas and chronicles abound in references to tyrannical abbots attempting, often in vain, to exert control over recalcitrant or argumentative monks. Control, or lack of it, usually depended on the strength of an

---

[1] St. Scothíne, "the Battle Hard," tempted fate more rashly. "Two maidens with pointed breasts used to lie with him every night that the combat with Satan might be the greater for him."

abbot's personality. Brian Moore's depiction of Father Abbot in his book *Catholics* does justice to the age-old difficulty of dealing with a collection of Irish monks. Some things never change. In general, however, we can say that life on Iona was austere though spiritually exhilarating. As I have suggested before, some of us may only imagine the latter; as to the former, "it is harsh, it is fierce, the order they serve."

A CHARMING POEM from the tenth century portrays an Irish monk daydreaming at his desk, amused at the regal pridefulness of Pangur, the monastic cat.

> Each of us pursues his trade,
> I and Pangur my comrade;
> His whole fancy on the hunt,
> And mine for learning ardent.
>
> More than fame I love to be
> Among my books and study;
> Pangur does not grudge it,
> Content with his own merit.

On equal footing with its reputation for piety and holiness, the Irish monastic system from earliest times was famed for the high level of academic achievement and erudition that supposedly characterized monks such as Columcille. That the Irish valued a life of scholarship is beyond dispute, though whether they merit any praise beyond that fact certainly is, for loving something and being good at it are two very different things. The distinction is an important one to the aim of this book, trying as we are to penetrate the very being of a type of personality so disfigured by traditional myths and legends. We know that Columcille was a man of hard labor. We also know that he was a religious zealot. These aspects of personality tell us something of the man but little of the range and sophistication, if any, of his mind.

Columcille, like the scholar who so loved his cat, enjoyed many hours in the privacy of his writing hut. Adomnán repeatedly describes the Saint in the various modes of reading or copying manuscripts. The final day of his life, in fact, Columcille spent transcribing the Psalms until he reached the passage that reads, "They who seek the Lord shall want no manner of thing that is good." "Here," he said prophetically, "at the end of this page I must stop; the rest let Baithine copy." Truly, as noted earlier, Columcille felt himself, through the Bible, as being in direct and personal communion with God. The Words themselves were small bits of magic which he, through learning, could see and understand, something his peers in the secular world could not. But was Columcille anything more than a rustic schoolchild? Did the word "scholar" really apply to him and those who followed in his calling?

The rudiments of whatever education Columcille received as a boy are unknown to us today, as indeed are many details from the turn of the fifth century in Ireland. Tradition has it that Columcille learned to read and write from the priest to whom he was fostered by his father, and this would seem likely as only clerics required the skills of literacy, without which the Bible could neither be explored nor interpreted for the people. But what level of competence this particular priest enjoyed is unfathomable. It is tempting, and unavoidable, to look at Patrick as some sort of guide in these matters, if for no other reason than his career, and the writings he left behind, are all we have for tangible evidence. Yet it would seem difficult indeed to see in Patrick the ideal of a teacher, for he declared in his *Confession* that he was "unlearned" and "greatly fearful to expose my unskillfulness, not being eloquent." Despite these disclaimers, Patrick's remarks do provide us with substantial hints as to what was going on in the minds of the missionaries, and the probable impact they may have had on their Celtic audience.

Patrick was no illiterate. Though he disparaged his own intellectual abilities (probably with some justification) his two letters produce several passages of considerable power, no matter how clumsy the Latin he employed. We have the picture here of an individual more concerned with preaching than literary instruction, which no doubt especially recommended him for the arduous assignment he had been given by his superiors in England: "to smash the head of the dragon, its paganism and idolatry." Two considerations occur, however. Patrick emphasized his deficiencies primarily when he compared himself to fellow clerics back home in Britain, "the others who have drunk in law and sacred literature in the best manner", who eloquently followed the advice of biblical wise men: "For by thy tongue is discerned understanding and knowledge and the teaching of truth." It would seem probable that from this body of men a small trickle of successors to Patrick's enterprise — monks sent later, after his death perhaps, or individually inspired to conduct missions on their own — could have provided a teaching nucleus more adept than the great Apostle himself. As Patrick's initial conversions took hold and matured, thereby providing a pool of possible students, this body of wiser, more skillful masters was perhaps available to nurture and school those brought to the faith by rougher men. Second, though exhibiting little in the way of profound learning, there can be little doubt that Patrick at least knew his scripture. "I am not ignorant of the testimony of my God", he said, and his writings are studded with biblical allusions and the apt selection of buttressing quotations, used to justify both his own particular failures in the missionary wars, and what he considered his embarrassing lack of communicative skills; as he put it, "Stammering tongues shall learn quickly to speak peace." If anything, the scenario seems possible that the first evangelists to Ireland, whether from Britain like Patrick or the Continent itself, were at least equipped to pass along, if nothing else, their enthusiasm for biblical writings, and that if they themselves were incapable of teaching the necessary skills that converts would require to join in that passion, more educated brothers certainly did exist, and that at several junctures during the late 400s and early 500s, some of these must have certainly passed into Ireland.

The men first instructed would have been those Celts who desired to become priests, and initial lessons must have been awkward affairs indeed, the equivalent of teaching the complexities of Japanese to a headhunter from Africa. Ireland, unlike most other regions of Continental Europe, had none of the external supporting structures that we have come to label most simply as Empire: no cultural base of poetry, business correspondence or political documentation bound by the single language of Rome, no vernacular Latin to connect the various occupations of the people in everyday affairs, be they merchants, grocers, soldiers, professors, fishmongers, lawyers or whatever, no commonality of reference or expression in terms of the historicity of Rome itself — in other words, the universal Latin heritage. The Irish were barbarians, temperamentally and intellectually distinct from the greatest civilization of its time, but they were not simpletons with minds as blank as a long, empty blackboard. To the chagrin, no doubt, of their earliest tutors, the Irish perversely had plenty to think about all on their own. They had developed, over centuries, a cultural reservoir so abstruse that an entire superstructure of professional custodians, the *filid*, had evolved just to preserve it. As there was no written Irish language, or written record of any kind, we must see in these highly honored scholars something equivalent to a living library of knowledge whose responsibility was to preserve and then pass along this lode of belief, law, custom, and genealogy to successors in exactly the form in which they initially received it. These men were walking computer chips, with data banks of prodigious capacity, who entered and retrieved their information in the form of poetry, highly dense and formulated by the most arcane conventions, usually delivered in drones or chants. In some ways, the earliest missionaries were dealing with a people more capable than themselves.

The critic and short story writer Frank O'Connor may well have disagreed. Much of this druidic body of learning and pedigree he lumped all together as "the dead weight of tradition," seeing in the tortuous machinations of this professional class an "obsession to produce not the man with the best brain, but the man with the best memory". Nevertheless, a training of high rigor did exist in Ireland, and alongside it a sense of curiosity and adventurism that eventually would mark the later scholarship of Christian Ireland.

Probably the only text of study used at first was the Bible itself, and these initial forays into the classroom seem certain to have been oral, writing materials being scarce and the earliest teachers perhaps stymied by the proverbial restlessness and quarrelsome nature of their students. Short sermons or lectures probably focused on three areas: simple story telling, which the Irish no doubt keenly enjoyed; genealogical forays into the family trees of biblical patriarchs, undoubtedly committed to memory as both an exercise and an accommodation to native methodology which specialized, after all, in memorizing dynastic pedigrees; and lastly, the singing of the Pslams.

If more than six centuries of primary emphasis within the Celtic Church is any guide, it appears that the Psalms of the Old Testament made the most telling impression on the Irish. King David, who allegedly wrote nearly half the one hundred and fifty compositions that make up this book of the Bible,[1] was especially attractive, a multi-faceted warrior prince whose career embodied grandiose feats on the battlefield as well as melancholic retreats to barren caves, whose skills ranged from diplomacy and generalship to poetry and music, in particular a mastery of that favorite Celtic instrument, the harp. A Norman cleric, whose esteem for the Irish in general was decidedly slight, could grudgingly note in 1185 that "it is only in the case of sweet and pleasant melody that I find any diligence in this people," and truthfully this "quick and lively talent" provided the only glimpse of "internal cultivation" that many visitors from civilization could discern. It was a gift the Irish turned full bore on the Psalms, merging their own tradition of chanting sacred druidic texts with the excitement of developing arrangements, as David called for them, in his instructions to singers and orchestra (Psalm 4, Joyful Confidence in God, "Sing with stringed instruments;" Psalm 5, For Divine Help, "A Song of David, with wind instruments" and so on). These were all committed to memory; when writing became more commonplace, and copying of manuscripts more customary, it was the Psalms to which the clerics first turned their attention. They delighted in creating the pocket-sized Psalters, and gloried in its Latin root *Psalterium*, "the musical instrument". It is virtually impossible to pick up any later Irish rule, penitential code, or saint's life without some reference to the glorious "Three Fifties". "This is what Maelruain used to say: 'There are three adversaries busy attacking me, my eye, my tongue, and my thoughts. The Psalter restrains them all.'" Another monk wrote: "It's like a glorious building with many shrines, various treasure houses with special keys to open each one of them."

IN APPROACHING THE years of Columcille's birth and early manhood, about the A.D. 530s, we sense the gradual decline of whatever influ-

---

[1] Modern scholarship dismisses even this attribution.

St. Martins' Cross
Iona
Scotland

With David and his harp, third panel up

ence Patrick and his British successors may have had on Irish Christianity. The signs are certainly faint. Patrick had brought with him a hierarchical structure inherited from Rome: he was a bishop, his role was to convert the people, build churches, ordain a native clergy, structure a diocesan network and then, in coordination with the Universal Church, establish a confederation of fellow bishops to oversee the entire operation. The earliest Irish chronicles record the names of many bishops, but starting at the midway point of the sixth century the accolade of annalistic recognition begins to include abbots in roughly equal number. By A.D. 600 there is barely a single bishop mentioned, the levers of ecclesiastical power having passed overwhelmingly from the episcopal configuration of Patrick's Roman usage to the native tradition that Columcille embodied, tribe and *paruchia*. The Venerable Bede, writing in c. 731 from Northumbria, could not comprehend the inferior status of bishops in the Irish system, the successors to St. Peter now rudely subordinate to abbots, kept in the wings of a monastery only for their liturgical monopoly in the rites of ordination. The Celts "had a zeal for God," Bede complains, "but not according to knowledge. Their ploughs do not run straight."

We are presented here with a picture of Celtic isolation, not only in Ireland but in Britain itself. Bede, though a historian of unusual perspicacity given the times, was certainly unaware of the complexities that had created what he saw as a peculiar and disjointed society, only partially civilized in the sense of a cosmopolitan Roman standard. He may never have realized that, before the sixth-century Anglo-Saxon dismemberment of Britain (of which he was a product), missions like those of the Briton Patrick had crossed the Irish Sea and implanted, however feebly, the rudiments of literacy in the northern reaches of that island. Nor would he have known, since his sympathies lay elsewhere, the suddenness with which these proselytizing voyages ceased. Patrick's church, dating from the second century, and an institution of considerable lineage, was now facing extermination.

The story of England's conquest by Angles and Saxons from the Continent is long and complicated. Before the Roman legions withdrew from the island in 410, Germanic freebooters had been employed, in typically desperate fashion, by Imperial paymasters to fight the battles Rome could no longer afford to wage itself — the old strategy of letting barbarians man the frontiers. Afterwards, the then bereft Britons continued this arrangement, but in 460 the Saxons, now plentifully settled at various points along the eastern coast of the island, turned colors and savaged their hosts. The terrible and sanguinary tides of battle surged for over a century, with both sides achieving periodic successes. In the latter half of the sixth century, however, Angles and Saxons routed the Britons and effectively destroyed their semi-Roman culture. Christianity — the ancient Church of Patrick — found itself penned against the sea in Strathclyde,

Wales, and Cornwall. The usage of Latin vanished for all practical purposes as the country was flooded with new and heathen settlers, "that miserable race", according to one Celtic monk, a people so warlike and indifferent to physical dangers that, in the words of the poet Sidonius, "shipwrecks, far from terrifying them, they regard as their training."

Whereas Patrick distrusted the Irish, thinking them liars, he was still willing to put all his prejudices aside "to be with them for the rest of my life." Not so his countrymen, who felt differently about the Anglo-Saxons. Bede peevishly chastises the Britons for refusing to convert the Germanic invaders, calling them "faithless", an epithet Patrick would have considered obscene. Bruised and humiliated in battle, the last thing a Briton would consider was the idea of sharing the joys of heavenly salvation with his mortal enemy. In bitterness, the Church of Patrick retreated to mountain hideaways and valley retreats. It had neither the time nor the energy for Ireland.

If one examines the conditions on mainland Europe at this same time, as illustrated, let us say, in the grim reporting of the bishop Gregory of Tours in his *History of the Franks* (a truly astonishing catalogue of garrotings, rapes, riots, murders, beatings, poisonings and tortures — indeed, in his own words, "every crime in the calendar"), it becomes clear why the Irish Church in Columcille's lifetime developed in a vacuum. As a proud and haughty race, the Irish probably interpreted this obscurity to advantageous terms by seeing themselves in the middle of what counted in this world, rather than off to one side at its periphery. They did not consider themselves an ignorant people, and were conceited enough to be indifferent when others thought them so.

THE FIRST MEN of the Irish race who learned to read and then to write did so in Latin, and these pioneers in turn taught others. They had the Bible as their primary tool, an eager, if select, audience with which to deal and the respect of their entire society which had, over its long history, never distrusted learning, oratory, or the pursuit of knowledge. Despite all these advantages the task was an arduous one, primarily due to the lack of precedent. There were no Irish/Latin dictionaries, grammatical primers or diagrammatic text books, no note pads or pens with which to copy down lessons and problems. In our own day and age, when we can teach the blind to read, the deaf to understand, and the dyslexic to function normally, perhaps these obstacles seem less extreme. Yet at that era they were almost insurmountable barriers to the learning process. The times were primitive and harsh, the perceptions of men to the world around them far different than those we entertain today. Education is a given in our modern, industrial society, and the instruction of even the disadvantaged and the handicapped (to continue using our example above) has become in itself an enormously specialized massif of that even greater subcontinent known as general education. In the Europe of c. 550 such would hardly have been the case. Literacy for most would have

168

seemed a frivolity when compared with the necessity of staying alive, staying sheltered, staying fed. There would have been little purpose to pursuing literacy, particularly as libraries and the country houses of the gentry went up in flames, put to the torch by ignorant Germanic barbarians wholly devoid of any insightful tradition, to whom a manuscript was worth nothing more than kindling, whereas a bottle of wine or a stolen chicken had a value more immediately satisfying. It is a remarkable piece of luck, though rarely mentioned today, that during those catastrophic times it was a Celtic people, and not a Germanic, that lived in Ireland, the final station, the last stop, of European classical culture. If the Anglo-Saxons had wasted their way through Ireland, our later intellectual heritage would have been drastically altered, for the Germans had no learned classes and little interest in anything but martial saga. The Celts were a different breed.

In the first place, they were an enthusiastic people, eager to garner honor and praise in those various pursuits which their society held in high regard. Unlike the Germans, who, Caesar complained, did nothing but prepare for war or the hunt — of anything else "they have not even heard a rumour" — the Celts were cheerfully diverse. They loved battle and carnage, the cruelty of blood sports and competition, yet they valued on an equal footing the exploits of wise men, their erudition and feats of memory. Much of this was show and pomp. The Celts were bombastic by nature and many times the fireworks of learning took precedence over content. "They often speak in riddles," wrote one observer in c. A.D. 25, "for the most part hinting at things and leaving a great deal to be understood." Perhaps this disguised what was, in some respects, a lack of originality in their makeup, but it suited them ideally as conservators. The greatest triumph of the Celtic system was that it initiated the effort to save from the rubble of European classical tradition some few tidbits here and there that later scholars more mature and perhaps more reflective could use in ways the Irish themselves might never have imagined possible. The druidic orders who were able to recite the pedigree of countless petty dynasties in any number of *tuaths* both famous and obscure unwittingly forged a standard of scholastic behavior that was antiquarian by nature, dedicated to preserving things of the mind or the spirit that might seem to others (and sometimes to themselves), to be of no value at all. In just this manner we see Irish scribes in the 800s, and far later during the early medieval era, painstakingly copy manuscripts in languages they did not understand — including the Old Irish of their ancestors — the equivalent, I suppose, of my tracing out a document like the Koran in Arabic. "Hard the labor," as one monk complained in the margins of a manuscript, "there's an end to that. And my seven curses go with it!"

The underlying basis for this type of training, especially the druidic, was repetition, and no wonder their adaptability to song made the Psalms such an Irish favorite, for chanting in general was highly regarded in pagan times as an aid to the retention of learning. And while it would be easy to reconstruct those early classroom scenes as periods of general drudgery – the recitation over and over again of prayer after prayer, Psalm after Psalm, – we should always keep in mind the parallel of sacred Vedas. These were the words of God, and power lay in their repeated supplication. This technique, not unnaturally, led to incredible familiarity with the texts themselves, which resulted in a scholarly free-fall seldom seen before, as the Irish ransacked their Bibles in a way totally revealing of their personality.

Commentators, many unfriendly to the Irish, have generally disparaged the critical apparatus with which these monastic novices – Columcille and his contemporaries – confronted their lessons. Discounting the achievements in attaining literacy (at first in a language totally foreign to their own in syntax, structure, and usage, a notable accomplishment by any standard) these critics have generally focused on the interpretive faculties brought to bear by the Celts on their biblical studies. Frank O'Connor, in the unkindest cut of all, said that "the Irish had the choice between imagination and intellect, and they chose imagination." An English observer, writing in 1907, felt the "Celt brings all heart and much fluency" to his work, but "with little mind." Even the sympathetic German scholar Rudolph Thurneysen believed it was an impossible task for Irish scholars to "develop their reasoning powers" at home. "They could only do so in closer proximity to the Mediterranean." These are all in accord with the aesthetic opinion of T. S. Eliot when he tried, in 1944, to define "What is a Classic?" Eliot, of course, had not the shred of interest in the Celts, barbarians whether Christianized or not, and in fact he was referring to the poet Virgil when he made these remarks. But they summarize the generally disparaging point of view that many intellectuals hold towards insular societies, the home-grown species of inverted wisdoms. What a "classic" requires is "maturity of mind," and

this needs history, and the consciousness of history. Consciousness of history cannot be fully awake, except where there is other history than the history of the poet's own people: we need this in order to see our own place in history. There must be the knowledge of the history of at least one other highly civilized people, and of a people whose civilization is sufficiently cognate to have influenced and entered into our own. This is a consciousness which the Romans had, and which the Greeks could not possess.

In this particular theory, the crustaceous accumulation in the typical druid's mind of God knows how many generations of heroic tradition is dismissable as "provinciality". The sequential power of one civilization (Greek) to heighten another (Roman) is seen as almost a cultural inevitability, and often relied upon by the expert as a general tool of rational explanation in all manner of historical judgments — architecture, commerce, social behavior, religious beliefs, military strategy, and so on. It is not an entirely accurate procedure, however, and in our narrow context of looking over the shoulder of a Columcille it is not conducive to a rounded portrait.

The Irish did not produce a textual scholar anywhere near the caliber of St. Jerome. Neither, for that matter, did anyone else. And I admit to using the word "ransacked" when referring to the Irish and their almost devouring attitude towards the Bible. They were untidy in their enthusiasms and often tangential in expressing opinions and attitudes.

Outsiders considered their verbosity charming and the evidence of a "quick mind", but tended to become fatigued rather quickly after their exposure to rivers of talk, concluding the Irish were difficult, obstinate, and perverse. As St. Patrick observed in some wonderment after sitting through an endless druidic monologue, "That's a very complicated story!" But what we really have here is the collision of cultures, and the inability of Latin to see eye to eye with Gaelic.

In some ways the Continental opinion, both ancient and modern, of the Celts is correct. There is truth in everything that O'Connor, Thurneysen, and Eliot had to say. Much of the Irish interpretation of Scripture seems foolish to us today: the emphasis on genealogy; the often demented search for oddity in language and usage, which result in word lists and tortured interpretations that veer to absurdity; a sometimes credulous approach to miracles and supernatural doings; and a mind-boggling ability to state two polarities of opinion and embrace both as positively true. But before accepting these divergencies as narrow truths, we should look at the language.

Latin may well have confused the Celts. What possible advantage did they really see in it? The missionaries who came first to the Irish (of whom Patrick, Palladius and four or five others are only the few whom we know and can identify; there were surely others), succeeded in convincing the Irish that in this medium they received the Word of God, and as such it was magic. To join in that magic the language had to be learned. But other than that, surely all the rest they saw seemed listless and deficient. "Was there not among the many languages something nobler to take precedence of Gaelic?" asked an Irish grammarian in the tenth-century *Scholars' Primer*. "Not hard," he answered himself, "no indeed, on account of its aptness, slightness, smoothness, and comprehensiveness", of which the last attribute stood out most boldly. Gaelic was the language of life. Befitting its ancient pedigree as an oral language (as opposed to literal or written), and in the hands of a gifted, imaginative people, there were seen to be no limits to what the simplest element in the world around them might wring from its speaker in either praise, damnation, or the many stops in between. "What was best, widest, and finest of every language was put in Gaelic," says the *Primer*, "to wit, what was easier and pleasanter to say. The Latinist has nothing to correspond with it."

Gaelic expresses and communicates emotional range in a fashion more pleasing to the ear than to the page. This tends not to help in garnering respect, for speech is transitory and evaporates in the air a second after leaving our lips. It deposits no records, leaving nothing to impress us. When seen in transcription it can often strike the reader as wordy, awkward, stilted, reaching, not the language best suited for both romance and hatred as the storytellers proclaim. Yet I am inclined to believe the sagas. To be cursed by a druid, to be damned by the saint — the high repute of these incantations is too historical to be denied.

Let us look at what the Grammarian meant by comprehensiveness. Gaelic has the power to run circles round its subject, providing countless variations on a single theme. In the hands of a skillful speaker the effect of being verbally abused would be akin to having one's head battered with regularity against a wall. Gaelic very often will not reach a crescendo or climax. It overwhelms with sheer weight and, while sinking beneath the waters, the person being drowned can only marvel at the flow of eloquence washing over him.

Looking at the color spectrum is a simple way of sensing this characteristic. Latin, as a matter-of-fact language, tells us red, blue, green, white, but Gaelic is more fulsome, interested in shades, tones, subtleties of difference. Negroes were not just blacks, they were *fir Gorma*, or "blue men". This would seem nonsensical to us, but the Irish saw more possibilities for the color blue *(gorm)* than we, and did not hesitate to plunge about finding an adjective more expressive, even if, to our minds, less accurate. In English we can easily associate the color red with bloody, and by extension, to violence, as in "bloody war" or "bloody hell". We can even extend ourselves by coming up with an associative phrase like "to catch a murderer red-handed", but that is as far as we generally will go. In Gaelic, no such restrictions apply.[1]

This rhetorical capacity perfectly suited a people who valued alert and ardent debate, since it provided its speakers with ready access to quick, pointed counterthrust, something the more tepid and impersonal Latin did not. No wonder to the duller Anglo-Saxon mind, the Greeks and Irish were brothers in deceit.

Their propensity for garrulity prevented the Irish from ever, in the words of one English critic, producing a *Divine Comedy* or any other work of "profound self-inquiry", though if we broaden our horizons to include modern literature (which this scholar did not) it seems plain that Joyce's *Ulysses* finally did reach the goal of fusing content to the body of a broader Celtic extravaganza, one devoted (though in English) to the

---

[1] As one observer put it to the English tongue, "In loving thou do'st well, in passion not."

traditional glee of word play and atmospheric effect. The Irish came to love the late Latin poets of the Empire, in particular Virgil, but they never could restrain themselves sufficiently to close the gap between their own expansive fertility of expression and the rigid emotional suppression of classicism. The seventh book of Lucan's *Pharsalia* describes Caesar's triumph over Pompey in 48 B.C. The victorious Roman general gloats over the death throes of one Domitius, "rolling his limbs," according to Lucan, "amid clotting blood." A Gaelic poet finds this description inadequate and freely translates the passage with more descriptive feeling: "So Caesar came to him while Domitius was at his last gasp, lying down on the battlefield with great, long, mangled wounds athwart him, and deep, intolerable gashes, and incurable scars, and he himself wallowing and bathing in the pools of dark blood and in the rivers of gore that were under the feet of the heroes in the battle." Lucan summarizes the great clash of armies with considerable color all his own:

> I scruple to expend tears at the downfall of the world upon deaths innumerable, and, tracing them out, to enquire into individual fates; through whose vitals the deadly wound made its way; who it was that trod upon entrails scattered on the ground; who, the hostile sword being thrust into his jaws, dying, breathed forth his soul; who fell down at the blow; who, while his limbs dropped down, lopped off, stood upright; who received the darts right through the breast, or whom the lance pinned to the plain; whose blood, the veins being severed, gushed through the air and fell upon the arms of his foe; who pierced the breast of his brother, and that he might be able to spoil the well-known carcase, threw afar the head cut off; who mangled the features of a parent, and by his extreme fury would prove to lookers-on that he whom he stabbed was not his father.

But the Irish transcriber cannot abide such restraint:

> Sad indeed it was in the battle afterwards. Abundant was the sound of an arrow against the trunk of nobles, and the sound of a sword piercing a body, and the sound of a spear penetrating a flank, and the sound of an axe hewing a champion, the sound of a hatchet crushing a foe, the sound of a club against a corselet, the sound of a stone against a helmet, and a ball over a soldier's temporal artery. Many, then, were red, headless trunks, and raw, freshly-cut carcases, and open, gaping wounds, and fresh, unmeasured lacerations, and deep, incurable gashes, and long, crooked manglings, and rough, dangerous blows, and felling strokes, and deadly knocks, and hurts of death. Many, too, were bodies torn, and skins slashed, and flanks pierced, and fierce warriors mangled, and hands injured, and heads broken, and youths severely wounded, and soldiers killed, and champions gored, and heroes' bodies in a bed of blood.
> Many, too, were men lying on their backs, and faces distorted pale, spectral, and heroes' countenances growing green, and deadened limbs starting, and eyes rolling wildly, and white lips tasting death, and necks dripping blood and cloven lungs oozing out, and gathered heads running together, and rent trunks groaning, and pure breasts heaving, and perfo-

Lane by the Bare Hill
Iona
Scotland

rated hearts pouring, and mangled hands twitching.

We see in Lucan a Latin that was crisp and professional. It came to the point, as Lucan intended. Gaelic refuses to do so. Latin had the necessarily international background to handle sophistication in religious metaphysics; Gaelic was ill-equipped, too parochial by far. Latin defined things; Gaelic, being rooted in everyday experience, could not, depending instead on the empirical school of giving examples instead. These limitations in the language were mirrored by similar types of deficiencies in the level of Irish scholarship, so bemoaned by some of the commentaries previously mentioned.

Because the advent of Latin was not accompanied by legionnaires and military subjugation (the case in Gaul and southern Britain), Gaelic had the opportunity to yield its ground gracefully. One ancient Irish law tract states that "Every speech of historians, poets, and brehon law givers is under the yoke of the men of the white blessed language, that is, the scriptures." But this overstates the case. The Gaels, with the pride of their own insularity to back them up, appropriated Latin and its superficial associations (Rome as the head of the Church, for example) for their own quite wayward purposes.

What type of scholar, then, was Columcille? As a matter of fact, was he a scholar at all? Are we certain he was even literate? And if so, did he exhibit a superior range of abilities than a St. Patrick, who continually lambasted himself "on account of my defect in learning"? These are impossible questions to answer definitively, but certain hypotheses seem more than likely. Columcille was certainly an educated man by Irish standards. The fact that a priest was responsible for his earliest lessons, and additionally that he was a prince as opposed to simple herdsman's son, seem fairly good indicators that the best there was had been placed before him. Aside from the Bible — and again, primarily the Psalms, which Adomnán records Columcille sang "like a terrible peal of thunder" — various Latin grammatical texts by Donatus and Priscian were probably fairly standard in the classroom by c. 525, and their value to the educative process should not be understated. The Irish, after all, were being confronted with a fairly difficult problem: the analysis of a completely alien language presented to them in a format (writing) which many of them had never seen. Grammar was therefore regarded as a manual, the key to unlocking the many levels of meaning, both allegorical and historical, that lay hidden in Scripture. It also allowed the decipherment of words describing artifacts and concepts which at first were well beyond the Celtic purview.

Though a source of current disputation among scholars, it seems more than likely that some classical poetry, pagan and worldly, was also introduced as an additional tool for understanding, with the strict proviso that one's attentions were not to stray unnecessarily from the holy road.

"If you work hard at secular learning," wrote one schoolmaster, "do so for this purpose: whereas the whole or almost the whole text of divine law obeys the rules of grammar, you will only understand easily the most profound and sacred meanings of divine eloquence in so far as you have fully learnt those rules beforehand. But what benefit can there be for orthodox truth in inquiring into the incests of the impure Proserpine, the adventures of the petulant Hermione, the bacchanals of Lupercus, or the parasites of Priapus?" These were remarks Cassian could have authored, and many Church Fathers spared no pains in warning of the perils in plunging too deeply into profane literature. But the Celts refused to listen. Many of the oldest legends say that Columcille was exceedingly well-versed in the contemporary poetry of his society, in fact may well have been a professional *filid*, however tainted that group certainly was with paganisms. In the gray stretches of Irish history between the introduction of Christianity and the final conversion of all the tribes — well over one hundred years of effort — it would not be incongruous to see such a mixture. That Columcille may have been a *filid*, however, is an extreme opinion.

It seems fair to say that Columcille had a more than satisfactory command of Latin, though his use of it may well have been stiff and formal, in keeping with its status in Ireland as a mandarin language known only to the privileged few. The fact that no one spoke Latin in the everyday life of market or court helped to ensure its exclusivity and, even more noteworthy in Celtic terms, the prestige of those who were its master. Again, we face a typically Irish contradiction here. Men like Columcille no doubt enjoyed the status they received as men of learning, yet only by increasing access to their religion that Latin provided could they hope to satisfy Christ's demands that the Word be spread to all nations (which most of the early Irish Saints interpreted in the restrictive sense of their own tribespeople). Columcille grew up, I would suspect, in the shadow of a maxim similar to that of a later monastic rule which said, "If the boys do not study in all seasons, the whole Church will die. For anyone who does not read, three hundred genuflections and three hundred honest blows with a scourge."

His library would certainly have been a limited one. It would have contained the Bible, of course, perhaps a few fragments of secular poetry from the Empire such as Virgil and, more certainly, bountiful selections from the early Patristic writers — "those ripples from the deep sea of the Fathers", as one annalist called them — Jerome, Augustine, and Cassiodorus. Before we are swept out to sea in the sweet raptures of orthodoxy, however, where many an Irish historian has endeavored to show us the way, we should assume that more evilly smelling works by Athanasius, Cassian, Sulpicius Severus, and Pelagius helped round out the meagre collection. Columcille's behavior, and that of his contemporaries, seems to guarantee it.

A TORRENTIAL DOWNPOUR drives me off *Torr an Aba* and into the restored monastery. I note the sequence and times of winter services in the Cathedral and then head off for my farmhouse on the other end of the island. Soaked through and pretty tired, I leave my bedraggled clothing near the kitchen stove and retire for the evening. Other visitors from times past found the accommodations on Iona crude and barely tolerable. Johnson and Boswell slept fully clothed in a barn on hay with their overcoats for pillows. A traveller in 1798 was more unfortunate, for by then an islander had taken it upon himself to open an inn, which in fact was little more than a "wretched hut, with a floor of liquid mire. Rain fell in all night through a hole in the roof, and we had plenty of companions; for besides the light infantry of bed bugs we had several chickens, a tame lamb, two or three pigs, a dog, and some cats, which last went and came at pleasure." Several dollops of whiskey helped them through the night. The worst that I can complain about is the technological bent of my host. Lying in bed I can hear various stereophonic rumblings as he plays a record while simultaneously tuning in a quiz show from God knows where on his Japanese color television set. Waking up several hours later when everyone is asleep, all I am aware of is the steady power of the western winds, shaking this house to its very foundations.

The next morning, I arrive for matins at the Cathedral. I must confess that I was not, at first, really aware of the current denominational status of the monastery, not to the degree that I am now at any rate. But even so I find myself shocked (which is rare for me) at the tomfoolery that I witness within. At the appointed hour an eclectic collection of castoffs from the era of Flower Power saunter to the choir stalls. Clothing is assorted oilskins, handkerchief turbans, mud-stained dungarees, Indian jewelry, batik shawls. So much for the anonymity of monkish attire. A hymn with puerile lyrics is sung to the strains of *Blowing in the Wind*, a juxtaposition that even Bob Dylan might find perplexing. Next a prayer to Our Lord: "We ask thy divine assistance to all those seeking to do good through the arts, dance and theatre." More deadly hymns:

> The astronauts shot into space
> and no one did they see.
> No angel sitting on a cloud
> with a harp upon his knee.
> At once man said there is no God
> and man is all supreme.
> But God was in the spaceship
> for it's all part of his scheme.

There is little drive to any of this proceeding, none of what Evelyn Waugh so aptly characterized as typical of "deep-thinking, pipe-sucking Christians". This is a twilight zone of murky self-indulgence, of just passing the

177

time. I approach a participant afterwards to ask just what sort of religion is practiced here, and "Ecumenical" is his reply. Is that really a religion I ask? "Yes, of course. We're Christian but nonsectarian. We aren't here to make anyone believe anything they don't want to believe."

"That's not religion in my sense of the word," I counter. "Religion is supposed to be the hard road, making people accept something that otherwise, in the plain light of day, they wouldn't. No sensible person would believe half the things religion asks them to, but through faith they do it."

"Whatever you say," is the final remark in this none too profound exchange, as my interlocutor hurries off to safety somewhere else in the compound. I am bemused. This is just the kind of thing one could surely discuss here, in church, but my opponent has fled.

This degeneration, in both thought and practice, is an outgrowth of Iona's more recent history. The Dukes of Argyll, hereditary landlords of Iona, rarely gave the place any attention. Whenever one or another of these grandees visited the place, the locals went wild tidying up the ruins, propping up dilapidated headstones, carting off manure from cloisters and altar sites. As tourism developed, and in large measure after the "discovery" of Staffa by Sir Joseph Banks in 1772,[1] antiquarians of gentlemanly persuasion beseeched the Aryglls to pay some attention to maintenance of the Abbey, now a derelict assemblage of tottering walls and crumbling masonry. Until the Eighth Duke of Argyll put up a few pounds for basic repairs, most conservation (largely cosmetic) had been underwritten by the steamship lines that plied out from Oban to Staffa and Iona. The Eighth Duke, George John Douglas Campbell, aside from being one of Scotland's largest landowners, was also a politician of some reputation, serving various Prime Ministers in lower echelon cabinet positions until 1868 when, as Secretary of State for India, his mulish mismanagement of affairs on the northern border of India contributed to events that eventually resulted in the Second Afghan War ten years later. His most memo-

---

[1] The naturalist Sir Joseph Banks, a veteran of Cook's first voyage of 1768, stopped at Staffa on his return from an expedition to Iceland undertaken in 1772. His reports on the geological phenomena of the island, primarily its spectacular sea caves and bizarre columns of hardened lava, reached a wider reading public through inclusion in Thomas Pennant's travel writings on Scotland. He did not, of course, discover Staffa in the accepted meaning of that word. Gaelic rovers had known of the island for hundreds of years and in fact the name Staffa derives from the Norse *Staphi-ey*, or "island of the pillars," indicating their familiarity with these waters as well during ancient times. The same circumstances apply to the Giant's Causeway in Ulster, part of the same lava eruption as Staffa. It had an ancient pedigree in Celtic tales of the underworld with its heroes and monsters, but it was not deemed "discovered" until an amateur geologist and antiquarian by the name of William Hamilton published his *Letters Concerning the Northern Coast of the County of Antrim* in 1786. These were enough to encourage Thackeray, for example, to visit the place during his Irish tour. Banks went on to a varied and esteemed career as scientist and financier of many exploratory sea voyages. He was, in fact, responsible for William Bligh's appointment to the Bounty, 1787. William Hamilton reaped little enduring fame. He was murdered by land agitators in 1797.

Irish Bishop
Kilmacduagh
County Galway

179

rable act thereafter, in the words of an observer, was to resign the office of Lord Privy seal. Socially, his greatest coup was the marriage of Princess Louise, Victoria's fourth daughter, to his eldest son.

The Duke was not a particularly keen connoisseur of Iona, seeing before him none of "the fire, the freshness, and the comparative simplicity of the old Celtic Church, but the dull and often corrupt monotony of medieval Romanism". Had he ever met Columcille, needless to say, his generous attitude towards the Celts would have evaporated. He was moved at the end of his life to some regard for the place, however, choosing the Abbey for his sepulcher, the monument of which quite impressively monopolizes an entire bay — "I Have Finished My Course" — and deeding the ruins over to the Church of Scotland, which was of course Protestant. Repairs to the Cathedral went along fitfully until the advent of George MacLeod in the 1930s.

MacLeod was a classic character from that long tradition of English, Irish, Welsh and Scottish eccentricity. A clergyman of pacifist and social-ist persuasions, he had resigned the ministry of a prosperous Edinburgh church to assume similar duties at Govan, an industrial slum on the Clyde outside Glasgow that had suffered an astounding unemployment rate of eighty percent during the Great Depression. MacLeod was disgusted at the inability of his religion to make any impress at all on the working people of such impoverished dump-sites, people for whom ecclesiastical decorum and parish hall socials had little relevance. MacLeod developed three objectives: language, community, politics. Clergymen had to learn the language of their constituencies, involve themselves in the central crises and concerns that affected day to day life there, and use the political system for social change. These were idealistic goals that swam marvellously through leftist circles of Cambridge academia, now so radicalized by events in Fascist Spain, Italy, and Germany, but which floundered when trotted out in the alleyways and tenements of Govan. The Iona Community evolved from MacLeod's conviction that an un-bridgeable gap existed between the pulpit on high and the last pew in church.

His concept was to join on the neutral (to him, anyway) plateau of manual labor, the idea being for workmen and ministers to gather together on Iona and, in Christian fellowship, restore the ruins during annual summer visits. The clergy would thus dirty their hands and learn the rudiments of a workman's point of view, and the workmen could see first hand the Church's commitment to sharing their toil. During the winter, all would return to their urban homes and seek to spread what they had learned to friends and colleagues.

The proposal was a hard one for MacLeod to sell. The Church of Scotland, trustee for Iona, was anxious for a restoration but distrustful of MacLeod's political leanings. The general populace saw Popery at work, a new monasticism and the revival of empty ritual. We are not "seeking hopelessly to play at being Franciscans", MacLeod wrote tartly in the press. His final offer to the Church was his services for free and his personal pledge to pay for any work on the site over and above what he could raise from sponsors. In 1939 four ministers, four divinity students, an architect, doctor, and nurse, along with seven unemployed workmen from the Glasgow area — "a slightly dazed company", in MacLeod's words — set up camp on Iona.

During the war years, progress was sporadic and tension among the workers high. They saw themselves, rightly, as societal guinea pigs for the well-meaning clergy who sported about the ruins in their gardening clothes playacting with shovels and wheelbarrows. But the conviction of MacLeod, and his insistent personality, kept the enterprise cluttering along through various ideological crises and the more practical difficulty of producing cash to fund construction. By 1967, when MacLeod abruptly severed connections with the Community, the entire monastic apparatus had been rebuilt: the Cathedral itself finished, the chapels, cloister, refectory, chapter house, Abbot's House, and infirmary restored, and all in superlative taste and to stunning effect. Haphazard summer work shifts evolved into year-long habitation of the site and at times almost continuous building. Lectures, sabbaticals, retreats, conferences — a whole range of intellectual activity — sprouted forth often drawing hundreds of visitors to the Abbey at a single time. Doctrinally, however, the effort to bring the Church into step with twentieth-century urban life produced a watery gruel of the lowest quality. Religion that is dragged into contemporary theatre without any connection to its past (however foolish or superstitious it may seem to us) is an operation too extreme for positive results. A community newsletter that I pick up from my pew says, "Give me the good news in the present tense. What happened nineteen hundred years ago may not have happened at all. How am I to know? Let's live! I long to see the living truth." This is humanistic, certainly ecumenical, but it isn't theology, faith, or dogma. MacLeod sensed this. The Community, in order to establish itself financially, conceded too much, opened the gates too freely and lost its evangelical fervor and purity. It went too far even for the maverick MacLeod who, by the sixties, revealed himself as a conservative man at heart with a deep affection for the establishment's Church of Scotland.

Wandering through the monastery I am struck by its secular tone. It reminds me of a youth hostel or college dormitory, empty for recess, full of old school plaques and supercilious commemorations:

On Friday 8th June 1984, Mrs. Jill Paterson, wife of the Very Reverend John M. K. Paterson, Moderator of the General Assembly of the Church of Scotland, Performed here the ceremony of switching on the Abbey heating system.

In a little gift shop off the cloister I purchase a couple of dish cloths for my mother, with scenes from the Book of Kells imprinted on them. Later on in the day, as I slog through various hermitages once peopled with holy anchorites, I wonder at the propriety of my little presents. Drying off plates with St. Matthew must certainly be a sacrilege, and if not that then at least a mockery to our spiritual laziness. An ancient Martyrology describes the testing of two Irish hermits:

> "We are on a search," says Moling, "on a search for Christ. Awful is that deed which the Jews have done, crucifying Christ."
> "We would spend all our might in saving Him," says Mael-doburchon.
> Moling then goes into the midst of a thornbrake and sets his cowl on a pole in the midst of the brake. "Supposing Christ were the cowl, how wouldst thou rescue him?"
> Mael-doburchon cast his raiment from him, and with his hands he put the brake past him till he reached the cowl, so that it was between his arms. "That is the way I would rescue Christ," says Mael-doburchon; and there were streams of blood out of his fingers.
> "Wondrous!" says Moling.

BY NOONTIME I have wandered all over the northern edge of the island. Many times the mist and drizzle clear off to allow truly immense panoramas of what was once Dál Riata. Climbing the *Dun* I find a sheltered spot and eat my lunch of cheese and stale crackers, the only fare I could find at the village store and appropriately meagre. As St. Columbanus advised, if the stomach is burdened, the mind is confused.

Most Irish histories regard Dál Riata as a kingdom of consequence, yet from a mainstream European point of view the place was a backwater of ignorance and heathenism. As far as Tacitus was concerned, the entire northern reach of Britain "was a land too poor to be worth plundering", so remote that it seemed "another island," inhabited by rabble "who made their best decisions when drunk." As warriors, the Dál Riata were cruel and brave — "I saw an array, they came from Kintyre, and splendidly they bore themselves", in the words of an admiring poet — but after A.D. 642 when Dál Riata suffered a grievous defeat at the hands of the Britons, their king's severed head "gnawed by ravens", they cease to merit the attention of any but the most provincial of historians.

The society from which Columcille sprang was in most respects crude and heavily pagan, not the Christian sanctuary of holiness that legends frequently suggest. The heroic tales so beloved by the people swarmed with grisly variations on battle gore and the taking of heads. In one dispute over who had the right to the meatiest shank of a pig, two warriors from Ulster and Connaught boast their prowess:

> "I swear what my people swear. Since I first took spear and weapons, I have never been a day without having slain a Connaught-

A'Mhachair
Iona
Scotland

man, or a night without plundering, nor have I ever slept without the head of a Connaughtman under my knee."

"It is true," said Cet, "thou art even a better warrior than I. But if Anlúan mac Mágach were in this house he would match thee contest for contest, and it is a shame that he is not in the house to-night."

"But he is," said Conall, taking Anlúan's head out of his belt and throwing it at Cet's chest, so hard that a gush of blood broke over his lips. After that Conall sat down by the pig, and Cet went from it."

It took time for Christian tales to develop more pious variations on these themes of martial glory. Two centuries after Columcille's death, in fact, we still see glee at the fact that St. Ciarán, in a saintly rage, could stab to death his opponents with a holy crozier. Sexual and other bodily matters were likewise treated in earthy fashion. Urinating contests between warrior-like women were commonly depicted and infidelities abound in the literature. King Aillil knows full well that his wife, the voracious Maeve, is sleeping with the warrior Ferdiad (among others) but his reaction is one of amusement. In a speech laden with phallic innuendo he taunts Ferdiad, who has "lost his sword" in the vain attempt to satisfy Maeve. "Why so wild," he asks, "without your weapon,"

> On heights of a certain royal belly?
> In a certain ford was your will
> worked, or your heroism, an empty
> shout to Maeve's oaths; tribes of men
> can bear witness, sucked dry in the
> struggle with giddy women, crawling
> entering battling with great, murky
> deeds under cover, everywhere.

"Now sit down," he commands, "and we will play *fidchell* (a board game). You are very welcome." Seeping into the Christian era, this salacious view of life was at first barely altered. Christian bishops and abbots are depicted swearing oaths in the heathen fashion, cupping their genitals. Saints routinely are born from incestuous unions or as the result of rape, sometimes both: "St. Cummíne, Fiachna begat him in a fit of drunkenness on his own daughter." Through bizarre twists of fate, God himself wreaks sexual havoc. Creda — "good was the woman, constant and pure" — washed her hands outside of church, little knowing that a thief lay hidden in the thorn tree above, so smitten by her beauty that he masturbates, his seed falling to a bed of watercress below which Creda unfortunately picks for supper and eats. "God's miracle caused it" and St. Báithín, "the bright, prolific man", was the result nine months later. The pagan custom of human sacrifice also penetrated early Christian legend.

> To Cormac said Columcille, "Abide here in Durrow."
> "I will not stay for long if you do not leave with me some of your

relics," says Cormac.

"Some of them shall go to thee."

"Thy hand for it," says Cormac. Columcille stretched out his hand. Cormac lopped the little finger off him.

"Bitterly hast thou visited me, O Cormac!" says Columcille.

"Wolves shall eat thee for it." And this was fulfilled.

It took countless generations for Christianity to launder these popular entertainments into a suitably moral context. In the same spirit we should not expect from a Columcille the behavior of a Cassiodorus or Boethius. He is, in fact, a transitional figure who straddles our demands for a picture without blemish.

Columcille operated from the middle ground, assimilating the broadest aspects of pagan belief and practice into a Christian context, though in many cases it seems that his own barbarianism (at least according to saga) was only slightly veneered by a Christian finish. As an example of the former, we have the vast body of voyage literature with which many admirers of Irish storytelling are so familiar. The most famous of these extravagant tales involve St. Brendan the Navigator who allegedly discovered the Bermudian Islands. As improbable as that seems, it is a fact that Scandinavian explorers were stunned to find Irish hermits in the Faroe Islands and even Iceland, hitherto unknown to any of the Viking seadogs. It has been suggested that this incredible impulse on the part of Celtic monks to set out to sea without any viable destination was the direct result of a Christian moral conviction wresting control of a hitherto pagan custom. Punishment for crime in heathen Ireland was customarily quick and summary, no matter the condition or sex of the offender. Clerical intervention is thought by some scholars to have generated an ameliorating influence whereby the lives of women and children in particular were spared or dealt a more humane sentence. Thus the judicial custom of placing individuals in curraghs without sails or oars, towing them out to sea "as far as a white shield will be visible", and leaving their fate to God. It was but a short step for fanatics like Columcille to go the extra step by inviting such a voyage, symbolizing as it would a punishment for their sins, yet exciting in the sense that it gave the Almighty the opportunity to intervene directly in their lives by beaching them wherever He wished, if at all. Columcille, not quite as bold as others, did choose to navigate his course; there are many instances, historically verifiable, of monks who did not. The capriciousness of this behavior is startling, further evidence that Columcille's voyage to Iona was one of hasty penance rather than a preordained missionary enterprise aimed at converting Scotland. The mental ethos of the desert was to stay within, to avoid contact with others. "A monk's function is not to teach, but to lament," as Jerome put it.

An opposite example, where Columcille's barbarism is only slightly affected by his religion, is the very strange tale of his follower Oran. On landing at Iona, Columcille feels the need for a blood sacrifice and asks for a volunteer. Oran says to him, "Take me, I am ready for it," whereupon he is slain and buried in much the same manner as druids, who were known to be selected by chance or rote for sacrifice to the Gods, and willingly endured a cruel death. Columcille opines that "it is well for us that our roots should go under the ground here, to consecrate it."

These extremes of dramatic myth (which, it must be stressed, may or may not have anything to do with the actual Columcille) reflect a more accurate picture of the obstacles Christianity faced here than do the more popularized legends. It was indeed a muddy century, and no single religious cult enjoyed unchallenged authority. As the preface to an old law tract stated, it took representatives from both Christian and pagan traditions to hammer out the eventual accommodation of the new religion to Celtic society, "to stitch together Church and tribe. Three bishops, three kings, and three *filid*, two of whom tied a thread of poetry round the law."

The evolutionary result, not surprisingly, proved a jumble so odd and unappealing to later visitors that it left many of them speechless that Ireland could have, over the years, conjured such a reputation for sanctity and the civilized pursuit of knowledge. As far as one priest was concerned, the Irish were the only people he knew "who stupidly contend against the whole world", little realizing (as he supposedly did) that they had no significance in the wider Christian society of mainland Europe, being mere inhabitants "of those two outermost islands of the ocean".

Whether such prejudiced opinions are really fair should not obscure from us the reality that the Irish were, in fact, all too busy in their relative isolation, and while the various aberrations that marked much of their activity may seem, over centuries, slight and even rather winsome, it would be misleading to gloss over them. I know of no other Catholic nation that has so rigorously praised itself for fidelity to orthodox canon, nor any that has earned the right of self-congratulation in quite such melancholic circumstances − countless generations of extirpation and blood letting. The very struggle to exist, however, has diminished its historical perspective, reducing to a dull blur those idiosyncrasies that initially shaped the tradition so many lives were expended to preserve. "The Irish Church today," wrote the novelist Rose Macaulay in 1953, "bemeaned and deflowered by the bitter centuries of persecution, has had plucked from it the proud flower of its intellect and breeding, reducing it to a devout provincialism." The by-products of fable − Patrick's saga, the saints' legends, the myth of Christian inevitability − are standards to grab hold of in times of trouble, the tip of the iceberg. When a Church goes underground, these are the things most easily preserved.

Proceeding on their own, the Irish had no one looking over their shoulders, no one, in St. Jerome's phrase, "to prune their vines severely when the shoots were too luxuriant". This can certainly be seen in the schoolroom, as the Irish embarked on the mysteries of self-education. Specialists have written fascinating treatises on this very narrow topic, many concentrating on the peculiar gyrations that Latin suffered at the hands of enthusiastic, albeit unbridled, students. Operating in a vacuum with few texts, little guidance and bare familiarity with the medium, it is remarkable the Irish gradually attained a praiseworthy ability to read and write tolerably correct Latin: It was not a free-flowing or conversational language in their hands, but more of a stilted, formal, artificial, rule-bound expression befitting its cloistered environment. Out of class, it grew like a multi-headed Celtic monster into something called Hisperic Latin, a mind-numbing stew of riddle and linguistic fantasy more pleasing to the vain pursuit of intellectual showmanship than a conveyance of information. This odd by-product of Irish educational mores stressed the bizarre: word inventions from ill-digested scraps of Greek and Hebrew, tinkering with accepted grammarian rules for suffixes to deflect or obscure true meaning, substitution of unexpected or abstruse verbiage over an alternative more predictable and appropriate, ostentatious "word-melody" at the expense of simple declaration, confusion just for the sake of it, or the monster devouring its tail. If this sounds like a druidic intrusion to the Christian domain of letters, so it should, since it is a typical contribution of ancient pagan methodology and literary standards of conduct to the new learning. Hisperic Latin, according to several scholars, was the hieroglyphics or "secret language" of the inner circle — in the old days, proprietary to the druids, transferred now to the Christian priesthood. Other than the stripe of the holy men involved, what else had changed? The Irish outlook was charaterized by the same behavioral modes, the same privileges and honors, and the same ingrained respect for wise men. Simple swineherds probably saw nothing at first to distinguish druid from priest.

The famous letter of Aldhelm, a seventh-century abbot of Malmesbury, to a fellow Anglo-Saxon who had just returned from six years of study in Ireland, gives some indication as to the intensity of academic gamesmanship that thrived among the Celts. "The fields of Ireland are rich in learning," Aldhelm notes, but these fellows are uncontrollable and without discipline. He mentions a famous teacher in England "surrounded by a crowd of Irish disciples who grievously badger him, as the truculent boar is hemmed in by a snarling pack of hounds", and tear him "with the tusks of grammar" and pierce him "with the sharp and deep syllogisms of chronography till he casts aside his weapons and hurriedly flees to the recesses of his den."

Grammar, of course, is a set of building blocks, a puzzle to be assembled and disassembled, an engineering science "which protects and controls articulate speech" in the words of one Irish scholar. I think it had the same hypnotic fascination for the Irish that video tapes seem to have held over at least one generation of children in our own times. If we can imagine the picture of a pasty, youthful face drained of healthful color by incessant concentration on a computer screen, we should also be able to see the same thing in fifth-century terms: students playing feverish matches of hide and seek within a language – cryptograms, puzzles, word games, hidden treasure. It became a "nit-picker's" paradise that, when applied to the letter of divine scripture, produced some very curious results where the original intent of a religious passage could be distorted with little or no disquietude, and at times with conscious invention. An episode from the *Life of Adomnán* typifies the prankster's approach. Adomnán and a king are shown disputing a breach of ecclesiastical sanctuary. They both perform ritualistic fasts against one another – Adomnán up to his neck in the frigid waters of the Boyne River – to the extreme point that whichever gives up the fast and loses face will certainly (given the histrionic strictures of saga) die a miserable, wretched death. Each evening the king asks Adomnán, "What will you do tonight, cleric?" Adomnán answers that he will fast "to shorten your life". The king, believing Adomnán would never mislead him, then knows that he too must fast until morning. Adomnán, tiring of this, disguises a common monk in abbot's garb, covering his face with its cowl, and instructs him to tell the king, when asked, that he intends to feast. The king, taken in by the ruse, himself orders a great dinner and breaks the fast unknowingly. The next morning Adomnán, who had spent the night in a river, victoriously condemns the ashen king to "go to hell", a fate which soon befalls him. There is no question in Adomnán's mind (or, to be accurate, that of the monk who invented this story) that the desirable end of deposing an evil king more than justified the devious means to accomplish it. As to the sin of deceit, Adomnán could explain that it was his monk, not himself, who told the falsehood, "for Adomnán deemed it more fitting that a member of his monastic family should lie rather than himself". Logic of this sort, which a distinguished British historian would label as "perverted ingenuity", earned for the Irish their reputation as subtle, though ultimately specious, debaters. They applied this talent to all facets of their training.

Hisperic Latin is a trademark of the ultimate outsider. Ireland, on the periphery, made do with such rudiments of continental learning that filtered through, but the paucity of original source material threw them back to their own devices. Hisperic Latin tells us about boredom, about students having mastered their lessons, pushing on to something further, something risque, daring, imaginative, fun. There was no classical master about to slap them down and make everyone return to their seats.

IONA, NOT UNNATURALLY, physically reinforces this notion of living on the edge, in isolation. This is both a help and a hindrance to coming to grips with just what it was that Columcille and his companions held to be the core of their religious belief. The Reverend John Ryan, an Irish

Jesuit whose distinguished writings on the Celtic Church won him wide scholarly praise, typifies the notion of a Columcille basking in orthodoxy, a pious member of the Universal Catholic Church. This ignores the more graphic reality that there was no Universal Church at that time, certainly nothing comparable, let us say, with the historical position of the Church these past three to four centuries. This is always the danger inherent in viewing the past as we stand rooted in the present. Today we have a Church devoid of heresy or doctrinal variation; we have a hierarchical situation where bishops everywhere barely deviate an inch from dogma delivered by Rome; and we have a pope instantly recognizable by Catholics as diverse as every corner of the world. This was hardly the case in A.D. 575. Columcille knew that a Rome existed. It was the great classical city so beloved by the poets he himself adored, it was the site of martyrdom for Saints Peter and Paul, and the pope himself had his seat there. Columcille no doubt firmly believed that he and that same pope held identical beliefs in harmonious agreement. If anyone had told him otherwise he would have exploded in anger. "No one of us has been a heretic," as St. Columbanus wrote to Gregory the Great, "no one a Jew, no one a schismatic."

But in fact, as "a dweller at the ends of the earth", Columcille had gone his own way without ever realizing it. No matter that a Rome could be imagined far to the south, Columcille would have been hard pressed to name the man who sat in St. Peter's Chair. No matter the Roman legends of glory and munificence that probably trickled through to Columcille's hearing. How was he to know that Rome was a jungle of fallen masonry and dilapidated ruin, the pope beleaguered by marauding intruders and doctrinal deviations so varied as to defy categorization. And the pope, whoever he might have been, knew nothing of Ireland. He did not make it a habit to send proclamations, reports, encyclicals, or statements of faith along to his dear son in Christ, the Abbot of Iona. He had never heard of the man. He was too busy trying to stockpile enough corn and grain in his city to avoid famine. Whatever pronouncements he might choose to make, be they doctrinal, financial, organizational, or devotional, hardly crossed the Alps. What arrived here in Iona were remnants, the oddities of information, rumor, superstition, and gossip that were hardy enough, or interesting enough, to make it this far. The Irish, given their background, welcomed what they received, however jangling or perverse it might seem to be. They had the exasperating ability to reconcile polarities of thought or behavior into a harmonious single unit that would strike us today as absurd. St. Scuithín "of the sweet stories", for example, "loved damsels beautiful and white bosomed", but he loved his virginity as well. St. Crónán of Roscrea pursued the hermit's life of solitary contemplation, yet was famed for his hospitality and love of company, miraculously turning meagre supplies of beer and butter into a drunken feast for one hundred and twenty guests — "the angels of God will say our prayers tonight", he says in a stupor. Irish monks, in ignorance of Christ's most basic message that brother love brother, not only joined in the bloody feuds of everyday Celtic life, but often initiated them. "Nobles of Munster," said one disgusted warrior, "fly from this abominable fray and leave it between the clergy themselves who could not be quiet without coming to battle." As late as the twelfth century foreign dignitaries could behold in astonishment the arrival for Mass of a Celtic abbot armed with sword and spear, followed by retainers similarly equipped. The Irish saw nothing untoward in any of this. In the words of one historian, "they expected diversity rather than uniformity", having the intuitive ability to reconcile contradiction.

Columcille believed himself totally orthodox. This conviction was buttressed by the absence of anybody foreign who might have said otherwise. Columcille stood in a societal vacuum where only his own traditions had any leverage. Those few from beyond his sphere who managed to infiltrate this shell therefore took on exaggerated influence.

He had before him the picture of Jesus Christ as portrayed in Scripture. This in many ways is where confusion can begin. The patriotic and deeply religious depictions of Columcille would stress the similarities here between Christ and this most popular Irish Saint: Columcille in his curragh, with twelve disciples in imitation of the twelve apostles, landing on Iona barefoot and in simple garb, staff in hand, prepared to preach to the multitudes. Visually, the similarities may well have been there, but that's about it. The only trait that Columcille and the historical Jesus may well have shared was their conviction to stay among their own. I tend to believe that Christ's original instruction to his disciples was that they should confine themselves to teaching the Jews. Columcille had no intention of reaching out either, following instead the advice of the desert fathers "to be an example, not a lawgiver". The Celts had a lively sense of hatred, they had no interest in saving those whom they detested, and it probably never occurred to them to try. The stunning achievement of the Irish, about which even British historians are united in their praise, was the conversion of Anglo-Saxon barbarians in what we call today Northumbria, the northernmost Germanic kingdom that bordered the highland territory of Dál Riata and the Picts. It is a fact, however, that the Irish never initiated that effort. They were asked to come.

The actual Christ who lived, preached, met his death on the cross, had no effect on Columcille. The disfigured portrait in the Bible did, and it segued comfortably into the exalted and traditional reaches of Celtic saga lore, with Jesus transformed into a Christian Cú Chulainn, fairies or spirits (both good and bad) turned into angels and devils depending on their penchant for good or evil, druidic magicians into saints with formidably dizzying powers — Christianity, in Carlyle's phrase, evolved to a higher form of hero worship. More subtle or considered analysis of what Christ stood for or what his life meant in day to day terms simply could not stand the onrush of enthusiastic adoration. With little else to choose from, the Irish absorbed with equal abandon the teachings of their own master, the heretic Pelagius, and the stern counsels of the desert. "It is passion," as Gibbon remarked, "that leads man to God."

These are matters of considerable debate among scholars who attempt to define with some degree of exactitude the varying impact of patristic writings on the direction of Irish monasticism. The clues are, as usual, slim, though certainly provocative. Many experts distrust the notion of linking various aspects or traits of a career with an assumption that it followed the course it did under the direct stimulation of a certain piece of writing or a specific school of thought. In Irish terms, however, we can often do little else. It seems to me that Columcille, and others like him, were almost vacuum cleaners for whatever came to them from far across the seas. They saw the command given Abraham, "Leave your country, your kinfolk and your father's house, for the land which I will show you." They saw that order obeyed by St. Antony, St. Martin, John Cassian, Pelagius and they, in turn, did the exact same thing.

THE *LIFE OF St. Martin* by Sulpicius Severus is thought to have circulated in Ireland as early as c. 450. From reading Martin the Irish had reinforced their own affection for soldierly fortitude and a disdain for the tunnel vision to which bishops and other administrators so narrowly adhered. Bishops wanted order, subservience, a loyal work force — all antithetical to individual action. For the same reasons was Cassian studied, for he had seen no benefit in a worldly Church. Ireland is truly a child of Cassian, the man who synthesized what he saw in the Egyptian desert and laid it out as a model pathway for those with the strength to pursue virtue. His writings were certainly known to the Irish by A.D. 575, and a specific reference in the *Amrá* may include remnants of an old tradition regarding Columcille, that while on Iona he "read books that Cassian loved". The story of St. Antony, referred to by Augustine in his *Confessions*, would have been known at the very least in story form. All of these traditions coalesced to legitimatize the obsession of the Irish "to seek a solitude in the pathless Ocean."

Interestingly enough, in the single Celtic soul there coexisted the two extremes of the desert, Greek vs. Copt. In Irish behavior we see the blind faith and simplicity of childlike worship that so characterized the vision of Antony and the Copts, while the desire to excel in studies and to pursue intellectual goals, so markedly Greek, is also evident, though without the tension so destructive in the Egypt of Cassian's young manhood.

And now, to Pelagius. The long and open affection for this singular individual on the part of the Celts is not open to question. Augustine's loathing, the humiliation of appearances before ecclesiastical tribunes, St. Jerome's vituperative attacks, the book burnings and exiles and sentences of anathema — none of this shook their bedrock respect for the

St. Martin, Abbey of Ligugé
Les Pays de l'Ouest, France

theories he espoused. While claiming orthodoxy from every convenient hilltop, the Celts nevertheless did not come out from under his shade until centuries later. How could this be so?

There are several answers, the first one simple vanity. No Celt had ever seen or met Christ in the Holy Land. No Celt had numbered as one of the Apostles, not one had fled to the desert with Antony, nor had any Celt worn the papal tiara. The only Celt to have ever, in over five centuries of Christian life, been singled out for attention by anyone among the intelligentsia of the Empire was Pelagius. Only he had made the great Augustine sit up straight in his chair to take notice; only he had commanded the attention of an otherwise self-absorbed St. Jerome; only he had caused popes and bishops to tremble. This was all perversely appealing to the Celtic temperament, and even as late as 731 the Venerable Bede could chastise the Pelagian Irish for remaining hidden under "the dark cloud of their ignorance"

More important, the doctrine made sense for them. Given the Celtic penchant for doing whatever pleased them best, the latitude for action within Pelagian notions of free will justified the wildest adventures and satisfied their longing for glory. The saints who fled to ocean sanctuaries in search of Cassian's "stillness of divine contemplation" did so looking for combat. Classical reporters routinely noted how often the Celts plunged into battle without clothing or body armor of any sort. So too did the hermits. They had no need for Augustine's grace; they were fully fit and able to deal with whatever Satanic siege machine might turn up in their desert hideaways. Nearly all the saga literature of the saints' lives display this violent belief in self. Individual hermits "rout the enemy, the devil flees and his host of allies with him", they become "monarchs of their places". When angels assist them, they do so in menial fashion, helping build walls, dig wells, plough fields, even entertain the saints when diversion or rest periods are required. But when it is time for action, the saints have all the power they need to vanquish Satan alone.

Developing this line of thought in their uncontrolled, disordered world, the Irish naturally went to extremes, a development St. Augustine most likely could have predicted. The Celts saw no terror in meeting God or conversing with Him. In their Pelagian excess, in fact, they could take a very hectoring, even demanding tone with the Almighty. Adomnán records that Columcille went to heaven once a week to negotiate with God. He was not overwhelmed, simply doing business along the usual lines. When ordered to crown Aedán the Wily as king of Dál Riata, in fact, he bluntly refused, preferring another. An angel "suddenly stretched out his hand and struck the holy man with a scourge, the livid scar from which remained on his side all the days of his life", saying "If you refuse this command I will strike you again." It took three visitations, with further corporal encouragement, before Columcille obeyed. "Take virginity around thee," another angel instructed him later. "I will not take it until a reward be given me," he replies. "What reward dost thou demand?" says the angel. "I declare it is not one reward but four that I must have!" Irish sagas show many instances where God struggled to control his saints. St. Patrick was waving his hands and screaming incantations so violently on one occasion (the murder of his charioteer) that God had to beg him to calm down. Patrick may well have noticed an indulgent streak in his deity from that moment on, for the famous *Tripartite Life*, an ancient collection of Patrician saga lore that embodies most of the legends we are so familiar with today, contains the interesting story of Patrick's fast on God to obtain a favor dear to his heart, wherein the devastating loss of face was not endured by the saint, as God caved in to his Apostle's demands. Through extreme and egotistical behavior, the Irish communicated with God on an equal footing. They did not, as Alfred North Whitehead observed, hold God in terror as "the enemy you conciliate", but rather subdued Him into being "the companion whom you imitate".

The venerable Book of Armagh, compiled in the early 800s and one of the holiest manuscript collections of ancient Ireland, is really a barometer of Celtic belief. It contains the writings of Patrick and biographical matter by various monks seeking to develop his cult; the *Life of St. Martin* by Sulpicius Severus, the influence of which has been suggested; the Gospels, which of course contain the Christian saga; various miscellaneous biblical tracts such as the Apocalypse; and lastly the Pauline Epistles. These last entries, most significantly, are largely prefaced with commentaries by the heretic himself, Pelagius. He was read and studied exclusively by the Irish until at least the year 900.

The Celts, of course, could explain all this. They were notorious for their ability to weasel a way out of any difficulty no matter how abstruse. A fine example of Irish logic can by found in Manus O'Donnell. A saint by the name of Cruimtheir Fraech excoriates Columcille over the slaughter of *Cúl Dreimne*.

> "It is not I who am to blame," replied Columcille "but the wrong judgment of the King against me."
> "It were more easy for a cleric to submit to a wrong judgment than to set about defending himself," said Cruimtheir.
> "When a man's wrath is up and he is sore tried, he cannot submit," said Columcille.
> "It is right to stifle wrath," said Cruimtheir, "lest it make matter for regret."
> "Though a man do much ill through anger," said Columcille, "yet will God pardon him therefore if he do penance."
> "It were better to shun evil than to seek forgiveness therefor."
> "Knowest thou not, O Cruimtheir Fraech," said Columcille, "that God and the folk of Heaven have more joy for a sinner that returneth to them with repentance, than for one that doeth no sin and remaineth continually in a state of virtue? For it is the wont of us mortals to have more welcome for those that are dear to us and

that have long been absent, than for those that are ever with us. And note thou well that in the world there is no one that shall sooner reach Heaven than the sinner that repenteth."

"If it be so," said Cruimtheir, "may God make us good men both together."

"Amen," said Columcille.

F OR THE NEXT three days I tramp around Iona, to the amusement of the farmer's wife who is gradually increasing my breakfast ration. "I can't get over you people," she remarks. "You all have a look on your faces like you've entered heaven or something. It's only a wee barren island where no one really wants to live." On a rainy morning she fills me in on what it is like here. Their croft is about twenty acres in size, seven of which are arable and planted with hay and potatoes. Behind their place, down towards *A'Mhachair*, is common moorland for everyone's stock. They have fifty sheep, four head of cattle, two milk cows. Without summer guests and subsidies from the British Government and E.E.C., they could not pay their bills or support themselves at anywhere near the poverty line, despite the fact that their rent has not been "reviewed" or raised since 1939. "How they manage on some of the outer islands where tourists seldom go is quite beyond me." Iona right now is fully crofted and fully stocked, in large part because three or four older retirees from the armed forces have recently come here to settle. Even so the arrangement is profitable for neither crofter nor landlord.

At one time, between the World Wars, there were sixty children in the school. Now there are twelve, though the figure has been as low as five. Young couples do not see a future as Hebridean farmers. Personally, she likes her life on Iona, though the monotony of long winters can be burdensome. Her husband is a local whom she met while waitressing one summer at the Columba Hotel near the Abbey. They have two small children. Neither of them would stay if the island lacked essential amenities such as running water and electricity. They are not homesteaders, "I'd go crazy without my television", she says. Nor do they ever go to church. "No one here does. The people at the Abbey have nothing to do with us and vice versa. They could be from another planet. From the looks of them, some are."

"What about the wind?" I ask her. "Do you ever get used to it?"

"I heard a story once where a farmer across the channel found a hen that had been blown across from Iona. That's about a mile, you know. In the old days, when the cottages were thatched, they had to be tied down with ropes and weights. One time my husband didn't leave the tractor in gear. It was blown fifty yards straight down the lane one night. I live with it, I'm used to it, but it can be very scary at times."

My last afternoon here I walk past the Abbey to the northern shore and a little eminence known as the Hill of the Seat. It was here, as an old man, that Columcille liked to sit on fine afternoons, taking in the view across the Strait of Storm.

T HE YEAR OF Columcille's death, A.D. 597, was also marked by the return of Rome to British shores, though I hasten to add the homecoming proved inconsequential in martial terms: no legionnaires with drums beating or banners flying imperiously in the air, only a paltry collection of Italian monks who had been brooding for weeks on the blood bath that lay waiting for them on the beaches of Kent in southern England. Given the character of their Anglo-Saxon hosts, such premonitions were probably justified.

Several rather amorphous Germanic kingdoms, set up along the usual lines of tribal configurations and the relative strengths of competing warlords, had grown up in the lowland plains of southern and central England, lapping as far north as the Scottish highlands where the Picts and Celts of Dál Riata contested their advance. Why Pope Gregory the Great, enveloped in monumental difficulties of his own back in Italy, chose to send a little band of twenty-five monks on the grandiose mission of re-converting Great Britain is a question much debated by historians. Cynics point out that Gregory was a miracle monger of the very worst sort, a man who believed in prayer as a form of supernatural intervention whereby floods of angels could descend from heaven to assist in any matter so holy as the spiritual reconquest of England. It is certainly true he gave his monks little else in support which is one reason, perhaps, why they balked in France refusing to proceed and sending their abbot, Augustine, back to Rome pleading release from this "idea of going to a barbarous, fierce, and pagan nation, of whose very language they were ignorant." Gregory declined to do this and the party continued. They were fortunate in landing among the more civilized of the Anglo-Saxon kingdoms, that of Kent, whose king had married a Christian some years before.

Two rather astonishing gaps in knowledge on the part of both Gregory and Augustine will help confirm the picture I have attempted to convey of a Church universal only in its ignorance. Gregory was somewhat put out that Augustine did not proceed to London to establish his see, settling instead in Canterbury. Pouring over old documents and maps in Rome, he had assumed that London still retained its dignity as a capital city, whereas nothing further from the truth could there have been, as the example of Rome itself might have suggested to anyone with a glimmer of imagination. And neither cleric had any idea that a Christian Church, descended from St. Patrick, even existed in Britain. Augustine, in fact, by attaching himself to the pagan court of King Ethelbert, procured its bitter enmity instead. When he learned that British Celts tucked away in Wales and Cornwall still followed the Christian way, he treated them as wayward and ignorant children. Under the flag of Ethelbert, a conference was arranged between the two parties (Bede states that Augustine "summoned" them to attend) which did not reach a happy conclusion. Augustine, utterly uninformed as to the ancient lineage of the insular Church, demanded recognition as archbishop with control of their affairs, and an end to provincial customs. He also insisted they join with him in seeking to convert the Saxons, hated enemies who had despoiled them of ancestral lands. The Britons requested time to reflect, though their resentment towards Augustine, whom they considered an Italian parvenu, is apparent in Bede's recounting of the episode. They consulted, in typically Celtic fashion, not with abbots, kings, warriors, bishops, or famous teachers, whose advice they could rely upon in formulating a response, but with a penniless holy hermit dressed in rags, living in a remote and forbidding wasteland.

> They inquired of him whether they should abandon their own traditions at Augustine's demands. He answered: "If he is a man of God, follow him." "But how can we be sure of this?" they asked. "The Lord says, 'Take my yoke upon you and learn of Me, for I am meek and lowly in heart,'" he replied. "Therefore if Augustine is meek and lowly in heart, it shows that he bears the yoke of Christ himself, and offers it to you. But if he is haughty and unbending, then he is not of God, and we should not listen to him." Then they asked, "But how can we know even this?" "Arrange that he and his followers arrive first at the place appointed for the conference," answered the hermit. "If he rises courteously as you approach, rest assured that he is the servant of Christ and do as he asks. But if he ignores you and does not rise, then, since you are in the majority, do not comply with his demands."

Augustine, of course, remained seated.

This was but the first angry exchange between the Celtic Church and the Roman mission begun by Gregory and Augustine. Of the Irish Church, naturally, the Italians knew even less than of the British. Iona had hardly (if ever) been heard of in Canterbury — to say nothing of faraway Rome — nor any other of the Irish *paruchia*. The Roman attitude was one of arrogance and suspicion. Augustine, for example, cursed the Celtic British and prophesied their destruction. Bede comments that a later battle, which saw the Saxons slaughter several hundred unarmed monks from the Welsh monastery of Bangor, was an appropriate punishment for the Celtic sins of obstinacy and pride.

THE IRISH MONK Columbanus, about whose life much is known (at least the last twenty or so years of it), is a figure we should contrast against those of Augustine and even Gregory. It would not, of course, be fitting to denigrate the efforts, nor indeed the courage, which marked Augustine's mission in Kent. Much can be made of the timorous foreboding of his group as they dawdled in France looking for some way to evade their instructions, but the fact remains they did cross the Channel and, in the face of inauspicious portents, succeeded in planting what eventually became a triumphant enterprise. Augustine himself, however, does not present an appealing figure. Though given substantial leeway in the conduct of his affairs by Gregory, he often appears hesitant, confused and unimaginative. Gregory sent him several letters full of pragmatic advice which at times seem to reflect exasperation with the dullness of his missionary. Crying for the use of common sense, he chides Augustine to adapt himself to the conditions he has found. "Correct some things strictly, and allow others out of leniency," he writes, and if miracles are to be employed, "clearly understand your own character; fear lest the frail mind becomes proud because of these wonderful events."

Gregory projects the more substantial personality, but also one that is typical of the age. A fervent believer in monasticism he had dispersed the fortune accumulated by his father, a Roman senator, and endowed seven ecclesiastical communities with the proceeds. He himself entered one of these, only to be dragged unwillingly by various popes into secular affairs, one of whom sent him to Byzantium for six years as ambassador. It is revealing of Gregory that he refused to learn Greek during his stay in the East. Never an innovative or daring scholar, he saw only temptation in the ancient classical language, a satanic medium cunningly equipped to lure the unwitting into heresy or worse. He is truly representative of the lackluster approach to learning that commentators bemoan as a hallmark of monastic scholasticism during the Dark Ages —incredulous fascination with the miraculous, complete and solitary attention to patristic writings above all others, abhorrence of anything pagan in literature.

He was, however, a man of extraordinary energy. Although he was pope for only thirteen years, we have records of over eight hundred letters from his pen, as he struggled with adversities so diverse that a lesser figure would have broken under the strain. Rome itself, over which Gregory, for all practical purposes, was ruler, threatened to slide over the edge into anarchy and starvation with a regularity that was depressing. Yet another heathen menace took up the game of periodic devastation, this time a collection of tribes known as the Lombards, and it took all of Gregory's skills to buy them off. The Eastern Empire had long since abandoned the notion of Rome as the capital, not even according it the dignity of an Imperial representative, who was sent instead to Ravenna. Since 476, in fact, the office of Emperor had stood vacant. Looking all about him, no wonder that Gregory could write, "My harp is tuned to mourning."

In the midst of this chaos, however, Gregory had the time and imagination to run the papal estates, direct the missionary enterprise to England, assume the civil responsibilities for other Italian cities and towns that lesser men could not handle, managed to write prolific biblical commentaries and indulged an interest for liturgical development along with the arrangements of religious music that now broadly carry his name.

The curious contradiction within this man was the blind detestation of heresy and paganism mingled with a streak of insistent practicality. Over and over he stressed to Augustine that he use restraint when dealing with the heathens, that he exercise give-and-take and not prove overly dogmatic with local custom. "We have been giving careful thought to the affairs of the English," he wrote in 601,

> and have come to the conclusion that the temples of the idols among that people should on no account be destroyed. The idols are to be destroyed, but the temples themselves are to be aspersed with holy water, altars set up in them, and relics deposited there. For if these temples are well-built, they must be purified from the worship of demons and dedicated to the service of the true God. In this way, we hope that the people, seeing that their temples are not destroyed, may abandon their error and, flocking more readily to their accustomed resorts, may come to know and adore the true God.

This is not the course of action a man such as Columbanus would have followed.

Columbanus was born for trouble. With his arrival in France c. 590, after years of study at the Irish monastery of Bangor and evidently some instruction at the feet of holy hermits, he too heard the calling to depart from Erin. Like Columcille he did not go as a preacher or missionary. Though settling near the court of a Frankish king, he at first evinced no interest in attracting pupils or any secular patronage. Inevitably his reputation, and that of his followers, for leading just and holy lives, began to spread and the people came to him — not just farmers or serfs or common herdsmen, but men of the court, noble women and even a monarch or two. Columbanus, on the edge of frontier life, refused any accommodation with pagan worship or behavior. He was like Christ in the Temple, scattering the moneylenders with curse and scourge. Columbanus put heathen sanctuaries to the torch. He singed immoral, ungodly behavior, with fierce reprobabion, no matter the social standing of the sinner. He was not a man to be trifled with.

The conditions into which he wandered were appalling, and justly famous are the chronicles of Gregory, Bishop of Tours, who catalogued the at times unbelievable behavior of the Franks, a Germanic tribe that under the leadership of Clovis had subjugated most of the old Roman province of Gaul by the early fifth century. The dynasty established by this most ferocious chieftain has been called Merovingian, after the semi-legendary king of that name, Merovaeus, from whom they claimed their lineage, and his career of depredation was, in Gregory's eyes, only slightly superior to that of other barbarians in that he at least allowed himself to be baptized. This was an event of glorious importance to the bishop, himself a member of the old Gallo-Roman aristocracy, even

St. Columbanus
Abbey of Luxeuil
Vosges
France

though he was painfully aware that all standards from the great days of the classical past had eroded appreciably. Clovis had not been an easy convert. His wife, a Christian, had begged her husband to abandon heathen rituals but her credibility vanished when their first child died within minutes of his baptism. "A great many things keep happening," as Gregory noted, "some of them good, some of them bad." Typically, Clovis could only be impressed by some drastic happenstance on the battlefield. During one of his innumerable combats, with the course of affairs turning against him, he pledged fidelity to Christ should victory be achieved. Providence intervened and Clovis kept his promise, which Gregory describes in language as grandiose as the Emperor Constantine's conversion two hundred years before, which in terms of the later destiny of Western Europe can probably be seen in hindsight as a not inappropriate comparison. Clovis and his successors, unlike many other tribes, did not adopt one or another of the many heretical sects then popular – most notably, Arianism – and the evolution of his descendants, however disjointed the journey, into what later became the Carolingian dynasty that produced Pepin le Bref, his son Charlemagne and eventually the Holy Roman Empire, ensured the triumph of orthodoxy and the Papacy. In the end, however, as Gregory only too regretfully had to concede, Clovis remained a barbarian at heart, regularly shattering the skulls of both enemies and friends alike with his double-handed battle-ax.

A short glimpse of the domestic difficulties of King Chilperic, a grandson of Clovis, and the solutions he devised to cure them, will suffice to explain the terror of the times. Chilperic was a contemporary of Gregory's. It is doubtful whether Gregory could speak the Germanic vernacular of the Frankish court, but through intermediaries and translators he frequently negotiated, consulted, begged and cajoled these warriors on all manner of business, both political and religious, in his role as bishop. He was therefore an eyewitness to much that horrified him. Chilperic had several wives, a not unusual circumstance of the times, and these of course busily vied for his attentions and pressed for the advancement of their respective children. We know the names of three consorts, the most formidable of whom was Fredegund. Her jealousy of Audovera, Chilperic's first wife, resulted in convoluted plotting for the deaths of all the sons this woman had borne the king. One conveniently dies in battle. The second, after picaresque adventures beyond description, is surrounded in a country manor and, fearing capture, orders his servant to kill him. This servile wretch is then rewarded by having his hands, feet, ears and nose cut off, followed by tortures Gregory does not choose to describe, and is finally "despatched in the most revolting fashion". The last son, Clovis, is sent to Berny where a plague is raging, in the hopes he will contract the disease and die. He does not, and Fredegund then inflates some childlike boastings by the boy into a conspiracy. She seizes the girl he loves, ties her to a stake in front of his lodgings and orders thugs to beat her. The girl's mother is tortured and burned alive. Chilperic, seeking to appease Fredegund, arrests his son, strips him of all his clothing and hands him over to her care. He is stabbed to death and Audovera is "murdered in the most cruel fashion". The last of Audovera's children, a daughter, is locked away in a nunnery and her property seized by Fredegund.

Chilperic's third wife, Galswinth, "he loved very dearly, for she had brought a large dowry with her." But Galswinth, unfortunately for her, grew envious of Fredegund, who returned the enmity. "She never stopped complaining to the King about the insults which she had to endure. Chilperic did his best to pacify her with smooth excuses" but in the end he tired of all the fuss, and ordered one of his servants to garrote her in his bed. Chilperic did not live long enough to dispose of Fredegund. "One day when he returned from the chase just as twilight was falling," Gregory writes,

> he was alighting from his horse with one hand on the shoulder of a servant, when a man stepped forward, struck him with a knife under the armpit and then stabbed him a second time in the stomach. Blood immediately streamed both from his mouth and through the gaping wound, and that was the end of this wicked man.

Queen Fredegund fled to the cathedral in Paris for sanctuary, "remaining all alone".

Her later career as Queen Dowager is a long and gruesome calendar of misdeeds, sandwiched between illicit affairs and pregnancies. She orders a priest to assassinate her stepson's wife, and murders him when he fails; she solicits the killing of a lover who rebuffs her, and sends two clerics to stab her nephew; after arguments with metropolitan bishops, she arranges for one to be stabbed and the other poisoned, both deaths she personally observes; twelve assassins are put on the road towards a rival court to do away with its king, and three Franks are routinely beheaded at her dinner table, seated one beside the other, "with one blow. Everyone then went home." In a final burst of vindictive behavior she attempts to kill her daughter, Rigunth, who

> would often insult her mother to her face, and they frequently exchanged slaps and punches. "Why do you hate me so, daughter?" Fredegund asked her one day. "You can take all your father's things which are still in my possession, and do what you like with them." She led the way into a strongroom and opened a chest which was full of jewels and precious ornaments. For a long time she kept taking out one thing after another, and handing them to her daughter, who stood beside her. Then she suddenly said: "I'm tired of doing this. Put your hand in and take whatever you find." Rigunth was stretching her arm into the chest to take out some more things when her mother suddenly seized the lid and slammed it down on her neck. She leaned on it with all her might and the

edge of the chest pressed so hard against the girl's throat that her eyes were soon standing out of her head. One of the servant girls who was in the room screamed at the top of her voice: "Quick! Quick! Mistress is being choked to death by her mother!" The attendants who had been waiting outside for them to emerge burst into the strong-room, rescued the princess from almost certain death and dragged her out of doors. The quarrels between the two were even more frequent after this. There were never-ending outbursts of temper and even fisticuffs. The main cause was Rigunth's habit of sleeping with all and sundry.

No wonder the German historian Heinrich Zimmer could label the Merovingians as "degenerate".

B Y THE YEAR 590, when Columbanus arrived in Gaul with twelve disciples, the territorial dominions of the Franks had been divided in three, with his earliest monastery, Annegray, situated in the Burgundian kingdom. Many commentators have traditionally seen in Columbanus, and the many Irish monks who followed after him, the salvation of European classical culture. In comparison with a Gregory of Tours, for instance, a product of the highest level of culture that Gaul could produce at this time, Columbanus must have seemed a character from the *Aeneid*, more familiar and conversant with Roman educative roots than they, the indigenous population were. Whereas Gregory quite rightly denigrated his own literary abilities — "My Latin may be provincial", he says — Columbanus took pride in the skill and emotive power clearly evident in the many writings he produced.

These, of course, have been scrutinized with almost microscopic intensity by scholars and linguists who attempt, with varying levels of success, to diagnose the intellectual capacity of the author. Their conclusions, some of them bitterly contested, interest us on two counts. On the one hand we seek to discover the level of skill and sophistication with which his native education endowed him; on the other, and by extension, we would wish to calculate the type and quality of learning that any monastery founded by him might reasonably have been expected to promote and preserve. Columbanus, after all, is a crucial test, the first of the patristic figures from the early Celtic Church to have left behind a body of work that we can run our fingers through and argue over. Unlike a Columcille or a Finnian, a Ciarán or a Brendan — all praised to the sky in saga lore as unrivalled scholars ("Columcille learned Greek grammar", as one claimed without proof) — Columbanus is present for inspection, and thus a generic Irish tradition that verges sometimes on braggadocio leaves itself open to the perils of exposure. The question of his scholarship is not an idle one: over seventy monastic foundations are said to have emanated from the three communities of Columbanus — Annegray, Luxeuil, and Fontaines, all within a twenty-mile radius in the mountains and forests of the Vosges in Alsace — a ripple effect of extraordinary breadth that unfolded over centuries until dissolution during the years of revolution in the seventeenth and eighteenth centuries. If Columbanus, the seminal figure, was a classicist of the first order, as some legends have claimed, one could expect his followers to treasure the tradition as he had, with far reaching effect, as European culture reconstructed itself after the collapse of Empire. If instead he was a buffoon or a character of limited breadth and abilities, then clearly the Irish incursion to the old Gaulish province has been seriously inflated, along with boasts for the old Ireland of Saints and Scholars. The verdicts vary, as should not be surprising.

This is a great deal of pressure to exert on a single individual. When last I looked we had been talking about Columcille, here on Iona. But Adomnán tells us nothing about him in a personal sense, and so we turn to his contemporary in Gaul, Columbanus. He is the one thin reed we can cling to, and only because ten letters (six prose works, four in verse), a rule, a penitential, four sermons, and some odd bits of poetry (one rather well known, a rowing song for boatmen that Columbanus composed as he moved up the Rhine into Switzerland after expulsion from the Vosges) have somehow escaped the tumultuous and, for want of understatement, destructive tendencies inherent in the European story. So much has been generalized from these lean literary remnants, so many extravagant claims made for hundreds, indeed thousands, of nameless Irish monks and *peregrini*. No doctor performing an autopsy has ever undertaken dissections more abstruse and convoluted than those indulged by scholars over sentences, phrases, even single words that Columbanus produced from his various cells and asylums. This shows to some degree how precious the few bits of evidence we have can truly be, and also illustrates the ingenuity that many specialists can bring to their trade. But the end result, really, is that we take a great leap into the unknown when we speculate too freely on the few bones we find scattered about. As I said earlier in this book, the story of history is not a smooth one.

Were the Irish intellectual paragons? Did they save the culture of the old Empire from ashes and tumult? Were they responsible for the salvation of Europe? Let us look at the extremes of opinion. The first can be labelled the Saints and Scholars approach, or Pass the Torch. Within the context of a trial, with Columbanus in the witness box, this body of analysis takes a very broad and generous approach to the writings we have before us as primary exhibits. His literary output, and especially the poems, reveal a meager list of influences if compared, let us say, to the contents of that great library in Alexandria that we saw earlier in this narrative. Even Gibbon, who generally practiced restraint, saw a library on Iona that was more heavily stocked with works of Latin, Greek, and Hebrew authors than was possible. But even so, Columbanus seems reasonably well educated, more versed in classical lineage than most

Cloisters
Abbey of Luxeuil
Vosges
France

205

people enrolled today in our colleges and universities. In the ten letters that we can ascribe to his pen (surely but a remnant of a far greater output) what do we see? An extensive and impressive knowledge of scripture and patristic writers, which hardly surprises us; familiarity with contemporary authors such as Gildas the Briton and Gregory the Great; and unabashed delight in, and use of, Ovid, Virgil, Horace, Prudentius, and Juvenal, with scattered references to Persius, Lucan, Juvencus, and Statius among others. This is all presented in perfectly respectable Latin that at times glistens with word play and inventive cheerfulness — what Columbanus called "our frivolities", described by one linguistic scholar as his occasional "purple patch".

The use of Horace in particular stands out, a poet whose work is quoted by no other writer of this period, allowing us the conclusion that he was studied, and thus preserved, only in Ireland, and that through Columbanus and other Celtic masters the work of this illustrious poet from the first century before Christ did not simply disappear, as Gregory of Tours fumbled with his syntax, but rather was exclusively nurtured and loved by this strange band of wanderers far from the Roman orbit. As Irish monks on pilgrimage began, as did Columbanus, to migrate eastwards in the late 500s and early 600s, they brought their love of the old classics with them (as well as the occasional manuscript), in effect passing the lighted torch of learning back again to Europe whence it had originally come, bringing the process round full cycle.

The opposing viewpoint accepts the accolade of Saint but debunks the Scholar, to devastating effect, I think, when it casts aspersions on the authenticity of the poems attributed to Columbanus, within which the meatiest use of classical poetry (in particular that of Horace) is to be found. In his prose work, moreover, these scholars conclude that classical allusions there were simply the "common coin" of the times, easily gleaned from the patristic writings of St. Augustine and St. Jerome, which the Irish clearly possessed, cherished, and studied. Even harsher judgments tend to deprecate the very root of the Scholastic legend, the proficiency exhibited by Celtic writers in Latin, suggesting that as self-taught novices they had produced, after one hundred years of effort, a hothouse aberration — forced and artificial — that could hardly be sustained outside the classroom. "The Latin they wrote," said one historian, "was, at its best, poor, thin in vocabulary and incorrect in idiom. At its worst, it was a linguistic nightmare, an unwitting reconstruction of the confusions of Babel," a typical case where "their achievements did not equal their ambitions." When Columbanus sprinkled his writings with classical allusions, poor as they were, these resulted from his Continental experiences and did not reflect an unusually heightened level of culture in Ireland itself. Historians of this persuasion tend to suggest that descriptions of collapse in Europe are overly dramatic and cataclysmic. Learning may have gone underground, but it was certainly not extinct. "Scholars, as a type," wrote one, "are not pioneers." Many in Gaul, as elsewhere, managed to come to terms with new Germanic overlords. Works by Horace lay tucked away in some corner of a villa still standing, to be unearthed again in more settled times.

Where is the truth, if indeed this question can ever be fully answered? As one might expect, both opinions hold the glimmer of an answer.

The Irish did not embark on a conscious mission to save or preserve anything when they departed, as Columbanus did, for the mainland of Europe. Like Columcille before him, he left Ireland for a selfish motive, "to seek seclusion for myself", not to proselytize anyone or to piece together, in some antiquarian urge, the scattered debris of a classical past. When he arrived he was fifty or so years of age, a formed and complete individual who quickly took himself off into the wilds of the Rhineland forests. He learned nothing from the people who lived there. They and their rulers were, in his far from gracious opinion, no better than "dogs". While not a conscious conservator he was the product of a tradition that had, as a matter of impulse, ingested whatever came its way, a scholasticism — for indeed, it was a discipline — born of playful curiosity that was unique to Irish schooling and Irish methodology. Celtic standards of learning, though static and bound by convention, looked to increase its sum of knowledge so long as new information bore some relationship to the old. Genealogy, for example, piled up fresh data with each passing generation, yet it was the same traditional lore that had been logged for countless years. Christianity and the Bible were new but not new. They mimicked, in charming fashion, what already was, the entire ramshackle apparatus of an almost indigestible pagan metropolis, so vast that many glaring inconsistencies (much remarked upon by later, shocked visitors) could not be wholly clothed in orthodox respectability. Irish scholarship would not explore avenues deemed radical or formidably innovative, nor discover anything fresh in the natural world around it. It would bore into the delights of pedantry instead: word lists, encyclopedias, countless variations on a single theme. When it decided to love something, it kept it alive. The process oiled itself and reproduced exponentially.

Columbanus was an above average product of a bizarre and idiosyncratic system that happened to value poetry and gathered together whatever remnants of poetical tradition that happened to come its way, whether through trade, war or travel hither and yon. This body of material was essentially the late Latin culture of fourth-century Gaul, the bits and pieces of which we hypothesize had entered Ireland through haphazard communications with Gaul and Britain and Spain. Christine Mohrmann, whose linguistic work on St. Patrick's *Confession* is widely admired, sees in the prose of Columbanus (wisely sensing that the verse is doubtfully his) a classicism that had largely died away in the Merovingian Gaul which Gregory of Tours found so toilsome. In fact, should Gregory have perused anything by Columbanus he would have found it nearly impenetrable, as anachronistic as a twentieth-century American butcher reading Cotton Mather's colonial script. Columbanus, sensing everything around him on the Continent as degenerate, would not have seen the local vulgar Latin as superior to his own. He would, and did, reject it as inferior, and in his letters to popes and ecclesiastical synods he used the styles and mannerisms that he had been taught – and later taught himself – in his native Ireland. Unlike Gregory of Tours (and even St. Patrick) Columbanus never apologized for any deficiencies in his learning – verbosity and the occasional "rough passage," perhaps, but he was smart and arrogant enough to see the cultural superiority that he possessed.

There should be little argument on the literary quality of the writing that Columbanus produced. It was artificial, more than a bit gaudy, often consciously self-important and frequently obscure. It reflects a Celtic (and druidic) personality squeezed into the more rigid confines of classical Latin expression. One is constantly aware of tension, a breaking apart at the seams, the urge to burst loose. A passage from Columbanus to Gregory the Great illustrates this well. "Therefore I shall speak out freely," he says to the Pope (meaning, of course, that he intends to tell him what to do),

> saying to those that are our masters and helmsmen of the spiritual
> ship and mystic sentinels: Watch, for the sea is stormy and
> whipped up by fatal blasts, for it is not a solitary threatening wave
> such as, even across a silent ocean, is raised to overweening
> heights from the ever-foaming eddies of a hollow rock, though it
> swells from afar, and drives the sails before it, while Death walks
> the waves. But it is a tempest of the entire element, surging indeed
> and swollen upon every side, that threatens shipwreck of the mys-
> tic vessel. Thus do I, a fearful sailor, dare to cry, Watch! For water
> has now entered the vessel of the Church, and the vessel is in peril-
> ous straits.

One can imagine the Pope's reaction to this assault from an obscure and contentious "barbarian" about whose homeland he knew nothing. But we see in just this short passage what Irish learning was all about. Its sentence structure and vocabulary reflects, according to Mohrmann, "the cultivated literary language of the fourth and fifth centuries", commingled with very ancient Christian and monastic terminology that reflect an Irish connection with the very beginnings of Christian tradition: namely, those of the desert. The ideas and expression (in other words, the literary value) is largely Celtic in its excess, particularly the use of unusual words and the general flavor of "grotesque turgidity" found therein. The impressive exterior of this Latin garnish, designed to convey an impression of scholastic profundity, cannot conceal the content which is decidedly in a sphere all its own, off to one side. The metaphors of wild sea and perilous voyage seem to reflect the Celtic obsession with pilgrimage from their faraway island home, through rough and dangerous passage, to the ironic reward of death in exile among a pagan people. Likewise their use of Greek and Hebrew, which were not studied as real languages, but rather as exotic expressions of magic. No one in Ireland could speak or read either. Their repertoire of Latin sources is also seen as decidedly slim. But as the German-born scholar Ludwig Bieler notes, "It was the intensity of study rather than its range that won for this country the name 'Island of Scholars'. Their fame would seem to rest not so much on the number of ancient texts they possessed (which, after all, was largely a matter of chance) as on the use they made of whatever texts they had. To own much money is nothing to be particularly proud of, but it is an achievement to make little money go far."

Columbanus did not engage in "frivolities" during spare moments at Annegray to preserve anything from his surroundings. He indulged himself now and again to satisfy the academic urges that he and his fellow Irishmen valued so highly and tossed about among themselves within their monastic community. As ignorant Franks and Burgundians gathered about them, drawn by rumors of Celtic oddities in behavior, morality, and general sanctity, these Irish preferences turned up in conversation, sermons, lectures — then lessons — as each monastery expanded its mission to include, as Columbanus said, "the salvation of many". In this fashion was the classical past, or what the Irish knew of it at any rate, preserved and regenerated, through an Irish love for what had become, over one century, their own experience back in Ireland. As decades and generations passed, long after the death of Columbanus in 618, much was probably unearthed or contributed from the locales themselves to supplement what the Celts had brought, perhaps to overwhelm it. But the core material at first was probably Irish.

IS IT FAIR to say that regeneration of learning and faith on the Continent was due more to the efforts of Anglo-Saxon converts from Britain than to the Celts? That seems to be the general consensus of most professional historians, though a few Irish experts see more than a little jingoism in some of their English colleagues who delight in denigrating the Celtic contribution. Certainly the pervasiveness of an Irish impact has been overstated. The Irish were an influence both as missionaries and teachers, but largely in the areas where their monasteries were first established. In the early 600s this would place them in what is today northeastern France, Switzerland, and northern Italy. Historians generally credit Anglo-Saxon missions from Britain with most of the praise for converting the Lowlands and interior portions of Germany, and intellectually they place these monks in the very heart of the seventh-century Carolingian Renaissance about which so much has been written. From the evidence available it would seem these conclusions are largely correct.

There cannot be any confusion as to who did the work in Northumbria. When Oswald, an Anglo-Saxon warlord, called for missionaries from Iona to convert his people, the Irish sent him Aidan in 634 as bishop, who founded on a tidal island the monastery of Lindisfarne. Typically, Aidan came on foot with staff in hand and book satchels over his shoulder, dressed in the rough garb of a hermit. There is a charming scene in Bede which shows the warrior prince Oswald sitting at Aidan's feet, translating his sermons into the Germanic dialect of his thanes. In just twenty years the conversion of Northumbria was so far advanced as to be irreversible. The great evangelical surge of the Anglo-Saxons in the eighth century back to the lands of their ancestors on the Continent saw its simple beginnings in the preaching of Aidan. By A.D. 700 Abbot Adomnán of Iona presents a personality far different from that of a Columcille or a Columbanus. Iona is a powerful monastic confederation by now, its ruler welcomed, with pomp and ceremony, in the courts of Northumbrian nobles. Adomnán is clearly more cultured and less contentious: reasonably educated, diplomatic in his dealings with secular and religious leaders, aware of ramifications beyond Northumbria in the wider Christian world. He signals an end, to some degree, of obstinate insularity.

Still, the chronicles and records of the times do record the picaresque adventures of a great many stray Irishmen, well beyond the byways of traditional pilgrimage routes from Ireland and Scotland to Luxeuil, St. Gall, and Bobbio, to whom many conversions are due. They came and went, as one annalist noted, "like uncharted comets."

A T 4:30 A.M. I GET UP, put on all my winter underwear and two pairs of socks, get dressed, and gather up my gear. The farmer's wife has left some sandwiches for me and I slip out into the dark. For several minutes I assume that my eyes are failing to adapt but soon it's pretty obvious that the night is absolutely pitch black outside. Not a light, a star or any guide whatsoever. I had anticipated a dream-like ramble through the early morning mist down to the ferry in *Baile Mór*. Instead I begin to panic that I'll miss the boat, as I am totally blind on the pathway. I stumble to the ground three times, immerse myself in every ditch, puddle, and gully along the way and am horrified at the chaos and terror of crashing over a cow asleep in the middle of the lane. Luckily the wind shrieking overhead obliterates that startled animal's bellows. In the fifteen minutes it takes me to reach the dock, I am totally soaked. A small band of school children, waiting in the drizzle by a solitary lamp, look at me without a word. They all school at Oban during the week, and seem impatient for their first illegal cigarettes of the day.

Through impenetrable murk we finally see twin spotlights from the ferry approach Iona. It is a strangely ethereal sensation, a few lonely passengers grouped in the small pod of light, watching a distant satellite ship coming on from afar. The analogy of being lost in space is apt, I think.

Iona stands on the edge, one of the farthest islands before an empty expanse of water reaches westward for hundreds of unobstructed miles. The only road we have is back towards where we came, towards the center, a return to the country of great cities and hurried commerce. What is left behind are the pages of the past, long-closed and sealed up tight, like the Battler in its shrine case, removed from our eyes. As much as we might try, it seems impossible to share the joy of Columcille in his island fortress. We really are just visitors for whom innocence is beyond our reach:

Columcille *fecit*
  Delightful it would be to me
    That I might often see the face of the ocean,
    That I might see its heaving waves over the wide sea,
    When they chant music to the Father upon the world's course.
    That I might see its level sparkling sand, it would be no cause of sorrow,
    That I might hear the song of the wonderful birds, source of happiness,
    That I might hear the thunder of the crowding waves upon the rocks,
    That I might hear the roar of the surrounding sea by the side of the church.
  Delightful it would be to me
    That I might search all the books, that would be good for my soul.
    At times kneeling to beloved heaven,
    At times at psalm singing,
    At times contemplating the King of Heaven, Holy the Chief,
    At times working without compulsion, that would be wonderful.
    At times plucking seaweed from the rocks,
    At times fishing,
    At times giving food to the poor,
    At times in a solitary cell.

Irish, poet unknown

iNishkea North

*"I am haunted
by numberless islands."*
W. B. Yeats

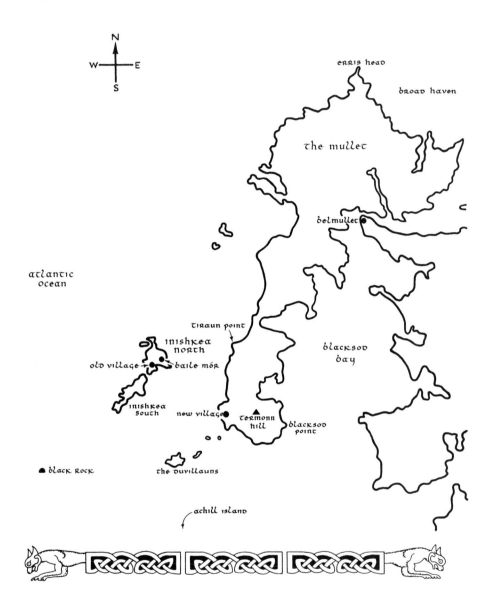

N
W   E
S

atlantic
ocean

erris head

broad haven

the mullet

belmullet

tiraun point

inishkea
north

old village → baile mór

inishkea
south

blacksod
bay

new village

termonn
hill

blacksod
point

black rock

the ouvillauns

achill island

MY TRIP BACK to Ireland is not without excitement. In Glasgow the train is boarded by that current bane of British existence, the soccer supporter, in this case Northern Irish fans of the Rangers. Hundreds mill about the station still drunk from celebrations of the previous afternoon. Some of these crowd about a distinguished gentleman wearing his kilt (the only kilt I saw in Scotland) mocking him and generally carrying on in abusive fashion. A couple of policemen rescue this seemingly impervious highlander. The ride to our ferry is unbelievably raucous. "We're the lads from Ulster," they sing, "We love to drink and fight." The men's room door is battered down off its hinges to retrieve a comrade who has passed out, his head in the toilet. Virulent songs trashing the I.R.A. and Catholics in general, which cannot be performed without liberal additions of the word 'fuck' — pronounced 'fook' — interspersed for effect at every stanza, are bellowed up and down the corridors. Conductors finally halt the train at a suburban station forty-five minutes into our ride, and dozens of police pile on. These separate the peace-loving passengers from the soccer trash. I am grateful, despite my shabby appearance, to be included in the former group. These custodians of order perversely desert us at the ferry, however, which negligently has left its bar open for business. After an hour or so of sheer terrorism the stewards essentially abandon ship, retreating behind the locked doors of the engine room, crew quarters, and bridge. Sane and rational passengers are reduced to herding themselves into a single lounge, where the entryways are barricaded with furniture pried up from the floor. The next officials we see when we dock in Larne are riot police, who assure our spokesperson that it's safe to open up. My last image in disembarking is the sight of innumerable fist fights and rumbles between the forces of darkness and light.

The next day, late in the afternoon, I pull into the small town of Belmullet, County Mayo. Should I bother to describe the weather, driving rain and high winds, or the miles of empty, barren land, the wastes of Connaught, that I had to drive through to get here? Aside from reaches in the far north of County Donegal, this projection of bog and sodden moorland is perhaps the most desolate region of the entire country.

Belmullet itself is the only village for miles in any direction, and was often noted for the filth and poverty of both its inhabitants and the hovels in which they lived. The motor car changed all that, and since the early 1900s its sudden accessibility made any gross manifestation of squalor too embarrassing for local officials to tolerate. Belmullet, when last I saw it twelve or so years ago, presented a most attractive facade. Ireland had recently joined the Common Market and was experiencing, for perhaps the only time in its modern history, a period of real prosperity, with the result that even this place had an upbeat and well-spruced air about it. The central street of the village, broad and handsomely laid out with a rather nice square as its central focus, boasted one or two decent restaurants to go with its multitudinous offering of pubs, a hotel, several attractive shops and guest houses, along with a handful of small entrepreneurial-type businesses that projected an optimism seldom seen in these parts. Those were the days when it was a common sight to see farmers herding cattle from the comfort of their new Mercedes road-cars. While it is not exactly back to the donkey cart for most of these expansive high rollers, Mercedes are clearly things of the past in backwaters like Belmullet. Walking about now through deserted streets swirling with garbage and trash, everything other than the aforementioned pubs seems boarded up, deserted, failed. Driving over the one-lane bridge onto the Mullet itself, a spot touristically geared for fine views and a good uplifting blast of ocean air, I am struck at the sight of an enormous dump, full of rusting cars and machine debris that I never recall seeing here before. It signals to me the abandonment of hope, and it is a dire psychological message indeed for the future of the West of Ireland.

Belmullet reminds me of a castle gate: once through the portcullis, you have abandoned all that is comfortable and safe. The Mullet, shaped like a fishhook turned upside down, is a monotonous expanse of country utterly devoid of anything save bog, water, and wind. A relatively low piece of land for the most part, it does, on the northern shore towards Erris Head, boast sea cliffs that are close to 300 feet high and predictably

216

put on quite a show in stormy weather. This area of the Mullet holds its own with the better-publicized Achill Island to the south, and in fact has some of that romantic melancholia for which Ireland is so famous. But the rest of this peninsula, as it straggles on for ten or so miles before reaching the southern terminus at Blacksod Point, is unrelievedly depressing. A single road passes one lonely concrete bunker farmhouse after another, interspersed here and there with unbelievably hideous modern chalets, most started years ago and never finished, various piles of cement mixers and stray equipment standing witness to enthusiasms long since abandoned. Few if any glimpses of the ocean open up as the road mostly runs along the eastern shore by Blacksod Bay, a large though shallow body of water that the Mullet protects from Atlantic depredations.

Driving along, carelessly inattentive to anything but the passing scenery, I am startled as a man runs through his gate nearly straight into my car, which I swerve across the road with brake pedal mashed to the floor. I am remotely aware that his arms are flailing, and remember questioning myself whether he was flagging me down or just reacting to being run over. In fact I have narrowly missed the lighthouse keeper who is frantic to reach his station down at Blacksod Point. We putter off as fast as this old car will take us. "Jesus, Mary and Joseph, is this all she can do?" he wails.

The Citroën is still moving as he leaps out the door and into the lighthouse. Back in a flash he hoists an oval wind sock, which immediately tears off from the flagpole and flies away into the bay. "Oh Christ," he says, "this is Force 9." He reenters the building and I follow, in time to catch him ranging from one set of instruments to another, ending at a radio set. The difficulty, as I begin to understand it, is the visitation of the weekly helicopter, which brings supplies, spare parts and, most importantly I presume, conversation to all the western lights. The chopper at this moment is flying "down the gut", meaning through the cleavage between Achill Island and the Nephin Beg Mountains on the mainland, and expects to set down here. The keeper is literally wringing his hands. "It's too much," he says to himself as much as to me, "I'll wave him off." After several tries he raises the pilot on his radio. Two minutes later we both stand outside on the jetty, in this primeval maelstrom, and pick him out, skimming across the open water, then streaking over our heads like a jet, fleeing inland to the refuge of some provincial airstrip. "That's enough excitement for today," yells the keeper.

Over a cup of tea we talk a bit about the Mullet. Here on the point a few families live, subsistence farmers for the most part who fish or lobster during the summer months. All their small craft are pulled up for the winter. There is one general store and one pub, both open at irregular hours. Tourists are few, outnumbered considerably by sport fishermen, who find the waters here teeming with varied species. In a barracks-type

217

building a few hundred feet from the lighthouse an annual visitation of students descend on the Mullet, environmental types who monitor the seal population that crowd the islands and rocks offshore in the Atlantic. "They call themselves Sea Shepherds," he says, "they stand guard over the herds during pup season. Three or four years ago the fishermen around here had a great hunt and killed hundreds of seals. They were making damage to their catch. The boats were hauling for salmon and getting nothing but dead heads, that's all they found in their nets, which the seals wrecked as well. Seals love those islands. All along the shore, you know, that's the only protection they have. There be seals every- where out there, nothing bothering them, lying around like bullocks in the sun. When the Government wouldn't cull them, the fishermen just went in for the terrible slaughter. And as a result we have these hippies here every spring in their rubber boats." He pauses and laughs. "People protecting seals! I don't know what's wrong with them." As I leave he points out the road to follow. "Go up that hill, which we call Termonn Hill, and you'll find the people you want. All the islanders, or those that be left, they all live on the other side. God be with ye."

Driving up, I pull over to a "scenic easement", something I never expected to see here, all neatly laid out with a trim stone wall, crushed gravel spread on the lot, trash baskets at regular intervals along the edge. Personally, I burn all the refuse I collect in my travels here. I have always had the sinister feeling that most of these barrels are just carted ten or twenty yards downwind and dumped. Nature has a way of dispersing this stuff pretty easily: whatever isn't tied down is blown away to someone else's front yard, which in this case is thousands of empty acres. The panorama is without limit. Dead south, six miles away across Blacksod Bay, is the heavily-brooding Achill Island, a tremendous mountain fast- ness plunging two thousand or so feet into the sea. North of it, and beneath Termonn Hill, are the small islands of Duvillaun More and Duvillaun Beg, beyond which a beacon far out in the ocean sends a piercing red light. Due west are the larger Inishkeas, about two miles offshore, once a single island but long since cut in two by the relentless Atlantic. Stretching off above them all I can see is the long battered coast of the Mullet, embroiled in clamor and broken surf.

The scene is certainly eclectic. Storms racing in from the sea with ten minutes of fury and lambast, followed by periods of total sunny calm; the sky as clear and unencumbered as though a poster from the Caribbean, the wind, a gentle breeze. As dusk approaches, however, a thick black wall of tempest, stretching over the entire horizon, advances from the west. Soon the lighthouse beacon is obliterated, then the Inishkeas and the Duvillauns, finally the cottages down on the shore of the Mullet below me.

"Understand the Creation," Columbanus once wrote, "if you wish to understand the Creator." Given the scene I am witnessing here, one of utter chaos, a humbling of the lone and insignificant traveller in the face of a natural world so extraordinarily powerful, I can to some degree understand the emotional surge that Irishmen such as Columbanus must have squeezed from their lives. Herbert Muller, in his book *The Uses of the Past*, noted that the faith of those ancient times "had a childlike simplicity and freshness that we cannot recover by an effort of the will", and he is correct. Page after page of theological disputation tells us the content of religious thought, but gives no insight to its drive. And while it is certainly unhistorical to link a visual feast such as this with a generalized explanation of somebody else's spiritual beliefs, somebody who lived in a time warp completely alien to our own, still, the connection seems to be there. Columbanus writes at one point that "I am thrusting my face into the fire." I cannot, as a believing Catholic, recall any point in my life when I ever did that. Fasting over and over again, Columbanus follows the Psalm's advice, "Open thy mouth wide and I will fill it." For me, it's only salty spray from the ocean storm bathing my face with stinging rainwater. Yet at least I'm wet; at least I'm standing here in Ireland, in a milieu little changed, in some respects, from those earliest eras of Christianity. I can feel this storm. I may not see or sense in it the mysteries of God as Columbanus did, but I know that whatever is behind this, it can blow me over in a second. I finally run for cover. That is something Columbanus would never have done. He may have felt dwarfed by what was happening here, but I doubt if he feared it.

Centuries of Christian experience have laundered such aberrant thoughts from Irish life. But in Columbanus' day this Pelagian streak remained alive, however blind that great cleric would have been to charges saying the opposite. The exasperating thing, of course, is that Columbanus saw himself as totally orthodox. Yet who can read from his work and not clearly see the self-determined streak of Pelagius lying everywhere, like radioactive debris contaminating the whole, rejecting all efforts at a cleanup? Columbanus shuns the pagan philosophers, says all the right things about grace and St. Augustine, yet reserves his most telling remarks for private effort. "He who perseveres up to the end shall be saved," he writes. "If you remove the freedom, you remove the worth." Within the body of his work one can see Cassian and St. Augustine battling hard. The grandeur of this lonely spot indicates to me that however solitary one man might seem, the Celtic spirit of wayward pride saw every conflict as a personal one that could be fought. The glories of victory, or the melancholic gratification that many a poet has found in being crushed, were opportunities too glistening to reject.

But another irony apparent here marks the end of our look at the Celtic spirit, for the purposes of this book anyway. One more wayward personality, one more exotic rogue, one more ecclesiastical heretic: John Scottus Erigena.

THERE IS A gap of some two hundred and fifty years between Erigena and the great patristic Fathers Columcille and Columbanus. Much of tremendous moment happened in that vast expanse of time, not the least of which was the stunning (if misunderstood) Carolingian Renaissance under the aegis of the great Charlemagne and his Anglo-Saxon tutor Alcuin, former headmaster of the cathedral school at York in Northumbria. The Irish role in that endeavor, while a matter of dispute, seems to have been significant though subordinate. In two disputatious clashes of will, one in England, the other on the European mainland that peaked in the Imperial city of Aachen, the Irish were severely trampled by the forces of moderation, papal control, episcopal order — in the words of Columbanus, by the Pharisees of this world. At Whitby in the year A.D. 664 the Northumbrian king Oswiu ordered the monks of Iona, indeed of all the Celtic *paruchiae* in his kingdom, to abandon their archaic customs that so offended the Holy See and its bishops.[1] The spokesman for the Roman party was even cavalier enough to indicate he had never heard of Columcille, mocking both his "primitive simplicity" and the sheepish nature of his descendants who followed that way so mutely. Periodic expulsions of recalcitrant monks from their monasteries (culminating in 717 when Iona was finally, with soldiers, cleared of dissidents) made Oswiu's decision of real moment in stifling the independent sprawl of Celtic monasticism. Eventually the ramifications of Whitby spread backwards into Ireland itself. By the eighth century it had largely conformed to the structure and customs of a Universal Church.[2]

The situation in Germany and the Frankish domains paralleled that of Northumbria. Second and third generation missionaries (usually of sober Anglo-Saxon stock) stumbling about in the forests and marshes of northern Europe, would sometimes find pockets of Christianity among the truly savage Germanic and Frissian heathen, the work of Irish monks from years ago. In general terms their reaction was one of horror that clergymen allegedly Christian could teach barbarians some of the uncanonical trash they uncovered. St. Boniface, for example, left his native England for Frisia in 716, initiating an evangelical career that continued until his martyrdom in 754. During that span he everywhere attacked Celtic irregularities, seeing in their wayward, haphazard traditions a threat as direct as pagan ignorance. In many ways, Boniface represents a reversal of

---

[1] Ostensibly these involved the dating of Easter, differing forms of tonsure and various procedural habits peculiar to the Celts. In real terms the disputes involved power and control of the Celtic Church itself.

[2] Though a diocesan system with bishops in the forefront of ecclesiastical affairs was not achieved until A.D. 1152.

Abbot's Effigy
Abbey of Luxeuil, Vosges, France

opinion on the Continent towards the Irish.[1] The old days when a semi-literate king or lord would happily entertain a hybrid, vagabond collection of monks and itinerant scholars at his court — "Greeks and Irish, speaking diverse tongues", as one medieval biographer put it, whom his hero "fed at his own expense", — were no longer seen as quite so exciting. Irishmen such as Columbanus had served their purpose on the front line. The 700s presented different priorities. Charlemagne initiated his educational reforms for specific, realpolitik ends: he saw the need for a literate clergy and a unified ecclesiastical system to pull together his enormous kingdom, to provide a network whereby he could manage all that he had won. The Holy Roman Emperor, though a warrior and freebooter to some extent, wanted order. He was civilized enough to see the difference between an army of soldiers and an army of clerks, and where lay the greater profit. Within these ambitions, diversity of opinion was no longer seen as a virtue. As an eighth-century pope remarked when told he had a visitor — a bishop from foreign parts — "These are people from whom we need protection." And Boniface carried out the papal initiative with single-minded zeal, oblivious to the achievements that Irish monks had amassed, both in his own homeland and the great new territories of the Germans, to whom he was sent, in succession, as a missionary, bishop, papal legate, archbishop and, finally, primate. The *peregrini* and vagrant churchmen that he found in his dioceses were a rabble of "false vagrants, adulterers, murderers, effeminates, pederasts, blasphemers, hypocrites, tonsured serfs who have fled their masters, servants of the devil transformed into ministers of Christ" and, worst of all, "subject to no bishop". The Irish practice of episcopal subordination, where an abbot held precedence in monastic communities and federations, was anathema to Boniface. Whereas Columbanus could write that "Churches of God planted in pagan nations should live by their own laws, as they had been instructed by their fathers," Boniface could tirelessly track down and secure from Rome the fitting punishment for churchmen who refused submission to his authority as bishop — "condemnation".

One such crusade involved the Irish scoundrel Clemens, who evidently was found preaching a variant on the Harrowing of Hell story. This apocryphal tale, one of a number the Celts found attractive, eventually ended up in the Apostles' Creed that Catholics even today universally recite — the sentence "And He descended into Hell," which follows the description of Christ's death on the cross. This unorthodox visit to the realm of darkness, unsubstantiated by any scriptural references in the

---

[1] Much of this antagonism can naturally be traced to ethnic differences. The Celts had no affection for Saxons in general, nor did a Christain commonalty have any effect on Saxon distaste for the Celts. Bede illustrates this quite normal state of affairs when he describes a Saxon abbey refusing to accept the holy relics of a saint from some other "alien" tribe.

Bible, naturally occasioned various explanations, the accepted version of which states that Christ freed those blameless souls imprisoned there whose only sin had been their birth and death before the redemption of Golgotha. This would have included the fathers and prophets of the Old Testament, for example. However, within the magical world of Celtic saga — indeed, of medieval miracle lore as a general category — this Harrowing of Hell had many versions, all involving the hypothetical question of who had been saved and who had not. The Irish missionary Clemens, according to Boniface, was preaching this tale in heretical fashion. He was emptying hell entirely of "both believers and unbelievers, God's witnesses at the same time as worshippers of idols", for which he deserved hunting down.

It has been plausibly suggested, however, that Clemens was following a technique of first generation missionaries, suspicious without a doubt to the new priorities of a Boniface, but in keeping with the spontaneity and inventiveness with which the Irish often approached their task of teaching. The Saxon missionary Wulfram had bungled the conversion of a Frisian king who had asked, just prior to baptism, whether his pagan forebears would join him in heaven. Wulfram replied, with singular tactlessness, that they were all in hell, whereupon the Frisian lost his temper and indicated he would join them there, for it would be intolerable to enter the afterlife separated from kinfolk. The Harrowing of Hell conveniently circumvents this problem, and no doubt missionaries like Clemens borrowed all sorts of leveraging and somewhat specious variants from the shadowland of mythology and Christian legend to squeeze themselves out of tight corners. But to Boniface, this sort of theological freebooting was heresy.

As the eighth century progresses, more and more Church councils, papal correspondence, and determined missions pen up the Irish. Their preeminent reputations decline, and the more abrasive aspects of Celtic temperament are noted, scorned, mocked, and satirized. The noble "Scottus", as one Frank wrote, is nothing more than a "Sottus". In 802, at an assembly of his bishops called in Aachen, Charlemagne had the Rule of St. Benedict minutely explained to the clergy. Its superiority to all other monastic regulations was manifest to the Emperor. It dictated subservience of all monasteries, no matter the origin or founder, to the bishop in whose diocese it lay. It preached sobriety of habit and discipline, it required order and labor, it radiated moderation and obedience. Even in Irish chronicles it soon came to be noted that "St. Benedict is lying in the bed of St. Columbanus." The Irish impetus as a primal moving spirit was coming to an end. "For a brief period," as one historian has written, "indeed, for the first and for the last time in her history, Ireland had become the most vital civilizing force in the West. Decline was inevitable. With the conversion of the Germanic peoples, the natural equilibrium of Western Europe was re-established, and the great centre no longer existed, paradoxically, on the outer perimeter." Even the traditional encouragements in Ireland itself for monks to undertake pilgrimage abroad diminished precipitously, as monastic rules and saints' lives counseled restraint. "To go to Rome is little profit, endless pain", wrote one. Another said, "If God could not be found on this side of the sea, I too would cross the water. But in every country there is a road which leads to Heaven." Kevin of Glendalough allegedly wanted to roam afield, but a holy hermit rebuked him, saying it was better to stay rooted in one holy place, "for have you ever known of a bird hatching its eggs on the wing?"

JOHN SCOTTUS ERIGENA, however, left home. As a matter of fact, so did great numbers of other monks, but this time, as an observer has noted, they seem to have come "at least as much to learn as to teach". By the early 800s, of course, an additional factor led many to flee Ireland — the Viking menace. "Whence are you from, learning's son?" asks the poet.

> "From Clonmacnoise I come;
> My course of studies done,
> I am off to Swords again."
>
> "How are things shaping there?"
>
> "Oh, things are keeping fair;
> Foxes round churchyards bare,
> Gnawing the guts of men."

Vikings coursed these waters that I see from here, descending on all the little islands stretched below me, looking for booty. They probably found little of anything on Inishkea North, a monastic community so inconsequential that no mention of it was ever recorded in any of the annals. But Inishmurray, just around Erris Head to the north, was sacked in 806, and Iona on several occasions, 795, 802, 806 and 825. Sixty-eight monks were slaughtered on one of those terrible visitations. It was no wonder that churchmen sought safety far away. They came more as refugees than as pilgrims seeking salvation.

John, following age-old tradition, arrived unannounced and unheralded to the Palace School of Charles the Bald, grandson to Charlemagne, at Laon in c. 845. He remained there as a resident scholar until c. 870, then disappeared from history. His earliest life, indeed, anything at all to do with his career in Ireland itself, is a mystery and little beyond his actual writings is known to us. The only colorful things that might be said of him are probably legendary, for these occur in the English chronicler William of Malmesbury's *Gesta pontificum* which was written some three centuries later. These include John's alleged response to a meddling remark of Charles the Bald who asked him, as they were drinking, what separated an Irishman from a drunkard. "The width of this table" was his cheeky retort. William also reported that Erigena ended his days in England as a teacher, that his pupils rebelled against their master and stabbed him to death with their thin, sharpened pens. They did so "because he forced us to think".

Erigena is the climax to this story, the last figure we can talk about, uniquely Irish, who links the Egyptian desert to this barren, wild piece of coast; to the ruined foundations of huts and *clocháns* and incised crosses which, for all their similarities, could be those of Nitria. This bond evaporates, as have the monasteries that once could be seen from here on the Inishkeas, after Erigena. Ireland, and Irish scholars, are no longer exotic beings. It is true that Ireland would remain, as always, a faraway land, mysterious because remote, vexing to established authority, but its standards and convictions would no longer be regarded with any interest, either as vestigial remnants of the most ancient Christian tradition or as the vanguard for whatever the newest heresy might be.

But nothing is ever neat in Irish history. Erigena is, at the same time, "the most considerable philosopher in the Western world between Augustine and Thomas Aquinas", yet also "one of the loneliest". In plainer English, he was one of the greatest, yet also one of the least important thinkers ever; relevant, but irrelevant; vital, though easily bypassed; a milestone in the history of metaphysical thought, yet unnoticed and totally obscure. Erigena matters, but does not. This is the Celtic mystery all over again: two propositions at loggerheads that we can fully support.

Certainly one remark is valid. Erigena kept the Celtic flirtation with heresy alive, albeit in a vacuum. When he completed his major work in 867, *De divisione naturae* ("On the Division of Nature"), he left behind him, in the words of the distinguished French historian Etienne Gilson, an air of utter "stupefaction". Not one of his contemporaries had the slightest notion what he was talking about. The only person influenced by *De divisione naturae* was Erigena himself. It was not until four centuries later that theologians figured out the dangers lurking in every page. He was then anathematized and his works burned on the pyre. Finally resurrected in the late 1600s when the first edition of *De divisione naturae* was printed, it took just four years for the work to be condemned again and placed on the Church's Index of forbidden books.

Certainly Erigena was a typical product of the Irish scholastic system when he arrived in France about 845; in fact, he may well have been considered above average, since it appears he secured the appointment of master to the Palace School quite soon thereafter, and at court received complimentary accolades as a man "scholasticus et eruditus". Although a lay brother, evidently, and not a priest, he had received a monastic education, knew his Latin thoroughly and was certainly well-versed in Patristic literature, particularly the works of St. Augustine. Though ostensibly an admirer of that great theologian from the African Church, there can also be little doubt that he had imbued the traditional affection of the Irish for Pelagius as well. Throughout Erigena's work there is praise for reason and man's ability to use it. Perhaps the most famous sentences he ever wrote were that "Authority proceeds from right reason, not reason from Authority. Rightful Authority seems to me nothing else than truth discovered by the power of reason." Man is "untrained and childish" — the Apostle Paul cannot give us solid foods, only "milk to drink" — but nevertheless it is up to us whether we swallow or not. "Do not be afraid," he writes, "for now we must follow reason, which investigates the truth of things, and is by no means prevented from proclaiming to all men the things which it zealously searches out and discovers with much toil."

For twenty or so years Erigena did not "search out" much of anything that might have tended to isolate him from his fellow schoolmasters or to launch him on some stray path into fields previously beyond reach. It is true that he had engaged in theological disputes, with repercussions that, luckily, his position as a favorite of the king's had deflected. But it seems that many of these years had simply been passed in reading, contemplation and, most importantly, the study of Greek. As maintained earlier, any Irishman in his native land would have been familiar only with exotic word lists and a general, vague idea as to the structure of Greek, but on the Continent the opportunity of meeting a native speaker or finding more useful pedagogic texts would certainly, by 850, have been more likely. Erigena had enough talent, it seems, to secure a commission from the king to translate the Greek texts of Dionysius the Areopagite into Latin, a gesture Erigena never forgot. In his note of dedication he thanked Charles for urging him to pass beyond the writings with which they were all now familiar in the West, the Augustines and the Jeromes, and to drink the "most pure and copious waters of the Greeks".

Dionysius was a stroke of luck for Erigena. As one of those quirks of history, in fact, the chance selection of such a work is really quite astounding. Dionysius, in an amalgam of medieval confusion and wishful thinking, was thought to be the learned Greek whom an "exasperated" Paul converted in Athens.[1] A rather turgid hagiographical biography of one St. Denis (Latinized to Dionysius, which may explain some of the resulting muddle) was compiled in c. 831 near Paris, in which the life and career of a local martyr was inextricably snarled with that of the Areopagite. The hybridized result was then granted credit as the author of several mysterious works in Greek that the Byzantine Emperor, Michael the Stammerer, had given Charles' predecessor, King Louis the Pious. These were accorded special honor though no one could read them, since they represented a direct link to the Apostolic Age when such men as Paul and Dionysius were believed to have heard (or had the opportunity to have heard) the living Words directly from Christ's mouth

---

[1] Areopagus is the hill west of the Acropolis where the law courts were situated. Paul, whom many Athenians regarded as "a babbler", naturally gravitated to where "all the city people and the visitors from abroad used to spend their leisure telling or listening to something new", standing among the crowds to dispute and argue over the tenets of Christianity.

or from those of his most intimate followers. In truth, Dionysius was something of a fraud, a sixth-century Syrian monk of decidedly suspect bent whose primary aim had been to refine the platonic meanderings of Greek philosophy (along with a goodly portion of very strange Middle Eastern fantasy) into a proper Christian context. Erigena, in an effort of considerable merit given the age, produced a serviceable text that even the Pope's librarian found striking, if somewhat amateurish. "It is a wonderful thing," he wrote, "how a barbarian, living at the ends of the earth, who might be supposed to be as far removed from the knowledge of this other language as he is from the familiar use of it, has been able to comprehend such ideas and translate them into another tongue."

The operative words here are "able to comprehend". Greek, the key to reading Scripture and some of the earliest Fathers, was also regarded with grave suspicion. Gregory the Great, we may recall, abjured its use, in fact lived in the East for six years as papal legate to the Eastern Court and still refused to learn it. Erigena was an easier prey. As he struggled with the text we can see, at the same time, something of a revelation come over him, his awareness that the Greeks were different, that within their language lay expressive opportunities so vast that Latin seemed juvenile in comparison. And in his hands lay this marvellous, though eccentric theologian called the Areopagite who used the language to wondrous effect. It is ironic that within this text, considered by everyone including Erigena to be totally orthodox, lay theories as heretical as any that had been condemned and burned. The Pope certainly did not know that, nor of course did Charles the Bald. Had they been able to read Greek, perhaps they might have seen that something was very wrong here. But they could not.

Erigena, in his study, grappled with Dionysius both linguistically and intellectually. In the end he mastered the book on both counts. His admiration for the Greeks, "who reason very subtly", simply exploded. After translating Dionysius he set his hand to another Greek, Maximus the Confessor, who had himself written extensively on the Areopagite. He then went off on his own.

In *The Division of Nature*, Erigena created an entire philosophic system from what he had gleaned from the Greeks. Some historians claim the result was not original since Erigena, in many ways, synthesized what he had learned and simply regurgitated a neoplatonic formula that, by now, should be familiar to us. This is partially true but it obscures the central point. Given the times and given the scanty resources available both materially, in terms of libraries, texts and familiarity with the medium of Greek, and fraternally, by which I mean the caliber of his contemporaries, Erigena had little of anything to rely on save his own intellectual ingenuity. Most of his knowledge of Greek philosophy was secondhand, what he read in Augustine and other early Fathers (such as small bits of Origen, in the expurgated edition by Rufinius) and these texts were all in Latin.

Aside from Dionysius and Maximus, and one or two other writers of lesser significance, Erigena had no direct access to the "shrewdest" of them all, Aristotle and Plato. Still he managed to isolate the primary themes by himself, construct a series of propositions based around them, build a sequential, logical roadway from one to the next, finally reaching the desired destination of God Himself. In many ways the progression — actually a forced march, which it more closely resembles — is clearly a precedent for the later analytical writings of Thomas Aquinas, over four hundred years into the future. Both searched for "perfect reasoning", but Erigena did so in a climate so crude and simplistic that we can only wonder at his achievement.

This is not the book (nor am I the writer) to fathom the intricacies of what Erigena put together in 867. Certain themes and certain highlights are sufficiently apparent to casual travellers such as myself, however, to merit attention, especially as they apply to the old monastic tradition of Ireland that we have been following about on this journey. From my reading of Erigena it seems obvious that the Greeks seduced him shamelessly, a fall from grace that Erigena would have admitted in the privacy of his study but not outside of it in the classroom or courtyard. He had faith, he believed in Christ, he did not doubt the resurrection, but like many complicated men before and after, he viewed the reality of religion as a matter that lay beyond, on the other side of the wall, a barrier that we poor mortals cannot understand. Quite simply, he believed in a God that could not be verbalized, recreated, imagined, or construed. "There is no way of signifying by verb or noun or any other part of articulated speech how the supreme and casual Essence of all things can be signified." Most trappings of religion are thus symbolic tools provided by the Church to help the least among us grapple, however clumsily, with the spiritual rudiments for living this life in a moral, saintly fashion. Eternal damnation in hellfire, therefore, is merely a convenient image. There is no fiery furnace. The penalty for sin is ignorance of God, distance away from Him. Likewise the Eucharist, only a symbol: "For we also, who after His incarnation and passion and resurrection have believed in Him, and understood His mysteries as far as is possible for us, do both in our spirits sacrifice Him, and in our minds — not our teeth — eat of Him."

How then are we to think of God? The mechanics are complicated, requiring patience, "for it is no trivial inquiry that we are embarked upon, nor one that can be investigated or brought to a conclusion except by many devious approaches of a most precise reasoning if, indeed, it can ever be wholly concluded." And in fact, it cannot be. Erigena, following the long tradition of the Greeks, and particularly those of the desert whom we have seen before — Evagrius and Cassian — sees no clarity at the end of this road, only the inexpressible, "Who is better known by not knowing, of Whom ignorance is the true knowledge." As Prudentius, bishop of Troyes, and a bitter adversary of Erigena bemoaned, all this was "the folly of Origen".

Erigena was a Hellenic Christian more suited to Mt. Athos than a rough frontier town like Laon. He paid lip service to the Holy Fathers of Scripture, quoting from the Bible frequently and from Augustine over sixty times. But these were offerings of straw, disingenuous in the extreme. When Erigena wanted real authority, when he found the Latin Fathers dull and deficient, he turned to Dionysius and to the East. Erigena's work is the fullest Neoplatonic expression that we have in Europe — unique, actually, in his isolation — until the Middle Ages were well advanced. He melded Greek inventiveness with his own Irish belief in self, that Pelagian stubbornness that saw him go his own way, "faith seeking to know" as St. Anselm of Canterbury put it. Prudentius viewed it differently, calling Erigena "perverse and insane". But Erigena found his opponents contemptible, demurely obeying Jerome's warning not to clutter the Bible with abstruse interpretation and nitpicking, not to stray too deeply into the boggy wetlands of overintellectualizing the Godhead. Simplicity, in Erigena's format, was for simpletons.

In a previous work on Irish history I wrote that Erigena is "still germane and still read." I realize now what a meaningless remark that was. Erigena is not germane — indeed, he never was — and he is certainly not read. As an oddity along that long road called the history of thought, as the subject for a learned monograph or a doctoral thesis, perhaps he finds an audience. But essentially he built on top of the world a gigantic structure that remained unoccupied. There was no one with sufficient stamina to make the climb and reach the top. And even later famous theorists such as Abelard and even Aquinas, may never have read anything he wrote. Erigena resides in obscurity.

THE NEXT SEVERAL days are idly, though pleasurably, spent awaiting calmer weather. Much of the time I tramp around near an old watchtower built in the eighteenth or nineteenth century with French Bonapartists presumably in mind. It overlooks the entire sweep of Blacksod Bay's disgorge to the Atlantic, and most particularly Inishkea North, directly seaward. The man on whose property the tower stands often comes out to chat. He is the son of an islander. "There isn't much to see on the island really," he says. "There was no dock or jetty. The people beached their curraghs on the strand there, the one facing us directly on the sheltered side of the place, and the village with its school and church and graveyard huddled around it. Actually, where the men landed on the island depended on the weather and wind. They came ashore wherever it was safest. When they came to the mainland their goal was the beach down here below, in other words the shortest distance between two points. They seldom rowed all the way around this headland to Blacksod

Point, too far entirely. So you can see it was a wet, chancy ride, both leaving and landing in surf, where the dangers of an accident, a rogue wave upsetting the curragh or knocking it sideways into another wave coming behind, were constant. After the evacuation in 1931 the people would still cross back and forth to their old homes. Sometimes in the summer they'd stay for a week or two, and until fairly recently all the islands out here were fully stocked for summer grazing. Not as much of that now. Most of the old-timers are dead. The only memorable feature on the place is *Baile Mór*, the great hill of sand, probably 70 or so feet high and 500 or 600 feet in diameter. You can see it just there sticking up like a finger. But that's it. Why in the name of God you want to get over there I can't understand. There was a priest here two months ago from America, and he went in to look at his parents' birthplace and to check some property there that belongs to him now, though the value of it be nothing. But ye've no stake in the place at all. Not to worry for you, I won't, because no one will take you over this time of year."

That is certainly true. Even the most skeptical Irish peasant will understand a stranger wanting to see an Inishmurray or an Iona. Both of these places are littered with ruins and artifacts from long ago, and no matter that these mean nothing to any of the locals, they can at least be polite enough when a stranger reveals an interest in them. But not so for Inishkea North. A few incised crosses, the foundations of a handful of *clocháns*, the shell of a rude and unmortared chapel are all that's left to indicate its monastic past. There are no round towers or high crosses, no cathedrals or chevroned mouldings, no statuary or decorative remains at all; no remnant worth noting, a blank page, not a single reference in any saga, genealogy, saint's story or legend. The place is a gap in our knowledge.

Because the island has no ornamental facing, I encounter more than the usual difficulties in finding a passage. Fishermen laugh in my face. A charter boat captain cannot conceal his bewilderment, and then outright scorn, that anyone could be thick enough to choose a destination so absurd. "Go back to Dublin for God's sake and have some fun. Leave it to the seals." I finally extract a semi-pledge from a lobsterman, whose house proclaims better days than these, that he will pick me up at Blacksod Point on the first calm day. He has no telephone, so every evening I stop at the door to report on weather bulletins that I have heard. On each visitation I am greeted more sullenly. At one point he asks for more money. I am never offered any tea or bread, but he is my only chance.

W E ALL HAVE our little peculiarities, and landing on Inishkea North has become mine. The only literature on the place dates from the

1930s when the distinguished French scholar Françoise Henry undertook a couple of season's work there. Using island men as laborers and staying in a cottage disused since the evacuation, she excavated the foundations of several *clocháns* either on or in the vicinity of *Baile Mór*. "Only a few of the objects found deserve study," she reported, "most of them are without interest" — a few pins, buttons, a comb, little else. A beached whale, decomposing on the strand nearby, made the work uncomfortable for her, though the islanders seemed indifferent to the nauseating odor.

What finally did pique her curiosity were the millions upon millions of little broken seashells that she found permeating the site. Identifying these as the marine snail *purpura lapillus*, it occurred to her that she had found on Inishkea North a monastic workshop of some sort, indirectly and unglamorously devoted to the creation of Ireland's most renowned artistic treasure, the illuminated manuscript.

Discussions of *purpura lapillus* in ancient literature are not uncommon, referring in general terms to its use in dying wool, a process evidently discovered by the Phoenicians, and also, in some amazement, to its exorbitant cost. Pliny the Elder, who needlessly perished at Pompei during the eruption of Vesuvius in A.D. 79 when he ordered his galley to close in towards the harbor for a better look, wrote a scathing denunciation of this "mad lust for purple", noting the irony of placing such inordinate value on a product derived from common shellfish, the smell of which was grossly offensive. In time its production was deemed a monopoly of the Roman State. In the Venerable Bede we find our first direct attribution for its use in the British Isles, the "beautiful scarlet dye which remains unfaded by sunshine or rain; indeed, the older, the more beautiful its color." He too was referring to wool.

The process of extraction was boring and laborious. A small gland behind the head contains the mysterious dye. In larger shellfish this sack can often be cut off from the body, saving time and effort. *Purpura lapillus*, however, is a mere half inch in length. Thus the shell was manually crushed using a rock or hammer and instantly placed in a large cauldron with salt. Dead or decayed mollusks had no value. These were then steeped for three days, according to Pliny. In its initial stages the extract gives no indication at all of its staining capacities. Indeed, it is colorless, but after a week of simmering over a wood fire, and with the careful addition of heated stones, the concoction begins to reveal a deep and splendid range of purples and deep reds. In its final form the compound may well have been reduced to a powder.

There is no question that the ancients were smitten by the hues, and overwhelmed by its resilience. One of its most frequently cited qualities, in fact, was longevity. The dye was most often used by the Romans in combination with gold leaf and silver, both for Imperial robes and manuscript decoration. Pliny described it as "strongly resembling the sea in a tempestuous state", and a friend of mine used the analogy of burgundy wine held up to sunlight.

By the Middle Ages the dye was no longer in use. The amount of liquid derived from a *purpura lapillus* was infinitesimal, necessitating enormous quantities of shellfish and fuel, and less expensive substitutes were found. Modern researchers have figured out with difficulty how the original recipe went. Folkloric memories totally lost sight of it, though in 1685 one interested antiquarian in Britain heard rumors of an Irishman "living by the sea-side in some Port or creek", who peddled marvelously colored handkerchiefs that he had stained "with a dye he boiled from some liquid substance taken out of shell fish."

I had a yearning to plunge my hands into a mound of sea shells, to go to the rocks where *purpura lapillus* can be picked by the bushel. I wanted to end my trip with the hardest and most ironical journey of all. Inishkea North was going to be difficult. I could see that, in both the demeanor of my recalcitrant guide and the state of the Atlantic from this perch up by the tower. Every circumstance was a negative, and yet the more foolish and idiosyncratic my goal — these insignificant mollusks — the more determined I became. I wanted to go where there was, in effect, nothing to see: no ruins for distraction, no tour books to lug along pointing out this and that, no lure of any sort. Just a place haunted, as Paddy Joe had remarked, by the past. The goal of seeing history where there was none became an obsession.

The sea shells, of course, are symbolic. They were to be a lesson to me of the bizarre little mazes through which a love of Ireland and its past can lead. There is nothing exotic about *purpura lapillus*. Even a blow-harding bus tour operator would find it hard indeed to glamorize such a puny life form. I see it as a source, as a way of removing the Book of Lindisfarne, the Book of Kells and the Book of Durrow straight from their atmospherically controlled display cases into my hands. Those manuscripts conceptually belong here, in the wild. This is where they were written, out to sea on the Inishmurrays, Ionas, and Inishkea Norths. In the middle of winter on days like this, monks in dank and drafty cells "weary with writing", nonetheless "travelled across the plain of shining books without ceasing."

IT MAY SEEM incongruous to compare a place like this with manuscripts universally regarded as among the masterpieces of human artistic expression. Lines form in the summer at the Library of Trinity College in Dublin to see the Book of Kells, and the Lindisfarne Gospel Book is reverentially displayed in London's mammoth British Library, surrounded by hundreds of other exhibits and all worth millions and millions of dollars. What we see are decorative pages of incredible delicacy and innovation, paintings with extraordinary coloration that at times are overwhelming in their emotive impact, a mastery of engineering precision that equals the greatest building or bridge. "Dense but delicate", as my wife once remarked to me in a whisper, and I remember the whisper as much as I do the insight. Anything sacred is usually pointed out in a hush.

But the noisy, wind-ridden severity of an Inishkea North is no museum. There are no whispers here, only shouts; no elegance, only mud; very little in the way of triumph, more likely wretched defeat and despair; no princely halls of a noble Tara, only the miry slime of a cattle stall.

THE BOOK OF Kells that the monks of Iona so elaborately scripted and painted on heavy sheets of vellum was born amid disaster. The Viking slaughters are laconically recorded in the old Irish annals, so too the flight of all the brothers back to Ireland, to their *paruchia's* more serene monastery at Kells in County Meath, given "to Columcille the musical, without battle." Abbot Cellach, who supervised the melancholy resettlement, resigned his office when the transfer was complete. He returned to Iona as a hermit, hiding in some corner of the island or another, avoiding heathen warriors as they periodically swooped down looking for more plunder. The ninth century records many Irish monks refusing to forsake Iona and its now ruined monastery. Many were murdered by the Vikings.

At Kells the Gospels were finished, a labor that scholars calculate must certainly have consumed many years. They are the work of several master painters and scribes, who as a class were among the most honored of any monastery's brethren. Old ecclesiastical laws often placed the scribe on the same legal footing as a bishop for they, and they alone, had the ability to "seize the light above". A Norman cleric over three centuries later imagined that these beautiful books were divinely drawn — "nothing seems to me more miraculous," he said when viewing them.

> If you look at them carelessly and casually and not too closely, you may judge them to be mere daubs rather than careful composi-
> tions. You will see nothing subtle where everything is subtle. But if you take the trouble to look very closely, and penetrate with your eyes to the secrets of the artistry, you will notice such intricacies, so delicate and subtle, so close together and well-knitted, so in-
> volved and bound together, and so fresh still in their colourings that you will not hesitate to declare that all these things must have been the result of the work, not of men, but of angels.

He would have been shocked to realize that many of the motifs and ornamentations which he found so stunning were in fact a direct trans-
ferral of pagan decoration, reworked to a Christian format.

Kells, though temporarily a successful refuge, was little spared later ravages of murder and desecration. Like most Celtic monasteries it was periodically plundered by roving packs of Scandinavian pirates, Irish

Market Cross, Kells, County Meath

renegades, Norman invaders and Scottish freebooters. One of its glorious high crosses, in fact, was used by the British as a gibbet in 1798.[1] The precious book was frequently bundled off to the round tower when alarm bells rang. In 1007 it was stolen, the jeweled cover ripped off (along with several pages) and the residue hastily buried. "The chief relic of the Western World" lay beneath the sod of a farm field for months before it was found again by chance. The thief was never caught.

It is certainly no wonder that few Celtic manuscripts have survived to our times. Were they but a residue of a far greater number? Most scholars think so. The Egyptian tradition of copying and decorating manuscripts was clearly practiced in Ireland on a large scale.[2] Adomnán, parts of whose biography of Columcille were transcribed directly from the *Life of St. Martin* by Sulpicius Severus, added the words "and writing" to Severus's description of Martin's day, namely "prayer" and "reading". Monastic documents that have survived are replete with instructions for scribes, most particularly that before finishing a document they recheck their work most diligently to its original, and not to make corrections or additions unless absolutely necessary. But fire and pillage made havoc of their many hours of labor. Even Brian Boru, the mighty warlord who died at the Battle of Clontarf on Good Friday, 1014, was aware of the tremendous losses, sending monks abroad with commissions to purchase manuscripts for the restocking of libraries in Ireland.

Today, just a handful of the great Gospels remain, their travels through centuries of Irish turmoil largely unknown to us. The writings of antiquarians from the seventeenth to nineteenth centuries offer some clues. Seemingly insignificant or unintelligible books (or those without decoration), appear to have just simply disappeared, either thrown away by ignorant individuals clearing out an attic, stolen by amateur scholars from Continental libraries and monasteries, or simply used as stuffing or binder covers for works deemed more important. Some of the finer manuscripts, or the more famous, such as the Books of Mulling, Dimma, and Armagh, largely evolved into the possession of hereditary custodians. In the case of the *Cathach*, or Battler, of Columcille, this turned out to be an O'Donnell sept from Donegal, and the ancient psalter passed down from hand to hand through countless generations, sharing that family's transformation from its once proud position of lordship and landowner to that of dispossessed mercenaries in France. Within the localized Gaelic society, of course, everyone knew who had what. One of the Four Masters, the monk Michael O'Cleary, was sent in disguise from Louvain back to Ireland in 1620 with specific instructions "to follow the track of old books". Using tips and barnyard gossip he chased down many a genealogy

---

[1] The Market Cross, transferred from the monastic site into town, 1698.
[2] It is interesting to note the opinion of Françoise Henry that the decorative habit of placing red dots in and around various letters, words and pages is directly attributable to Egyptian models.

and prayer book and saga, which were dutifully copied. Many of these custodians continued the old habit of equating their ancient Gospels with magic, renting out what scrapes of tattered manuscripts they still possessed to farmers, who would soak them in buckets of water and tie the pages round a sick cow's neck. That any vellum or brilliant ink survived such treatment is more the miracle.[1]

By 1700 there were enough antiquarian gentlemen about that a market developed in ancient manuscripts. This was a fairly select group of collectors, however. The poet Tom Moore, for instance, wrote his *History of Ireland* with no inkling whatever of the manuscript sources then available that might have given some backbone to what was otherwise a work of fluff. When confronted with the Books of Ballymote and Lecan in the study of a learned acquaintance, he was shocked and embarrassed. "I never knew anything about them before," he said. "I had no right to have undertaken my history." But scholars of a more serious bent searched for and purchased what remnants they could find. "I wish to save as many as I can from the wreck which has overwhelmed everything that once belonged to us," as one enthusiast noted.

Curiously enough, Protestant antiquaries were heavy contributors to the rescue effort, the earliest and most famous being James Ussher, appointed Primate of All Ireland by James I in 1625. Ussher detested Catholicism — the Pope is declared to be Antichrist, he once wrote, "that man of sin foretold in the Holy Scriptures" — but he was a learned cleric of reasonable disposition and quiet, scholarly habits. He wrote widely on the religious questions of his day, which were considerable and disputatious, and managed on more than one occasion to find himself at the very center of catastrophic political happenings. He stood on the execution platform when the controversial Thomas Wentworth, Earl of Strafford, was beheaded in 1641, an event many consider the beginning of Charles I's precipitous decline. He also whispered final words to Archbishop Laud when he too lost his head to the ax, and watched the King's execution four years later which, as a Royalist, he considered a disaster. From an old Norman family (his surname derived from an ancestor who accompanied John Plantagenet to Ireland in 1185 as that knight's usher) he had a keen interest in Irish religious history and the rather modern conception that original source material was far to be preferred over other peoples' written commentaries and second-hand opinions. He began collecting at an early age and, while stingy with household purse strings ("Phebe's apparel cost £40!" he scribbled on the back of an envelope), a friend once noted that "for books he had a kind of laudable

---

[1] Resistance to water was a noted attribute of these books. The Lindisfarne Gospel was allegedly dropped in the sea by monks fleeing for Ireland. It was recovered four days later with no ill effects. And an annalist reported that "Whatever book Columcille would write, it might be ever so long under water and not even a single letter in it would be drowned (i.e., washed away)."

covetousness, and never thought a good one, either manuscript or printed, too dear." He purchased the Book of Kells, it is believed, from one or another of the Plunkett family, who had regularly served as Abbots of Columcille's old monastery of Kells until forfeited to the crown in 1539.

There is no reason to think he paid too much for it.[1] The infamous Florence MacMoyer, for instance, pawned the Book of Armagh for £5 to a "Protestant gentleman". MacMoyer was another hereditary custodian. In fact his family name, Maor na Canóine, translates from the Irish as Steward of the Canon. In pre-Elizabethan times this carried with it stipends of considerable value, the MacMoyers holding over seven thousand acres in County Armagh that generated something like £3500 in rental income a year. With the Plantation of Ulster, however, they lost it all, and Florence MacMoyer spent his adult years leasing a miserable croft on property that had once been his. It was the lure of "an estate as good as ever your grandfather had" that compelled him to give false testimony in London against the Catholic Primate of Ireland, Oliver Plunkett, whose trial, a grave travesty, ended in martyrdom on Tyburn Hill, July 1, 1681. It is ironic that the venerable and sacred Book of Armagh, when translated into cash by MacMoyer to cover his travelling expenses to the trial, was indirectly responsible for the creation of yet another Catholic saint.

MacMoyer never saw the Gospel book again. It is known to have travelled through at least four Protestant families since that unholy transaction, finally reaching safe haven at the Royal Irish Academy in 1854.

The Book of Lismore was fortunate to survive at all. Workmen smashing through a wall in Lismore Castle, County Waterford, found the rat-gnawed manuscript in a dank wooden box, along with an ancient Irish crozier. They and subsequent examiners purloined several folios until at last the Duke of Devonshire, on whose property the Book had been discovered, was convinced to take some steps for its protection, most notably by Eugene O'Curry, whose diligence as a detective in this matter is legendary.

Many antiquarians, however, had no luck. "I went to visit old Flaherty," wrote one Doctor Molyneux in 1709 about a famous hedge scholar, "who lives, very old, in a miserable condition at Park, some 3 hours west of

---

[1] Ussher's collection of ten thousand pieces, along with some plate and jewelry, was all that survived the Rebellion of 1641, which saw his estates and country houses burned to the ground. Ussher lived a penurious existence thereafter. Even his library was confiscated by the Puritans, though when offered for sale a friend purchased the collection and returned it to him. When Ussher died in 1656 these books represented his daughter's sole inheritance, and she in turn auctioned the library for £2200, that sum, ironically enough, raised by subscription from Oliver Cromwell's Irish forces and given in bulk to Trinity College, where it was largely lost track of. A notation dated 1705 reads, "The Library of Trinity College, Dublin, where the noble Study of Bishop Ussher was placed, is quite neglected and in no order, so 'tis perfectly useless; the Provost and Fellows of that college having no regard for books and learning."

Galway in West Connaught. In my life I never saw so strangely wild a country; nothing appeared but stones. I expected to have seen here some old Irish manuscripts, but his ill fortune has stripped him of these as well as his other goods, so that he has nothing now left but some few of his own writing, and a few old rummish books of History, printed."

The learned literature on these manuscripts is, not surprisingly, wide and argumentative. Françoise Henry, in fact, until her relatively recent death, was probably the world's foremost authority on the Book of Kells. There was not a brush-stroke in that entire book that escaped her severe scrutiny, and memorably literate dissections could range from elegant, Francophile generalities on artistic aesthetics ("Enriching its rather meager initial repertory with various borrowings from Oriental or Germanic patterns, it went on using principles of composition and methods of drawing which went back to its early past, and so evolved one of the most successful abstract arts which the world has ever known"); to a clinician's report on the chemical properties in each of the paints used by the monks — mineral pigments such as red and white lead, orpiment and verdigris for yellows and greens, ultramarine from the stone, lapis lazuli, and organic dyes from vegetable or animal matter: *purpura lapillus*,[1] of course, carmine red extracted from an insect known as the kermes, various leaves and foliage (woad, indigo, holly) that produced blues, pinks, purples. This is all fascinating material. It smells of quiet studies and cups of tea, open binders full of scribbled notes, sedate libraries and bow-tied custodians, all images that I enjoy immensely. But the picture that an Inishkea North delivers is somewhat different. I see the interior of a small stone chapel, perhaps a *clochán*, though possibly one of the larger boat-shaped oratories such as Gallarus down on the Dingle Peninsula. At the altar, by the eastern window, the great Mass book opened to one of the Gospels, with only the light of a candle or two to supplement the dim grey of a winter dawn. Amidst these somber tones and shades, would not the streak of color in the robe of Matthew, or the luminous halo surrounding the head of Christ, not seem indeed a gift from heaven? Would not the ink from *purpura lapillus* seem a beauty that only God could create? "Nightfall and time for supper", a scribe once wrote in the margin of his manuscript. "How much vellum, O Hand, hast thou written? You will make famous the vellum, while you yourself will become the bare top of a pile of bones."

---

[1] Curiously enough, the Book of Kells is the only insular illuminated manuscript for which Henry questioned the use of *purpura lapillus*.

St. Luke the Evangelist
Codex 51, Stiftsbibliothek, St. Gallen, Switzerland

FROM THE TOWER a narrow road runs downhill to a small beach that faces the Duvillauns. On either side modest cottages and bungalows stand in line, the homes of those who once lived out to sea on Inishkea North and South. Some are deserted and falling apart, others send thin wisps of peat or coal smoke into the gale through squat and chubby chimneys. Walking down the lane I look for the house of John Riley, a survivor of October 28, 1927.

The cataclysmic event for Galway and Mayo fishermen these past hundred and fifty years had nothing to do with land league agitation, the revolution for independence, black and tans, World War I or II, the great depression of the twenties, entry into the Common Market or even the Virgin Mary's apparition in the tiny village of nearby Knock. It was the "Terrible Western Tragedy" of an October evening in 1927, the "most sudden, the most remarkable, the most disastrous storm on record". Forty-five fishermen, all in curraghs weighted down with tons of nets full of mackerel, were obliterated in an avalanche of wind and wave. Nine islanders from Inishbofin in Galway, seventeen from Cleggan Bay, nine from Lacken and ten from the Inishkeas died in a span of thirty to forty minutes.

Excerpts from the various Official Inquests:
Festy Feeney stated he was in one of the boats that left Cleggan. There were four other men and they carried nets weighing almost a ton. These occupied about one fifth of the boat, leaving no room for working her. "We started shooting the nets after 6 o'clock, and were engaged at it when the gale came on. We were about a quarter mile out from the shore at the time. All the boats were shooting their nets together, and were about 400 yards apart." Asked if he had any indication of the gale, or if it was expected, the witness replied, "No. It was a grand calm night, the sea being like a lake. Then suddenly the gale came along roaring, and the sea was lashed into huge breakers. We had two nets hauled into the boat at the time but we had to cut the others and make off."
Question: "During the time you were hauling and cutting nets, did you see other boats?"
Witness: "It was impossible to see anything when the gale came on. There was nothing but spray and salt water flying over us. This was the fiercest gale I was ever in. I never experienced anything like it before."
Question: "If you had not seven nets in the boat, would you have been able to have brought your boat home?"
Witness: "I could not tell you. It was God who brought us home."

Remarks of the local doctor:
"Curraghs are small miserable craft. They are suicide tubs. It was criminal folly to allow people to risk their lives in this manner in order to obtain their supper."

Testimony of the coroner:

"Bodies are gradually being discovered, many in advanced stages of decomposition. The body of a headless man was found on Tuesday at Blacksod. Through a birthmark on the finger it was identified. It was coffined that evening and buried."

A reporter, *The Ballina Herald*:

"One of the Kearneys was observed getting up on a rock and waving his hand towards the shore, when a wave dashed him off the rocks and he disappeared immediately. All yesterday the fisher folk scanned the waves for any trace of the men, but their vigil has been unrewarded. The scene at the pier baffles description."

A reporter, *The Galway Observer*:

"The night was beautifully fine and clear, but very dark. Dark nights are best for fishing in the bay. The hurricane swept down on the boats with frightful suddenness. The balance of the nets that had not been boarded were hurriedly cut adrift and the fight for life began. The boats, all curraghs, made for the pier. At first slight progress was made but after an hour's fruitless effort the crews found themselves being carried towards the cliffs in a tempestuous sea. Heavy waves broke over the boats, which soon became half full of water. In some cases the oars were wrenched out of the crews' hands. All hope was abandoned. The boat soon cracked against the rocks and the whole bottom fell out of her. The crew were precipitated into the raging sea."

Thomas Williams, fisherman, *The St. Patrick*:

"I went down twice, and when I came up the second time I caught hold of some floating wreckage. The next place I found myself was on the shore, being swept in by a huge wave." That same wave had also swept the remainder of the crew onto the shore as well, but Anthony Kearney, who was lame, was swept out again by a receding wave and was seen no more.

A reporter, *The Ballina Herald*:

"Carrying stable lamps, the men and women of the village were loudly shouting the names of their friends, and imploring God to save them, and when all hope was given up for the drowned fishermen, Fr. Quinn, raising his hand in the darkness of the night, pronounced conditional absolution. The scene was heartrending and impressive. Three boats had been smashed on the rocks, and the pieces of them had been washed ashore. The strand was littered with the boards of the boats along with coats, caps, and other articles of clothing belonging to the lost crews. On Saturday morning and even on Friday evening, thousands of seals could be seen on the cliffs and shore, being driven in by the storm. Their roaring and whining added to the horror of the scene."

A reporter, *The Ballina Herald*:

"It is only on Monday that their relatives on Inishkea Islands

Curraghs
Doolin
County Clare

---

learned of the tragic deaths of their breadwinners on Friday night last. On Saturday nine men from the islands risked the crossing to the mainland seeking information that some of the men might have landed safely elsewhere, but weather conditions were so bad that it was not until this morning that two of them, the harbingers of bad tidings, were able to return with the bad news, 'Not so.' Several women fainted, and many became hysterical. Those who had more fortitude and restraint prevented several women and girls from plunging into the sea. Last night, the lights on the islands continued to shine brightly as signals to the absent fishermen, indicating the usual landing places for themselves and their curraghs. Tonight, those lamps are dimmed for fishermen who will never return."

An interview with Fr. Dodd, parish priest of the Inishkeas:
"No finer Christians could be found anywhere; clean living, industrious, and honorable, they were an asset to any nation. No tragedy such as this has ever occurred in this district, and I am fearful of the results. Ten of the most experienced and able fishermen have been lost, and this will mean the end of the fishing industry here. In addition to losing their breadwinners, their families have lost curraghs and gear, they face starvation."

Inishkea obituaries:
"John Monaghan was the only married man among the ten deceased. He leaves a wife and seven children, the eldest being eleven.
Michael Kean, though only nineteen, was the sole breadwinner of his family, supporting an aged father and younger brother.
The deaths of Michael and John Monaghan practically wipe out this family, as there is none left but a crippled brother and an aged mother and father.
The body of John Riley, twenty-one, is the first to be recovered, washed to shore entangled in nets. Clenched in his hand was his little brother's cap, a young lad of fourteen, and also lost."

The Fisher Folk's Calvary:
"These poor people live in wretched conditions. Their heritage is hardship. They live, most of them, in cabins not considered good enough to house the least considered livestock. There are hundreds of one-roomed, tumbledown hovels in which at night the cow, the ass, and oftentimes the pig, are sheltered at one end, and the family live in the other end. The kitchen is at once the bedroom and stable. His stock is everything he has. Food: potatoes, tea, salt fish. No butter. Meat and fowl on Christmas, Easter and the first of November. Eggs are never eaten, but traded for tea. Most of the men go harvesting in Scotland each fall, and depend heavily on money from relations back in America. The young people who have any life in them emigrate abroad."

Mr. O'Connor, M.P.:
> "I knew a young doctor once whose duties brought him to this part of the world for a while. He told me one of his experiences, how he saw a woman delivered of a child, and her bed was a pile of seaweed."

A reporter, *The Connaught Telegraph*:
> "It is quite true to say that today the Gael in his compounds and reservations is as much isolated, ostracized, submerged and degraded as he was in the Penal days. The only things he has freely now are the consolations of his religion. In all else he is much the same — same starvation diet, same old hovel, same old bog. The fish which poor men and boys of the Inishkeas lost their lives in catching were not being sought for sale — there is no market within their reach — but for food, the salted mackerel, which would tide their families over the winter. One might well disbelieve that such conditions could exist widespread in parts of the 26 Counties. It is plainly manifest that many people have drifted into the English mentality which inspired a one-time Chief Secretary, in answer to a question in the British House of Commons, to reply: 'The honourable member need not expect the Government to feed the people of the West of Ireland on chicken and champagne.'"

And a month after the disaster:
> "Bodies are still appearing on the shore. The sea is too rough for islanders to cross over to the mainland for the purposes of identification. But later, with the aid of sweaters and other bits of clothing, they can usually determine who the victim was. Yet another body was found by a man working the seaweed, near Tiraun Point, Blacksod. Two girls were there, and with their aprons they made a stretcher and carried it up the beach to the priest's house."

JOHN RILEY IS over eighty years of age. He is the father of eleven children, who in turn have presented him with thirty grandchildren. Two daughters live in New York (one in the Bronx, the other in Queens). His wife has been over to visit them twice. "I wouldn't live in it," she says stoking the fire, "it's way too fast. You'd want to be young when you go there, do you know. You can't be falling asleep in America, you'd want to be running, running, running for the Dollar."

"I never went across myself," says Mr. Riley, "I never left the holy land."

I ask him what life was like on Inishkea North. "There were about two hundred people living on the islands, maybe thirty families on each. We had roughly ten acres in all, after the Congested Districts Board took away the land from Mr. Welch, who had a large estate out here. In fact, he owned most of the Mullet. Cleared off to England, he did. Along with that we had a share of the common grazing land. Each family had two or three sets of pigs apiece, and every man kept two donkeys. For six months of the year they'd manure your fields, because without that nothing would grow for you. As it was we could raise any kind of cereals and turnips and for a long time potatoes. It was the best land in all the parish for potatoes but for some reason, the potato began to fail on Inishkea. A divine message, maybe, I don't know. We had no canned goods on the island. Plenty of fish, mostly mackerel, that we'd salt each winter, plenty of kelp and limpets, even whaling. And we had poteen. There were two pubs on the place! And a fine school we had, with fine teachers. We learned both languages, English and Irish, though you'd hear no English spoken outside of class. When we came out here to the mainland we were amazed at the people we met, they had no education at all. They couldn't speak either tongue, really, it was more like a broken language they had. We really lived far better than the mainland people, I can tell ye. We ate better and, oh, there was money away making a shilling in there, even as kids. When I was young we used to be looking for bronze pins and bronze needles in the big shell mound. The English used to come over from the colony there to buy them from us. We were happy until disaster happened.

"There was fifty-two of us out, from both islands, in twenty-six boats, the old-style curragh, the ones with tar. They're still going around, there's an odd one you'll see once in a while. And oh, it was the finest night we ever went out, the fish were everywhere. Very dark, though, we could hardly see the glass to see it was dropping. I was about five or six hundred yards off the island, on the ocean side, others more out. Luckily for me, we had pulled up all our nets and were heading back to shore around nine, and in like the blink of an eye there was this great roar and it was on us. The storm just stood up from the ocean."

"Was it stronger than today's winds?"

"Oh, praise God, this is nothing. When the blast came up on my boat it didn't capsize us or flip us over. It just threw us up on the shore like a box of matches. One minute I was in my boat, the next I was sitting on the beach. We lost ten men that night, all of them young. The oldest was only forty, he wasn't old. Left a family of seven. Two lads had the grace of God with them that night, they were put on the shore at Tiraun, down here a ways. As bad as it was, they survived, they two came out. There's that old saying that someone will come out of every war alive, and they did. But ten of our lads, they were gone. Then the Government came in and told us to move. They built us houses over here and just cleared us out."

"Were you anxious to leave?"

"Oh well, not very. This place here on the mainland we thought was no good. Nothing in it, no work, nothing going. Most of the men off the island didn't live long. They died young, because they had to go to work, you know: stockmen, hooking for potatoes, lifting baskets, filling lorries, everything. That's hard work and they weren't used to it. Some of them went to England and America, but they weren't used to going anywhere but where they were. The boys and girls here are still at it, they still emigrate. They come home for Christmas, or never at all. They're not the type to get homesick anymore. The world is too fast now, Ireland has lost them.

"I stayed a fisherman and went back to the island all the time. Many's the winter night I slept in it, I had to. I had to go back, it's there my family made a living, anything to take a shilling out of it. We still have livestock on Inishkea. Not much on it now, we cleared them out before winter. The wide boats make a mess of it, they can't land on the beaches very well, but they've got motors and the job is easier than it was when I was a young lad. No more rowing. We park the boats way down into Blacksod Bay. It's a long way around but no matter. It's worth going where you're safe."

"What about the future out here?" I ask.

"Well, island life is dead. We're too old now to be in there, it's no place for pensioners. And the young people? They're not hardy enough, they have no interest in it or anything else, for that matter, except what money can buy. They don't have the Gaelic any more, which is all we speak in this house. The old people use it, but not the younger ones. And they have no religion. You take the family rosary. It's dying out, I tell ye, it's dying out. I'm still on to it, thanks be to God, but these smart youngsters want nothing to do with it. There's no fear of God in them, and you can't live in at Inishkea without it. It's a queer thing, I say this many times to my wife, but here are these young lads with far better educations than we ever had, and they really aren't educated at all. And no manners. If you were working and they were passing you by all the day long, they'd never say 'God bless the day', 'God bless the world', 'God bless the work'. They have no values at all, and it's the death of old Ireland."

After leaving Mr. Riley's I return to my car and drive down the lane through this community of island exiles. It is early evening. The ocean is one immense cauldron of white caps and boiling water. All of a sudden at a small gully the road ends, immersed in sand and runoff from the hillside of Termonn. I get out to wade through in my Wellingtons to see if it is shallow enough to pass.

IT SEEMS APPROPRIATE to me now, being at the end of this road that simply trails off into the water, in what must be the most cheerless and dreary corner of this entire island, to think of the other niche in the Celtic persona, the one that coexisted, paradoxically, with the sometimes boyish joy that Irish monks could bring to their studies and the demanding run for knowledge of almost any sort that they craved. Some might call it the dark side to the Irish soul, the penitential urge.

Former Catholics may well cringe from this topic. What more grisly memories from their childhoods can they dredge up than those of waiting in a long line, in the dimmest corner of church, for their turn to offer confession in hushed and embarrassed whispers to an unseen though perhaps familiar priest? For some, this archaic ritual may well be the road too far, the final, undignified step they will no longer tolerate having anything to do with. Like fasting and going on retreats, it all has to do with memories far and distant.

But of course we come again to a place like this, rich in heavy, mordant, cheerless overtones, all browns, grays and sodden greens, all dank and heavy with nature's bombast, the very parody of death. Walking along the shore I really have to laugh out loud, more at myself than anything else. Am I slipping too purposefully into a wallow of gloom? Am I remaining faithful to my genuine (and Catholic) remembrance of things in my own sinful past that did not go well, or is this all a phony, touristic exercise, just wading through an obligatory, funereal afternoon because I have no ride out to Inishkea and am waiting for the pub to open so I can warm up? It was a penitent, as I recall, out on Banna Strand in County Kerry, in the middle of the night on Good Friday, 1916, who stumbled over the raft that Roger Casement and his two companions had rowed in from a German submarine offshore. Any other evening, any other country, and Casement might never have been arrested. But it had been Good Friday, and the conscience-striken farmer had been searching his soul as he trudged along the beach. That's an image I can understand. I remember all those vigils and retreats myself. And I rather like this walk.

For all my Catholic brethren, we have the Irish to thank for these muddled feelings, and many of us are better off for them I think. A goodly measure of regret over errors from "this dead life" and the resolution to avoid repeating them is a valuable ingredient in any human being, though badly out of fashion today, where we are admonished to do as we like as often as we like and to ignore the consequences. For a Catholicism so devastated by modern thought, so often ridiculed by intellectuals and, paradoxically enough, many of its own adherents, a religion "self-satisfied and unfertilized" by any "deeper meaning", it is ironic indeed that so archaic a tradition as penance offers some of us the only meaning still left in the old hulk.[1] Penance, or more properly, the penitential impulse, is all that stands between us and a venal society pulling its people the other way. It is the only force that I see saying "no". It says it to me all the time. In that great burst of Celtic energy towards both England and the Continent that we witness in the historical record of the seventh century, the Irish brought more with them than a love for learning and a knack for teaching. They brought this heavy conscience as well.

THE SACRAMENTAL STATUS of penance has little foundation in Scripture, and in fact it was not until the Fourth Lateran Council of 1215 that the Church codified the various steps for the remission of sin into anything at all resembling legislation. Jesus was vague on the subject.

---

[1] The poet Philip Larkin derided Christianity as "That vast moth-eaten musical brocade."

He certainly spoke in general terms about sin and forgiveness, on the charity required to herd stray sheep back into the fold. But the closest he ever came to direct instructions was his remark to the disciples, "Whose sins you shall forgive, they are forgiven them; and whose sins you shall retain, they are retained." Paul, in his letters to the Corinthians, speaks vaguely about a congregation "gathered together" to punish individuals guilty of serious sin, but nothing more.

In its earliest practices the ancient Church apparently improvised, using the biblical images of sackcloth and ashes for its most useful expression of remorse and punishment. Sinners were dunned in public before the entire congregation. They stood in the rear at services dressed as though in mourning, were refused any sacraments and often found themselves formally expelled from attendance for a specified period of time. Publicity and humiliation were keynotes, and penitents were generally unanimous in wanting something more private, a squeamishness ridiculed by that great moralist Tertullian when he asked, "Is it better to be damned in secret than to be absolved in public?"

The procedure was usually confined to errors of substantial gravity, and Tertullian even thought that some offenses to God were so extraordinary as to be deemed "irremissible". The early Fathers were also harsh on recidivism — "As one baptism," wrote Ambrose, "so one penance." With the Church's growth in power this tended to place enormous pressure on bishops, whose ceremonial preeminence made them, in public, the natural dispensers of divine forgiveness, thereby focusing the enmities of warlords and recalcitrant kings (guilty of more than a few transgressions against people and places) on God's anointed leaders.

As the ascetic movement developed in parallel with the day-to-day Church, a separate tradition grew as well. In Egypt and the deserts of the Holy Land, monks and hermits lived a life of continual remorse, "as though at the mouth of Hell". Abstinence, mortification of the flesh, continual prayer, the magnification of any failure into a sin so horrific that eternal damnation was foreordained[1] — all these extreme positions, reflecting as they did the harshness of the environment, tended to develop a custom and attitude towards penance more reminiscent of John the Baptist than of Jesus Christ. The notions of pervasive sin naturally encouraged the habit, and ideal, of perpetual atonement.

In Ireland, as we have suggested throughout this book, the rigor of these desert principles emerged as it did nowhere else, and in the matter of penance the Celts made perhaps their most fundamental impact on the body of Catholic canon. It was a dubious and entirely fruitless contribution in the opinion of many, but historical and interesting nevertheless.

---

[1] A hermit in Egypt condemned himself to six month of nakedness in a swamp infested with insects after he had slapped a mosquito on his foot. In a moment of reflection he had seen this act as one of sinful revenge.

Hermit's Cell
Saul
County Down

When the ethos of the Desert Fathers reached their shores, the Irish were ready with a system to codify and spread it. As has been remarked in many examinations of Celtic law and custom, its heritage was in large measure uninfluenced by Roman or Latin culture. Ascetic traditions, those still seen in India, for example, were natural to Celtic society, the most common instance being that of the fast. In socio-political terms individuals could ritualistically fast on others, either on people of higher caste, such as princes or kings, in order to redress wrongs or collect debts. Dishonor fell on those who allowed a faster to suffer so ostentatiously on his doorstep, perhaps to death. Often disagreements could be settled in such formalized fashion, a clearly superior resolution than armed assault or the minor warfare that calling up one's kinfolk for support often entails. In Ireland the transference of this custom into the religious arena was natural. We have seen the saints fast on God, we have seen Adam, burdened with sin, shamelessly doing the same thing, and these stories merely reflect that penitential extremes were routine in the daily life of pagan Ireland. Another characteristic shared with the Brahmin was the admission and atonement for sin. "By confession," said one Brahminic code, "and by repentance, by austerity and by reciting the Veda, a sinner is freed from guilt." If one exchanged "Psalm" or the "Three Fifties" for the word "Veda" you could as likely be reading a Celtic penitential composed by Columbanus or Maelruain. In fact, two very archaic words in the Irish vocabulary were so entrenched in usage and familiar custom that missionaries and even later teachers were unable to replace them with Latin equivalents: *aithrige*, Irish for "penance", and *anmchara* (in the Brahmanic lexicon, *acharya*) which translates as "spiritual guide" or "confessor".

The Merovingian Gaul through which Columbanus travelled had little use for penance. Gregory of Tours did not record seeing any of the butchers with whom he had to deal making amends before bishop and congregation. Vengeance and retaliation were the standard rules of conduct. Confession was generic, the repetition of the *Confiteor* or "I confess to Almighty God . . ." that cropped up during Mass. The example from Rome was little different. Gregory the Great saw Christ's exhortation, "Lazarus, come forth!" as a confirmation that public penance was still the way. But the Celtic missions changed all this.

Columbanus and his contemporaries took a very hard line on sin, and not just the temple-crashing, devil-baiting disorders of dire consequence, but of everyday, small infractions as well, in keeping with exhortations of St. Antony to "die daily". "The diversity of faults," wrote Columbanus,

> needs to be cured by the remedy of a diversity of penance. Accord-
> ingly, brethren, it is so prescribed by the Holy Fathers that we
> should make confession of all things, not only of capital crimes.
> Thus neither are even little sins to be neglected from confession,
> because as it is written, 'He who neglects little things, falls little by

little.' Confession and penance liberate from death.

Thus when Columbanus settled in the Vosges, he came as more than just a monk, or a missionary, or a teacher, or a scholar. He came "as a disturbing element." Franks and Germans were used to the ardor of warfare: the hardships of battle, forced marches, sacrifice, and pain. They even suffered some of those discomforts in their sport, primarily the chase, afterwards (or so contemporary stories of the times relate) falling into the reverse condition of drunken, pleasurable stupors. They had no idea what to make of a Columbanus. This man was a warrior who fought himself, not some hated foe, who chastised his flesh through fasting and self-inflicted privations (at Annegray he often lived on bark and herbs, "fearsome, cold water, let this be thy drink!"), a man who whipped himself with a scourge, genuflected hundreds of times while at prayer, who stood alone with arms outstretched in the famous Irish cross vigil, sometimes up to his neck in a frigid stream "to crucify myself" for sins; a man who slept on the bare ground in caves, with a stone for his pillow, a man who had exiled himself from tribe and kinfolk for no apparent reason. An oddity, Columbanus attracted the curious; then an audience; then emulation; then conversions and followers. The popularity and endowments of Annegray, Luxeuil, and Fontaines all attest to that. And to these people, Columbanus gave the Celtic view on penance. "Confession should be taken," preached Columbanus in his most dramatic break with Continental custom, "before meal-time, going to bed, or howsoever it may be easy to give it." With confession no longer viewed as an extraordinary or singular experience, taken up but once or twice in a lifetime, its more dramatic trappings were dispensed with as well. Frequent confession meant informal confession: no histrionic ceremonies before assembled congregations and bishops' regalia, just conferences and daily remonstrance with a trusted *anmchara*. In the Irish system confession became a resolutely private exercise, and tremendous stress was placed on the selection of one's confessor, usually referred to as a "soul friend". Celtic penitentials and rules abound in their praise — "a man without an *anmchara* is a body without a head," says one — and this stress on individual counsel has certainly come down intact to us today in Catholic custom.

So too has the categorization of sin. Cassian analyzed the various grades of sin and discussed each in turn, but he nowhere filed away the appropriate punishment for committing them. Nor did Antony, Athanasius, the Greek Fathers (they were too subtle for that), or even Martin. But the Irish did. With their highly structured Brahmanic legal codes, their penchant for encyclopedic lists and classifications, their love for distinguishing straw from straw, it was natural for them to satisfy the more austere turn of mind that desert theology demanded by compiling their little dictionaries of penance.

These books, and there are many versions by many different authors still extant, offer in some ways an opportunity for mocking the Irish, and indeed many commentators have enjoyed rummaging through them to find the odd and ridiculous entries:

> He who fails to guard the host carefully, so that a mouse eats it,
> shall do penance for forty days.

> He who indents with his teeth the cup of salvation is commanded
> to make amends by six strokes.

Then too we have the pitiless, harsh, and extreme modes of punishment — the multiplicity of verdicts calling for "one hundred lively blows" for the most meager of offenses — which some critics emphasize as illustrating a Celtic lack of sanity, a mental chaos that can usually be contrasted to a Benedictine's "well-balanced mind". Also evident are the gross inconsistencies and contradictions between the various penitentials, some calling for this, some for that. And finally, the matter of sexual candor. The penitentials do not shirk in this regard. The seventh-century compilation of Cummean, third oldest on record, differentiates quite specifically between the multiplicity of offenses within this genre: the idle daydream, the earnest desire, the acts derived from both, those that cannot be helped ("unintentional pollution"), those that can, sin resulting in issue, sin that flouts the helpless condition of a participant (slave girl with master, for instance), the difference between those in orders (a very great sin indeed) and those who are not. Others delve into unseemly aberration: drinking blood or urine, the eating of excrement or scabs, intercourse with animals or members of the same sex. Some nineteenth-century historians often regarded such explicitness as reflecting a lack of refinement in the Celtic temperament, amounting to the endorsement, as it were, of just those sins which the holy monks were attempting to regulate. Philip Schaff even refused to translate John Cassian's Book VI of the *Institutes*, "On the Spirit of Fornication".

In fact, the penitentials had a lasting influence on European practices. They were disorganized to some degree, it is true, but we must keep in mind that there was no universal custom or writ that applied to penance in the sixth and seventh centuries. Each rule was the product of an individual abbot. These rules would differ in specifics, though unified, in most cases, by their attitudes towards the various sins they catalogued. Barely literate village priests cherished the penitentials. They were an easy reference book from which appropriate penances could be uniformly disbursed. The people could tolerate them as well; no more untidy self-abasements in public. Only the bishops had a quarrel with the Irish system, and that may have had more to do with their dislike of the Irish in general than with the penitential system itself. Although being a bishop in unruly times was not without hazard, they rather enjoyed the notion of publicly humiliating a haughty king or nobleman, especially when the crimes committed may have been against the Church, its clergy or property. The groveling of Henry IV, Holy Roman Emperor, at Canossa in 1077 comes to mind here. Notwithstanding this unusual instance of the bureaucratic Church giving up one of its powers, in the long run it solidified the ecclesiastical grip over society, especially as rules regarding penance were extended from clergy to laity.

With its highly stratified sense of order, and with a legal system to quantify it, the Irish had every notch of the societal hierarchy pegged as to worth: the honor price of fifteen men in Patrick's time, for instance, is thought to have equalled that of one-hundred-five slave women, which in turn were worth three-hundred-fifteen cows and so on. Eventually, with every sin described, annotated, glossed, assessed, and graded, it was a natural turn of events to give each an equivalency or price. And from there it was but a minor leap towards accepting financial gifts as atonement for sin. "If the offender can pay fines," in the words of an old Irish penitential, "his penance is less in proportion." This appears to be an illogical step, morally speaking, but the Irish quite naturally had their own way of looking at things. They could be sly. Many of the Frankish clergy thought them little more than hustlers and sharpers. An amusing abridgement of the Psalter, for example, which recorded two or three verses from each Psalm, legitimizes a short cut should the monk oversleep or be too busy for his daily "Three Fifties" — reading the one is pronounced just as efficacious as reading the whole. The same was true for reciting hymns: if in a hurry, scan only the finale, "its grace shall be on the last three *capitula*" is the disingenuous advice. As we all know, this sort of mental contortion and specious arithmetic infected the later history of penance with devastating consequences for the Catholic faith. As Luther was to write in 1519, "There is nothing in the Church which needs reform so much as Confession and Penance."

I HAVE NOW been here for five days waiting on the weather. At news-time I always manage to be in a pub to catch the latest vague and generally inaccurate forecasts on the television news. Tonight the new church, which resembles a drive-in bank, is packed for Benediction. This is one of the few times that I see any bicycles on the road, as the old-timers struggle in through wind and rain for the service. The pub is empty save for three or four toothless reprobates, who mostly talk about fishing and the recent visit of Ronald Reagan to Ireland. While he was here, the President evidently drank Smithwick's Ale and not the famous Guiness stout, which one of these fellows considers "a tremendous let-down altogether." No tourist poster or picture book on Ireland will be tempted to record this place: a grimy, filth-ridden bar, cold and dank, with a cheerless and crudely-poured concrete floor littered with cigarette butts, match sticks, candy and potato chip wrappers, l.p. gas canisters, milk cartons, a crate of bananas and the mud and dung of foot traffic from several years past. And yet here is the essence of the place in many ways: good conversation, peasant wisdom, generosity of spirit and glasses of thick porter to beat off the chill. Some women come in from church in high spirits, one of them wife to one of the drinkers here. "You should have come, John," she says. "It was truly lovely, the bells and candles, the incense and a priest dowsing the crowd with it. Waving away our sins. 'Twas grand." Behind her back a thick bull at the counter tweaks his friend. "When the priest be over I'll send him after you, John, or are ye past it?" Whatever mood existed here dissolves, however, when a new barmaid comes in with her cassette player and buries the place in American country-western music. To make matters worse, she sings along. "The evening train's a'coming, Kick off your shoes, Turn out the lights, Make love to me tonight." "Christ, Paddy," says one of the fishermen, "there's never been any trains out here." We all pay up and leave.

Good weather is due tomorrow. My man says he'll pick me up at Blacksod Point, 9:00 A.M.

After several evenings camping out on top of Termonn Hill, I decide to sleep down by the jetty at the lighthouse. There were times up there when I thought the Citroën would be tumbled over on its side by the heavy gusts of wind or, worse still, down into the sea. I park between the skeletons of two curraghs, partially buried in sea sand, and spend a comparatively peaceful night.

The next morning I'm up early, gear packed. Today's the day, clear weather, seems calm. Unfortunately I spot a fairly large tramp steamer anchored deep in Blacksod Bay. Not a good sign, I say to myself, nor the appearance of another one two hours later, probably Spanish or Portuguese. These gentlemen, I fear, know something I do not. At 9:00 o'clock I see my passage chugging down the bay, but instead of coming to me he putters back and forth among his traps. At eleven he ties up to the jetty. We have a short, though heated, discussion. He has work to do, traps he wants cleared to more sheltered waters. I ask repeatedly if he intends to take me out, as promised. Again more talk about pots, swells, wrack, deep water, rocks, "clog'em in sand and that's it, you never see them again." He no longer looks me in the eye at all. I press him further, is he going to take me out? No direct response. I am reminded here of an exasperating lack in the Gaelic vocabulary. There is no word for either yes or no.

We finally agree that his pots are mostly safe; that he has the time to go, but not in this boat, there's nowhere on the island he can land with it; but that he does have a curragh which can put us on at the beach, he has an outboard motor to stick on the back of it, he even has some petrol; but unfortunately the curragh is back at his house, if he returns back in his lobster boat to get it the day will be over; but, again unfortunately, his car is inoperable, he has no ride to his house, and no, it's no use for me to drive him to the curragh because there's no hitch on the Citroën; Seamus, however, "over there", has a hitch and presumably his vehicle is in running order; but Seamus undoubtedly isn't home now, though there is the possibility, slight as it may be, that he is; if he were, would I tip him for the use of his car; if I would, maybe we could knock on his door.

At 2:00 P.M. we haul a heavy old curragh into the water at Blacksod Point and start off. It will take an hour, I'm told, to reach Inishkea North.

There were two or three moments in this improbable voyage, begun under circumstances that would have daunted any saint, when I noticed in the back of my mind that things were not looking good. Those little premonitory warnings were soon to be obliterated by overwhelming fear, a condition not ameliorated by my companion's incessant pessimism. Entering the open water of the bay we were first hit by very fresh winds from the infamous southwest. These were chopping up the water into ugly, backslapping waves which hit our boat with abrasive whacks and drenching spray. "I don't like this," the captain shouted. More worrisome was the view of a third vessel, a large trawler, cruising past us towards shelter. "Are they from here?" I yell?

"Never seen them before. You can bet he has the ear of God."

"You mean a wireless? They know of a storm or something?"

"That too, I'm sure. No, he's got the sixth sense. We should turn back."

"Keep going!"

As we near the Duvillauns, the wind is just a steady long whistle, the waves bigger and more menacing, the boat filling up with water. I am tossed an old paint can and bail it out. The curragh, about 20 feet long, seems utterly seaworthy and I continue to deceive myself that this is just a normal seafaring exercise, well in the tradition of a marine prowess for which these islanders were and still are properly regarded. But after shooting through the Duvillauns into the open ocean I change my tune.

For some reason, heroic visions and memories from adventure (and disaster) books that I had read long ago, many of them children's stories, crowded my head as we took in our first rollers. This was being face to face with enormous danger and it left me speechless. Alpine peaks, the Matterhorn in a gale, clipper ships driven onto sand bars and rocky cliffs and, yes, October 28, 1927. I have been in rough water before, but never in a small craft. My tongue was so thickened that I couldn't talk. What we had ventured into were waves so large and so broad that it seemed to take minutes to traverse a single one. They were gigantic loaves, in my estimation about 25 feet high and easily 10 feet or so across. At the peak, menacing little filigrees of foam and curling water spouts, reminiscent of those famous Japanese woodcuts, added just the right touch of doom, followed by a long and dizzying plunge back into the trough. "Oh Jesus

Christ," shouted the captain, "no chance, mister, no chance today!"

"You're right," I yelled back to him, "a wasted run. Keep her into the weather for a few minutes more." Disbelieving, he nods agreement.

Storm banks on the horizon come to view as we take in a few more suicide runs up and down the rollers. This is what Riley meant when he mentioned watching the glass fall and being nowhere close to land. Before turning back I recall what my mission was before all this turmoil hit us. I can see the Inishkeas to the north of us. I'd like to say that I picked out *Baile Mór*, or the strand, or some of the old cottages still there, but I cannot. The place is shrouded in sea mist. Without any word from me, the captain carefully sidles between two waves and reverses course. He is positively merry on the way back.

S AVE FOR A lone t-shirt, I no longer possess a single piece of dry clothing. I will drape my trousers, socks and underwear up by the car's heater, a meager contraption indeed, simply a vent direct from the motor, and arrange some shirts and sweaters on hangers in the back. Maybe by the time I reach Galway late tonight I can resume a normal appearance. I know these roads so well now that in the glowering dusk I simply head off to Termonn Hill, down to the little village, straight across the wash, water flying, and on up past John Riley's place to the watch-tower. Inishkea North sits out to sea in my last view of it before heading off down the Belmullet road, not in a defiant, majestic pose but rather as a stolid piece of the scenery, a minor player, a bit part in the incredible operatic performance about to be unleashed, if the pattering of raindrops on my windscreen is any indication. In the *Martyrology of Donegal* there is a reference to one St. Kieran: "It is he that used to go to the sea rock that was far distant in the sea, and used to return again." Well, I tried. The sea rock was there, the good intentions were there, but I returned having never set foot on the place. If I were in a confessional mode, what imagery there could be for a failure so pointed. But right now, I'm just tired.

"What really exists is not things made but things in the making," William James once wrote. By that yardstick nothing is alive here. Religion is dead, language is dead, memory is dead. Only a few shards remain in the graveyards of old Erin, to be chewed and licked by strays who wander about in battered old cars and leaking boots. To them belongs the joy of the search.

> There are three northern gates of the heavenly city which Saint James guards, that is baptism, penitence, martyrdom.
> Irish, ninth or tenth century

Afterword

17 September 1985

Dear Jim,

Thank you for your letter and i do hope you are all right and not too depressed after the Death of your poor mother God rest her soul. My mother will be saddened to hear that news as she is up in the midlands at the moment with my sister for a months holidays and i have written to tell her you wrote.

However i am glad you have had a new addition to the family so it might Balance things after your great loss as i can well imagine. Also the loss of the home place to fire must be a further blow as it was the hearth you set out from and no doubt it grieved you to part with it.

I have always believed that no matter what you own or get in this world will be taken away sooner or later as that is how this cruel world works.

Well Jim i am glad to inform you that i had great luck about the armada since last i met you, as i got an English team to dive in the area and we found all 3 ships the second day out and managed to salvage 3 cannon and 1 cannon ball to stake our salvage claim with the receiver of wrecks about 4 months ago. I thought you might see it on television in the states as it was televised world wide back in may last. I have a third of the claim legally signed and hope we can have the full licence to salvage the artefacts by April next with a bit of luck.

The biggest vessel lies out center way at streedagh beach and the other two lies equal distances west of her as we managed to be able to tell her name from the origin of her guns which were made in Italy and have the date stamped on their front 1571 and a Bishop holding a staff. Her name is the Juliana of 862 tons. And we have found gun carriage wheels to the number of six and 3 large anchors and two other guns we have no permission to lift yet.

I hope this news will raise your spirits and put an end for good and for all the confusion as to the location where those ships were wrecked.

We had a bit of trouble with the Irish government over the matter but we have great maritime solicitors and they are taking care of that end of it.

Well i do hope to see you soon again as i think This business would fascinate you owing to your love of history and things connected with the past, seeing things in reality that have been lost for four Centuries and now lying for all to view.

Jim i will say cherio now and send my deepest regrets as to your recent misfortunes. Our summer here was the worst in living memory, not one good week since July. Tell your wife i asked for her and the baby.

Yours truly
Paddy Joe Brady
Bye

257

Appendix

Some Thoughts on the Careers
of Jesus and St. Paul

I SLANDS OF STORM is a book about the Celtic world of Ireland and Western Scotland at a time when Christianity was first gaining acceptance there. One of the pertinent questions I initially sought to explore when thinking about the first Irish monks was to ask to whom did these early converts devote their lives, the Jesus who actually lived and died in the arid, sun-baked periphery of Palestine, or some artificial permutation that later generations of misguided though imaginative believers constructed from bits of rumor, intellectual flotsam of the period, or the well of personal inventiveness? In this era of religious turmoil these are questions of real interest to a great many people, witness the deluge of books, articles, movies, and television specials on the subject. Identifying the real Jesus (and then appropriating him according to whatever narrow cause it is for which his services are required) has become an international pursuit. Not surprisingly, the various portraits that emerge can vary greatly.

This is a personality that never interested me, I should admit, when I was younger. Perhaps, stereotypically, this resulted from learning the catechism in the company of unusually determined nuns, or later finding myself mutely seated at pews and desks before Benedictine monks with whom, as a teenager, I was lodged for several years. Whatever the cause, I became in college, an easy prey to rationalism, that "most detestable error" according to Pope Leo XIII but more readily understood by the Irish writer Sean O'Faolain in his remark that "thinking is pure poison to innocence". All of this lead to a perfect drought where thoughts of religion never entered my mind.

Why should this be so, not only to myself personally but for countless individuals over the past several hundred years? In large measure because of Christ's extreme familiarity, resulting in a cultural intimacy so pervasive that many people could justifiably feel almost bludgeoned by his persona. This has, not surprisingly, generated warm and somewhat repulsive reams of cliche and bedrock fantasias about the man and his life that no one in Western Europe or America has ever been able to evade. He became so common that he defied any urge to think about him, with every facet of his career prediagnosed by tradition and, in Catholic circles, canonical instruction. Jesus became as interesting as a light bulb.

In fact, this is hardly fair. We cannot blame Jesus for the disservices done him over the course of two thousand years by a varied cast of servants, both obscure and famous. It should help to realize that within just a few days of his death this process of obscuration was well into motion, that there have never been any strata of pure information on the man that came down to us untainted. The life and sayings of Jesus were pretty much propaganda right from the start (even some Catholic theologians now concede this) though to put hope, as many skeptics have, in the theory of some historians that Jesus is an entirely mythical person seems rather perverse.

W HEN WE ENTER our investigation into the life of Jesus we most certainly do not walk alone; we do not go where no man has feared to tread. If anything the road has been so worn down and rutted — washed away, repaired, washed away again — that we can be forgiven should despair afflict us as it has so many others. Consider the poor Germans, for instance. In 1906 Albert Schweitzer dutifully catalogued the theological efforts, mostly by his own countrymen, to produce an untainted version of the "Historical Jesus" whose message could prove as viable for the twentieth century as it was when first preached. Nothing could have been more futile. He would not stay, Schweitzer lamented, Christ "passes by our time and returns to His own." Not only that, the logical culmination of these many and often brilliant studies, certainly not foreseen at the time by Schweitzer and the others, was the aforementioned conclusion that Jesus never existed, was in fact a second-century invention. This seems a disspirited final judgment, leaving the field open to commentators like George Bernard Shaw who professed indifference to an actual Jesus, "as it is the doctrine and not the man that matters," since "one symbol is as good as another provided everyone attaches the same meaning to it." Even Schweitzer could agree with that. "It is not the Jesus as historically known, but Jesus as spiritually risen within men who is significant for our time and can help it," he wrote; which fits rather neatly into a position the monks taught me many years ago and is, I believe, the official stance of Catholicism on this subject — the high road and the low road as I called it then, meaning it was fine and good to inquire into the historical Jesus but that when, inevitably, fact clashed with dogma, never let it confuse you to the point of failing to close the door firmly on one in favor of the other. When fact becomes too obtrusive follow St. Augustine's advice: take the dogma, take your faith, and "without the smallest hesitation, believe it to be so." This was a short leash, sophistically presented as no leash at all. Or to use Schweitzer's metaphor, "fact" ends up encircling "religion without touching it, and, like a lake surrounding some ancient castle, mirrors its image with curious refractions."

Is it possible to know a factual Jesus? Is it even desirable? To the first question no easy answer exists. Everything I may say can, with as much good evidence, be refuted and disposed of with long lists of impressively cited authorities. What it probably all comes down to is what sits best alongside common sense and a dignified avoidance of sectarian bias. And to the second I personally feel that for those to whom religion is a profession, the public response would be a very queasy yes, when in fact the heartfelt reply would be no.

Who was Jesus? Let us be blunt and agree with the Benedictine historian Gregory Dix's assessment that Jesus was "an untutored peasant." That sounds harsh but there is little point in trying to make an intellectual out of him, or for that matter to overstate the capacities of the twelve Galileans he chose for his disciples. They too were men of hard toil and little or no standing in the community, either as scholars or people of substance. In a social sense, master and disciples alike were nobodies. Let us also agree that Jesus was a Jew. Many times a Catholic will forget this, or decide to ignore it, thinking that Jesus rejected Judaism, stalked off on his own into the desert to think things over and returned to found, with his followers, a new and higher religion that took the world by storm. This is false. Jesus lived and died a Jew.

His active career, if we follow its course as described in the Gospels, was relatively meteoric and short-lived. The outline is so familiar that I will dispense with all but a brief outline: Jesus as a young man receives baptism from John the Baptist, he retreats to the desert, is tempted by Satan, returns to Galilee and begins his mission of public ministry. The disciples are called, Jesus preaches in the synagogue but falls out with the Jewish establishment, he turns instead to open

260

air meetings with the multitudes, he enters Jerusalem to purify the Temple and is greeted by the mob as a Messiah, or "Son of David." He is treacherously taken by the authorities, tried before both Jewish and Roman authorities and executed, all to the hysterical approval of that same mob that had glorified him just a few days previously. The Gospels all conclude with a description of his resurrection from the dead. These bare facts – indeed, all there is to know of what Jesus said and did – come from the words of Mark, Matthew, Luke, and John, the Four Evangelists.

Pilate posed the right question, it seems to me – "What is truth?" he asked.[1] For most believing Christians one certain answer would be the Bible. At least there, no error is allowed. If we become confused by anything in it we can cheerfully, as Luther said, "just let it alone" and continue unimpeded as though doubt, even when entertained, can be willed from existence. The Bible, over many centuries, developed an infallibility almost uncontested and, a tribute to the book's power, virtually on its own merits. St. Jerome put it bluntly: "To be ignorant of the Scripture is not to know Christ." But unfortunately in this era of skepticism and loss of faith, to say nothing of merciless, unsentimental scholarship, that remark has now been turned around. We learn about Christianity from the Bible, to be sure. But do we really learn anything about Christ?

Most scholars now feel that we do not receive any genuine eyewitness accounts of Jesus in the Gospels. Attribution of authorship to the Four Evangelists is convenient though misleading, as it would appear that anonymous chroniclers – perhaps disciples of the disciples – were in fact responsible for gathering together from oral recollections and anecdotes that which emerged as the Gospels. The attribution of authorship to a group of later, unknown individuals may appear outlandish, but we should keep in mind several seemingly reasonable conclusions.

First, the original Twelve were not sophisticated men; nor, I think, were many of the first Christians (as Kirsopp Lake, a distinguished professor of religion at Harvard University in the 1920s and 1930s said, Mark's Gospel "would have pained the feelings of any educated Greek"), so much so that the notion of actually writing down, if indeed they could write, the activities and beliefs of Jesus was probably as daunting a task as they could conceive. And second, the Apostles saw no reason to record a life of Jesus. The Prophet's message was basic: Repent, the Kingdom is at hand. It seems a fair deduction, though this is disputed, that both Jesus and his followers sensed an immediacy to this prediction. The End was, quite literally, in sight, so the need for a written record did not seem to exist. The earliest writings we have in the New Testament, after all, are letters – Paul's letters – and they were crisis oriented, composed to confront immediate problems and controversies. The Gospels were more of an afterthought (and composed, it is believed, anywhere from thirty to fifty years after Paul) a result perhaps of the spreading realization that the End had been postponed, and that now was the time to preserve what was left in the memories of old people concerning the

---

[1] "Quid est veritas?" Asked of Jesus at his interrrogation by Pilate. The mystical aura of the Bible led many Christian theologians to search for hidden meanings within various well-known passages, usually anagrams whereby the rearrangement of letters in a sentence might reveal a different meaning altogether. Pilate's query was thus twisted into a cosmic reply, "Est vir qui adest," or "It is he who is before you."

tradition of Jesus.[1] And in fact some theologians dispute whether the Gospels were ever really meant to be vitae at all. They see their intention not as instruments of record but more as creed and teaching — propaganda in fact. While this may appear harsh, a critical examination of the Gospels does seem to reveal varied layers of intent. The bedrock data upon which all else builds would of course be the actual teachings of Jesus. But stacked all over this central core are virtually impenetrable encrustments of alteration, distortion, amendment, accretion, interpretation, opinion, and even prevarication, much of it composed to address the changing circumstances of the early Church. The eminent German theologian Rudolf Bultmann despairingly concluded that "strictly speaking, we can know nothing of the personality of Jesus."

This gloomy assessment would seem to justify Shaw's complaint that it was impossible to read the Gospels "without fantastic confusion of thought," and indeed this must now be true for those whose conception of Jesus strictly follows the traditional portrait with which we are all, believers and nonbelievers alike, so familiar. Shaw was not bothered by that. He felt that no one in the twentieth century paid attention to the Bible anyway, that religions as a public service should warn off the public with a sign: "The Gospels Now Unintelligible to Novices." And he may have been right. What a few cloistered academics think about Jesus will not exactly jibe with what a pope says about him, and to which authority are most people predisposed to listen? The Bible may well have peaked in its influence. It may have done its task so thoroughly that it can be shelved away for the private pleasures of determined scholastics, with the faithful idly skimming those few and fabled passages that most of us can probably recall automatically, the rest of the great book falling away as a hidden mass of verbiage.

Nevertheless, the marvels of quiet and single-minded scholarship continue to impress observers such as myself — the novices — with their insight. It has been established (though again, not without argument) that the Gospel of Mark is apparently the senior of the four. Together with Matthew and Luke these are known as the Synoptic Gospels, from the Greek *synoptikos* or "seen together," the idea being that these three, when diagrammatically compared, have nearly all their content in common. The theory is that Matthew and Luke were both familiar with Mark (and a second set of sayings, since lost, known as "Q" from the German *Quelle* or "source") and, for different reasons, borrowed heavily from what he had written when they put together their separate accounts of Jesus. Matthew, for example (and I use these proper names generically) is a compendium of Mark and "Q", and evidently composed with an eye to straightening out some problems of logic that understandably might have arisen in the missionary work of the first Apostles. Lake points to a revised version of John the Baptist's attitude to Jesus as an example. In the original of Mark's Gospel, the Baptist is seen excoriating the Judeans for wickedness and offering baptism for the remission of their sins. In this spirit he baptizes Jesus. But if Jesus was a God, some may well have asked,

---

[1] The early Church was very much vexed on this technicality by "deceitful scoffers" who mocked Christian converts for their belief in a prophesy that never transpired, arguing "where is the promise of His coming? For since the fathers fell asleep (i.e. the original Apostles), all things continue as they were from the beginning of creation." The author of St. Peter's Second Epistle counseled patience, suggesting God had delayed the great event "for your sake, not wishing that any should perish but that all should turn to repentance."

how could he sin and why did he require baptism? Matthew conceivably addressed this problem by introducing an element of hesitation within John: "It is I who ought to be baptized by thee," he says, but Jesus, for symbolic effect, insists that John baptize him even though he has no need of it.

Luke, some feel, is a major effort to break new ground. Written approximately fifteen years after Mark, it plunders the first Gospel freely but with condescension. Luke comments in his prologue that while others have tried their hand at the sacred narrative (meaning, no doubt, Mark and "Q") he intends to present "an orderly account" based on the most "careful" research. There is the impression here that whoever this author may have been, he intended to do a better job than his predecessors.

The picture of Jesus these three convey is very similar and, I am inclined to believe, generally accurate. His Jewishness, for example, rings especially true. We have here, to my mind, a man running wild. He is obsessed with God, the God of that most Jewish creation, the books of the Old Testament. This Yahweh is dissatisfied; this Yahweh is coming soon. All his prophet Jesus can say is: Beware, Beware and Repent. The Law of the Pharisees, the Law of the Temple, is no longer vitalized, it no longer breathes life, it no longer pleases God, it requires regeneration. Humble your heart and come to God. If you fail to do so, when he comes on the Day of Judgment, now imminent, he will sweep you away.

This is a message from one Jew to another and the Synoptics make this very plain, not only in the famous remark in Matthew — "Do not think I have come to destroy the Law or the Prophets. I have not come to destroy, but to fulfill" — but in several telling episodes, such as that of the Canaanite woman, a gentile or non-Jew, who badgered Jesus to cast out the devil from her daughter. Jesus, operating from a conventional Jewish contempt for infidels, "answered her not a word," complaining to his disciples that "I was not sent except to the lost sheep of Israel." The woman continued to harass Jesus who, losing his temper in the most narrow-minded Pharisaic fashion, exclaimed "It is not fair to take the children's bread and cast it to the dogs." This is not exactly brotherly love but the Canaanite, in Shaw's words, "melted the Jew out of him and made Christ a Christian" by replying "Even dogs eat the crumbs that fall from their master's table," and thereupon Jesus did as she asked. This was exceptional, however. Jesus' directive to the Apostles, "Do not go in the direction of the Gentiles," was quite predictable within the context of his background and intentions.

Did he consider himself a God? This, of course, is a question of some magnitude (though distinct from another, Was he God?) and involves to a large degree what we choose to believe are the meanings of several key words of salutation and description applied to Jesus in the Gospels, words such as Messiah, Christ, Son of Man, Son of God, Logos, Lord, Servant of God. My own memories from childhood and, after that, the sermons and religious instruction that I endured as a teenager, revive for me now what a dreadful linguistic mishmash these terms were put through then. The idea, I suppose, was to reduce everything to essentials, but unfortunately this tended to confuse the very real and often separate implications characteristic of each. Contributing to mental blur were the various languages involved: the Aramaic that Jesus and his followers in all likelihood spoke, the Greek (or pidgin Greek, a blend of the two) that most experts now feel was the everyday language of the Diaspora Jewish community, the pure Greek of the Peloponnesus, where Paul spent so much of his time, the

Hebrew of the Old Testament, the Latin of the Empire — all this finally penetrating my dull ears in English. Imagine the confusion in technical terms as some very subtle theological hairsplitting was transferred (and lost in the process) from one language to the next and later again, to another. It had never been clear to me that Christ — which I had been taught meant simply God the Son — was actually the literal translation of the Aramaic "Messiah" into Greek. Messiah, of course, never meant "God" but "appointed by God," "anointed," i.e. "prophet" if you will. "God," as another example, meant little to the ears of a Greek, but "Lord" did. Logos, or The Word, had no meaning of importance to Jewish ears, but it did to the Greeks, so we read in John that God is The Word. This was interpreted for me as having something to do with the Holy Spirit. Son of Man pretty easily interchanged itself in meaning with Son of God (though the two were distinct) which dovetailed, in the classroom anyway, into a convenient explanation as to what the Trinity was all about.

Since this is not a theological exercise I do not think a long discussion on religious philology would be appropriate here. The point I am trying to convey is that depending on how these particular words strike you, therein lies the answer as to whether Jesus thought himself a god. Most detached scholars (by that I mean secular scholars, or those who make it plain they favor no particular creed or sect) seem to conclude that good arguments can be made for either case, arguments good enough to convince a person to change his mind. However, common sense and an objective study of the Gospels (which should not be read too dogmatically because of the doubts, already mentioned, as to whether Jesus actually said what the chroniclers wrote down) would tend to confirm the impression that Jesus considered himself a prophet, not a god.

We should note that Jesus never said himself, "I am God." He never said, "I am a prophet" either, though he clearly had a message and did not hesitate to preach it. The keynote was basically eschatological, from the Greek *eoxara* or "the last things". Jesus was predicting the end of the world. He was telling Jews to repent before it was too late. He was warning them they could not hide beneath formulas and legalisms of the established Jewish religion, with its pedantic reverence for the Law or Torah, and hope to achieve mercy when the End came. Jesus, quite simply, was a street person, a revivalist, someone who reserved his most passionate tantrums not for sinners (he was always ready to forgive them, no matter the offense) but for the Pharisees, the ultimate hypocrites. If Jesus had a mission it was to reform Judaism. He was, in effect, a Jewish Luther.

He was also, it can be argued, unsure of himself, at least in the beginning. As a Jew, Christ was certainly aware of the prophetic tradition. Progressing from one enthusiastic camp jubilee to another we can see him begin wondering about himself — "Just who am I?" — and gradually he seems to let what others think of him provide the answer. "Who do the crowds say I am?" he asks the disciples, "Who do you say I am?" He is probably both disturbed and thrilled when he hears the reply from Peter, "The Son of the Living God."

Jesus always spoke of this Son in the third person, the Son who would come again on the terrible Day of Judgment. His growing conviction that perhaps he and this Son of God were in fact one and the same was outrageous enough that he continually warned his Apostles not to breathe a word of this fantastic news to any of the multitudinous rabble who were by now thronging about him. He was also formulating and predicting the torment that was to come: "The Son of

Man is to be betrayed into the hands of men, and they will kill him; and on the third day he will arise again." This news (which may well have been a later interpolation by the chroniclers) made the Apostles "exceedingly sorry", but if in fact Jesus said these words, there are some commentators who feel that he was setting up a test. Jesus had come to feel that perhaps he was a Messiah, a prophet, divinely touched by God. No one was to know this until he had proved it by rising from the dead. Many scholars have argued convincingly that, dying on the cross, Jesus realized that his notions were hallucinatory, that in fact, through megalomania or just human vanity, he had deceived himself and that he was dying for nothing. They usually point to the dreadfully despairing "My God, my God, why hast thou forsake me?" as proof. But others, with a latitude the Bible often provides, can point out more optimistic final words, particularly in his promise to the good thief ("This day thou shalt be in Paradise with me") or the more simple and prophetic, "It is consummated."

One could hope that on at least one particular point almost every student of religion or the Bible could agree, that in fact Jesus did die on the cross. But emerging from the relatively straightforward account of the crucifixion we now enter a different realm altogether, that of the Resurrection, and it is beyond my purposes to linger long in a discussion as to whether such an event actually happened. The Resurrection, of course, is probably the central tenet of Christianity, so ingrained in its universal consciousness that few believers probably give it much thought, blinding them, in the words of a Protestant theologian, to the predominate challenge of their religion, "the outrageousness of Christ's claim. Traditional reverence inhibits them from properly assessing it. If He did not in fact rise, His claim is false, and He was a very dangerous personality indeed . . . without question, a lunatic." Those who have considered the problem, and could not bring themselves to accept it, have offered various theories that range from the offhand and simplistic (the Apostles stole the body and later claimed to have seen the risen God) to the exceedingly complex, which hypothesized that Jesus never quite died on the cross. This explanation sounds like something from the outer fringes but the man who propounded it, Heinrich Paulus, was a soberminded believer in God (on his deathbed in 1842 he said, "There is another world") who labored forty years as a professor of theology at Heidelberg University. Paulus noted that victims of a crucifixion generally took hours to die, and even then one could never be certain until putrefaction of the body became apparent. He recalled the experience of Josephus after the fall of Jerusalem in A.D. 70, who on returning from a reconnaissance several miles south of the city came across several hundred crucified Jewish prisoners. He recognized three of these as former friends and managed, after a personal plea to Titus Caesar, to have them cut down. One of these, despite his lengthy ordeal, survived the torture. But Jesus, according to all accounts, had suffered only three hours. It is true he had been nailed to the cross, not trussed to it, and been stabbed in the chest by a centurion with his lance (which Paulus believed may have been therapeutic in the fashion of bleeding a patient with leeches), but nevertheless the end had been too swift. Jesus in effect lapsed into a deathlike coma. He just passed out.

What revived him was the invigorating cool of the mausoleum, and perhaps the oils and herbs that had been rubbed all over his body (one hundred pounds of myrrh and aloes, it seems). Then an earth tremor rolled away the entry stone, Jesus stripped off the burial linens in which he had been wrapped, stumbled out into the fresh air and dressed himself in work clothes he found lying about. When Mary Magdalene came to keep vigil at the tomb, she mistook Jesus as a gardener (a curious detail that John includes in his Gospel) but then fled in terror and joy to inform the disciples. As St. Mark reports, this was news so wondrous they could hardly believe it.

D ESPITE THE VARIOUS moods that ever-changing weather patterns can give this place (and which, leaving the impression of motion, ask us to believe that we too are always seeing something new) there is a sense in this enormous panorama of being frozen in step. This is not the same thing as saying we've entered a time capsule and have now returned to the Inishmurray of A.D. 600. That would involve some kind of touristic miracle, where we could meet a monk and he might give us a tour (as opposed to stoning us to death on suspicions of demonic wizardry, which I think would be more likely). By frozen I mean static, as I imagine Antarctica to be — unchanged and unchanging, regardless of era, despite weather and seasons, in defiance of evolutionary progressions in nature. It is a stifling feeling, like a heavy cloak over our heads, and dependent on the absence of people.

People generally add vitality to a place like this. They certainly make it bearable for everyone else. Most visitors here would hate it if they were alone – too much like prison – and would take some comfort in seeing others behaving as they do: picnicing perhaps, running about, shooting photographs, scratching initials on the stones, reading guide books, looking for rare species of sea birds, littering, talking, playing. To be here in the sense of a mission requires too much of a change in metaphor and can seriously strain one's own feelings of self-importance. Inishmurray (and again, I would think, Antarctica, which I have not visited) strikes me as an immense theatre. The solitary visitor to this place becomes the solitary actor, expecting in this grand arena that something important, something really big, is going to happen in front of this audience of no one. Some gigantic breakthrough in thought, an intense religious vision, a meaningful choice taken here that will alter one's life – all the signs point to it and one expects it, because we're facing here something eternal. Just how a person responds depends largely on what he brings with him.[1]

Perhaps this is all fantasy on my part, complicating something that would otherwise seem matter of fact – an island difficult of access, five or so miles from the coast of Sligo; some monastic ruins from long ago, interspersed with remains from more recent times; long vistas of ocean and mountains; constant gales and seaborne clatter of bird and wave – nothing all that special. Except for time, the notion that here in this wilderness, this faraway speck of rock and bog and water, the solitary visitor can stand as though on the highest Himalayan peak, in a vacuum should he wish. For time has reached a standstill here. As the Psalm says, "A day with the Lord is as a thousand years." And also the remark of an old desert hermit that "Unless a man say in his heart, Only I and God are in the world, he

---

[1] St. Jerome warned that "in solitude pride quickly creeps in, and when a man has fasted for a little while and has seen no one, he thinks himself a person of some account."

shall not find rest." This is as good a place as any to see if this is true.

What is not timeless, I think, is the mystery of the Mass, and in that sense the monks of the sixth and seventh centuries who lived here would certainly have had the advantage over us. They possessed an enviable faith in imponderables, which surely helped them in coping with the lonely and inhospitable life of Inishmurray. During the course of Mass, when the moment came to change bread and wine into the body and blood of Jesus Christ, who could not be envious of the thrill and supreme exhilaration that must flow from being the architect of such a stunning transformation. By defeating idolatry and superstition, Protestant reformers of the past have in a sense taken much of the awe out of life. Their rejection of the Eucharist as the physical body and blood of Jesus, and its replacement as a mere re-enactment, might at some point in the history of mankind be the position of the Catholic Church. But when that day comes it will have no effect on this island. It belongs to the past, and the sacrifice of the Mass (a barbaric term which reveals in an unintended way how close to pagan ritual Christianity really is) will always be appropriate here.

Of the seven sacraments of the Church, the Eucharist and baptism enjoy the superior lineage, but it is with difficulty that either can be absolutely tied to the teachings of Jesus. Jesus, we should repeat, was not intending to found a new religion, with new forms of ritual or new dogmas or new conceptions of who or what God was about. His frame of reference was completely Jewish, and it is fair to say that nearly all his instruction involved the Torah or Law, and his belief that over generations this essential ingredient of Jewish life had utterly lost its vitality. "The Sabbath was made for man," he preached, "not the man for Sabbath." His message was clearly a moral one, as indeed Judaism was, and is, a moral religion.

The ethics of Judaism, in fact, were extremely attractive to those outsiders from the gentile world in search of a value system both pedigreed and sophisticated. Judaism did not toy with men, asking them to believe in a pantheon of foolish gods with more than their share (or so it seemed) of human weakness, vice and triviality. Theirs was one god, a stern god, who demanded that man put value in his life by living it in a just and decent fashion. It was a legalistic outlook, a cold one at times, but it honored virtue and righteousness in all aspects of man's behavior, particularly the sexual. Judaism stood for something, could substantiate its tenets in ancient writings, jealously guarded, that no other religion could claim, and offered its people the pleasures of self-denial.

That Judaism was exclusive proved a problem, however. It had definite foibles, in peculiar dietary laws for one and, more troublesome, an insistence on circumcision as the price of conversion. This custom was deemed repulsive and primitive to most outsiders, and it proved to be the issue that pushed the new sect of Jesus outside the Temple confines of orthodox Judaism into the wider Roman world. In doing so it left Jesus and most of the disciples back in its wake.

We have many fanciful legends for each of the Apostles' post-crucifixion careers, but in specifics, as one observer wrote, they largely "disappear from history," and in fact only the barest pictures of Peter, James, and John survive today as factually probable. As we attempt to reconstruct what happened to the disciples in those fearful days after the death of Jesus, I am afraid our varied responses to the facts of the Resurrection will color our views. All can certainly agree that these most intimate followers of Jesus fled in sheer terror after the dreadful events on Golgotha, fearing that if a witch hunt developed they would follow their master up the same hill. In hiding, according to the Bible, a risen Jesus appeared to them and reinvigorated their wavering faith. With an apparition as astounding as that, they shed their timidity and began the mission laid out for them: "Go unto the whole world and preach the gospel to every creature."

This was not the picture that early skeptics presented, the first of note being a German historian, Hermann Reimarus, who wrote *The Aims of Jesus and His Apostles* sometime in the late eighteenth century. The views therein were so antagonistic to organized religion that Reimarus feared to publish openly, and it passed in manuscript form, four thousand pages in all, from friend to friend and was not printed until 1774-78, some six years after his death. It is a work of startling modernity and Schweitzer, that great student of German theological revisionism, wrote glowingly in praise that "seldom has there been a hate so eloquent, a scorn so lofty; but then it is seldom that a work has been written in the just consciousness of so absolute a superiority to contemporary opinion . . . (a work of) dignity and serious purpose."

Reimarus agrees with the picture of terrified disciples. They were certainly frightened and dispirited because Jesus had never predicted his death or his resurrection (Reimarus believed that references to these events in the Gospels were later insertions). And alas, they were all too frail. As Luke points out, when Jesus stood at the height of his popularity, he and his disciples were mobbed by well-wishers. Many patrons had left behind both family and business to follow the Master, forming a household of sorts and providing "out of their means" for all the material needs he required. Thus when Jesus sat down to dinner the disciples kept him company, eating and drinking from the same bounty. In fact, Reimarus writes, these meals became a source of notoriety, many Jews observing that Jesus and his cadres seemed unusually popular among the lower classes of publicans and prostitutes. In the happy atmosphere of these gatherings the disciples argued with each other as to who would sit on either side of Jesus at the places of honor. The only one of them with a job was Judas, who acted as treasurer for the group and carried the purse. Carpentry tools, farming gear, fishing boats and nets by which the Apostles had previously earned a living were all abandoned in their pell-mell disintegration into freebooters. They were chasing the life of plenty.

Reimarus is probably most remembered for his scathing reconstruction of the disciples' behavior after the arrest of Jesus. "From the moment they saw that he was taken and likely to be condemned in earnest," he writes, "they became cowards." Peter, who at least had the courage "to look on from a distance," disgraced himself by denying Jesus on three separate occasions, while the others fled "to secret places, locking the doors." They even refused to fetch the body, dispatching women and two converts of more adventuresome disposition to beg it from Pilate and to arrange the burial. In this frightful time "they no longer desired to sit at His right and His left," but grieved instead for their imminent return to toil, drudgery, poverty, and disgrace.

At this juncture — "Such is human nature," said Reimarus — the disciples assess their prospects. A life of beggary awaits them. They have no tools or money to start life anew, and anyhow common labor is now repugnant to them. But they saw how Jesus could move the crowd, how he could, without effort, unleash in people the urge to shower them with money, food and gifts. Why could they not continue this cycle? Preaching "was not an unremunerative occupation"; there was no reason they could not make it pay as Jesus had. And to further that aim they determined a bold stroke indeed: they removed his body from the tomb and hid it away, waited forty days without saying a word, then appeared in public on the Pentecost with glad tidings that Jesus had arisen, spoken with them, performed numerous miracles and then drifted away out of sight into heaven on the purest white cloud. In the chaotic proceedings of this announcement, whereby the Apostles appeared possessed by the Holy Spirit and suffered convulsive fits as they gibbered "in foreign tongues", Reimarus could see only a carefully orchestrated charade, one so outrageous, in fact, that it threatened their credibility, as many bystanders believed them drunk, "full of new wine". [1] But the intent, he felt, was clear. The long delay between the actual fact of the Resurrection and its disclosure was a calculated strategy. The body, no longer in evidence, could not be retrieved by those who might question the disciples — the trail had long since gone cold. And the span gave ample time for the Apostles to agree on what the risen Jesus had said and done, as well as providing a definite time frame for a start and finish. By the time the Apostles had broken their silence Jesus had come and, more importantly, had gone. There was no opportunity for an independent verification of their story. To Reimarus, proponent of "sound reason", this was the most damning evidence of all. "The witnesses of the resurrection are unable to bring forward any others, but are the only ones who pretend to have seen that which for other honest people remained invisible. We have no good grounds that Jesus arose from the dead. The witnesses are his disciples and followers, people who are not in good repute." Over the course of centuries, through long habit of faith and indoctrination, people have come to accept the Resurrection as an uncontested fact, "skipping all too softly over its real foundation", a series of imaginative lies.

Is there a middle ground between these extremes? One rather doubts it, in the sense of pleasing everybody. If a Christian accepts the Resurrection as fact there is no need to compromise with doubters: the disciples, seeing Jesus risen, have no choice but to believe and behave accordingly. Those who reject the Resurrection may conversely proceed from the premise that if everything was concocted from the start, with the Apostles inventing this most essential article of faith, then all proceeding from that falsehood must be suspect. People can grimly choose either position, but it seems to me a moderation of the second is our best chance for a reasonable reconstruction of plot.

"No sooner is a great man dead than legend is busy with his life", wrote a theologian in 1835 referring to Jesus. But was Jesus a great man in the Jewish community? He was a curiosity, to be sure, as the entry into Jerusalem showed, but the atmosphere on that occasion was circus-like and undignified, his appeal restricted to the lowest classes. Yet something about him, according to the French scholar Charles Guignebert, induced the Apostles "to endow an apparently ordinary life, a very restricted success and a degrading death with profound meaning." What was it that kept the disciples together? What was it that enabled them — common men of no great intelligence (though incapable, I think, of conscious invention or grave robbing) — to maintain their faith and, indeed,

---

[1] Peter was not amused by these charges. "These men are not drunk," he said, "it is only the third hour of the day."

vitalize it to the point where it converted other men of much higher talent (St. Paul, for example) who put the new sect on a true path of dominance? The answer to this must place the credit with Jesus.

We should accept the premise that Jesus was a remarkably persuasive and inspiring man. History is full of such people. The instances of ability in one individual to persuade thousands to follow him are so numerous and culturally diverse that, as a pattern, we have ample historical record. Jesus inspired men. He inspired these twelve, anyway, within a tradition of the Messiah or prophet that was certainly familiar to each of them. He preached an end to the world, he preached that the Son of Man would come with it to oversee the destruction of sin and to help judge those left on earth. It is not too incredible to believe that the disciples, afraid and despondent but convinced nonetheless that Jesus was a Messiah, could conclude as a balm to their depression over the crucifixion that Jesus would come again, in his good time, that he was indeed the Son of Man whom he had referred to so many times in connection with the End. Perhaps Jesus, having come to believe this himself, had even presented the association to them personally, but many observers are inclined to think the disciples inferred this from what he said. And as the danger passed and time went by, as the disciples emerged from hiding and began circulating through the community again, in the course of argument or discussion, perhaps the tenses became confused, from "will come" to "has come".

The disciples, like their master, were Jews. In the aftermath of the crucifixion it appears that no further persecution of their number was deemed necessary and that they and all the followers of Jesus went about their affairs unimpeded, including the habit of worship in the Temple. The disciples were still considered within the religious mainstream. Even the men who had done away with Jesus probably saw them as orthodox, and the disciples certainly gave no signs to the contrary. They, like other Jews, believed in the Law and generally obeyed its regulations. They were regarded as a splinter sect, perhaps, because of the claim they knew the identity of the Messiah, but in other respects they were just another troublesome synagogue. The Jews, almost beyond all others, were at home with the notion of disputatious congregations, and these followers of the Rabbi Jesus had certainly been a nuisance, even to the point of necessitating (for the preservation of social order, it was no doubt argued) a judicial execution.[1] But they were certainly Jews and not seen as heretics.

A reasonable conjecture sees them as coexisting with the Jewish establishment,

---

[1] The dilemma faced by men like Herod was complex. Roman policy towards the provinces usually placed considerable administrative power in the hands of the indigenous aristocracy. It was their duty to preserve the peace, thwart separatist or nationalistic tendencies among the lower classes and border tribes, maintain close and harmonious relations with the various branches of Imperial machinery. Herod was an orthodox Jew but, like most members of his class, did not regard his religion as anything more than an instrument for social control. He was too cosmopolitan and too much a "Roman" to believe in it spiritually, however much he honored Judaism's external or ceremonial forms. He wished Jesus removed from the scene for political not religious reasons. He saw the prophet as an agitator, a threat to the state's stability, even though Pontius Pilate regarded the matter as inconsequential. Despite the craft, intrigue and various bloody plots in which Herod and his contemporaries indulged (he was referred to as a "fox" by Jesus) the demands of accomodating both Imperial and Jewish interests proved too delicate a balance to maintain, and these semiRomanized noblemen were swept away in the turmoil of the late first century A.D.

discoursing with their fellow Jews, including Pharisees, just as Jesus had done. And as even ancient reporters verify, these exchanges were more often than not extremely argumentative and contentious. Judaism, being a Law with regulations and codes, invites the study of legalisms and definitions (it has often been described as "stern and cold"). It presents ripe ground for the quarrelsome at heart, and it seems reasonable that the theory of the Resurrection may well have seen its first spark in this milieu, at a point where an argument may have gone too far, where passion and anger and faith in everything that a martyred Jesus had come to stand for occasioned some remark or position that defied logic, something on the order of "Jesus came back, and will come again on the Day of Judgment." When asked to prove it I could well imagine a reply on the order of, "Well I saw him. And so did Philip, John, Luke, Matthew and the others." In the pit of open argument or the heat of passion, many things can be said that might be regretted later but impossible to retract given the necessity to save face or honor. These should not be classed as outright lies, but should instead be regarded as pious exaggerations, probably in the spirit of the wondrous medieval saints' lives. Or perhaps some metaphorical remarks were taken too literally by random listeners. "Jesus appeared to us in our thoughts as though alive" could well lose something by the time it reached the farthest rows of an audience, seeming to mean instead that Jesus appeared alive, period. I think in some such accidental or offhand fashion the germ of this idea might well have developed, and from there on we could attribute its spread, in the words of an old Gaelic poet, to "the old tradition of one ear to another." In a society dependent for its news on gossip, which could vary with each telling, there is no way to judge how quickly the tale might catch on, or in what form it might take, but we can hypothesize that within the context of Middle Eastern town and country life, with its well-established mania for all things religious, a story such as this would have stirred considerable interest, and possibly confirm a later remark by William James that "Faith in a fact can create the fact." And the people most caught by surprise may well have been the disciples.

The impression we gather of the Apostles from the Book of Acts is really one of stupefaction. Of course if the Resurrection actually happened they could be excused for being in a state of perpetual shock. But it seems more likely that the death of Jesus was an event so demoralizing to the group as a whole that most of them turned inward. They maintained their Jewishness and maintained their belief in Jesus as the Messiah, but they may have been aghast at what they saw happening about them.

Jesus, on frequent occasions, seems to have been exasperated by the dullness of his disciples ("Are you even yet without understanding?" he once said to Peter who could not follow the Master's meaning in a parable). And in Acts what little we see of the Twelve (aside from the Pentecost story and another relating their improbably miraculous release from prison) seems to suggest a similar confusion as events unforeseen overtake their synagogue. As most scholars now reconstruct events, there appear to have developed two problems with which the Apostles had to cope: one to do with more liberal Jews, freshly joined members of the "Christian" synagogue, who enjoyed repeatedly clashing with the same priestly hierarchy that had so bluntly disposed of Jesus; the second with spiritually inclined Gentiles who also clamored to follow the new sect.

In the first matter, an argument can be made that the Apostles just threw up their hands in dismay. These more revolutionary Jews, many of whom were apparently Hellenized, or from the more worldly reaches of the Diaspora, had little reverence for the Law, regarding it as archaic. They made such a clamor, both within the Apostles' congregation and towards the Temple itself, that the disciples refused to expose themselves to their personal abuse in the course of performing everyday charitable work, declaring in aggrieved fashion that "it is not desirable we should wait on tables." Instead they chose seven of the trouble-makers (called Deacons in Acts) to administer whatever monies or services they were due as members of the flock. Winning positions of leadership at the expense of the original Twelve was not sufficient for the liberals, however, and as they ostentatiously bruited their beliefs throughout the wider context of Jerusalem's population, that most feared (to the Apostles, anyway) and predictable calamity ensued: the Temple reacted with a general persecution, highlighted by the martyrdom of Stephen, leader of the Deacons (whose speech before the high priests, if anywhere near verbatim as reported in the New Testament, could have resulted in no other fate). The Book of Acts makes note that while Stephen's followers were scattered throughout Judea and Sumaria, the Apostles were spared and left in peace. How did this come to be? Had they made an accommodation with the Temple? Had they betrayed their principles in the process? Were they quislings?

These are uncomfortable questions and no certain answers are available. We can conclude that this crisis reinforced the shell shock or bunker mentality of the Apostles. They had had enough turmoil. They were good Jews who had little use for the wider world of the gentile Roman Empire — indeed, for little else but the environs of Jerusalem — and they had no vision of reaching out, with whatever message they conceived Jesus to have had, to anyone but their fellow Jews. The episode reveals their rather limited capabilities. They lived in perpetual hesitation, fear and immobility. The future of Christianity lay with those who fled Jerusalem, not those who stayed behind.[1]

I HAVE ALWAYS been deeply impressed by the spirituality of the Irish panorama. Perhaps I am too familiar with this country's long Christian history, and too fond of the eccentric little scraps of religious ruins that lie scattered throughout these off coast islands and their contemporaries back on shore — the deserted valleys, the inaccessible boglands, the river shores and mountain sides. Wherever a man could trudge he left a remnant of his belief, in a now broken *clochán*, a ruined cross perhaps, a pillar stone incised with devotional carvings, or just in a prayer, cast to the wind or sprinkled through an idle conversation ("I'll say a Hail Mary for you tonight," as a toothless old hitchhiker said to me after a lift). Man and God have lived side by side in this place for hundreds of years, and no matter where I view it, from the speed of a cruising train or the sloppy drench of a walk in the night down a wet and leaf-strewn lane, I am aware of this union. I never have that kind of feeling at home.

---

[1] St. Columbanus of Ireland wrote in the sixth century that "Jerome bade bishops imitate the Apostles, but taught monks to follow the fathers, who were perfect."

These thoughts occur to me now as I turn to the frantic and often bizarre career of St. Paul. Though I have not intended in this appendix to write a history on the development of Christianity, St. Paul is both a worthy man to consider in and of himself and an indispensable link in what I hope is not a tenuous attempt to connect the meaning of Jesus with those who came centuries later to live and die on islands like Inishmurray, Iona, and the Inishkeas. I had always assumed that the lure of a hermitage was its tranquillity, its removal from the world of men. I think I was mistaken. Monks — or anyone, even today's visitor — can come to an Inishmurray in confusion of thought (this is normal) but not in the spirit of irresolution or timidity. To many a monk it was more severe to test himself alone in exile, than back in the world, despite the allure and seeming multiplicity of threats from a secular society. "An hour's sleep is enough for a monk," wrote one hermit, "that is, if he is a fighter." And again, "If a man wills, in one day he can come by the evening to a measure of divinity."

St. Paul, who it is believed never met, saw, or heard Jesus in person, was a man who spent his life in commotion. In some ways this was the result of his being Jewish, and a Pharisee at that, but more likely, it seems to me, is that he lived at the very crossroads of culture at a time when spiritual concerns were of more vitality and moment than at almost any other age. He lost himself to the spiritual chaos of the marketplace, each strand of prevalent thought and attitude taking a share of his intellect. Though Jewish, for example, he was also a citizen of the Empire (hence his Roman name, Paulus); and though both Jewish and "Roman" he could reflect, under varying conditions, the attitudes of his urban backgrounds as well — his place of birth and early childhood, the city of Tarsus, near the Mediterranean in what today is Turkey, and later Jerusalem, Antioch, Corinth, all stewing pots of Greek and Oriental viewpoint, never pure, in all probability mongrelized and confused beyond comprehension. In this disjointed atmosphere Paul studied to be a rabbi, adhered to the Law with near fanaticism and early on joined in the persecution of the liberal Christian Jews. He is said to have held the clothes of those who had stripped in order to stone Stephen the Deacon with more dispatch (or perhaps not to soil their garments).

But in fact Paul's enthusiasm for rabbinical propriety was all bluster. He realized, as Jesus had before him, that the Law could in certain circumstances be a sham: one could adhere to its principles, live its life, follow its dictates with utter scrupulousness, but still lead an inner life of sensuality and sin. The Law, in other words, governed one's outward behavior, how one acted. That was the sort of religion Judaism was, concerned with action. Man sinned; his religion (the Law) told him this was wrong and corrected him; he repented. In many ways this could degenerate into a vicious cycle, a swing between doing the right thing and the next minute indulging in its opposite, back and forth through a man's life until, it was hoped, in the final walk, the way of the Law was the choice made and the path taken.[1] This utilitarian view of life was at variance with the Greek, more subtle in many ways but often sophomoric in some of the remedial approaches it embraced. The Greeks were less concerned with act than they were with being.

---

[1] As a Jewish writer has noted, "It is observed in the Talmud: 'The Rabbis have taught that a man should always regard himself as half guilty and half innocent.' The inference which you are intended to draw is, that while it is never too late to mend, it is also never too late to sin."

Paul saw this when he realized that his own soul was not righteous, that he sinned in thought and attitude, no matter how diligent his outward or physical attention to the Law. He behaved in a holy fashion but was not holy in his heart, the Greek notion of "how you are" as opposed to "what you do."

I am, of course, simplifying these distinctions, which were probably not all that clear to Paul, sensitive, high-strung, and self-absorbed as he undoubtedly was. But as generalities I think they work. To the Greeks, repentance did not mean changing your ways. You had instead to change your nature, which is probably the most difficult task any human being can undertake. And that, as we shall see, is where Paul went off on his own into the polyglot cloud of Middle Eastern thought and produced what is essentially the Catholic tradition we have today.

I do, in some ways, envy Paul his nervous breakdown. That is what I feel happened to him on the road to Damascus where it is claimed he was knocked to the ground, saw and conversed with the risen Jesus and, in a kind of stupor wherein he also lost his sight, somehow managed to stagger into the city still alive. This sounds like an hysteric collapse to me and indeed, Paul repaired himself to the countryside for rest and recovery. But the cause of this disintegration was noble – the clash of ideas, the collision of values and definitions, the resolution of spiritual crisis. Paul was obsessed with the state of his soul, his worth as a human being. He was grappling with the big issues, and I admire him and his society for that. It doesn't require being here on Inishmurray, which is powerfully suggestive, as I mentioned before, to thoughts of a religious or introspective nature, to realize how barren our Western culture, and particularly American culture, has become. Notions of soul, of being, are meaningless and never debated except in classrooms where I can visualize the boredom. Our concerns are certainly ethical: abortion, war, fights on poverty, "save the seals" and so on. But spiritually, have we graduated or advanced from the past, solved its questions (as most would probably feel)? Or have we regressed into the vacuum of being entertained (an achievement of modern times, I do not question that), where we become incapable of reflection or even of the slightest inclination to wonder, as Paul did, what we are, in the sight of righteousness? I confess to the latter, dreary conclusion. It is disputable, I'm sure.

It is amazing, from a retrospective viewpoint, to consider how the mental processes of one man can, over centuries, influence in an almost reflexive manner the spiritual outlook of countless generations. It would be a happy conclusion if we could say the mind of that singular individual was in most respects "normal", taking into account, of course, that we may all have different definitions of what normalcy is. To me words like "well-adjusted", "balanced", "happy in outlook" and "steady" come to mind, not one of which applies itself adequately to the character of St. Paul. He was a man on the move, both emotionally and physically, and an extremist in every sense of that word. He has been described as the first, and perhaps the greatest theologian of the Church, and though he never systematized his thought into an ordered presentation, he certainly littered the landscape with immense ideas and schemes that later scholars such as Augustine refined and justified. Paul was the Thomas Edison of the early Church: its finest inventor, its "peculiar apostle".

Alfred North Whitehead wrote in 1926 that "Men knew a lot about dogs before they thought of backbones and vertebrates." If one applies this notion to religion (as Whitehead did in his own abstruse way) one can see the intended sarcasm:

man felt in his heart there had to be a god — what a lonely, dangerous life without one! Details, however, were elusive, hard to come by. God, it seems, could be uncooperatively reticent. So man supplied the necessary details and what results is theology, the science of God, which tells us more about human beings than it does about the deity. "Gods never mix with men", Plato warned. Theology never learned that.[1]

Paul's theology is certainly a fascinating collection of ideas and, as I mentioned previously, it reflects to a large degree the curious and splendidly diverse streams of thought which plied the religious bazaars of the time. But in the long run, again, it tells us more about Paul than anything else. It certainly reveals very little about the street prophet named Jesus. He disappears from sight, replaced by the God we all know today as Jesus Christ. Bernard Shaw, like many skeptics, could not believe the transformation. "Fantastic", he wrote, and in reference to Paul's experience on the road to Damascus he noted that this conversion "was no conversion at all. It was Paul who converted the religion", turning his own private hallucination into a dogma of immense attraction, the "ghastliness of a beautiful thing seen in a false light".

What Paul achieved was largely a substitution. He transferred his enormous powers of respect, devotion, and servitude from the rigors of the stylized Jewish Law to the rigors of Golgotha. He stated this himself bluntly. "Through the Law I have died to the Law. With Christ, I am nailed to the cross." Why did he do this, especially when the Jewishness of his nature must have revolted, at least in the beginning, from the notion of a Messiah strung up and killed on the cross, an act of butchery? The answer is that Paul saw the way out of a personal dilemma, and allowed himself (which I am certain he would deny) to be seduced by the Greeks. The Jewish notion of "act" inherent in the Law had defeated Paul, pushed him over the edge. Perhaps he felt overwhelmed by the responsibilities the Law imposed: when he failed it he had only himself to blame, and yet to repair the damage — or repent — he again had only himself to depend on. It seems that Paul became obsessed by the understandable but almost compliant notion of recurrent sin. He wanted to break the pattern, break man's unconstrained willfulness that could allow him to sin, repent, sin again, repent again, down the road of life. This is where the Greek notion of gaining forgiveness, so alien to the Jewish, came to his aid. He realized, conceptually at least, that you could break the cycle of repeated sinfulness only by removing individual freedom of action, by forcing the sinner into complete dependence on a third party without whom atonement was impossible. Paul, being an excitable, rather neurotic individual given to extremes, certainly knew the value and power of guilt. He realized that people regret committing sin, and want forgiveness for that sin in the end. There's something very human about cleaning the slate. In Jewish consciousness that obligation was the sinner's. In Paul's notion it could only be achieved through an application to someone or something else. Paul provided that figure in the resurrected Jesus, not the historical Jesus, I should quickly add, but a divine Jesus Christ, the God, Son of the Father. Through Christ, who suffered the humiliation of death on the cross through love of mankind, a permanent alteration of nature was made

---

[1] Updated by Hegel, "The true knowledge of God begins when we know that things as they immediately are have no truth."

possible. Man could stop his sinning only through faith in Christ, never alone, a transference by Paul of emphasis from action (which had always bothered him personally in his bouts with sin) to faith, where he felt controlled and thus comfortable. In effect, Paul wrote himself a prescription, and gathered up the considerable effort of will it must have required to believe in it every inch of the way. This momentous theory that man could not be "saved" by good works alone (as opposed to the Law, which superficially appears to suggest the opposite) had interesting consequences for the little island of Inishmurray.

C ERTAINLY PAUL'S EARLY conversations with the first Christians – indeed, with the Apostles themselves who had, after all, intimate knowledge of Jesus and his character – must have been curious affairs. Many theologians question whether Peter, John, Mark, James and the others considered Paul sane, though they probably agreed that the spirit was in him. However intriguing their speculative discussions may have been, however, a matter of more pragmatic nature probably consumed most of their meetings, and that was the question of gentiles.

The liberal Christian Jews of Stephen's wing, it is argued – dispersed by persecution from the environs of Jerusalem, scattered like seeds through the various trading cities of the Middle East – predated Paul's efforts among the gentiles, and to them goes the credit for discovering that among the larger general population lay the future of their sect. This is very much a gray area, of course, and it is unclear precisely what their message entailed. It remained, however, demonstrably unattractive to conservative Jews, who regularly expelled these people from their synagogues. Probably a combination of frustration with the narrow world of the Jews, unvarying no matter the town or city, and zeal for the person of Jesus drove these zealots to seek contact with gentiles. It is fairly certain they met with considerable initial success.

The religious atmosphere of the times, as I have suggested, was ideal for the curious gentile – he had a veritable blizzard of creeds, faiths, superstitions, cults, and prophets to choose from, dominated by the bland and by now crustaceous folk mythology of the Greeks. One of the few religions to offer any sort of higher morality was Judaism, but it seemed so private a pursuit, so ostentatiously exclusive and haughty, that it discouraged many gentiles from ever considering an approach. This changed dramatically in just a few years with the seepage into religious circles of these exiled Christian Jews. They offered Gentiles the morality of Judaism without its Law, the rigidity and legalism of which they ridiculed, replacing it as a standard of conduct with the more spiritual and aesthetic humanism of Jesus. In effect, these first missionaries preached the same desired end result – righteousness – but softened Judaism by abandoning the gloomy, misanthropic Law. At some unknown point, probably when they realized the effect they were having on their audience, they began the wholesale abandonment of Jewish custom. They rejected circumcision.

There is certainly nothing bashful about circumcision. Ancient cultures besides the Jewish have for centuries touched man at his most basic private place in order to seal a covenant with God. No other piece of flesh would do: ear lobe, toe, finger, whatever. Only the penis. [1] That many adult gentiles would find such a

---

[1] Some societies even today also practice female circumcision, whereby outer portions of the female genitalia are removed.

276

practice abhorrent is not a surprise. More than most preconditions this enabled Judaism to remain ethnically pure.

By waiving this entry ritual, needless to say, these early proselytizers succeeded in traumatizing the original disciples, for indeed this was heresy. Paul, by now a leading spokesman for those wishing to work among the gentiles (but who may, or may not, have yet developed his ideas on Jesus and the redeeming cross) took few pains to spare them on this matter, or any other, and in the various conferences, synods, and meetings which were called to consider the controversy he regularly thrashed and bullied them into submission. Robert Graves, in his singularly entertaining novel *King Jesus*, envisions Paul throwing the Apostle James bodily down the stairway of the Temple. And Paul himself, in his letter to the Galatians, admits that "I withstood Peter to his face, because he was deserving of blame." Later on, he would angrily cast Mark aside as well.

In the person of Peter, in fact, we probably see the fullest picture of Apostolic futility. When visiting the gentile missions in his role as inspector general he could, on cue from Paul perhaps, adopt the liberal stance. But once back in Jerusalem he would reverse himself, under pressure from the other disciples, and question Paul's procedures. Peter cuts a sad figure indeed: vacillating, weak, depressed. Paul never met his match from him or any of the Twelve.

The history of the Christian Church, unique and separate from Judaism, can generally be pinpointed to the resolution of this crisis in Paul's favor. The gentile mission surged forward into the Empire, the original Christian synagogue of the Apostles cast behind, inert and disregarded, lingering in the Temple's shadow, utterly dissolved when Jerusalem was destroyed in A.D. 70 by Roman legions. From this period as well, we can probably date the baleful distrust and loathing these two religions developed for each other: [1] the Jewish opinion that Christians stole all they had from Judaism without ever acknowledging their debt — the monolithic Jewish God, the Jewish scriptures, the Jewish notion of a Chosen People; the Christian, that Jews were "uncircumcised in heart" and had, in typically perverse fashion, slaughtered the one true God.[2] These are confusions of thought which still plague us today.

Paul's missionary travels, three in number though uncertainly dated, were perilous and exacting affairs. More than once he was scourged, thrown in prison, threatened with execution, yet time and again he returned to the street corner or synagogue, forum or secret chapel, there to preach to the willing yet also, dangerous though it was, to spar with those who either ridiculed him or sought his death. The public arena, what we might consider the media context of the time, saw Paul engaged in what probably amounted to several hundred debates, and in this fevered atmosphere his theological positions gradually took form. I am here reminded of what an Irish monk of the seventh century said in his prologue to a life of St. Patrick, a man already three to four hundred years in his grave and about whom little but oral tradition had anything to say. "I have led my boyish skiff with its unskilled oar," he wrote, "into this deep and dangerous gulf

---

[1] As Kirsopp Lake observed, "In religion, as in other things, a really lively hatred requires some degree of relationship."

[2] The attitude of St. John Chrysostom was a standard of the early Church, that a chief result of the crucifixion was punishment: "the casting out of the Jews, the calling of the Gentiles."

of sacred narrative, with its mounds of waves surging wildly amidst the sharpest rocks fixed in uncharted waters, a gulf hitherto entered and occupied by no boats." Certainly as Paul travelled from city to city, from one difficult oration or debate to the next, he cast and recast his theories as probes, questions, clarifications, and circumstances dictated. He may have felt many times that he too had been cast to the stormy seas, surrounded as he was by Jews, Greeks, Romans, Orientals, queasy converts, mistaken companions, friends and foes alike, all badgering and pressing him for certitude and a guaranteed reply to their often sophistic and hostile queries. In these harried circumstances he frequently groped for the right answer. We see this clearly in his letters, as he tried to form tailored approaches to whatever particular audience he addressed. In these quite frantic conditions, both physically and intellectually, it is not surprising that Paul and his coterie eventually surfaced with an almost jerry-built construction for their religious dogma. It borrowed freely from the currents of the time and also reflected the understandable fatigue and stress that Paul endured. He needed something to lean on. He could not have gone forward otherwise.

The "mystery" religions of the Orient, as they are called, about whose number, variety and content most experts can only speculate, were certainly an active and popular element in Middle Eastern life. It would be too facile a comment to dismiss these doctrines as grossly superstitious, though many undoubtedly were. In assessing their influence on early Christian tenets we should probably consider them as just an ingredient, one among many, the exact proportion of which we can only surmise, that made up the finished whole. Scholars of Paul and his thought are correct in this instance to warn against hasty conclusions. Paul took what he needed from several traditions, many of these interwoven one to another, and it would be erroneous to apply mathematical exactitude in dissecting which influence was which or in what proportion to one another or the end result. It is safer to generalize which is, quite clearly, the least offensive course, because when we discuss the mystery religions we are, in effect, discussing the sacraments.

Paul, though a Jew, abandoned the Law, turned his back on circumcision. He embraced instead Jesus, a Jew himself as we have seen, with Jewish ideas of morality and conduct which Paul retained. But notions of incarnation, whereby a god becomes man, were alien to Jewish thought. Not so to the Greeks, who could take it the extra step: they could accept the idea of a god "dying" in its human manifestation, but then emerging again in the heavens to greater glory. Paul's adoration of the divine Jesus, not the human, seems clearly to be a Greek touch.

How the next permutation occurred can never be precisely explained, but it seems reasonable to conclude, given the rather murky and indefinable nature of anything "miraculous", that some features of the mystery cults were appropriated rather liberally by the Christians. Paul did not invent the sacraments. Perhaps he merely refined or legitimatized a process he saw already underway, but he certainly valued their place in his scheme, either conceptually (he just liked the idea) or pragmatically (they were popular and proved useful in gaining converts), maybe both. The sacraments, and in this instance I refer to baptism and the Eucharist, were unexplainable mysteries, secret initiations without which no avenue to the divine Jesus was available, and only through Jesus, according to Paul, was a private, personal salvation for each individual even remotely possible.

It is suggested by some, that in many ways the quasi-Oriental and Greek hybridizations preached much the same thing, and in neither case was it the intention to liberate mankind. Paul's critics, and he has had many over the years, will often accept his insistence that man subject himself to Jesus for the sake of an eternal reward, but condemn him in the same breath for pandering to the baser instincts (as they perceive them) of ritual and superstition as preconditions for this dependence.

Whatever the merits in these complaints, it is a fact that within the thought processes of Paul (or his clique) these various strands coalesced into what became the Christian and Catholic tradition — high morality, the divinity of Jesus, the mysteries of sacramental practice. Certainly the last of these, the sacraments, were not clearly defined or satisfactorily explained during Paul's ministry. When dealing with mystical matters, in fact, he could often appear as much in the dark as everyone else.[1] But he clearly crossed the line when it came to the Eucharist, most interesting of the sacraments. Whereas a case could be made that Jesus — the historical Jesus — never intended the breaking of bread as anything more than a commemorative ceremony, Paul quite clearly viewed it as the literal transformation of matter into God. "The cup of blessing that we bless," he wrote in Corinthians, "is it not the sharing of the blood of Christ? And the bread that we break, is it not the partaking of the body of the Lord?" These are not the words of a man thinking. They are of a man believing.

The fourth gospel of the New Testament, John's, is a tribute to Paul's success. Whereas the three Synoptic gospels of Matthew, Mark and Luke are Jewish in their orientation, John is unabashedly Greek and sacramental. Scholars tend to date John at c. 100 A.D., and many feel it postdates the last Synoptic, Luke, by ten to twenty years. Certainly the bias in John illustrates the widening separation of Christian from Jew, with Jesus at one point angrily saying to the Chosen People, "Why do I speak to you at all!" And it devotes great energy to the Eucharist, "the living bread that has come from heaven". Many of the Jewish disciples around Jesus, after a long harangue, found the notion incredible, complaining "This is a hard saying. Who can listen to it?" which, of course, is the whole point of a mystery.

Like circumcision, the idea behind the Eucharist is very ancient indeed, perhaps a throwback to the primeval warrior's custom of eating his enemy (or parts of him) in order to steal his valorous spirit.[2] Shaw, in fact, parodied the notion when he spoke of Englishmen eating beefsteak (rare and bloody, we may assume), thinking they could possess for themselves the strength of a bull, and facing instead "the most ignominious defeats by vegetarian wrestlers, racers and bicyclists." Sarcasm and disbelief aside, many practicing Catholics would probably be offended at the suggestion of such a primitive origin for what is probably the holiest, and certainly the most mysterious of the sacraments. My own belief as a Catholic is that we in the West, after centuries of habit, have accepted it to the

---

[1] The resurrection of the dead, for example. Paul gave this substantial thought, but his conclusions or, rather, ruminations, were refuted in the later books of Luke and John.

[2] Edward Gibbon, in *The Decline and Fall of the Roman Empire*, described an incident from A.D. 378 when the Visigoths threatened Constantinople: "A Gothic soldier was slain by the dagger of an Arab, and the hairy, naked savage, applying his lips to the wound, expressed a horrid delight while he sucked the blood of his vanquished enemy."

point of cultural certitude, whereby anthropological questioning of a custom so holy and so sanctified by its ancient lineage seems without question sacrilegious. That is why reverse certitude is at times so revealing. A recent novel by Brian Moore, born in Belfast but now living in California, is the latest example. In *Black Robe*, which deals with the heroic attempts of French missionaries (called by the Indians Blackrobes or Normans) to preach the gospel to "Les Sauvages", we see a similarity in point of view. The Iroquois, Huron, and Algonquin all tortured their captured enemies mercilessly, and regularly ate them in ritualized frenzy. They could understand the notions of Eucharist, which they hated and feared only in terms of its rivalry with their own forms of witchcraft, and the strength imparted to these foreign priests who ate it. They could see in Catholic ritual vestiges of their own. By drawing allusions from both traditions together, Moore established the common source for both, which springs from a dark and long-forgotten pool of primitive belief:

> "The Blackrobes are the worst of sorcerers," said old Ontitaraic. "I have heard they live in separate habitations, always. When they live among the Huron they will not allow the Huron to sleep in their dwellings. In each of the Blackrobe habitations there is a special room. In that room there is a small box placed on a high ledge. Inside the box there are pieces of corpse which they brought from France. They say this corpse is the body of their god. They have secret ceremonies in which they eat little pieces of this fucking corpse."
> "That is true," said another council member. "I have heard the same story. And by a Huron."

References

Page #

3. "Domus deliciis . . . ": *The Antiphonary of Bangor, An Early Irish Manuscript in the Ambrosian Library at Milan*, ed. F. E. Warren, Part II, London 1895, p. 28. Trans. in Françoise Henry, *Irish Art in the Early Christian Period (to 800 A.D.)*, Ithaca 1965, p. 203.

3. "Si tollis hostem . . .": *Sancti Columbani Opera*, trans. G. S. M. Walker, Dublin 1957, p. 33.

Part I

7. "Pittance . . .": "Three words Diarmaid, abbot of Iona, left with bishop Cathrach: pittance, perseverance, cross-vigil." Trans. E. J. Gwynn and W. J. Purton, "The Monastery of Tallaght," in *Proceedings of the Royal Society of Antiquaries of Ireland*, Vol. XXIX, Section C, No. 5, p. 144.

7. "Who could show me . . . ": *Vita Beati Antonii*, as quoted in F. Henry, op. cit., p. 23.

10. "bare Ben Bulban's head": W. B. Yeats, "Under Ben Bulban," in *Selected Poems and Two Plays of William Butler Yeats*, ed. M. L. Rosenthal, New York 1965, p. 193.

10. "Cast a cold eye . . . ": ibid.

10. Swift's epitaph: "He lies where furious indignation can no longer rend his heart." See Yeat's poem, "Swift's Epitaph," in *The Winding Stair And Other Poems* (1933).

12. Yeat's lecture tour: see Francis Russell, "The Archpoet," in *Horizon*, Vol. III, No. 2, November 1960, pp. 66-69.

14. "a dingy, desolate looking country . . . ": Thomas Carlyle, *Reminiscences of My Irish Journey in 1849*, New York 1882, p. 194.

14. "low moory expanse . . . .": Terence O'Rorke, *The History of Sligo: Town and County*, Vol. II, Dublin 1889, p. 30.

14. "degraded superstition": Caesar Otway, *Sketches in Ireland: Descriptive of Interesting, and hitherto unnoticed Districts, in the North and South*, Dublin 1827, p. 150.

15. William Thackeray, *The Irish Sketch Book*, London 1869, p. 235.

17. "a king's son . . . ": St. Cormac, as quoted in W. D. Simpson, *The Historical Saint Columba*, Aberdeen 1927, p. 5.

18. "the first action in the annals of law . . . ": Douglas Chrétien, *The Battle Book of the O'Donnells*, Berkeley 1935, p. 1.

18. "The Book of Finnian is none the worse . . . ": Manus O'Donnell, *Betha Colaim chille, Life of Columcille*, trans. A. O. Kelleher and G. Schoepperle, Urbana 1918, p. 179.

18. "the wrong decision of a judge . . . ": "Miscellanea," E. J. Gwynn, in *Ériu*, Vol. IX, 1921-23, p. 29, as quoted in Chrétien, op. cit., p. 9.

19. "St. Molaise of Inishmurray . . . ": *The Martyrology of Donegal, A Calendar of the Saints of Ireland*, trans. John O'Donovan, Dublin 1884, p. 217. See also Manus O'Donnell, op. cit., p. 185.

19. "he made these quatrains" . . . and following: Manus O'Donnell, op. cit., p. 195.

19. "a rare thing . . . ": Ashley Powell, "An Outline of Irish History," in *Ireland*, ed. L. Russell Muirhead, London 1962, p. xix.

20. *Agricola*, Cornelius Tacitus, trans. Maurice Hutton, London 1925.

20. Strabo, Posidonius, Diodorus Siculus: see "The Celtic Ethnography of Posidonius," trans. J. J. Tierney, in *Proceedings of the Royal Irish Academy*, Vol. 60, 1959-1960, pp. 189-275.

21. "to the Irish believing in Christ ": Prosper of Aquitaine, "Chronicon," trans. James Kenney, in *Sources for the Early History of Ireland: Ecclesiastical*, New York 1929, p. 165.

21. "unaided and alone . . . ": *The Writings of Patrick*, trans. Rev. Charles H. H. Wright, London 1889, p. 62.

23. Druid barrier: see *Annals of Ulster, A Chronicle of Irish Affairs From A.D. 431 to A.D. 1540*, trans. William Hennessy, Vol. 1, Dublin 1887, p. 57; "The Annals of Tigernach, Third Fragment A.D. 489-766," trans. Whitley Stokes, in *Revue Celtique*, Vol. XVII, No. 1, January 1896, p. 144; and A. O. and M. O. Anderson, *Adomnán's Life of Columba*, London 1961, p. 84.

23. "Its sound is a drink of death . . .": Erich Poppe, "A Middle Irish Poem on Eimíne's Bell," in *Celtica*, XVII, 1985, p. 63.

24. "had grasped our womenfolk . . . ": "Advice to a Prince," trans. Tadhg O'Donoghue, in *Ériu*, Vol. IX, 1921-1923, p. 51.

24. "Woe to brothers . . . ": Gerald of Wales, *The History and Topography of Wales*, Harmondsworth 1982, p. 108.

25. A "red-draped doomsday": "A Poem of Prophecies," trans. Eleanor Knott, in *Ériu*, Vol. XVIII, 1958, p. 73.

25. Columcille's shrewd political intent: see author's *The Road Wet, The Wind Close: Celtic Ireland*, Dublin & Chester Springs, Pennsylvania 1986, pp. 128-135, regarding the Convention of Druim Cett.

25. Forty priests . . . : see *The Irish Liber Hymnorum*, trans. J. H. Bernard and R. Atkinson, Vol. II, London 1898, p. 53.

26. "barbarous nations": Edmund Spenser, *A View of the Present State of Ireland*, ed. W. L. Renwick, Oxford 1970, p. 7.

27. "I saw an old woman . . . ": ibid., p. 62.

28. "Brighton in the West": The Special Correspondent of *The Times, Letters from Ireland, 1886*, London 1887, p. 130. See also William B. Pemberton, *Lord Palmerston*, London 1954, and Jaspar Ridley, *Lord Palmerston*, London 1970.

29. "a piece of civilization . . . ": ibid., p. 129.

30. "bare, barren, dreary island": O'Rorke, op. cit., p. 38.

31. Women of the island hurling stones at the rates collector: see "Notes of Home Rambles: Sligo and Innismurry," in *The Irish Monthly*, November 1883, p. 603.

33. Aerial photographs: see E. R. Norman and J. K. S. St Joseph, *The Early Development of Irish Society, The Evidence of Aerial Photography*, Cambridge 1969, pp. 56, 57, 94-119.

34. "The men of this country . . . ": Gerald of Wales, op. cit., p. 91.

34. Several of the finest specimens . . . taken away: The King, Michael Waters, complained in 1897 that "some tourists have taken away a slab from the altar." In *J.R.S.A.I.*, Vol. VII, 1897, p. 72.

37. "very innocent . . . ": W. R. Wilde, "Memoir of Gabriel Beranger, and his labours in the Cause of Irish Art, Literature, and Antiquities, From 1760 to 1780, With Illustrations," in *P.R.S.A.I.*, Vol. I, 1870, p. 134.

37. "the islanders believe . . . " and following: John O'Donovan, *Letters containing information relative to the Antiquities of the County of Sligo, Collected during the progress of the Ordnance Survey in 1836*, Bray 1928, pp. 10, 21, 8, 12.

40. Saints "could see nothing . . . ": Anonymous monk, *Two Lives of St. Cuthbert*, trans. Bertram Colgrave, Cambridge 1940, p. 97.

40. "prisons of hard, narrow stone" and following: *Martyrology of Donegal*, op. cit., p. 83.

41. Here "no Protestant lives . . . ": John Healy, Archbishop of Tuam, "A Pilgrimage to Inishmurray," in *Papers and Addresses: Theological, Philosophical, Biographical, Archaeological*, Dublin 1909, p. 487.

41. "four very wild men": J. O'Donovan, op. cit., p. 9.

41. "I dwell among barbarians": *Writings of Patrick*, op. cit., p. 67.

42. "a pimple . . . ": Cummian, Abbot of Durrow (?), as quoted in Kathleen Hughes, *The Church in Early Irish Society*, London 1966, p. 107.

42. "never let yourself bog down . . ": "History as a Literary Art," in *History*, eds. O. Handlin, A. M. Schlesinger, S. E. Morison, F. Merk, A. M. Schlesinger Jr., Cambridge 1954, p. 49.

42. "Will the reader turn the page?": Catherine Drinker Bowen, as quoted in Barbara

Tuchman, "In Search of History," in *Practicing History: Selected Essays*, New York 1981, p. 17.

43. "This is not a time . . . ": Marcel Duchamps, as quoted in Anaïs Nin, *The Diary, 1931-1934*, ed. Gunther Stuhlmann, New York 1966, p. 357.

44. "They seek their own interests . . . ": Philippians 2:21.

46. "You who are called to be saints . . . ": Romans 1:7,13.

46. "twilight world": Chadwick, *The Early Church*, op. cit., p. 33.

46. "the triumph of barbarism . . . ": Edward Gibbon, *The Decline and Fall of the Roman Empire*, New York 1932, p. 685.

46. "surrender": M. Rostovtzeff, *Rome*, trans. J. D. Duff, New York 1960, p. 322.

46. "Transportation . . . ": "Provincialism the Enemy," as quoted in Sven Birkerts, *An Artificial Wilderness: Essays on 20th-Century Literature*, New York 1987, p. 17.

47. "Our caution . . . ": Philip Rousseau, *Pachomius: The Making of a Community in Fourth-Century Egypt*, Berkeley 1985, p. 74.

47. "After two or three hundred years of talking . . . ": James H. Robinson, *Mind in the Making*, New York 1921, p. 111.

47. "the gifts of the river": Herodotus, as quoted in H. Idis Bell, *Egypt From Alexander the Great to the Arab Conquest: A Study in the Diffusion and Decay of Hellenism*, Oxford 1948, p. 2.

49. "the consummation, yet also the collapse . . . ": Adolf Harnack and John M. Mitchell, "Neoplatonism," in *The Encyclopedia Britannica*, Thirteenth Edition, Vol 11, London 1926, p. 372.

50. "An immature and youthful mind.": "The Church History of Eusebius," trans. Rev Arthur McGiffert, in *A Select Library of Nicene and Post Nicene Fathers of the Christian Church*, eds. Philip Schaff and Henry Wallace, Second Series, Vol. 1, New York 1886-1900, p. 254. See also St. Matthew 19:12: "There are eunuchs who were born so from their mother's womb; and there are eunuchs who were so made by men; and there are eunuchs who have made themselves so for the sake of the kingdom of heaven. Let him accept it who can."

50. "Who could ever read . . . ": St. Jerome, as quoted in Vincent of Lérins, "A Commonitory For the Antiquity and Universality of the Catholic Faith Against the Profane Novelties of all Heresies," trans. C. A. Heurtley, in *Nicene Fathers*, op. cit., p. 144.

50. Primary blame for the library's destruction varies. See Luciano Canfora, *The Vanished Library: A Wonder of the Ancient World*, trans. M. Ryle, Berkeley 1990.

50. "well stated by the Greeks" and following: Origen, as quoted in R. P. C. Hanson, *Origen's Doctrine of Tradition*, London 1954, p. 167.

50. "Away with all attempts . . . ": Tertullian, op. cit., p. 9.

50. to "cut off the impulse . . . ": R. P. C. Hanson, "A Note on Origen's Self-Mutilation," in *Vigiliae Christianae*, Vol. 20, No. 2, 1966, p. 81.

51. Origen's system "owed nothing to Jesus . . . ": E. De Faye, *Origene, sa Vie, son Oeuvre, sa Pensée*, Vol. III, Paris 1923, p. 160, as quoted in Hanson, op. cit., p. 186.

51. Though "one nature . . . ": Maximus of Tyre, as quoted in Origen, *Contra Celsum*, trans. Henry Chadwick, Cambridge 1953, p. xvii.

52. "seducing the Church . . . ": Vincent of Lérins, op. cit., p. 144.

52. "I have marked rejected . . . ": Cassiodorus Senator, *An Introduction to Divine and Human Readings*, trans. Leslie W. Jones, New York 1969, p. 77. See also remarks by George Scholarius as quoted in Henry Chadwick, *Early Christian Thought and the Classical Tradition: Studies in Justin, Clement, and Origen*, New York 1966, p. 95: "The Western writers say, 'Where Origen was good, no one is better, where he was bad, no one is worse.' "

52. "he thought like a Greek" or "He played like a Greek": Eusebius, *The Ecclesiastical History*, Book VI, 19, trans. H. J. Lawlor, Vol. II, London & New York 1932, p. 59.

56. "Two girls in silk kimonos . . . ": "In Memory of Eva Gore-Booth And Con Markievicz," from *The Winding Stair And Other Poems* (1933), in *The Collected Poems of W. B. Yeats*, New York 1974, p. 229.

61. "customers in *shebeens* . . . ": E. B. McGuire, *Irish Whiskey: A History of Distilling, the Spirit Trade and Excise Controls in Ireland*, Dublin 1973, p. 424. See also K. H. Connell, "Illicit Distillation: An Irish Peasant Industry," in *Historical Studies 3*, London 1961, pp. 58-91.

64. "At my late being in Sligo . . . ": Geoffrey Fenton to Burghley, October 28, 1588, in *Calendar of the State Papers Relating to Ireland, of the Reign of Elizabeth — 1588, August to 1592, September*, Vol. CXXXVII, London 1885, p. 68.

64. "Now all this country is gone lonesome . . . ": as quoted in F. H. A. Aalen and H. Brody, *Gola: The Life and Last Days of an Island Community*, Cork 1969, p. xv.

66. Robert Sténuit and the *Girona*: see his book, *Treasures of the Armada*, trans. Francine Barker, New York 1973.

67. "Take great care . . . ": *State Papers*, op. cit., as quoted in Caoimhín Ó Danachair, "Armada Losses on the Irish Coast," in *The Irish Sword*, Vol. II, No. 9, 1956, p. 321.

67. "Nearly three hundred anchors . . . ": David Howarth, *The Voyage of the Armada*, Harmondsworth 1982, p. 173.

68. If the view is gloomy . . . : Thackerary, *Irish Sketch Book*, op. cit., p. 191.

70. "your majesty may occupy yourself . . . ": see either J. P. O'Reilly, "Remarks on Certain Passages in Capt. Cuellar's Narrative of his Adventures in Ireland After the Wreck of the Spanish Armada in 1588-89, Followed by a Literal Translation of That Narrative," in *P.R.I.A.* Vol. III, Third Series, 1893-96, pp. 175-217; or *A Letter Written on October 4, 1589 by Captain Cuellar of the Spanish Armada to His Majesty King Philip II Recounting his Misadventures in Ireland and Elsewhere After the Wreck of his Ship*, trans. Henry D. Sedgwick, New York 1895.

76. "Be as cautious as a stranger . . . .": *The Wisdom of The Desert — Sayings from the Desert Fathers of the Fourth Century*, trans. Thomas Merton, New York 1970, p. 53.

77. "truly a desert land": Giraldus Cambrensis, *Topography of Ireland*, trans. Thomas Wright, London 1913, p. 20.

78. "all say the same thing . . . ": I Corinthians 1:10.

78. "unspoiled and undivided . . . ": Caecilius Cyprianus, *The Unity of the Catholic Church*, trans. Maurice Bevenot, London 1957, p. 48.

78. "All things are permitted to bishops . . . ": Tertullian, "De Monogamia," in *Treatises on Marriage and Remarriage*, trans. William P. Le Saint, S. J., Westminster 1951, pp. 99, 70. The ascetic Vincent of Lérins, however, felt that Tertullian "was a great trial to the Church" and "obnoxious." See "A Commonitory," op. cit., p. 145.

78. Country "no monk ever knew" and following: St. Athanasius, *The Life of St. Antony*, trans. Robert Meyer, Westminster 1950, pp. 20, 22, 41, 53, 54, 31, 64, 60, 17, 60, 33.

78. "for the mark of the true monk . . . ": *Western Asceticism*, op. cit., p. 85.

81. "the squalor of the Orient" and following: Herbert J. Muller, *The Uses of the Past, Profiles of Former Societies*, New York 1957, p. 204. See also "Baths," *Britannica*, Vol. 3, op. cit., pp. 514-520.

82. "Whose feet wilt thou wash?": St. Basil the Great, as quoted in Maisie Ward, "Saint Basil and the Cappadocians," in *Word and Spirit: A Monastic Review — I, In Honor of St. Basil the Great, d. 379*, Still River, Massachusetts 1979, p. 10.

82. "perfect men . . . ": John Cassian, "The Institutes of the Coenobia," Book VIII, Chapter 19, as quoted by Owen Chadwick, *John Cassian: A Study in Primitive Monasticism*, Cambridge 1950, p. 51.

82. "The monk's cell . . . ": *Western Monasticism*, op. cit., p. 93.

83. "These four are the stars . . . ": as quoted in Hugh G. Evelyn White, *The History of the Monasteries of Nitria and of Scetis*, New York 1932, p. 96.

84. Unruly hedonists "without object or rules . . . ": St. John Chrysostom, op. cit., p. 919.

84. "Worldy men have ruined Rome . . . ": Abbot Arenius, *Wisdom of the Desert*, op. cit., p. 49.

84. "altar against altar": as quoted in Cardinal Jean Daniélou, S. J., "The Fathers and Christian Unity," in *Word and Spirit*, op. cit., p. 101.

84. Monks coming in contact with harlots: See Palladius Hieronymus and Others, *The*

Book of Paradise, Being The Histories and Sayings of the Monks and Ascetics of the Egyptian Desert, trans. E. A. Wallis Budge, Vol. I, London 1904, pp. 412-417.

84. "Self-willed, authoritarian . . . ": H. Idris Bell, op. cit., p. 106.

84. No cult of sainthood followed his death: though Cassian was canonized, see David Hugh Farmer, The Oxford Dictionary of Saints, Oxford 1987, for analysis of his narrow appeal.

84. One visitor estimated that on Mt. Nitria . . . : Palladius, The Lausiac History, trans. Robert T. Meyer, London 1965, p. 40.

85. "Prince of the Origenists": Merton, Wisdom, op. cit., p. 69.

85. "The most eloquent Cassian": Cassiodorus, op. cit., p. 70.

86. "who are indeed athirst . . . " and following: "The Twelve Books of John Cassian on the Institutes of the Coenobia," trans. Edgar C. S. Gibson, in Nicene Fathers, Second Series, Vol. XI, op. cit., p. 200.

86. "shed all matter . . . " and following: Evagrius Ponticus, The Praktikos, Chapters on Prayer, trans. John E. Bamberger, OCSO, Spencer, Massachusetts 1970, pp. 66, 75, 16, 24, 18, 23, 56, 57, 59, 61.

87. "An old hermit . . . ": "Apophthegmata patrum," as quoted in White, op. cit., p. 108. Cassian relates a different version in "Institutes," IV, 24, where the hermit perversely uproots the tree and casts it aside.

88. accidie: Psalm 90:6.

88. "like some fever": Cassian, "Institutes," op. cit., p. 266.

88. "The great religious conceptions . . . ": Alfred North Whitehead, Religion in the Making., Cleveland 1964, p. 19.

89. "to experiment with him . . . ": Athanasius, op. cit., p. 80.

89. "to change the glory of the incorruptible God . . . ": Romans 1:23.

89. "with the inner eyes of the soul . . . " and following: "The Conferences of John Cassian," trans. Gibson, in Nicene Fathers, Second Series, Vol. XI, op. cit., p. 403.

89. Abbot Sarapion: ibid., p. 402.

90. "no affinity with the morality of the Bible . . . " and following: Philip Schaff, History of the Christian Church: Nicene and Post- Nicene Christianity, Vol. III, New York 1884, p. 166.

91. "he was not bewildered": Athanasius, op. cit., p. 120.

91. "There can be no other valid reason . . . " and following: Merton, Wisdom, op. cit., pp. 23, 31.

91. "imprudent" sympathy: Chadwick, Cassian, op. cit., p. 37.

92. "The coarse excretions . . . ": Bamberger, Praktikos, op. cit., p. 1.

92. "beyond the capacity . . . " and following: Cassian, "Conferences," Nicene Fathers, op. cit., p. 492.

92. "the want of youth . . . ": Edward Gibbon, The History of the Decline and Fall of the Roman Empire, Vol. IV, London 1923, p. 104.

92. Charles V: ibid., p. 108. See also Andre Chastel, The Sack of Rome, 1527, Princeton 1983.

93. "subject to no royal authority . . . " and following: Ammianus Marcellinus, trans. John C. Rolfe, Vol. III, Cambridge & London 1936, pp. 385, 381, 383, 403, 405, 328, 475, 477, 405.

95. "The numbers . . . " and following: Gibbon, Decline and Fall, 1923 edition, Vol. III, op. cit, pp. 316, 322, 323, 329.

96. "When a frontier between civilization and barbarianism . . . ": Arnold J. Toynbee, A Study of History, London 1946, p. 143. For interesting views on Toynbee's work see George F. Kennan, "The History of Arnold Toynbee," in The New York Review of Books, June 1, 1989, pp. 19-22, and H. R. Trevor-Roper, "The Prophet," N.Y.R.B., October 12, 1989, pp. 28-34.

97. "final and long impending punishment . . . ": Paulus Orosius, The Seven Books of History Against the Pagans, trans. Roy DeFerrari, Washington 1964, p. 353.

97. "The city which has taken captive . . . ": Ep. 127, as quoted in St. Augustine, Concern-

ing the City of God against the Pagans, trans. Henry Bettenson, Harmondsworth 1984, p. 44.

99.   "running away": St. Jerome, "Against Vigilantius," trans. W. H. Fremantle, G. Lewis, W. G. Martley, *Nicene Fathers*, Vol. VI, op. cit., p. 423.

99.   "snakeling, bred in black caverns": Prosper of Aquitaine, as quoted in Bede, *A History of the English Church and People*, trans. Leo Sherley-Price and R. E. Latham, New York 1985, p. 50.

99.   "peculiar satisfaction": Gibbon, *Decline and Fall*, 1923 edition, Vol. III, op. cit., p. 103.

100.   "Britannicus noster": Orosius, as quoted in J. N. L. Meyers, "Pelagius And The End Of Roman Rule In Britain," in *The Journal of Roman Studies*, Vol. L, 1960, p. 22.

100.   "north of the wall": John Ferguson, *Pelagius*, Cambridge 1956, p. 40.

101.   "a literary genius . . . ": Rebecca West, "St. Augustine," in *The Essential Rebecca West*, Harmondsworth 1983, p. 211.

101.   "most stupid fellow . . . ": trans. Kenney, op. cit., p. 162. For complete letter see *Nicene Fathers*, Vol. VI, op. cit., p. 499.

101.   A "very strong and active mind . . . " and following: *The Anti-Pelagian Works of Saint Augustine, Bishop of Hippo*, trans. Peter Holmes and Robert Wallis, Vol. I, Edinburgh 1872-76, pp. 240.

102.   "excited" and following: "A Treatise on the Gift of Perseverance," trans. Holmes and Wallace, in *A Select Library of the Nicene and Post-Nicene Fathers of the Christian Church*, ed. Philip Schaff, First Series, Vol. 5, New York 1886-1900, p. 547.

102.   "Everything good . . . ": Pelagius, as quoted by Augustine, "A Treatise on the Grace of Christ, And on Original Sin," in *Nicene Fathers*, ibid., p. 241.

103.   "fatally opposed . . . ": *Anti-Pelagian Works*, op. cit., p. 73.

103.   "Why should I ask God . . . ": Letter CLXXXVIII to the Lady Juliana, A.D. 416, trans. Holmes and Wallace, *Nicene Fathers*, First Series, op. cit., pp. 548-552.

103.   "to the best of my recollection . . . ": *Anti-Pelagian Works*, op. cit., p. 409.

103.   "We say . . . ": Pelagius, as quoted in B. B. Warfield, *Nicene Fathers*, First Series, op. cit., p. xv.

104.   "good and praiseworthy" and following: *Anti-Pelagian Works*, op. cit., pp. 134, 132, 361, 409.

104.   Followers of both men: as Jerome observed, "You are a crafty fellow Pelagius, you let others write and talk, keeping your own tongue quiet." As quoted in Hugh Williams, "Heinrich Zimmer on the History of the Celtic Church," in *Zeitschrift Für Celtische Philologie*, IV, 1902, p. 533.

104.   "creeps into houses": "The Confessions and Letters of St. Augustine, with a Sketch of His Life and Works," trans. J. Cunningham, *Nicene Fathers*, First Series, Vol. I, op. cit. See also 2 Timothy 3:6.

105.   "as a powerful threat to reason . . . ": Rebecca West, op. cit., p. 165.

105.   "The Apostle": *City of God*, op. cit., p. 736.

105.   "It's his favorite pun again!": D. L. T. Bethell, "The Originality of the Early Irish Church," in *J.R.S.A.I.*, Vol. 111, 1981, p. 42.

106.   "that all men, as long as they be mortals . . . " and following: *City of God*, ibid., p. 359.

106.   "All are governed . . . ": "The Principal Works of St. Jerome," trans. W. Fremantle, *Nicene Fathers*, Second Series, Vol. VI, op. cit., p. 462.

106.   "rendering the cross . . . " and following: *Anti-Pelagian Works*, op. cit., pp. 240, 98.

106.   "the complete egotist . . . ": West, op. cit., p. 219.

106.   "enemy of grace": Augustine, Letter CXCI, A.D. 418, trans. J. Cunningham, *Nicene Fathers*, Vol. I, First Series, op. cit., p. 555. See also "On Heresies," as quoted by Warfield, op. cit., p. lxiii.

107.   "You, O God, are my stronghold": Psalm 58:10.

107.   "It is God . . . ": Philippians 2:13.

107.   "inscrutable": *City of God*, op. cit., p. 216.

107.   He "was condemned . . . ": Etienne Gilson, *Reason and Revelation in the Middle*

Ages, New York 1954, p. 23.

107. "Unless I see . . . ": St. John 20:25. See also *City of God*, Book II, Chapter 7, op. cit., p. 54, where Augustine comes close to describing this process himself. The difference between himself and the pagan philosophers is faith. A modern description of this dichotomy can be found in Jean Daniélou, *God and the Ways of Knowing*, New York 1957, pp. 54-57.

108. "We cannot, except in intellectual chaos . . . ": K. Lake, *Landmarks*, op. cit., p. 77.

108. "And so the Apostles departed . . . ": Acts 5:41. Pelagius was officially condemned in 431 during the First Council of Ephesus.

109. "proud and haughty people": *Anti-Pelagian Works*, Vol. II, op. cit., p. 243.

109. "lord of all donkeys": Julian of Eclanum, as quoted in Peter Brown, *Augustine of Hippo*, London 1967, p. 383.

109. "joyful conclusion": Chadwick, *John Cassian*, op. cit., p. 62.

109. "How incomprehensible . . . ": Romans 11:33.

109. "of resistence to . . . ": Warfield, op. cit., p. xxi.

109. "Work out your salvation . . . ": Philippians 2:12.

110. "Survey the path . . . ": Proverbs 4:26.

110. "With one mind . . . ": Acts 2:46.

110. "Virtue has need of our will . . . ": St. Athanasius, op. cit., p. 37.

110. "irresistable": Warfield, op. cit., p. xxi.

110. "semi-Pelagians": also called "Reminders of Pelagianism" by Prosper, among others. See Warfield, ibid.

110. "We are no match . . . ": Prosper of Aquitaine, *Defense of St. Augustine*, trans. P. De Letter, London 1963, p. 45.

110. "That each may arrive at knowledge . . . ": *Anti-Pelagian Works*, Vol. 1, op. cit., p. 29.

112. Augustine's proposals "against the teaching of the Fathers": See Vincent of Lérins, "A Commonitory," Chapter XXVII, op. cit., p. 152.

112. "Let there be no innovation . . . ": Pope Stephen I (254- 257), as quoted by Vincent, ibid., p. 135.

112. "When God sees in us . . . ": Cassian, "Conferences," *Nicene Fathers*, op. cit., p. 426.

113. A land "remote . . . " and following: *The Writings of Patrick*, op. cit., pp. 62, 54, 55.

113. "ministering to the people nothing . . . ": Cassian, "Institutes," *Nicene Fathers*, op. cit., p. 200.

113. "The response of utterly foreign peoples . . . ": Peter Brown, *Augustine*, op. cit., p. 398.

114. "dazed": *The Principal Works*, op. cit., p. 499.

115. "The one city . . . ": *City of God*, op. cit., p. 593.

115. "clear, charming, abstruse . . . ": Cassiodorus, op. cit., p. 120.

115. "tools of virtue" and following: *St. Benedict's Rule for Monasteries*, trans. Leonard J. Doyle, St. John's Abbey, Collegeville, Minnesota 1948, p. 100.

116. "You ought to exercise caution . . . ": Cassiodorus, op. cit., p. 132.

123. "Bordgal": Kuno Meyer, *Learning in Ireland in the Fifth Century and the Transmission of Letters*, Dublin 1913, p. 11; "Miscellanea Hibernica," in *University of Illinois Studies in Language and Literature*, Vol. II, No. 4, November 1916, p. 34; "Gauls in Ireland," in *Ériu*, Vol. IV, 1910, p. 208. See also Kenney, op. cit., p. 142; Séan Ó Ríordáin, "Roman Material in Ireland," in *P.R.I.A.*, Vol. LI, Section C, 1945-48, p. 38; and "Colloquium on Hiberno-Roman Relations and Material Remains," in *P.R.I.A.*, Vol. 76, Section C, Nos. 6-15, 1976, pp. 171-292.

123. A "convenient" place to visit: Tacitus, op. cit., p. 71. See also "A Catalogue of the Roman Coins from Newgrange, Co. Meath and Notes on the Coins and Related Finds," in *P.R.I.A.*, Vol. 77, Sec. C, No. 2, 1977, pp. 35-55.

124. "tepidly": Gildas, as quoted in Dom Louis Gougaud, *Christianity in Celtic Lands: A History of the Churches of the Celts, their origin, development, influence, and mutual relations*, London 1932, p. 21.

124. Regions "inaccessible to the Romans": Tertullian, "Adversus Judaeos," Chapter 7, as quoted in Nora Chadwick, *The Age of the Saints in the Early Celtic Church*, London 1961, p. 21.

124. "infiltrated": Ludwig Bieler, *St. Patrick and the Coming of Christianity*, Dublin 1967, p. 3.

124. "quick of mind . . . ": Diodorus Siculus, op. cit., p. 251.

124. "flourishing academies": *Select Letters of St. Jerome*, op. cit., p. 405.

125. "entirely unexpected" and following: Robin Lane Fox, *Pagans and Christians*, New York 1987, pp. 609, 655.

125. "I have prayed enough . . . ": *Ausonius*, trans. Hugh G. Evelyn White, Vol. I, London 1919, p. 23.

126. "being carried away . . . " and following: "The Dialogues of Sulpicius Severus," trans. Bernard M. Peebles, C.S.B., in *The Fathers of the Church: A New Translation*, Vol. 7, New York 1949, p. 161.

126. "the price of what he ate . . . " and following: *The Lausiac History*, op. cit., p. 113.

126. "Better than all else . . . ": Merton, *Wisdom*, op. cit., p. 33.

126. "read with a passionate interest . . . ": Nora Chadwick, *Poetry and Letters in Early Christian Gaul*, London 1955, p. 16.

126. "The elders had their time free . . . " and following: "Life of St. Martin, Bishop and Confessor," trans. B. Peebles, in *Fathers of the Church*, op. cit., p. 117.

128. "exuberance and glitter": *Select Letters*, op. cit., p. 405.

128. "This compels us to recognize . . . ": "Dialogues," op. cit., p. 194.

128. "contemptible" and following: "The Works of Sulpitius Severus," trans. Alexander Roberts, *Nicene Fathers*, Second Series, Vol. XI, op. cit., pp. 8, 13, 14, 36.

129. "Stand in line of battle . . . ": St. Jerome, "Against Vigilantius," op. cit., p. 423.

129. "Hearts consecrated to Christ . . . ": Paulinus of Nola, in *Ausonius*, Vol. II, op. cit., pp. 125-127.

129. These "wanderers and strangers . . . ": Celestine, Bishop of Rome, trans. Myles Dillon and Nora Chadwick, *The Celtic Realms*, London 1967, p. 167.

129. "While they were looking . . . ": *The Lausiac History*, op. cit., p. 46.

130. "ill will . . . ": "Works of Sulpitius Severus," op. cit., p. 37.

130. "This is an old maxim of the fathers . . . ": "Institutes," op. cit., p. 279.

130. "Every word of the Lord . . . ": Cassiodorus, op. cit., p. 133.

131. "It is high time . . . " and following: *The Letters of Sidonius*, trans. O. M. Dalton, Vol. II, Oxford 1915, pp. 51, 188-91. See also C. E. Stevens, *Sidonius Apollinaris and His Age*, Oxford 1933.

131. "The devastation . . . ": "The Leyden Glossary," trans. Kenney, op. cit., p. 142.

Part II

137. "It is time for me to pass . . . ": as quoted in Kathleen Hughes, "The Changing Theory and Practice of Irish Pilgrimage," in *The Journal of Ecclesiastical History*, Vol. XI, No. 2, October 1960, p. 150.

139. "That is too much!": as quoted in J. L. Campbell, "The Tour of Edward Lluyd in Ireland in 1699 and 1700," in *Celtica*, #5, 1960, p. 221.

139. Lough Neagh: Muirhead, op. cit., p. 133.

139. Arboe high cross: see D. A. Chart, E. Estyn Evans, H. C. Lawlor, eds. *A Preliminary Study of the Ancient Monuments of Northern Ireland*, Belfast 1940, pp. 241-242; and Her Majesty's Stationery Office, *Ancient Monuments of Northern Ireland: In State Care*, Belfast 1969, pp. 95-97, 91.

141. "tiny curraghs . . . " and following: Gildas, *The Ruin of Britain*, trans. Hugh Williams, London 1899, p. 45. For curraghs in general see James Hornell, *British Coracles and Irish Curraghs*, London 1938, Parts I & II, pp. 148-178, and Part III, pp. 5-39; also Timothy Severin, *The Brendan Voyage*, New York 1978.

142. "converted that people . . . ": Bede, op. cit., p. 146.

142.	"For the fear of hell . . . ": *Liber Hymnorum*, op. cit., p. 75.

142.	"Christianity preaches a doctrine of escape . . . ": Whitehead, op. cit., p. 51.

142.	"What Saint ever won his crown . . . ": "Epistle XXVII to Eustochium," as quoted in Kenneth E. Kirk, *The Vision of God: The Christian Doctrine of the "Summum Bonum,"* New York 1966, p. 176.

142.	"helmets of salvation . . . ": "Bede's Prose Life of St. Cuthbert," in *Two Lives of St. Cuthbert*, op. cit., p. 215. See also Walafridus Strabus, "Life of Blathmac," in *Early Sources of Scottish History A.D. 500 to A.D. 1286*, ed. M. O. Anderson, Vol. I, Edinburgh 1922, p. 263.

142.	An "island soldier": *Adomnán's Life of Columba*, op. cit., p. 79.

142.	"a warrior and cleric": "Berchan's Prophesy," as quoted in Anderson, *Sources*, op. cit., p. 46.

143.	"The sweet district of Ireland": *Adomnán's Life of Columba*, op. cit, p. 313.

143.	"The custom of travelling . . . ": Walahfrid Strabo, *Life of St. Gall*, trans. Kenney, op. cit., p. 551.

143.	"Rest like a doomed man . . . ": *Early Irish Lyrics, Eighth to Twelfth Century*, trans. Gerard Murphy, Oxford 1956, p. 21.

143.	Martin "achieved martyrdom . . . ": Sulpicius Severus, "Life of St. Martin," trans. F. R. Hoare, in *The Western Fathers*, London 1954, p. 54, as quoted in Clare Stancliffe, "Red, white and blue martyrdom," in *Ireland in Early Mediaeval Europe, Studies in Memory of Kathleen Hughes*, ed. D. Whitelock, R. McKitterick, D. Dumville, Cambridge 1982, p. 31.

143.	"the abbot of a strange tribe over you . . . ": Whitley Stokes, "On the Calendar of Oengus," Dublin 1880, p. CLXXXV, as quoted by Frank O'Connor, *The Backward Look: A Survey of Irish Literature*, London 1967, p. 20.

145.	"The meaning is difficult": "The Bodleian Amra Choluimb chille," trans Whitley Stokes, in *Revue Celtique*, Vol. XX, 1899, p. 135.

145.	"A brave man . . . " and following: "A Poem in praise of Columb Cille," trans. Fergus Kelly, in *Ériu*, Vol. XXIV, 1973, pp. 15, 9, 11.

145.	"Good is her blushing" and following: "Amra Choluimb cille," op. cit., pp. 285, 49.

146.	"with face afire . . . ": "Some Saints of Ireland," trans. E. J. Gywnn, in *The Church Quarterly Review*, Vol. LXXIV, April 1912, p. 74.

146.	"full of demons": "Amra Choluimb cille," op. cit., p. 43.

146.	"whatever business he loved . . . ": "Cuimmin's Poem on the Saints of Ireland," trans. Whitley Stokes, in *Zeitschrift Für Celtische Philologie*, Vol. I, 1897, p. 67.

146.	"My brothers . . . ": Bede, op. cit., p. 73.

147.	"Slain by the power . . . ": *Adomnán's Life of Columba*, op. cit., p. 385.

147.	"although they are beautiful . . . " and following: Diodorus Siculus, op. cit., p. 252.

148.	"It is a pity . . . ": Eugene O'Curry, *Lectures on the Manuscript Materials of Ancient Irish History*, Dublin 1861, pp. 641-2.

148.	"To open it . . . ": Manus O'Donnell, op. cit., p. 183.

148.	Celts "must have longed . . . ": Constantine FitzGibbon, *The Irish in Ireland*, London & New York 1983, p. 61.

149.	Oban: Malcolm Ferguson, *A Trip from Callander to Staffa and Iona with Brief Descriptive Sketches of the Route by Sea and Land, and the Sacred Rock-Bound Isle of I-Colm-Kill*, Edinburgh 1894, p. 39.

149.	"And bring out from the murmuring sea . . . ": as quoted in Ferguson, op. cit., p. 39.

149.	"To knock men in ye head . . . ": E. Lhuyd, as quoted in J. L. Campbell and D. Thomson, *Edward Lhuyd in the Scottish Highlands 1699-1700*, Oxford 1963, p. XX.

150.	"a witch . . . ": Joanna Baillie, *The Family Legend: A Tragedy in Five Acts*, New York 1810, p. 36. See also Sir Walter Scott, "Prologue to Miss Baillie's Play of The Family Legend," in *Poems and Plays of Sir Walter Scott*, Vol. I, London 1911, p. 25.

150.	"a most dolorous countryside": James Boswell, *The Life of Samuel Johnson & The Journal of a Tour to the Hebrides with Samuel Johnson, L L.D.*, ed. F. V. Morley, New York 1966, p. 557.

150. "A most wretched walk . . . ": John Keats to his brother Tom, 23 and 26 July 1818, in *Letters of John Keats*, ed. Robert Gittings, London 1970, p. 141.

152. A miserable whelter of weeds: Boswell, op. cit., p. 563.

155. "Wednesday, Oct. 20 . . . ": ibid.

155. Iona visitations: for general survey, Derek Cooper, *Road to the Isles, Travellers in the Hebrides 1770-1914*, London 1979, and Elizabeth Bray, *The Discovery of the Hebrides, Voyages to the Western Isles 1745-1883*, London 1986. Sir Walter Scott: see Edgar Johnson, *Sir Walter Scott, The Great Unknown*, New York 1970. John Keats: see Claude Finney, *The Evolution of Keat's Poetry*, Vol. II, Cambridge 1936, pp. 407-428; Walter J. Bate, *John Keats*, Cambridge 1963, pp. 339-362; *Letters of John Keats*, op. cit., pp. 137, 140-145,150-151. William Wordsworth: see Mary Moorman, *William Wordsworth, A Biography: The Later Years 1803-1850*, London 1968, pp. 497-500; *The Complete Poetical Works of William Wordsworth*, London 1893, pp. 721-723. Joseph Turner: see Jack Lindsay, *J. M. W. Turner, His Life and Work*, New York 1966, p. 173; M. Butlin, E. Joll, *The Paintings of J. M. W. Turner*, New Haven 1977, Vol I (Text), pp. 180-181, Vol. II (Plates), #329 — "Staffa, Fingal's Cave," 1832. Boswell and Johnson: See W. Jackson Bate, *Samuel Johnson*, New York 1977, pp. 467-474; Boswell's *Tour of the Hebrides*, op. cit., pp. 557-566; Johnson's *A Journey to the Western Islands of Scotland*, ed. R. W. Chapman London 1951, pp. 124-143. Felix Mendelssohn: see Heinrich E. Jacob, *Felix Mendelssohn and His Times*, Englewood Cliffs 1963, pp. 199-203, 236-241; Eric Werner, *Mendelssohn, A New Image of the Composer and His Age*, London 1962, pp. 214, 417-420.

155. "I and the ladies sketched": David Duff, *Victoria in the Highlands, The Personal Journal of Her Majesty Queen Victoria*, New York 1969, p. 71. Also quoted in Ferguson, op. cit., p. 140.

155. "innocent, simple, and crouching . . . ": Mrs. Murray, as quoted in John Stewart, *The Official Guide To The Islands of Staffa and Iona*, Glasgow 1888, p. 84.

155. "Whatever withdraws us . . . ": Johnson, *Journey to the Hebrides*, op. cit., p. 134.

156. "Where is Duncan's body?": William Shakespeare, *Macbeth*, Act II, scene iv.

156. "men who did not expect . . . ": Johnson, *Journey to the Western Isles*, op. cit., p. 137.

156. "a general rudeness": John Macculloch, *A Description of The Western Islands of Scotland, including The Isle of Man: Comprising An Account of their Geological Structure, with Remarks on their Agriculture, Scenery, and Antiquities*, Vol. I, London 1884, p. 5.

156. "At the end of three days . . . ": Thomas Pennant, *A Tour in Scotland and Voyage to the Hebrides*; MDCCLXXII, London 1775, p. 249.

156. "the most stupid" and following: ibid, pp. 244, 246.

156. "purloined a piece of it": Stewart, *Official Guide*, op. cit., p. 83.

157. *Annals of Ulster*, Vol. II, op. cit., entry for year 1204.

160. Fifty-five voyages: John Bannerman, *Studies in the History of Dalriada*, Edinburgh 1974, p. 149. See also *Adomnán's Life of Columba*, op. cit., pp. 116 and following.

160. "princely malt": "The Rule of Ailbe of Emly," trans. Joseph O'Neill, in *Ériu* Vol. III, 1907, p. 105.

160. "As long as I shall give the rules . . . ": "The Monastery of Tallaght," op. cit., p.129.

160. "in a hard prison of stone": "Cuimmin's Poem on the Saints of Ireland," op. cit., p. 63.

160. "where the seven roads meet": *Vitae Sanctorum Hiberniae*, trans. Charles Plummer, Vol. I, Oxford 1910, p. cxiii.

160. "Dry bread and cess . . . ": "Rule of Ailbe of Emly," op. cit., p. 105.

160. "Without ploughing . . . ": *The Martyrology of Oengus the Culdee*, trans. Whitley Stokes, London 1905, p. 189.

160. "Where there is a cow . . . ": *Vitae Sanctorum Hiberniae*, op. cit., p. cxxi.

160. "thirty victorious . . ": "The Life of St. Columba From the Edinburgh Mss.," trans. Paul Grosjean, in *Scottish Gaelic Studies*, Vol. II, Pt. 2, February 1928, p. 141. In *The Annals of Clonmacnoise, being Annals of Ireland from the earliest Period to A.D. 1408*,

trans. into English A.D. 1627 by Conell Mageoghagan, ed. Rev. Denis Murphy, S.J., Dublin 1896, the figure becomes three hundred books (p. 95).

160. "Go through the herds . . . ": *Martyrology of Oengus*, op. cit., p. 203.

161. "To go and say the office . . . ": "The Rule of the Grey Monks," trans. Dom Louis Gougaud, *Christianity in Celtic Lands*, op. cit., p. 334.

161. "Shame to my thoughts . . . ": "A Religious Poem," trans. Kuno Meyer, in *Ériu*, III, 1907, p. 15.

161. "the freedom of the desert . . . ": Cassian, "Conferences," op. cit., p. 490.

161. "Senán loved lasting illness" and following: "Cuimmin's Poem," op. cit., pp. 5, 67; Gougaud, op. cit., pp. 94-95.

161. "What should be shunned . . . ": "Apgitir Chrábaid: The Alphabet of Piety," trans. R. Vernam Hull, in *Celtique*, Vol. VIII, 1968, p. 63.

161. "Battle hard . . . ": *Martyrology of Oengus*, op. cit., p. 407.

162. Brian Moore, *Catholics*, New York 1972.

162. "it is harsh . . . ": "Rule of Ailbe of Emly," op. cit., p. 105.

162. "Each of us pursues his trade . . . ": trans. Frank O'Connor, *The Backward Look*, op. cit., p. 52.

162. "They who seek the Lord . . . ": *Adomnán's Life of Columba*, op. cit., p. 525. See also *Vitae Sanctorum Hiberniae*, op. cit., p. cxiv.

163. "unlearned" and following Patrician quotations: *The Writings of Patrick*, op. cit., pp. 38-40.

163. "smash the head of the dragon . . . ": Muirchú, "Vita Patricii," trans. Ludwig Bieler, in *The Patrician Texts in the Book of Armagh*, Dublin 1979, p. 83.

164. "the dead weight of tradition" and following: O'Connor, *The Backward Look*, op. cit., pp. 2, 14.

165. "it is only in the case of sweet melody . . . ": Gerald of Wales, op. cit., p. 103.

165. David and the harp: see Helen M. Roe, "The David Cycle in Early Irish Art," in *J.R.S.A.I.*, LXXIX, 1949, pp. 39-59.

165. *Psalterium*: Martin McNamara, "Psalter Text and Psalter Study in the Early Irish Church (A.D. 600-1200)," in *P.R.I.A.*, Vol. 73, Section C, #7, 1973, p. 229.

165. "The three fifties": See "Life of St. Columba From the Edinburgh Mss.," op. cit., p. 165.

165. "Maelruain used to say . . . ": "Monastery of Tallaght," op. cit., p. 142.

165. "It's like a glorious building . . . ": *Hibernica Minora, Being a Fragment of an Old-Irish Treatise on the Psalter*, ed. Kuno Meyer, Oxford 1894, p. 29.

167. "had a zeal for God . . . " and following: Bede, op. cit., pp. 144, 283. He is quoting from Augustine's "A Treatise on Nature and Grace Against Pelagius," in *Anti-Pelagian Works*, op. cit.

168. "shipwrecks, far from terrifying them . . . ": *Sidonius, Poems and Letters* trans. W. B. Anderson, Vol. II, Cambridge 1965, p. 431, as quoted in Henry Mayr-Harting, *The Coming of Christianity to Anglo-Saxon England*, London 1972, p. 13.

168. Irish as liars: see W. B. Stanford, "Towards A History of Classical Influences in Ireland," in *P.R.I.A.*, Vol. 70, Section C, #3, 1970, p. 27.

168. "to be with them . . . ": *The Writings of Patrick*, op. cit., p. 57.

168. "faithless": Bede, op. cit., p. 103.

168. "every crime in the calendar": Gregory of Tours, *The History of the Franks*, trans. Lewis Thorpe, Harmondsworth 1983, p. 285.

169. "they have not even heard a rumor": Julius Ceasar, *Bellum Gallicium*, trans. Tierney, in "Celtic Ethnography," op. cit., p. 272.

169. "They often speak in riddles . . . ": Diodorus Siculus, op. cit., p. 251.

169. "there's an end to that . . . ": as quoted by W. B. Stanford, op. cit., p. 38.

170. "the Irish had the choice . . . .": O'Connor, *The Backward Look*, op. cit., p. 5.

170. "Celt brings all heart . . . ": Edmund Bishop, as quoted by Kathleen Hughes, "Some Aspects of Irish Influence on Early English Private Prayer," in *Studia Celtica*, Vol. V, 1950, p. 48.

170. "What is a Classic?": *An Address delivered before the Virgil Society on the 16th of*

October 1944, London 1946, p. 19.

171. "quick mind": Diodorus Siculus, op. cit., p. 251.

171. "That's a very complicated story!": *Vitae Sanctorum Hiberiae*, op. cit., p. cxxxi.

171. "Was there not among the many languages . . . ": *Auraicept Na N-Éces — The Scholars' Primer, being the texts of the ogham tract from the Book of Ballymote and the Yellow Book of Lecan, and the text of the Trefhocul from the Book of Leinster*, trans. George Calder, Edinburgh 1917, p. 5.

172. Color spectrum: See Stancliffe, "Red, white and blue martyrdom," op. cit., p. 28-29.

172. Greeks and Irish brothers in deceit: see A. J. Simpson and E. S. C. Weiner, *The Oxford English Dictionary*, Second Ed., Vol. VI, Oxford 1989, pp. 804, 807.

172. "profound self-inquiry": Rachel Bromwich, *Matthew Arnold and Celtic Literature*, Oxford 1965, p. 26.

172. "In loving thou do'st well . . . ": Anonymous, written for and published by Thomas Cook, *Releig Orain, The Royal Cemetery of Iona*, Leicester 1889, p. 13.

173. "I scruple to expend tears . . . ": Lucan, *The Pharsalia*, trans. H. T. Riley, London 1903, pp. 281-282.

173. "Sad indeed . . . ": *In Cath Catharda: The Civil War of the Romans. An Irish Version of Lucan's Pharsalia*, ed. and trans. Whitley Stokes, Leipzig 1909, p. 441.

175. "Every speech of historians . . . ": *Senchus Mor*, as quoted in Robin Flower, *The Irish Tradition*, Oxford 1947, p. 4.

175. "my defect in learning": *The Writings of Patrick*, op. cit., p. 60.

175. "like a terrible peal of thunder": *Adomnán's Life of Columba*, op. cit., p. 289.

176. "If you work hard . . . ": Aldhelm, Abbot of Malmesbury and Bishop of Sherborne, as quoted in H. Mayr-Harting, op. cit., p. 214.

176. A mandarin language: D. A. Binchy, "Semantic Influence of Latin in the Old Irish Glosses," in *Latin Script and Letters, A.D. 400-900. Festschrift presented to Ludwig Bieler on the occasion of his 70th birthday*, ed. John J. O'Meara and Bernd Naumann, Leiden 1976, p. 168.

176. "If the boys do not study . . . ": "Rule of the Celi De," trans. E. Gwynn, in *Hermathena*, No. XLIV, 2nd Supplement Volumn, Dublin 1927, p. 83.

176. "For anyone who does not read . . . ": "An Old-Irish Treatise De Arreis," trans. Kuno Meyer, in *Revue Celtique*, XV, 1893, p. 495.

176. "those ripples . . . ": "Annals of Bavaria," A.D. 1074, trans. Martin McNamara, op. cit., p. 253.

177. A "wretched hut . . . ": T. Garnett, *Observations on a Tour through The Highlands and part of the Western Isles of Scotland*, Vol. I, London 1811, p. 243.

177. "deep-thinking . . . ": Evelyn Waugh to Dudley Carew, 31 May 1922, in *The Letters of Evelyn Waugh*, ed. Mark Amory, Harmondsworth 1980, p. 11.

178. Staffa: see Edward Smith, *The Life of Sir Joseph Banks*, London 1917, pp. 32-3, and H. C. Cameron, *Sir Joseph Banks: The Autocrat of the Philosophers*, London 1952, pp. 57-8.

180. Resignation of Lord Privy seal: see P. C. Yorke and H. Chisholm, "Earls and Dukes of Argyll," in *Britannica*, Vol. I, op. cit., p. 486.

180. "the fire, the freshness . . . ": George Douglas, Eighth Duke of Argyll, *Iona*, London 1878, p. 103. See also the same author's *Autobiography and Memoirs*, ed. The Dowager Duchess of Argyll, New York 1906.

180. "seeking hopelessly to play . . . ": George MacLeod, "The Coracle," No. 2, May 1939, p. 18, as quoted in T. Ralph Morton, *The Iona Community: Personal Impressions of the Early Years*, Edinburgh 1977, p. 17.

181. "a slightly dazed company . . . ": MacLeod, as quoted by Morton, ibid., p. 33.

182. "We are on a search . . . ": *Martyrology of Oengus*, op. cit., p. 153.

182. if the stomach is burdened . . . : *Sancti Columbani Opera*, op. cit., p. 127.

182. "a land too poor . . . ": as quoted in H. M. Chadwick, *Early Scotland: The Picts, The Scots and The Welsh of Southern Scotland*, Cambridge 1949, p. xix.

182. "another island": as quoted in M. O. Anderson, *Kings and Kingship in Early Scotland*,

Edinburgh 1973, p. xvii.

182. "who made their best decisions . . . ": *Germania, The Earliest Beginnings and the Land of the Germans*, as quoted in J. F. Killeen, "Ireland in the Greek and Roman Writers," in *P.R.I.A.*, Vol. 76, Section C, No. 9, 1976, p. 211.

182. "I saw an array . . . ": The Welsh poem "Gododdin," as quoted in Archibald A. M. Duncan, *Scotland, The Making of the Kingdom*, Edinburgh 1951, p. 44, and H. M. Chadwick, *Early Scotland*, op. cit., pp. xxi, 126.

182. "I swear what my people swear . . . ": "The Story of Mac Dáthós' Pig and Hound," in *Hibernica Minor*, op. cit., p. 62. See also O'Connor, op. cit., p. 50.

184. St. Ciarán's rage, urinating contests, and churchmen swearing oaths in heathen fashion, see O'Connor, op. cit., pp. 56-7, 45-6.

184. "lost his sword" and following: *The Tain*, trans. Thomas Kinsella, Oxford 1970, p. 104.

184. "St. Cummíne . . . " and following: *Martyrology of Oengus*, op. cit., pp. 243, 135, 157.

185. Faroe Islands and Iceland: "In the book of the Course of Ages which the priest Bede the holy made, there is spoken of an island which is called *Thile* in books of Latin, and it is said that it lies 6 days' sailing north of Britannia. Wisemen hold that *Thile* is Iceland . . . But before Iceland was settled by Northmen there were there those people whom the Northmen call *Papar*. They were Christian men, and people think they must have been from the West of the Sea because there were found after them Irish books and bells and crooks, and yet more things, by which it might be perceived that they were West men . . . And it is also spoken of in English books that at that time men went (i.e. sailed) between the lands (i.e. between the British Isles and Iceland)." Arev the historian (1067-1148), "Landnama-book, The Book of the Settlements," in *Origines Islandicae: A Collection of the More Important Sagas and other Native Writings Relating to the Settlement and Early History of Iceland*, trans. Gudbrand Vigfusson and F. York Powell, Vol. I, Oxford 1905, p. 13.

185. "as far as a white shield will be visible ": "On the Punishment of Sending Adrift," trans. Mary E. Byrne, in *Ériu*, XI, 1932, p. 98. See also *Martyrology of Donegal*, op. cit., p. 83: "Énda founded a church on Aran, and afterwards assumed the abbacy thereof. Thrice fifty was his congregation. The test and proof which he used to put upon them every evening to clear them of sins, was to put every man of them in turn into a curragh without any hide upon it at all, out upon the sea; and the salt water would get into the curragh if there was any crime or sin upon the man who was in it. It would not get in if he was free from sins; and Énda, the abbot, was the last who entered the curragh. There was not found any man who did not escape the wetting except only the cook. What hast thou done, said Énda. He said that he did nothing but put a little addition to his own share from that of another brother. Énda ordered him to leave the island. There is no room for a thief here, he said, I will not permit this at all."

185. "A monk's function . . . ": "Against Vigilantius," op. cit., p. 423.

186. "Take me . . . ": "The Life of St. Columba From the Edinburgh Mss.," op. cit., p. 147.

186. "stitch together Church and tribe . . . ": "The Pseudo-historical Prologue to the Senchas Már," in *Studia Celtica*, X/XI, 1975/76, p. 19.

186. "who stupidly contend . . . " and following: St. Wilfrid at Whitby, as quoted in Bede, op. cit., p. 188.

186. "The Irish Church today . . . ": Rose Macaulay, *Pleasure of Ruins*, London 1953, p. 363.

186. "to prune their vines . . . ": *Select Letters*, op. cit., p. 405.

187. "word-melody": Stanford, "Towards a History," op. cit., p. 21.

187. "secret language": F. M. Stenton, *Anglo-Saxon England*, Oxford 1971, p. 178.

187. "The fields of Ireland . . . ": Aldhelm, as quoted by Françoise Henry, "The Lindisfarne Gospels," in *Antiquity*, XXXVII, 1963, p. 102.

187. Grammar "protects and controls . . . ": *Johannis Scotti Eriugenae: Periphyseon (De Divisione Naturae)*, ed. and trans. I. P. Sheldon-Williams, Ludwig Bieler, collaborator, Vol. I, Dublin 1968, p. 111.

188. "What will you do tonight, cleric? . . . ": "Life of St. Adamnán," as quoted in D. A. Binchy, "A pre-Christian survival in mediaeval Irish hagiography," in *Ireland in Early Mediaeval Europe*, op. cit., p. 176-7.

188. "perverted ingenuity": M. L. W. Laistner, *Thought and Letters In Western Europe A.D. 500 to 900*, London 1931, p. 105.

189. "No one of us has been a heretic . . . " and following: trans. Kenney, op. cit., p. 193.

189. St. Scuithín: "Cuimmin's Poem," op. cit., p. 65.

189. St. Cronan of Roscrea: Eoin Neeson, *The Book of Irish Saints*, Cork 1967, p. 85; E. J. Gwynn, "Some Saints of Ireland," in *The Church Quarterly Review*, LXXIV, April 1912, p. 68.

190. "Nobles of Munster . . . ": as quoted in Kathleen Hughes, "The church and the world in early Christian Ireland," in *Irish Historical Studies*, Vol. XIII, No. 50, September 1962, p. 105.

190. Celtic abbot in arms: Giraldus Cambrensis, *The Itinerary through Wales and the Description of Wales*, trans. W. Llewelyn Williams, London 1908, p. 112.

190. "they expected diversity . . . ": Kathleen Hughes, *Church in Early Irish Society*, op. cit., p. 99.

190. "to be an example . . . ": as quoted in Hughes, ibid., p. 14.

190. "if Christianity be the highest instance . . . ": Thomas Carlyle, *On Heroes, Hero-Worship, and The Heroic in History*, Boston 1907, p. 19.

191. "Leave your country . . . ": Genesis 12:1. See also "Life of St. Columba, by the Monk Jonas," in *Translations and Reprints from the Original Sources of European History*, trans. Dana C. Munro, Vol. II. No. 7, Philadelphia 1902, p. 5.

191. "read books that Cassian loved": *Liber Hymnorum*, op. cit., p. 367.

191. "Antony, the Egyptian Monk": *The Confessions of St. Augustine*, trans. Edward Pusey, New York 1949, p. 155.

191. "to seek a solitude . . . ": Adomnán, as quoted in Nora Chadwick, *The British Heroic Age*, Cardiff 1976, p. 48.

193. "the dark cloud . . . ": Bede, op. cit., p. 137.

193. "stillness of divine contemplation": Cassian, "Conferences," op. cit., p. 490.

193. Celts fought without armor: Diodorus Siculus, op. cit., p. 250.

193. "rout the enemy . . . ": see Plummer, *Vitae Sanctorum Hiberniae*, op. cit., p. clxxxi.

193. An angel "suddenly stretched out his hand . . . ": *Adomnán's Life of Columba*, op. cit., pp. 474-5.

193. "Take virginity . . . ": *Martyrology of Oengus*, op. cit., p. 147.

194. St. Patrick waving his hands: See Binchy, "The Pseudo-historical Preface," op. cit., p. 18.

194. "the enemy you conciliate . . . ": Whitehead, op. cit., p. 40.

194. "It is not I who am to blame . . . ": Manus O'Donnell, op. cit., p. 189.

196. This "idea of going to a barbarous nation . . . " and following: Bede, op. cit., pp. 66, 100, 102, 103, 75, 86.

198. "My harp is tuned . . . ": as quoted in H. Mayr-Harting, op. cit., p. 55. See also F. H. Dudden, *Gregory the Great, His Place in History and Thought*, London 1905.

201. "A great many things keep happening . . . " and following: Gregory of Tours, op. cit., pp. 63, 144, 283, 75, 222, 379, 381, 587, 521, 263.

203. "degenerate": Heinrich Zimmer, *The Irish Element in Mediaeval Culture*, trans. Jane Edmands, New York 1891, p. 22.

203. "Columcille learned Greek grammar": "Amra Choluimb chille," op. cit., p. 405.

204. Torch of classical learning passed on by Celts: Edward James summarizes the theories of Zimmer and his school in "Ireland and western Gaul in the Merovingian Period," in *Ireland in Mediaeval Europe*, op. cit., pp. 362-386. For opposite opinion, Johannes Wilhelmus Smit, *Studies on the Language and Style of Columba the Younger (Columbanus)*, Amsterdam 1971.

204. Iona library: Edward Gibbon, *The History of the Decline and Fall of the Roman Empire*, Vol. III, Boston 1861, p. 526.

206. "our frivolities": as quoted in Stanford, "Towards a History," op. cit., p. 18.
206. "purple patch": Ludwig Bieler, "The Humanism of St. Columbanus," in *Mélanges Columbaniens: Actes du Congrès International de Luxeuil, 20-23 juillet 1950*, Paris 1952, p. 100.
206. "common coin": Ludwig Bieler, ibid., as quoted in Smit, op. cit., p. 208.
206. "The Latin they wrote . . . ": R. R. Bolgar, *The Classical Heritage and its Beneficiaries*, Cambridge 1954, p. 93.
206. "Scholars as a type . . . ": Ludwig Bieler. "The Island of Scholars," in *Revue Du Moyen Age Latin*, VIII, No. 3, 1952, p. 219.
207. "to seek seclusion . . . ": *Sancti Columbani Opera*, op. cit., p. 29.
207. "dogs": The Monk Jonas, op. cit., p.26.
208. "rough passage": as quoted in Christine Mohrmann, "The Earliest Continental Irish Latin," in *Vigiliae Christianae*, Vol. XVI, 1962, p. 228.
208. "Therefore I shall speak out . . . ": trans. G. S. M. Walker, as quoted by Mohrmann, ibid., p. 224.
208. "the cultivated literary language . . . ": Mohrmann, op. cit., p. 221.
208. "grotesque turgidity": ibid.
209. "It was the intensity . . . ": Bieler, "Island of Scholars," op. cit., pp. 230, 223.
209. "the salvation of many": *Sancti Columbani Opera*, op. cit., p. 29.
209. Aidan and Oswald: Bede, op. cit., p. 145.
210. "like uncharted comets": Laistner, op. cit., p. 251, as quoted in Dillon and Chadwick, *Celtic Realms*, op. cit., p. 192.
211. "Delightful it would be . . . ": trans. Eugene O'Curry, as quoted in William F. Skene, *Celtic Scotland: A History of Ancient Alban*, Vol. II, Edinburgh 1871, p. 92-3.

Part III

213. "I am haunted . . . ": W. B. Yeats, "The White Birds," in *W. B. Yeats, The Poems*, ed. Richard J. Finneran, New York 1983, p. 42.
218. "Understand the Creation . . . ": "Sermon Concerning Faith," *Sancti Columbani Opera*, op. cit., p.65.
219. "a childlike simplicity . . . ": Muller, *Uses of the Past*, op. cit., p. 238.
219. "I am thrusting my face . . . ": *Sancti Columbani Opera*, op. cit., p. 39.
219. "Open thy mouth wide . . . ": Psalm 81:10.
219. "He who perseveres . . . ": *Sancti Columbani Opera*, op. cit., p. 33.
220. The Pharisees: G. S. M. Walker, op. cit., p. 21. See St. Matthew 23:13.
220. "primitive simplicity": Wilfrid, op. cit., p. 191.
222. "Greeks and Irish . . . ": as quoted in Gougaud, *Christianity in Celtic Lands*, op. cit., p. 178.
222. "These are people . . . ": ibid., p. 165.
222. "false vagrants . . . " and following: *The Letters of St. Boniface*, trans. Ephraim Emerton, New York 1940, pp. 144, 146.
222. "Churches of God . . . ": *Sancti Columbani Opera*, op. cit., p. 25.
222. "alien" tribe: Bede, op. cit., p. 158.
223. "both believers and unbelievers . . . ": Boniface, as quoted in D. N. Dumville, "Biblical Apocrypha and the Early Irish: A Preliminary Investigation," in *P.R.I.A.*, Vol. 73, Section C, No. 8, 1973, p. 302. See also William H. Hulme, *The Middle-English Harrowing of Hell and Gospel of Nicodemus*, London 1907, pp. lx-lxx, and J. A. MacCulloch, *The Harrowing of Hell: A Comparative Study of An Early Christian Doctrine*, Edinburgh 1930.
223. "Scottus . . . ": as quoted in Zimmer, *Irish Element*, op. cit., p. 48.
223. "St. Benedict is lying . . . ": as quoted in James O'Carroll, "Monastic Rules in Meroving-ian Gaul," in *Studies*, XLII, No. 4, 1953, p. 418.
223. "For a brief period . . . ": James Carney, "The Impact of Christianity," in *Early Irish Society*, ed. Myles Dillon, Dublin 1954, p. 68.

224. "To go to Rome . . . ": Sedulius Scottus, trans. O'Connor, op. cit., p. 51.
224. "If God could not be found . . . " and following: trans. Gwynn, op. cit., p. 71.
224. "have you ever known of a bird . . . ": as quoted in *Some Saints of Ireland*, op. cit., p. 71.
224. "at least as much to learn . . . ": Carney, op. cit., p. 68.
224. "Whence are you from . . . ": *Early Irish Metrics*, trans. Gerald Murphy, as quoted in O'Connor, op. cit., p. 69.
224. Erigena's "bon mot": see Kenney, op. cit., p. 589.
225. "because he forced us to think": as quoted in Sheldon-Williams, op. cit., p. 5.
225. "the most considerable philosopher . . . ": John J. O'Meara, *Eriugena*, Cork 1969, p. VII, as quoted in Pa il Oscar Kristeller, "The Historical Position of Johannes Scottus Eriugena," in *Latin Script*, op. cit., p. 156.
225. "the loneliest": Henry Bett, *Johannes Scotus Erigena: A Study in Mediaeval Philosophy*, Cambridge 1925, p. 1.
225. "stupefaction": Etienne Gilson, *History of Christian Philosophy in the Middle Ages*, New York 1955, p. 127.
225. "Scholasticus . . . ": as quoted in Sheldon-Williams, op. cit., p. 3.
226. "Authority proceeds . . . ": *Periphyseon i*, 69, as quoted in Alice Gardner, *Studies in John the Scot (Erigena), A Philosopher of the Dark Ages*, New York 1900, p. 16.
226. "untrained and childish . . . ": *Periphyseon* i, 64, trans. Sheldon-Williams, Vol. I, op. cit., p. 189.
226. "most pure and copious waters . . . ": as quoted by John Edwin Sandys, *A History of Classical Scholarship*, Vol. I, Cambridge 1921, p. 494.
226. An "exasperated" Paul . . . : Acts 17:10-21.
227. "It is a wonderful thing . . . ": Anastasius, trans. Kenney, op. cit., p. 582.
227. "who reason very subtly . . . " and following: *Periphyseon*, trans. Sheldon-Williams, op. cit., Vol I, pp. 117, 85, 81, 69 (quoting the Areopagite), 191; Vol. II, p. 105.
228. "For we also . . . ": *Periphyseon*, as quoted in Gardner, op. cit., p. 84.
229. "the folly of Origen": as quoted in Sandys, op. cit., p. 493.
229. "faith seeking to know": from the original title to Anselm's *Proslogium*, "Fides quaerens intellectum," or "Faith seeking understanding."
229. "perverse and insane": as quoted in Gardner, op. cit., p. 67.
229. Jerome's warnings: see Sandys, op. cit., p. 493.
231. "Only a few of the objects . . . ": Françoise Henry, "Remains of the Early Christian Period on Inishkea North, Co. Mayo," in *J.R.S.A.I.*, Vol. LXXV, 1945, p. 146.
231. "mad lust for purple": Pliny, *Natural History*, trans. H. Rackham, Vol. III, Cambridge & London 1938, p. 249; quoted in F. Henry, "A Wooden Hut on Inishkea North, Co. Mayo," in *J.R.S.A.I.*, Vol. LXXXI, Part I, 1951, p. 174.
231. "beautiful scarlet dye . . . ": Bede, op. cit., p. 37.
231. "strongly resembling an angry sea . . . ": Pliny, op. cit., p. 174.
232. "living by the sea-side . . . ": as quoted in F. Henry, "A Wooden Hut," op. cit., p. 175.
232. "weary with writing . . . ": "St. Columcille the Scribe," trans. Kuno Meyer, in *An Anthology of Irish Literature*, ed. David Greene, New York 1954, p. 33.
233. "to Columcille the musical . . . ": *Annals of Ulster*, Vol. I, op. cit., p. 289.
233. Scribe on the same footing as bishop: Gougaud, *Christianity in Celtic Lands*, op. cit., p. 361.
233. "seize the light above": *Aethelwulf De Abbatibus*, ed. A. Campbell, Oxford 1967, p. 19, as quoted in Kathleen Hughes, "Evidence for contacts between the churches of the Irish and English from the Synod of Whitby to the Viking Age," in *England Before the Conquest, Studies in primary sources presented to Dorothy Whitelock*, ed. P. Clemoes and K. Hughes, Cambridge 1971, p. 56.
233. "Nothing seems to me more miraculous . . . ": Gerald of Wales, op. cit., p. 84.
235. "The chief relic . . . ": *Annals of Ulster*, op. cit., p. 519.
235. "and writing": *Adomnán's Life of Columba*, op. cit., p. 187.
235. "to follow the track . . . ": W. W. Heist, "Over the Writer's Shoulder: Saint Abban," in

Celtica, XI, 1976, p. 78.

236. The Gospels as magic: "Which Books have a strange property which is that if they or any of them had sunk to the bottom of the deepest waters they would not lose one letter, sign, or character of them, which I have seen partly myself of that book of them which is at Durrow in the King's County, for I saw the ignorant man that had the same in his custody, when sickness came upon cattle, for their remedy put water on the book and suffered it to rest there a while and saw also cattle return thereby to their former or pristine state and the book to receive no loss." *The Annals of Clonmacnoise*, op. cit., p. 96. And Bede reports, "I have seen that folk suffering from snake-bite have drunk water in which scrapings from the leaves of books from Ireland had been steeped, and that this remedy checked the spreading poison and reduced the swelling." Bede, op. cit., pp. 39-40.

236. "I never knew anything . . . ": as quoted in Euguene O'Curry, *Lectures*, op. cit., p. 154.

236. "I wish to save . . . ": Charles O'Conor (1710-1791), as quoted in Kenney, op. cit., p. 56.

236. "that man of sin . . . ": as quoted in William Urwick, *The Early History of Trinity College Dublin 1591-1660, As told in Contemporary Records on occasion of its Tercentenary*, London 1892, p. 83.

236. "Phebe's apparell . . . ": as quoted in Constantia Maxwell, *A History of Trinity College Dublin 1591-1892*, Dublin 1946, p. 55.

236. "for books . . . ": ibid., p. 58.

236. "Whatever book . . . ": "Life of St. Columba From the Edinburgh Mss.," op. cit., p. 141.

237. "Protestant gentleman": Alice Curtayne, *The Trial of Oliver Plunkett*, New York 1953, p. 56.

237. "an estate as good . . . ": ibid.

237. "I went to visit old Flaherty . . . ": Dr. Thomas Molyneux, as quoted in A. Smith, "Journey to Connaught, April 1709," in *The Miscellany of the Irish Archaeological Society*, Vol. I, Dublin 1846, p. 171.

237. "The Library of Trinity College . . . ": as quoted in Urwick, op. cit., p. 94.

238. "Enriching its rather meagre repertory . . . ": Françoise Henry, *Irish Art in the Early Christian Period*, op. cit., p. 203.

238. "Nightfall and time for supper . . . ": Gougaud, *Christianity in Celtic Lands*, op. cit., p. 363.

240. "The Terrible Western Tragedy": all accounts from *The Connaught Telegraph*, issues of November 5, 7, and December 10, 1927; *The Galway Observer*, issues of November 5 & 19, 1927; *The Ballina Herald*, October 29, November 12, 19, & December 3, 1927.

247. Banna Strand and Casement's arrest: a farmer named John McCarthy discovered the raft, and had the information passed along to police barracks in Ardfert. See Captain Robert Monteith, *Casement's Last Adventure*, Dublin 1953, p. 158; Denis Gwynn, *The Life and Death of Roger Casement*, London 1930, p. 384; and B. L. Reid, *The Lives of Roger Casement*, New Haven 1976, p. 353.

247. "this dead life": as quoted in Dorothy Whitelock, "The Interpretation of The Seafarer," in *The Early Cultures of North-West Europe, H. M. Chadwick Memorial Studies*, ed. Cyril Fox, Bruce Dickins, Cambridge 1950, p. 266.

247. "self-satisfied . . . ": Whitehead, op. cit., p. 141.

247. "That vast . . . ": "Aubade," in *Collected Poems*, ed. Anthony Thwaite, New York 1988, p. 208.

248. "Whose sins you shall forgive . . . ": St. John 20:22,23.

248. "gathered together . . . ": I Corinthians 5:4.

248. "Is it better . . . ": as quoted in John T. McNeill, *The Celtic Penitentials and their Influence on Continental Christianity*, Paris 1923, p. 79.

248. "irremisible": as quoted in *Medieval Handbooks of Penance*, op. cit., p. 5.

248. "As one baptism . . . ": ibid., p. 14.

248. "as though at the mouth of Hell": *"De Arreis,"* op. cit., p. 494.
248. A hermit in Egypt . . . : See *The Road Wet*, op. cit., p. 12.
250. "By confession . . . ": as quoted in *Celtic Penitentials*, op. cit.
250. *"Aithrige,"*: ibid., p. 108.
250. "Lazarus, come forth": ibid., p. 89.
250. "die daily": St. Athanasius, op. cit., p. 36. See I Corinthians 15:31 for source of Antony's quotation.
250. "The diversity of faults . . . ": "The Penitential of St. Columbanus," as quoted in Oscar D. Watkins, *A History of Penance, Being a Study of the Authorities*, Vol. II, London 1920, p. 619.
251. "as a disturbing element": Julius von Pflugk-Harttung, "The Old Irish on the Continent," in *Transactions of the Royal Irish Academy*, Vol. V, 1891, p. 76.
251. "fearsome, cold water . . . ": Myles Dillon, "Laud Misc. 610," in *Celtica*, VI, 1963, p. 137.
251. "to crucify myself": Gougaud, *Christianity in Celtic Lands*, op. cit., p. 93.
251. "Confession should be taken . . . ": "Penitential of Columbanus," op. cit., p. 287.
251. "a man without an *anmchara* . . . ": Gougaud, *Christianity in Celtic Lands*, op. cit., p. 287.
252. "He who fails to guard the host . . . ": *Handbooks of Penance*, op. cit., pp. 14, 260.
252. "one hundred lively blows": ibid., pp. 33, 115.
252. "well balanced mind": Pflugk-Harttung, "The Old Irish," op. cit., p. 79.
252. "unintentional pollution": *Handbooks of Penance*, op. cit., p. 104.
252. Book VI of the "Institutes": "We have thought it best to omit altogether the translation of this book," *Nicene Fathers*, Second Series, Vol. XI, op cit., p. 248.
253. Equivalencies: *Celtic Penitentials*, op. cit., p. 123.
253. "If the offender can pay . . . ": *Handbooks of Penance*, op. cit., p. 36.
253. "its grace shall be . . . ": : *Liber Hymnorum*, op. cit., pp. 98, 216.
256. "It is he . . . ": as quoted in Edwin, Third Earl of Dunraven, *Notes on Irish Architecture*, ed. Margaret Stokes, Vol. I, London 1875, p. xviii.
256. "What really exists . . . ": William James, *A Pluralistic Universe*, Gloucester 1967, p. 263.
256. "There are three northern gates . . . ": as quoted in Kathleen Hughes, "Some Aspects of Irish Influence," op. cit., p. 51.

Appendix

259. "detestible error": "The Study of Holy Scripture," in *The Great Encyclical Letters of Pope Leo XIII*, New York 1903, p. 282.
259. "thinking is pure poison . . . ": Sean O'Faolain, *The Vanishing Hero*, New York 1957, p. 44.
260. Christ "passes by our time . . . ": Albert Schweitzer, *The Quest of the Historical Jesus*, trans. F. C. Burkitt, New York 1948, p. 399.
260. Conclusion that Jesus never existed: see Charles Guignebert, *Jesus*, trans. S. H. Hooke, New York 1935, p. 264.
260. "as it is the doctrine and not the man . . . ": Bernard Shaw, "Preface on the Prospects of Christianity," in *Androcles and the Lion: An Old Fable Renovated*, Harmondsworth 1983, p. 11.
260. "It is not Jesus as historically known . . . ": Schweitzer, op. cit., p. 401. See also Rudolph Bultman, "The cross is not redemptive in its own right: it becomes so only when it is preached and believed in as such," as quoted in Reginald Fuller, *The New Testament in Current Study*, New York 1962, p. 265.
260. "without the smallest hesitation . . . ": as quoted in "Study of Holy Scripture," op. cit., p. 294.
260. Fact encircles "religion without touching it . . . ": Schweitzer, op. cit., p. 27.
260. "an untutored peasant": Dom Gregory Dix, *Jew and Greek: A Study in the Primitive*

Church, Westminster 1953, p. 22.

261. "What is truth?": St. John 18:38.

261. "just let it alone": as quoted in Schweitzer, op. cit., p. 13.

261. "To be ignorant of the Scripture . . . ": as quoted in "Study of Holy Scripture," op. cit., p. 274.

261. Mark's Gospel "would have pained the feelings . . . ": Kirsopp and Silva Lake, *An Introduction to the New Testament*, New York & London 1937, p. 23.

262. Gospels as propaganda: see K. and S. Lake, op. cit., p. 18.

262. "strictly speaking . . . ": Rudolph Bultmann, *Jesus and the Word*, New York 1936, as quoted in Fuller, op. cit., p. 27. Bultmann's views caused tremendous consternation within theological circles and in 1959, some twenty-three years later, he felt compelled to offer a grudging and partial retraction. As Fuller reports (p. 48), "He admits that the Gospels, against their direct intention, do disclose something of the character and content of Jesus' history."

262. "without fantastic confusion . . . " and following: Shaw, op. cit., pp. 14, 15.

262. "deceitful scoffers . . . ": 2 St. Peter 3:4.

263. "It is I . . . .": St. Matthew 3:14.

263. "an orderly account . . . ": St. Luke 1:3.

263. "Do not think that I have come to destroy . . . ": St. Matthew 5:17.

263. Canaanite woman: St. Matthew 15:21-28.

263. "melted the Jew out of him . . . ": Shaw, op. cit., p. 33.

263. "Do not go in the direction of the Gentiles": St. Matthew 10:5.

264. Attitude of Jesus towards the Pharisees: see St. Matthew 15 and St. Luke 12:1-2.

264. "Who do the crowds say I am?": St. Luke 9:18 and St. Matthew 16:16.

264. "The Son of Man is to be betrayed . . . ": St. Matthew 17:21-22.

265. "My God, my God . . . ": St. Matthew 27:46.

265. Latitude the Bible often provides: "Divine Scriptures are more fruitful in resources of all kinds for this sort of facility," as Tertullian noted. "Nor do I risk contradiction in saying that the very Scriptures were even arranged by the will of God in such a manner as to furnish materials for heretics." *The Writings of Quintus Septimius Florens Tertullian*, trans. Peter Holmes, ed. A. Roberts, J. Donaldson, Vol 11, Edinburgh 1870, p. 47.

265. "This day thou shalt be in Paradise . . . ": St. Luke 23:43.

265. "It is consummated": St. John 19:30.

265. "the outrageousness of Christ's claim . . . ": J. B. Phillips, *Your God is Too Small*, New York 1962, pp. 114-115.

265. "There is another world . . . ": as quoted in Schweitzer, op cit., p. 49.

265. The crucifixion: ibid., pp. 51-55. See *Josephus*, trans. H. St. J. Thackeray, Vol. I, Cambridge & London 1961, p. 155.

266. Jesus as a gardener: St. John 20:15.

266. "A day with the Lord . . . ": Psalm 89:4.

266. "Unless a man say in his heart . . . ": Abba Allois, as quoted in *Western Asceticism*, trans. Owen Chadwick, Philadelphia 1958, p. 132.

266. "in solitude . . . ": *Select Letters of St. Jerome*, trans. F. A. Wright, Cambridge 1954, p. 413.

267. "The Sabbath was made for man . . . ": St. Mark 2:27.

267. Apostles largely "disappear from history": Henry Chadwick, *The Early Church*, Harmondsworth 1982, p. 17.

268. "Go unto the whole world . . . ": St. Luke 16:15.

268. "seldom has there been a hate . . . ": Schweitzer, op. cit., p. 15.

268. "out of their means": St. Luke 8:3.

268. "From the moment they saw that he was taken . . . " and following: Hermann Samuel Reimarus, *Brief Critical Remarks on the Object of Jesus and His Disciples As Seen in the New Testament*, trans. G. E. Lessing, London 1879, pp. 88, 89, 92, 90, 44, 31, 87.

269. "in foreign tongues" and following: Acts 2:4, 13, 15.

269. "No sooner is a great man dead . . . ": David Friedrick Strauss, as paraphrased by Schweitzer, op. cit., p. 79.

269. "to endow an apparently ordinary life . . . ": Charles Guignebert, *Christianity, Past and Present*, New York 1927, p. 22.

270. Herod "a fox": St. Luke 13:32.

271. "stern and cold": Kirsopp Lake, *The Earlier Epistles of St. Paul: Their Motive and Origin*, London 1930, p. 44.

271. "the old tradition . . . .": *Senchus Mor*, trans. O'Donovan, O'Mahony, Hancock, eds. The Commissioners for Publishing the Ancient Laws and Institutes of Ireland, Dublin 1865, p. 31.

271. "Faith in a fact . . . ": William James, *The Will to Believe, and other essays in popular philosophy*, New York 1956, p. 25.

271. "Are you even yet without understanding?": St. Matthew 15:16. See also 16:21-23.

272. "It is not desirable . . . ": Acts 6:2.

272. Stephen's speech: Acts 7:1-53.

272. "Jerome bade bishops . . . ": *Sancti Columbani Opera*, op. cit., p. 21.

273. "An hour's sleep is enough . . . " and following: *Western Asceticism*, op. cit., pp. 49, 132.

273. "It is observed in the Talmud . . . ": C. G. Montefiore, "Rabbinic Judaism and the Epistles of St. Paul," in *The Jewish Quarterly Review*, Vol. XIII, January 1901, p. 196. See also the same author's "First Impressions of Paul," *JQR*, Vol. VI, April 1894, No. 23, pp. 428-474, where he discusses from a Jewish point of view the Apostle's theories, "utterly strange and unexpected not only that you cannot attain righteousness by the Law because you can never fulfill the Law, but that, even if you fulfilled the Law, you would not attain righteousness. This amazing paradox shows that we are dealing with an ideal, an ideal of evil. No Jew ever looked at the Law from this point of view."

274. "Men knew a lot about dogs . . . ": Whitehead, op. cit., p. 129.

275. "Gods never mix with men": as quoted in St. Augustine, *The City of God*, op. cit., p. 324.

275. "Fantastic . . . ": Shaw, op. cit., p. 83.

275. "Through the Law I have died . . . ": Galatians 2:19.

275. "The true knowledge of God . . . ": *Logic*, trans. William Wallace, New York 1874, p. 181.

277. Robert Graves, *King Jesus*, London 1966, p. 11.

277. "I withstood Peter . . . ": Galatians 2:19.

277. "uncircumcized in heart": Acts 7:51.

277. "I have led my boyish skiff . . . ": Muirchú, "Vita Patricii," trans. Kenney, *Sources*, op. cit., p. 333.

277. "In religion, as in other things . . . ": Kirsopp Lake, *Landmarks in the History of Early Christianity*, London 1920, p. 17.

277. "the casting out of the Jews . . . ": Homily LXVIII, Matthew 21:33-44, from "The Homilies of S. John Chrysostom, Archbishop of Constantinople," in *A Library of Fathers of the Holy Catholic Church, Anterior to the Division of the East and West*, trans. Rev. George Prevost, Oxford 1851, p. 914.

279. "The cup of blessing . . . ": I Corinthians 10:16.

279. "Why do I speak to you at all?": St. John 8:26.

279. "the living bread . . . ": St. John 6:59.

279. "This is a hard saying . . . ": St. John 6:61.

279. "the most ignominious defeats . . . ": Shaw, op. cit., p. 22.

279. "A Gothic soldier . . . ": Gibbon, *Decline and Fall*, 1923 edition, Vol. III, op. cit., p 339.

280. "The Blackrobes are the worst of sorcerers . . .": Brian Moore, *Black Robe*, New York 1985, p. 169. This work is largely based on Francis J. Parkman's monumental *France

and England in North America, in particular Vol. II, *The Jesuits in North America in the Seventeenth Century*, New York 1965 [1867], itself dependent on hundreds of letters, memos and reports from the missionary fathers themselves, who sought to evangelize Huron tribes in the northern Canadian wilderness during the 1600s. These papers are collected in the Jesuit *Relations* and abound in references to cannibalism and the Indians' view of the Eucharist. See Parkman, pp. xxxix and 114 for examples. Other interesting discussions on the Eucharist can be found in R. P. C. Hanson "Eucharistic Offering in the Pre-Nicene Fathers," in *P.R.I.A.*, Vol. 76, Sec. C, No. 4, 1976, pp. 75-95; Caroline Bynum, *Holy Feast and Holy Fast: The Religious Significance of Food to Medieval Women*, Berkeley 1987; Pietro Redondi, *Galileo: Heretic*, trans. Raymond Rosenthal, Princeton 1987.

Select Bibliography

Islands of Storm is an attempt to re-explore more personally some of the material covered in *The Road Wet, The Wind Close: Celtic Ireland* that was published in 1986. Rather than burden these present pages with a bibliography that would largely be a repetition of that in my earlier book, I have decided instead to acknowledge a collective indebtedness to those many authors I first consulted, and to encourage readers interested in further researches to explore *Celtic Ireland's* reference sections as an initial step. With the exception of just a few indispensable books, such as James Kenney's *Sources for the Early History of Ireland*, I have not repeated any titles, even though the barest understanding of the Irish past would be impossible without fully reading D. A. Binchy, Ludwig Bieler, Myles Dillon and Eóin MacNeill.

Having said that I must add that many scholars will certainly notice omissions in the present bibliography, most particularly in the areas of early chruch history and the careers of Jesus Christ, St. Paul, and St. Augustine. I did not list every book that passed through my hands nor every author that I may have read, as I had no desire to present an inflated list of authorities that might give the mistaken impression that I am an expert in any of the topics addressed here. I confess that I am a rover. The books and articles that significantly contributed to this work are the only ones I chose to mention.

This book was barely finished before several distinguished works were released that I was unable to use: Paula Fredriksen, *From Jesus to Christ, The Origins of the New Testament Images of Jesus*, New Haven 1988; Neil Forsyth, *The Old Enemy, Satan and the Combat Myth*, Princeton 1987; Hyam Maccoby, *The Mythmaker, Paul and the Invention of Christianity*, New York 1986; Peter Brown, *The Body and Society: Men, Women and Sexual Renunciation in Early Christianity*, New York, 1988; Barry Cunliffe, *Greeks, Romans and Barbarians: Spheres of Interaction*, New York 1988; Elain Pagels, *Adam, Eve, and the Serpent*, New York 1988; and Robert Alter and Frank Kermode, editors of *Literary Guide to the Bible*, Cambridge 1987, where emphasis veers away from the often dreary detective work of the nineteenth-century German theologians whom I have chosen to discuss in this book, reflecting instead the current urge to study the Bible more joyfully as literature and poetry. A new book by Colin Martin and Geoffrey Parker, *The Spanish Armada*, New York 1988, has on page 207 a fine reproduction, in color, of a map drawn on 20 April, 1589, of Spanish wrecks on Inishnagore. Parts II and III, completed in 1989, were written without the benefit of Hugh Trevor-Roper's discussion of Ussher in *Catholics, Anglicans and Puritans: Seventeenth Century Essays*, Chicago 1988. Projects such as this one — barely financed, worked on when snatches of time can be wrested free — cannot afford the luxury of stopping presses whenever one would wish to take advantage of new insights and conclusions. And thus the titles below form the foundation of this book. Asterisk (*) indicates a work heavily relied upon by the author.

Part I: INISHMURRAY

A. The Island

Specific:

Anonymous, "A Visit to Inismurray," in *The Protestant Penny Magazine*, No. V, Vol. 1, October 25, 1834, pp. 65-69, 102-104.

Anonymous, "Notes of Home Rambles: Sligo and Innismurry," in *The Irish Monthly*, November 1883, pp. 595-606.

Champneys, Arthur C., *Irish Ecclesiastical Architecture*, London 1910, pp. 16-18.

Clark, Wallace, *Sailing Round Ireland*, London 1976, pp. 57-69.

Edwin, Third Earl of Dunraven, *Notes on Irish Architecture*, ed. Margaret Stokes, Vol. I,

London 1875, pp. 45-54.

Frazer, W., "On 'Holed' and Perforated Stones in Ireland," in *J.R.S.A.I.*, Vol. VI, Part II, 1896, pp. 166-7.

Hayward, Richard, *Connacht: Mayo, Sligo, Leitrim and Roscommon*, London 1955.

Healy, John, Archbishop of Tuam, "A Pilgrimage to Inishmurray," in *Papers and Addresses: Theological, Philosophical, Biographical, Archaeological*, Dublin 1909, pp. 487-496.

*Heraughty, Patrick, *Inishmurray, ancient monastic island*, Dublin 1982.

Kiley, Benedict, *Ireland from the Air*, New York 1985, pp. 152-3.

Leask, Harold G., *Irish Churches and Monastic Buildings*, Vol. I, Dundalk 1977, pp. 11-14, 51, 56.

Lionard, Pádraig, "Early Irish Grave Slabs," in *P.R.I.A.*, Vol. 61, Section C, No. 5, 1961, pp. 151-153.

Logan, Patrick, *The Holy Wells of Ireland*, Chester Springs, Pennsylvania 1980, pp. 83-4, 141-3.

Lubbock, John, "On the Preservation of our Ancient National Monuments," in *The Nineteenth Century*, April 1877, pp. 259-261.

MacLeod, Catriona, "Some Mediaeval Wooden Figure Sculptures in Ireland: Statues of Irish Saints," in *J.R.S.A.I.*, Vol. LXXVI, Part IV, 1946, pp. 155-161.

Mason, Thomas H., *Islands of Ireland*, London 1936, pp. 25-33.

McTernan, John C., *Historic Sligo: A Bibliographical Introduction to the Antiquities and History, Maps and Surveys, Mss. and Newspapers, Historical Families and Notable Individuals of County Sligo*, Sligo 1965.

Ó Danachair, Caoimhín, "An Rí (The King): An Example of Traditional Social Organization," in *J.R.S.A.I.*, Vol. 111, 1981, pp. 14-28.

O'Donovan, John, *Letters concerning information relative to the Antiquities of the County of Sligo Collected during the Progress of the Ordnance Survey in 1836*, Bray 1928, pp. 8-16. See also "John O'Donovan, Irish Historical Scholar 1806-1861," in *Irish Men of Learning, Studies by Father Paul Walsh*, ed. Colin O Lochlainn, Dublin 1947, pp. 263-272; and "John O'Donovan, the Man and the Scholar," in *Talamh An Eise: Canadian and Irish Essays*, ed. C. J. Byrne and M. Harry, Halifax 1986, also published as Vol. XII, No. 2, June 1986, of *The Canadian Journal of Irish Studies*.

O'Rorke, Terence, *The History of Sligo: Town and County*, 2 Vol., Dublin 1889.

Pochin Mould, Daphne D. C., *Ireland from the Air*, New York 1973, No. 105.

Stokes, George T., *Ireland and the Celtic Church. A History of Ireland from St. Patrick to the English Conquest in 1172*, London 1886, pp. 184-188.

Wakeman, W. F., *A Survey of the Antiquarian Remains on the Island of Inismurray*, London 1893.

Westropp, Thomas Johnson, *The Ancient Forts of Ireland: Being A Contribution Towards Our Knowledge of Their Types, Affinities, and Structural Features*, Dublin 1902.

Wilde, W. R., "Memoir of Gabriel Beranger, and his Labours in the Cause of Irish Art, Literature, and Antiquities, From 1760 to 1780, With Illustrations," in *P.R.S.A.I.*, Vol. I, 1870, pp. 131-136.

Wood-Martin, W. G., *History of Sligo, County and Town, from the earliest ages to the close of the reign of Queen Elizabeth*, 3 Vol., Dublin 1882.

General:

Aalen, F. H. A. and Hugh Brody, *Gola: The Life and Last Days of an Island Community*, Cork 1969.

Arensberg, Conrad M., *The Irish Countryman*, New York 1937.

Arensberg, Conrad M. and Solon T. Kimball, *Family and Community in Ireland*, Cambridge 1968.

Brody, Hugh, *Inishkillane: Change and Decline in the West of Ireland*, London 1973.

Fox, Robin, *The Tory Islanders — A People of the Celtic Fringe*, Cambridge 1978.

Luce, J. V., "Homeric Qualities in the Life and Literature of the Great Blasket Island," in *Greece and Rome*, Vol. XVI, No. 2, October 1969, pp. 151-168.

The Battler:

Betham, Sir William, *Irish Antiquarian Researches*, Dublin 1827, pp. 109-121.

Chrétien, Douglas, *The Battle Book of the O'Donnells*, Berkeley 1935.

Crawford, O. G. S., "The Magic of Columba," in *Antiquity*, Vol. VIII, 1934, pp. 168-175.

Lawlor, H. J., "The Cathach of St. Columba," in *P.R.I.A.*, Vol. 33, Section C, 1916, pp. 241-443.

Lucas, A. T., "The Social Role of Relics and Reliquaries in Ancient Ireland," in *J.R.S.A.I.*, Vol. 116, 1986, pp. 5-37.

O'Curry, Eugene, *Lectures on the Manuscript Materials of Ancient Irish History*, Dublin 1861, pp. 327-332.

Petrie, George, *Christian Inscriptions in the Irish Language*, Vol. II, Dublin 1878, pp. 91-93, Plate 90.

Phair, P. B., "Betham and the Older Irish Manuscripts," in *J.R.S.A.I.*, 1962, pp. 75-78.

Armada:

Allingham, Hugh, *Captain Cuellar's Adventures in Connacht and Ulster, A.D. 1588*, London 1892.

Hardy, Evelyn, *Survivors of the Armada*, London 1966.

Howarth, David, *The Voyage of the Armada, The Spanish Story*, Harmondsworth 1982.

Mattingly, Garrett, *The Armada*, Boston 1959.

Ó Danachair, Caoimhín, "Armada Losses on the Irish Coast," in *The Irish Sword*, Vol. II, No. 9, 1956, pp. 320-331.

O'Reilly, J. P., "Remarks on Certain Passages in Capt. Cuellar's Narrative of his Adventures in Ireland After the Wreck of the Spanish Armada in 1588-89, Followed by a Literal Translation of That Narrative," in *P.R.I.A.*, Vol. III, Third Series, 1893-96, pp. 175-217.

Sedgwick, Henry D., trans., *A Letter Written on October 4, 1589 by Captain Cuellar of the Spanish Armada to His Majesty King Philip II Recounting his Misadventures in Ireland and Elsewhere After the Wreck of His Ship*, New York 1895.

Spotswood Green, William, "The Wrecks of the Spanish Armada on the Coast of Ireland," in *The Geographical Journal*, No. 5, Vol. XXVII, May 1906, pp. 429-451.

B. Early Christian Era

Christ:

Bultmann, Rudolf, *Primitive Christianity In Its Contemporary Setting*, trans. Reginald H. Fuller, Philadelphia 1980.

Fuller, Reginald H., *The New Testament in Current Study*, New York 1962.

Guignebert, Charles, *Christianity, Past and Present*, New York 1927.

Guignebert, Charles, *Jesus*, trans. S. H. Hooke, New York 1935.

Guignebert, Charles, *The Jewish World in the Time of Jesus*, trans. S. H. Hooke, London 1951.

Lake, Kirsopp, *The Stewardship of Faith: Our Heritage from Early Christianity*, New York & London 1915.

*Lake, Kirsopp, *Landmarks in the History of Early Christianity*, London 1920.

Lake, Kirsopp, *The Religion of Yesterday and To-Morrow*, Boston & New York 1925.

*Lake, Kirsopp, *The Earlier Epistles of St. Paul: Their Motive and Origin*, London 1930.

Lake, Kirsopp, *Paul: His Heritage and Legacy*, New York 1934.

*Lake, Kirsopp and Silva, *An Introduction to the New Testament*, New York & London 1937.

Lampe, G. W. H., ed. *The Cambridge History of the Bible*, 3 Vol., Cambridge 1969.

Robertson, John M., *Pagan Christs, Studies in Comparative Hierology*, London 1911.

Santayana, George, *The Idea of Christ in the Gospels or God in Man: A Critical Essay*, New York 1946.

*Schweitzer, Albert, *The Quest of the Historical Jesus*, trans. F. C. Burkitt, New York 1948 [1910].

Schweitzer, Albert, *Paul and his Interpreters*, trans. W. Montgomery, London 1950.

Shaw, Bernard, "Preface on the Prospects of Christianity," in *Androcles and the Lion, An Old Fable Renovated*, Harmondsworth 1983.

Wilken, Robert L., *The Myth of Christian Beginnings: History's Impact on Belief*, New York 1972.

Wood, H. G., *And Did Christ Really Live?*, New York 1938. Primarily an argument with John M. Robertson, in particular his *Christianity and Mythology*.

Nitria:

Butler, Alfred, *The Ancient Coptic Churches of Egypt*, 2 Vol., Oxford 1884.

Clarke, Somers, *Christian Antiquities in The Nile Valley, A Contribution Towards The Study Of The Ancient Churches*, Oxford 1912.

Curzon, Robert Jr., *Ancient Monasteries of The East*, New York 1856.

Falls, J. C. Ewald, *Three Years in the Libyan Desert*, London 1913, primarily pp. 61-111.

Sonnini, C. S., *Travels in Upper and Lower Egypt: undertaken by order of The Old Government of France*, trans. Henry Hunter, Vol. II, London 1799, pp. 138-179.

*White, Hugh G. Evelyn, *The Monasteries of The Wadi 'N Natrûn*, 3 Vol., New York 1926-33.

Spread of Christianity:

Bell, H. Idris, *Egypt From Alexander the Great to the Arab Conquest: A Study in the Diffusion and Decay of Hellenism*, Oxford 1948.

Bonner, Gerald, *St. Augustine of Hippo: Life and Controversies*, Philadelphia 1963.

Brennan, Brian, "Athanasius' Vita Antonii: A Sociological Interpretation," in *Vigiliae Christianae*, Vol. 39, No. 3, 1985, pp. 209-227.

Brown, Peter, *Augustine of Hippo*, London 1967.

Bury, J. B., "The Origin of Pelagius," in *Hermathena*, No. XXX, 1904, pp. 26-35.

Chadwick, Henry, *Early Christian Thought and the Classical Tradition: Studies in Justin, Clement, and Origen*, New York 1966.

*Chadwick, Henry, *The Early Church*, Harmondsworth 1967.

Chadwick, Henry and J. E. L. Oulton, *Alexandrian Christianity*, Philadelphia 1954.

*Chadwick, Owen, *John Cassian, A Study in Primitive Monasticism*, Cambridge 1950.

Chitty, D. J., *The Desert A City: An Introduction to the Study of Egyptian and Palestinian Monasticism under the Christian Empire*, Oxford 1966.

Daniélou, Jean, "Gospel Message and Hellenistic Culture," Vol. II of *A History of Early Christian Doctrine Before the Council of Nicea*, London & Philadelphia 1973.

Evans, Robert F., *Pelagius, Inquiries and Reappraisals*, New York 1968.

Evans, Robert F., *Four Letters of Pelagius*, New York 1987.

Ferguson, John, *Pelagius*, Cambridge 1956.

Fox, Robin Lane, *Pagans and Christians*, New York 1987.

Fuller, J. F. C., *The Generalship of Alexander the Great*, New Brunswick, New Jersey 1960.

Gibbon, Edward, *The History of the Decline and Fall of the Roman Empire*, 6 Vol., London 1914.

Gilson, Etienne, *The Christian Philosophy of Saint Augustine*, trans. L. E. M. Lynch, New York 1960.

Grant, Robert M., *Augustus to Constantine, The Thrust of the Christian Movement into the Roman World*, New York 1970.

Hanson, R. P. C., *Origen's Doctrine of Tradition*, London 1954.

Hanson, R. P. C., *Allegory and Event: A Study of the Sources and Significance of Origen's Interpretation of Scripture*, Richmond, Virginia 1959.

Hanson, R. P. C., "The Reaction of the Church to the Collapse of the Western Empire in the Fifth Century," in *Vigiliae Christianae*, Vol. 26, No. 4, 1972, pp. 272-287.

Hanson, R. P. C., *The Attractiveness of God*, London 1973.

Jones, A. H. M., *The Later Roman Empire, 284-602: A Social Economic and Administrative Survey*, 2 Vol., Oklahoma 1964.

Ladner, Gerhart B., *The Idea of Reform: Its Impact on Christian Thought and Action in the Age of the Fathers*, Cambridge 1959.

Laistner, M. L. W., *Thought and Letters In Western Europe A.D. 500 to 900*, London 1931.

Munz, Peter, "John Cassian," in *The Journal of Ecclesiastical History*, Vol. XI, April 1960, pp. 1-22.

Nock, A. D., *Conversion: The Old and the New in Religion from Alexander the Great to Augustine of Hippo*, Oxford 1933.

Nock, A. D., "Early Gentile Christianity and its Hellenistic Background," in *Arthur Darby Nock: Essays on Religion and the Ancient World*, Vol. I, Cambridge 1972.

Norris, R. A., *God and World in Early Christian Theology*, New York 1965.

O'Meara, John J., *The Young Augustine, The Growth of St. Augustine's Mind up to his Conversion*, London 1954.

Palanque, J. R., G. Bardy, P. de Labriolle, G. de Plinval, Louis Brehier, *The Church in the Christian Roman Empire*, trans. E. G. Messenger, 2 Vol., New York 1953.

Pelikan, Jaroslav, *The Christian Tradition: A History of the Development of Doctrine*, Vol. I: *The Emergence of the Catholic Tradition (100-600)*, Chicago & London 1971.

MacMullen, Ramsay, *Christianizing the Roman Empire: A.D. 100-400*, New Haven 1984.

Rousseau, Philip, *Ascetics, Authority, And The Church In the Age of Jerome and Cassian*, Oxford 1978.

Rousseau, Philip, *Pachomius: The Making of a Community in Fourth-Century Egypt*, Berkeley 1985.

Souter, Alexander, "The Commentary of Pelagius on the Epistles of Paul: The Problem of its Restoration," in *Proceedings, The British Academy*, 1905-06, pp. 409-432.

Souter, Alexander, "Pelagius and the Pauline Text of the Book of Armagh," in *The Journal of Theological Studies*, Vol. XVI, 1915, p. 105.

Souter, Alexander, "The Character and History of Pelagius' Commentary on the Epistles of St. Paul," in *P.B.A.*, 1915-16, pp. 261-296.

Souter, Alexander, "Pelagius And His Commentary. Introduction. A Record of Previous Research," in *Pelagius's Expositions of Thirteen Epistles of St. Paul*, Cambridge 1922.

Souter, Alexander, *The Earliest Latin Commentaries on the Epistles of St. Paul: A Study*, Oxford 1927.

TeSelle, Eugene, *Augustine the Theologian*, New York 1970.

Vogt, Joseph, *The Decline of Rome: The Metamorphosis of Ancient Civilization*, trans. Janet Sondheimer, London 1967.

Weil, Simone, *Intimations of Christianity among the Ancient Greeks*, trans. Chase Geissbuhler, London 1957.

Early Christian era in Ireland:

*Anderson, A. O. and M. O., *Adomnán's Life of Columba*, London 1961.

Carney, James, "The Impact of Christianity," in *Early Irish Society*, ed. Myles Dillon, Dublin 1954.

*Chadwick, Nora, *Poetry and Letters in Early Christian Gaul*, London 1955.

*Chadwick, Nora, *The Age of the Saints in the Early Celtic Church*, London 1961.

Coffey, George, "Archaeological Evidence for the Intercourse of Gaul with Ireland before the First Century," in *P.R.S.A.I.*, Vol. XXVIII, Section C, 1910, pp. 96-106.

Crawford, O. G. S., "Western Seaways," in *Custom is King: Essays Presented to R. R. Marett on his seventieth birthday*, June 13, 1936, London 1936, pp. 181-202.

Gougaud, Dom Louis, *Christianity in Celtic Lands: A History of the Churches of the Celts, their origin, their development, influence, and mutual relations*, London 1932.

Healy, Most Rev. John, *Insula Sanctorum et Doctorum; or, Ireland's Ancient Schools and Scholars*, Dublin 1890.

Green, Alice Stopford, "The Trade Routes of Ireland," in *The Old Irish World*, Dublin 1912.

*Hughes, Kathleen, *The Church In Early Irish Society*, London 1966.

Jackson, Kenneth, *Language and History in Early Britain: A Chronological Survey of the Brittonic Languages, First to Twelfth Century A.D.*, Cambridge 1953, pp.3-261.

*Kenney, James F., *The Sources for the Early History of Ireland: Ecclesiastical*, New York 1927.

MacCaffrey, James, "Rome and Ireland: Pre-Patrician Christianity," in *The Irish Theological Quarterly*, Vol. I, No. 1, January 1906, pp. 47-66.

Meyer, Kuno, *Learning in Ireland in the Fifth Century and the Transmission of Letters*, Dublin 1913.

O'Connor, Frank, *The Backward Look: A Survey of Irish Literature*, London 1967.

Ó Ríordáin, Séan, "Roman Material in Britain," in *P.R.I.A.*, Vol. LI, Section C, 1945-48, pp. 6-82.

Ryan, John, *Irish Monasticism: Origins and Early Development*, London 1931.

Sheehy, Maurice P., "Concerning the Origin of Early Medieval Irish Monasticism," in *The Irish Theological Quarterly*, Vol. XXIX, No. 2, April 1962, pp. 136-144.

Zimmer, H., *The Irish Element in Mediaeval Culture*, trans. Jane Edmands, New York 1891.

Part II: IONA

A. The Island

Specific:

Argyll, Eighth Duke of, *Iona*, London 1878.

Campbell, J. L. and D. Thomson, *Edward Lhuyd in the Scottish Highlands 1699-1700*, Oxford 1963.

Chapman, R. W., "Johnson in Scotland," in *The Portrait of a Scholar and other Essays written in Macedonia, 1916-1918*, Oxford 1920, pp. 127-140.

Emery, Frank, *Edward Lhuyd F.R.S. 1660-1709*, Caerdydd 1971.

Fergusson, Malcolm, *A Trip from Callander to Staffa and Iona with Brief Descriptive Sketches of the Route By Sea and Land, and the Sacred Rock-Bound Isle of I-Colum-Kill*, Edinburgh 1894.

Garnett, T., *Observations on a Tour through The Highlands and part of the Western Isles of Scotland*, Vol. I, London 1811, pp. 217-272.

Hannan, Thomas, *Iona: And Some Satellites*, Edinburgh 1928.

Iona visits by Scott, Keats, Wordsworth, Turner, Mendelssohn, Boswell and Johnson: see reference listing for p. 155.

Leyden, John, *Journal of a Tour in the Highlands and Western Islands of Scotland in 1800*, ed. James Sinton, Edinburgh 1903, pp. 36-50.

Macculloch, John, *A Description of The Western Islands of Scotland, including The Isle of Man: Comprising An Account of their Geological Structure, with Remarks on their Agriculture, Scenery, and Antiquities*, Vol. I, London 1819, pp. 5-21.

Macmillan, A. and R. Brydall, *Iona: Its History, Antiquities, etc.*, Edinburgh 1898.

Macnab, P. A., *The Isle of Mull*, Newton Abbot 1970.

Martin, M., *A Description of the Western Isles of Scotland c. 1695*, London 1884.

Morton, T. Ralph, *The Iona Community: Personal Impressions of the Early Years*, Edinburgh 1977.

Murray, W. H., *The Islands of Western Scotland: The Inner and Outer Hebrides*, London 1973.

Pennant, Thomas, *A Tour of Scotland and Voyage to the Hebrides*; MDCCLXXII, London 1774, pp. 241-269.

Pennant, Thomas, *The Literary Life of the late Thomas Pennant Esq., By Himself*, London 1793.

Royal Commission on the Ancient and Historical Monuments of Scotland, *Argyll, Vol. I, Kintyre*, Glasgow 1971.

*Royal Commission on the Ancient and Historical Monuments of Scotland, *Argyll, An Inventory of the Monuments, Vol. 4, Iona*, Edinburgh 1982. By far the most complete bibliographical listing on the island and its history.

Steers, J. A., *The Coastline of Scotland*, Cambridge 1973. Geological data.

Stewart, John, *The Official Guide to the islands of Staffa and Iona*, Glasgow 1888.

B. Early Christian Era

Ireland, Scotland, the Continent:

Anderson, A. O., *Early Sources of Scottish History A.D. 500 to 1286*, Vol. I, Edinburgh 1922.

Anderson, M. O., "Columba and other Irish Saints in Scotland," in *Historical Studies V*, London 1965, pp. 26-36.

Anderson, M. O., "Dalriada and the creation of the kingdom of the Scots," in *Ireland in Early Medieval Europe, Studies in Memory of Kathleen Hughes*, ed. D. Whitelock, R. McKitterick, D. Dumville, Cambridge 1982, pp. 106-132.

Bannerman, John, *Studies in the History of Dalriada*, Edinburgh 1974.

Bethell, D. L. T., "The Originality of the Early Irish Church," in *J.R.S.A.I.*, Vol. 111, 1981, pp. 36-49.

*Bieler, Ludwig, "The Island of Scholars," in *Revue Du Moyen Age Latin*, VIII, No. 3, 1952, pp. 213-231.

Bieler, Ludwig, "Hibernian Latin," in *Studies*, Vol. XLIII, No. 1, 1954, pp. 92-95.

Bieler, Ludwig, "The Celtic Hagiographer," in *Studia Patristica*, Vol. V, 1962, 243-65.

Bieler, Ludwig, "The Christianization of the Insular Celts During the Sub-Roman Period and its Repurcussions on the Continent," in *Celtica*, VIII, 1968, pp. 112-125.

Binchy, D. A., "Semantic Influence of Latin in the Old Irish Glosses," in *Latin Script and Letters A.D. 400-900. Festschrift presented to Ludwig Bieler on the occasion of his 70th birthday*, ed. John J. O'Meara and Bernd Naumann, Leiden 1976, pp. 167-173.

Binchy, D. A., "A pre-Christian survival in Mediaeval Irish hagiography," in *Ireland in Early Mediaeval Europe*, op. cit., pp. 165-178.

Bolgar, R. R., *The Classical Heritage and its Beneficiaries*, Cambridge 1954.

Bowen, E. G., *The Settlements of the Celtic Saints in Wales*, Cardiff 1956.

Bowen, E. G., *Saints, Seaways and Settlements in Celtic Lands*, Cardiff 1969.

Bowen, E. G., "The Irish Sea in the Age of the Saints," in *Studia Celtica*, Vol. IV, 1969, pp. 56-71.

Bowen, E. G., "The Geography of Early Monasticism in Ireland," in *Studia Celtica*, VII, 1972, pp. 30-44.

Bowen, E. G., *Britain and the Western Seaways: A History of Cultural Interchange Through Atlantic Coastal Waters*, New York 1972.

Bullough, D. A., "Columba, Adomnan and the Achievement of Iona," in *The Scottish Historical Review*, Vol. XLIII, October 1964, pp. 111-130; Vol. XLIV, April 1965, pp. 17-33.

Byrne, Francis J., "The Ireland of St. Columba," in *Historical Studies V*, London 1965, pp. 37-58.

Chadwick, Hector M., *Early Scotland: The Picts, The Scots and The Welsh of Southern Scotland*, Cambridge 1949.

Chadwick, Nora, "Intellectual Contacts between Britain and Gaul in the Fifth Century," in *Studies in Early British History*, Cambridge 1954, pp. 189-263.

Chadwick, Nora, "Introduction," "Early Culture and Learning in North Wales," and "Intellectual Life in West Wales in the Last Days of the Celtic Church," in *Studies in the Early British Church*, Cambridge 1954, pp. 1-182.

Chadwick, Nora, *Contributions to Celt and Saxon, Studies in the Early British Border*, Cambridge 1963, pp. 1-19, 138-166, 167-185, 323-354.

Chadwick, Nora, *Celtic Britain*, London 1963.

Chadwick, Nora, *The Celts*, Harmondsworth 1970, pp. 64-109.

Chadwick, Nora, *The British Heroic Age*, Cardiff 1976.

Chambers, R. W., *England Before the Norman Conquest*, London 1926.

Charles-Edwards, T. M., "The Social Background to Irish Peregrinatio," in *Celtica*, Vol. XI, 1976, pp. 43-59.

Charles-Edwards, T. M., "Bede, The Irish And The Britons," in *Celtica*, XV, 1983, pp. 42-52.

Collingwood, R. G., and J. N. L. Myres, *Roman Britain and the English Settlements*, Oxford 1937.

Deanesly, Margaret, "The Anglo-Saxon Church and the Papacy," in *The English Church and the Papacy in the Middle Ages*, ed. C. H. Lawrence, New York 1965, pp. 29-62.

Dickinson, William Croft, *Scotland, from the earliest times to 1603*, London 1961, primarily pp. 22-51.

Dillon, Myles, "The Irish Settlements in Wales," in *Celtica*, XII, 1977, pp. 1-11.

Dowden, John, *The Celtic Church in Scotland; Being an Introduction to the History of the Christian Church in Scotland down to the Death of Saint Margaret*, London 1894.

Duke, John A., *History of the Church of Scotland To The Reformation*, Edinburgh 1937, primarily pp. 1-70.

Dumville, D. N., "Biblical Apocrypha and the Early Irish: A Preliminary Investigation," in *P.R.I.A.*, 73, Section C, No. 8, 1973, pp. 299-338.

Duncan, Archibald A. M., *Scotland, The Making of the Kingdom*, Edinburgh 1975, primarily pp. 17-100.

Dunleavy, Gareth W., *Colum's Other Island: The Irish at Lindisfarne*, Madison 1960.

Esposito, Mario, "The Knowledge of Greek in Ireland During the Middle Ages," in *Studies*, Vol. I, No. 4, December 1912, pp. 665-683.

Esposito, Mario, "On the New Edition of the *Opera Sancti Columbani*," in *Classica and Mediaevalia*, XXI, 1960, pp. 184-203.

Evans, Claude, "The Celtic Church in Anglo-Saxon Times," in *Études Celtiques*, XVIII, 1981, pp. 215-226.

Farmer, Hugh, "The Studies of Anglo-Saxon Monks," in *Los Monjes Y Los Estudios, IV Semana De Estudios Monasticos Poblet 1961*, Abadia de Poblet 1963, pp. 87-103.

FitzGibbon, Constantine, *The Irish in Ireland*, London & New York 1983.

Finlay, Ian, *Columba*, London 1979.

Flower, Robin, *The Irish Tradition*, Oxford 1947.

Fraser, J., "The Question of the Picts," in *Scottish Gaelic Studies*, Vol. II, Part II, 1928, pp. 172-201.

Fuhrmann, Joseph, O.S.B., *Irish Medieval Monasteries on the Continent*, Washington 1927, primarily pp. 1-13, 54-57.

Giblin, Cathaldus, *Irish Franciscan Mission to Scotland 1619-1646*, Dublin 1964.

Gougaud, Dom Louis, *Gaelic Pioneers of Christianity. The Work and Influence of Irish Monks and Saints in Continental Europe*, Dublin 1923.

Gougaud, Dom Louis, *Modern Research, With Special Reference to Early Irish Ecclesiastical History*, Dublin 1929, primarily pp. 5-18.

Gwynn, E. J., "Some Saints of Ireland," in *The Church Quarterly Review*, LXXXIV, April 1912, pp. 62-81.

Hamlin, Ann, "*Dignatio diei dominici*: an element in the iconography of Irish crosses?" in *Ireland in Early Mediaeval Europe*, op. cit., pp. 69-75.

Heist, W. W., "Over the Writer's Shoulder: Saint Abban," in *Celtica*, Vol. XI, 1976, pp. 76-84.

Henderson, Isabel, *The Picts*, New York 1967.

Herbert, M. and A. O'Sullivan, "The Provenance of Laud Misc. 615," in *Celtica*, X, 1973, pp. 174-192.

Herren, Michael, "The Pseudonymous Tradition in Hiberno-Latin," in *Latin Script*, op. cit., pp. 121-131.

Hughes, Kathleen, "Some Aspects of Irish Influence on Early English Private Prayer," in *Studia Celtica*, V, 1950, pp. 48-61.

Hughes, Kathleen, "The Changing Theory and Practice of Irish Pilgrimage," in *The Journal of Ecclesiastical History*, Vol. XI, No. 2, October 1960, pp. 143-151.

Hughes, Kathleen, "The church and the world in Early Christian Ireland," in *Irish Historical Studies*, Vol. XIII, No. 50, September 1962, pp. 99-113. An interesting appendix by Bannerman, pp. 113-116.

*Hughes, Kathleen, "Irish Monks and Learning," in *Los Monjes Y Los Estudios*, op. cit., pp. 61-86.

Hughes, Kathleen, "The Celtic Church and the Papacy," in *The English Church*, op. cit., pp. 1-28.

Hughes, Kathleen, "The Golden Age of Early Christian Ireland (7th and 8th centuries)," in *The Course of Irish History*, ed. T. W. Moody and F. X. Martin, New York 1967, pp. 76-90.

Hughes, Kathleen, "Evidence for contacts between the churches of the Irish and English from the Synod of Whitby to the Viking Age," in *England Before the Conquest, Studies in primary sources presented to Dorothy Whitelock*, ed. P. Clemoes and K. Hughes, Cambridge 1971, pp. 49-67.

Hughes, Kathleen, "Sanctity and Secularity in the early Irish Church," in *Sanctity and Secularity: The Church and the World, Papers read at the Eleventh Summer Meeting and the Twelfth Winter Meeting of the Ecclesiastical History Society*, ed. Derek Baker, Oxford 1973, pp. 21-38.

Hughes, Kathleen, "Synodus II S. Patricii," in *Latin Script*, op. cit., pp. 141-147.

*James, Edward, "Ireland and western Gaul in the Merovingian Period," in *Ireland in Early Mediaeval Europe*, op. cit., pp. 362-386.

Kendig, Perry Fridy, *The Poems of Saint Columba*, Philadelphia 1949.

Kenney, James F., "The Earliest Life of St. Columcille," in *The Catholic Historical Review*, V, 1926, pp. 636-644.

Laistner, M. L. W., *Thought and Letters in Western Europe A.D. 500-900*, London 1931.

Lehmann, Paul, "The Benedictine Order and the Transmission of the Literature of Ancient Rome in the Middle Ages," in *The Downside Review: A Quarterly of Catholic Thought*, Vol. 71, No. 226, 1953, pp. 407-421.

MacCana, Proinsias, "The Three Languages and the Three Laws," in *Studia Celtica*, V, 1950, pp. 62-78.

*McNamara, Martin, "Psalter Text and Psalter Study in the Early Irish Church," in *P.R.I.A.*, Vol. 73, Section C, No. 7, 1973, pp. 201-298.

McNamara, Martin, *The Apocrypha in the Irish Church*, Dublin 1975.

MacNeill, Eóin, "Beginnings of Latin Culture in Ireland," in *Studies, An Irish Quarterly Review*, Vol. XX, No. 77, March 1931, pp. 39-48; Vol. XX, No. 79, September 1931, pp. 449-460.

McNeill, John T., *The Celtic Churches: A History A.D. 200 to 1200*, Chicago 1974.

Marcus, G. J., "Irish Pioneers in Ocean Navigation of the Middle Ages," in *The Irish Ecclesiastical Record*, Vol. LXXVI, 1951, pp. 353-363, 469-479.

Marcus, G. J., "Further Light on Early Irish Navigation," in *The Irish Ecclesiastical Record*, Vol. LXXXI, 1954, pp. 93-100.

*Mayr-Harting, Henry, *The Coming of Christianity to Anglo-Saxon England*, London 1972.

Meyer, Kuno, "Gauls in Ireland," in *Ériu*, IV, 1910, p. 208.

*Mohrmann, Christine, "The Earliest Continental Irish Latin," in *Vigiliae Christianae*, Vol. XVI, 1962, pp. 216-233.

Morison, Stanley, *Politics and Script: Aspects of authority and freedom in the development* of *Graeco-Latin script from the sixth century B.C. to the twentieth century A.D.*, Oxford 1972, primarily pp. 149-170.

Morris, C. D., "The Vikings and Irish Monasteries," in *Durham University Journal*, New Series Vol. XL, No. 2, June 1979, pp. 175-185.

Ní Shéaghdha, Nessa, "Translations and Adaptations into Irish," in *Celtica* VI, 1984, pp. 107-124.

Ó Briain, Felim, "Saga Themes in Irish Hagiography," in *Essays and Studies Presented to Professor Tadhg Ua Donnchadha (Torna) on the Occasion of His Seventieth Birthday September 4, 1944*, Cork 1947.

Pepperdene, Margaret W., "Bede's Historia Ecclesiastica: A New Perspective," in *Celtica*, IV, 1958, pp. 252-262.

Pflugk-Harttung, Julius von, "The Old Irish on the Continent," in *T.R.I.A.*, V, 1891, pp. 75-102.

Plummer, Charles, "Introduction," *Vitae Sanctorum Hiberniae*, Vol. I, Oxford 1910, pp. ix-clxxxviii.

Raby, F. J. E., *A History of Secular Latin Poetry in the Middle Ages*, Vol. I, Oxford 1957, particularly pp. 147-258.

Reeves, William, ed., *Life of St. Columba, Founder of Hy. Written by Adamnan, Ninth Abbot of That Monastery*, Edinburgh 1874.

Rhys, J., *Celtic Britain*, London 1904.

Simpson, W. Douglas, *The Historical St. Columba*, Aberdeen 1927.

Skene, William F., *Celtic Scotland: A History of Ancient Alban*, 3 Vol., Edinburgh 1876-80.

*Smit, Joannes Wilhelmus, *Studies on the Language and Style of Columba the Younger (Columbanus)*, Amsterdam 1971.

Smyth, A. P., "The Earliest Irish Annals: Their First Contemporary Entries, and the Earliest Centres of Recording," in *P.R.I.A.*, Vol. 72, Section C, No. 1, 1972, pp. 33-43.

Stancliffe, Clare, "Red, white and blue martyrdom," in *Ireland in Early Mediaeval Europe*, op. cit., pp. 21-46.

Stanford, W. B., "Early Hiberno-Latin and Irish Hymns," in *Latin Script*, op. cit., pp. 113-118.

*Stanford, W. B., "Towards A History of Classical Influences in Ireland," in *P.R.I.A.*, Vol. 70, Section C, No. 3, 1970, pp. 13-91.

Stanford, W. B., *Ireland and the Classical Tradition*, Dublin 1977.

*Stenton, F. M., *Anglo-Saxon England*, Oxford 1971.

Sullivan, Richard E., "The Papacy and Missionary Activity in the Early Middle Ages," in *Mediaeval Studies*, Vol. XVII, 1955, pp. 46-106.

Swanton, Michael, ed., *The Dream of the Rood*, Manchester 1970, primarily pp. 42-47.

Various authors, *Mélanges Columbaniens: Actes du Congrès International de Luxeuil, 20-23 juillet 1950*, Paris 1951.

Various authors, *The Irish Sea Province in Archaeology and History*, Cardiff 1970.

Various authors, "Colloquium on Hiberno-Roman Relations and Material Remains," in *P.R.I.A.*, Vol. 76, Section C, No. 6-15, 1976, pp. 171-292.

Wainwright, Frederick, *The Problem of the Picts*, Edinburgh 1955.

Walker, G. S. M., "On the Use of Greek Words in the Writings of St. Columbanus of Luxeuil," in *Archivum Latinitatis Medii Aevi, Bulletin Du Cange*, Bruxelles, Vol. 21, 1951, pp. 117-131.

*Walker, G. S. M., *Sancti Columbani Opera*, Dublin 1957.

Whitelock, Dorothy, *The Beginnings of English Society*, Harmondsworth 1952.

Winterbottom, M., "Columbanus and Gildas," in *Vigiliae Christianae*, Vol. 30, No. 4, 1976, pp. 310-317.

Williams, Hugh, "Heinrich Zimmer on the History of the Celtic Church," in *Zeitschrift Für Celtische Philologie*, IV, 1902, pp. 527-574.

Workman, Herbert B., *The Evolution of the Monastic Ideal From the Earliest Times Down to the Coming of the Friars*, Boston 1962, primarily pp. 138-217.

Zimmer, Heinrich, *The Celtic Church in Britain and Ireland*, trans. A. Meyer, London 1902.

Part III: INISHKEA NORTH

A. The Island

Specific:

Browne, Charles R., "The Ethnography of The Mullet, Inishkea Islands, and Portacloy, County Mayo," in *P.R.I.A.*, Vol. III, Third Series, 1893-96, pp. 587-649.

Cooke, A. H., "Molluscs," in *The Cambridge Natural History*, ed. S. Harmer and A. Shipley, Vol. III, New York 1895, pp. 89-91. Figure 7, Plate 35, is common to Inishkea North.

Crawford, Henry S., "A Descriptive List of Early Cross-Slabs and Pillars," in *J.R.S.A.I.*, Vol. XLIII, 1913, p. 157.

Henry, Françoise, "Early Christian Slabs and Pillar Stones in the West of Ireland," in *J.R.S.A.I.*, Vol. LXVII, Part II, 1937, pp. 273-275.

Henry, Françoise, "Remains of the Early Christian Period on Inishkea North, Co. Mayo," in *J.R.S.A.I.*, Vol. LXXV, 1945, pp. 127-155.

Henry, Françoise, "New Monuments from Inishkea North, Co. Mayo," in *J.R.S.A.I.*, Vol. LXXXI, Part I, 1951, pp. 65-69.

Henry, Françoise, "A Wooden Hut on Inishkea North, Co. Mayo," in *J.R.S.A.I.*, Vol. LXXXII, 1952, pp. 163-178.

Skerrett, R. A. Q., "Notes on the Dialect of the Inishkea Islanders," in *Studia Celtica*, Vol. II, pp. 196-201. Specialist.

Synge, J. M., *In Wicklow, West Kerry and Connemara*, Totowa, New Jersey 1980, primarily pp. 111-156.

General:

Otway, Caesar, *Sketches in Ireland: Descriptive of Interesting, and Hitherto Unnoticed Districts, in the North and South*, Dublin 1827.

Otway, Caesar, *A Tour in Connaught: Comprising Sketches of Clonmacnoise, Joyce Country, and Achill*, Dublin 1839.

Otway, Caesar, *Studies in Erris and Tyrawly, Illustrative of the Scenery, Antiquities, Architectural Remains, and the Manners and Superstitions of the Irish Peasantry*, Dublin 1850.

Erigena:

Most general histories on philosophy, such as Gordon Leff's *Medieval Thought: St. Augustine to Ockham*, Harmondsworth 1962, will have some discussion on Erigena. There are also useful summaries in specialist encyclopedias, i.e., *Evangelical Dictionary of Theology*, ed. W. A. Elwell, Grand Rapids, Michigan 1984, pp. 362, 983; *New Catholic Encyclopedia*, Vol. VII, New York 1967, pp. 1072-74; *The New Schaff-Herzog Encyclopedia of Religious Knowledge*, Vol. X, Grand Rapids, Michigan 1957, pp. 303-307. The only complete translation of *Periphyseon, On The Division of Nature*, is by Myra L. Uhlfelder, Indianapolis 1976, with an introduction and summary (dry) by Jean A. Potter.

Bett, Henry, *Johannes Scotus Erigena: A Study in Mediaevel Philosophy*, Cambridge 1925.

Gardner, Alice, *Studies in John the Scot (Erigena) A Philosopher of the Dark Ages*, New York 1900.

Gilson, Etienne, *History of Christian Philosophy in the Middle Ages*, New York 1955, primarily pp. 111-128.

Kristeller, Paul Oskar, "The Historical Position of Johannes Scottus Eriugena," in *Latin Script*, op. cit., pp. 156-164.

Laistner, M. L. W., "The Revival of Greek in Western Europe in the Carolingian Age," in *History*, Vol. IX, No. 33, October 1924, pp. 177-187.

Laistner, M. L. W., *The Intellectual History of the Early Middle Ages: Selected Essays of M. L. W. Laistner*, ed. Chester G. Starr, Ithaca 1957, primarily pp. 93-149.

Liebeschutz, H., "John Eriugena and his cosmological interpretation of Martianus Capella," in *The Cambridge History of Later Greek and Early Medieval Philosophy*, ed. A. H. Armstrong, Cambridge 1967, pp. 576-586.

O'Meara. John J., *Eriugena*, Cork 1969.

*O'Meara. John J. and Ludwig Bieler, eds., *The Mind of Eriugena: Papers of a Colloquium Dublin, 14-18 July 1970*, Dublin 1973.

Sandys, John Edwin, *A History of Classical Scholarship*, Vol I, Cambridge 1921.

Sheldon-Williams, I. P., "Johannes Scottus Eriugena," in *Cambridge History of Later Greek and Early Medieval Philosophy*, op. cit., pp. 518-533.

*Sheldon-Williams, I. P., ed., and Ludwig Bieler, collaborator, *Johannis Scotti Eriugenae: Periphyseon (De Divisionae Naturae)*, 3 Vol. (Books 1 to 3 only), Dublin 1968-1981.

Irish Gospel Books:

Henry, Françoise, *Irish Art in the Early Christian Period (to 800 A.D.)*, Ithaca 1965, primarily pp. 58-65, 159-224.

Henry, Françoise, *The Book of Kells: Reproductions from the Manuscript in Trinity College Dublin*, New York 1974.

*Hughes, Kathleen, "The Distribution of Irish Scriptoria and Centres of Learning from 730 to 1111," in *Studies in the Early British Church*, op. cit., pp. 243-271.

Mahaffy, John P., *An Epoch in Irish History, Trinity College, Dublin, Its Foundation and Early Fortunes 1591-1660*, London 1903, primarily regarding Ussher's library.

Maxwell, Constantia, *A History of Trinity College Dublin 1591-1892*, Dublin 1946, primarily regarding Ussher's library.

Urwick, William, *The Early History of Trinity College Dublin 1591-1660 As Told in Contemporary Records on occasion of its Tercentenary*, London 1892, primarily regarding Ussher's library.

Penance:

McNeill, John T., *The Celtic Penitentials and their Influence on Continental Christianity*, Paris 1923.

McNeill, John T., and Helena M. Garner, *Medieval Handbooks of Penance*, New York 1938.

Mitchell, Gerard, "The Penitential of St. Columbanus And its Importance in the History of Penance," in *Mélanges*, op. cit., pp. 143-151.

Oakley, Thomas P., "English Penitential Discipline and Anglo-Saxon Law in their Joint Influence," in *Studies in History, Economics and Public Law*, Vol. CVII, No. 2, 1923, primarily pp. 13-104.

Oakley, Thomas P., "Cultural Affiliations of Early Ireland in the Penitentials," in *Speculum, A Journal of Mediaeval Studies*, Vol. VIII, No. 4, October 1933, pp. 489-500.

Oakley, Thomas P., "Alleviations of Penance in the Continental Penitentials," in *Speculum*, Vol. XII, No. 4, October 1937, pp. 488-502.

Oakley, Thomas P., "Neglected Aspects in the History of Penance," in *The Catholic Historical Review*, October 1938, pp. 293-309.

O'Carroll, James, "Monastic Rules in Merovingian Gaul," in *Studies*, XLII, No. 4, 1953, pp. 407-419.

Watkins, Oscar D., *A History of Penance, Being a Study of the Authorities*, London 1920, primarily Vol. II.

Acknowledgments

My debt to the many Irish people interviewed for this book is self- evident, and in particular I would like to express appreciation to Paddy Joe Brady.

All photographs are the author's with these exceptions: Molaise's "House" was taken c. 1875 by a photographer in the employ of Edwin, Third Earl of Dunraven, and appeared in his book *Notes on Irish Architecture*. The Monastery of Bishôi and the Tree of Obedience were shot c. 1921 and first published in Hugh G. Evelyn White's *The Monasteries of The Wady 'N Natrûn*. They are reproduced courtesy of The Metropolitan Museum of Art in New York.

Rockwell Kent's 1927 oil painting, *Coast of Ireland (And Women Must Weep)*, is reproduced by kind permission of his widow, Sally Kent Gorton, and by The Rockwell Kent Legacies and Rockwell Kent Gallery, State University of New York at Plattsburgh. The line drawing by Harold Leask of Inishmurray's cashel is reproduced by kind permission of his widow, the late Ada K. Longfield Leask, and Dundalgan Press of Dundalk in County Louth. One unpublicized disaster of recent "troubles" in Ireland was the destruction of many Leask originals when the editorial offices of his publisher were burned during bomb attacks on a neighboring pub. My thanks to Jan V. Roy for her reconstruction of Leask's sketch.

For guiding me again through the labyrinth of today's computer technology, my appreciation to Susan Bailey and Ralph Brown. Maps are by Alex Wallach, and assistance in photographic matters was provided by William Lane.

It is unfortunate that indigent writers can usually offer no more than thanks for artistic services that many talented friends so freely offer. William Rudy saved me considerable embarrassment by his diligence in proofreading the finished manuscript, and Wendy Oppel spent many hours creating and preparing the design for this book. I am in their debt.

I am grateful once more to Katherine Dibble and the research staff of the Boston Public Library.

Finally, a word of thanks to the publishers of this book, Kristin Dufour and Christopher May. I will not pretend that my meanderings through the Irish past are matters in which all general readers should take an interest, nor even that people familiar with Ireland must, out of duty, grapple with them as well. This is, I suppose, a narrow book with narrow appeal, and having said that I acknowledge what many writers working on arcane subject matter know all too well: publishers are few in this day and age who have any interest at all in wandering along the stony path.

JCR
8 November, 1989
Newburyport, Massachusetts

314

Index

316